Hot Connections

Hot Connections

Why Sexual Platforms Matter

Jenny Sundén, Susanna Paasonen, and Katrin Tiidenberg

The MIT Press
Cambridge, Massachusetts
London, England

The MIT Press
Massachusetts Institute of Technology
77 Massachusetts Avenue
Cambridge, MA 02139
mitpress.mit.edu

The MIT Press would like to thank the anonymous peer reviewers who provided comments on drafts of this book. The generous work of academic experts is essential for establishing the authority and quality of our publications. We acknowledge with gratitude the contributions of these otherwise uncredited readers.

This book was set in Stone Serif and Stone Sans by Westchester Publishing Services. Printed and bound in the United States of America.

Library of Congress Cataloging-in-Publication Data

Names: Sundén, Jenny, 1973– author | Paasonen, Susanna, 1975– author |
    Tiidenberg, Katrin author
Title: Hot connections : why sexual platforms matter / Jenny Sundén,
    Susanna Paasonen, and Katrin Tiidenberg.
Description: Cambridge, Massachusetts : The MIT Press, [2026] | Includes
    bibliographical references and index.
Identifiers: LCCN 2025019736 (print) | LCCN 2025019737 (ebook) |
    ISBN 9780262052061 paperback | ISBN 9780262052085 epub |
    ISBN 9780262052078 pdf
Subjects: LCSH: Sex | Sexology—Research | Online dating | Fetishism
    (Sexual behavior) | Social media
Classification: LCC HQ21 .S8175 2025 (print) | LCC HQ21 (ebook)
LC record available at https://lccn.loc.gov/2025019736
LC ebook record available at https://lccn.loc.gov/2025019737

EU Authorised Representative: Easy Access System Europe, Mustamäe tee 50, 10621 Tallinn, Estonia | Email: gpsr.requests@easproject.com

Contents

Acknowledgments

This book would not have come together without funding from The Foundation for Baltic and East European Studies (Östersjöstiftelsen) for the project *Rethinking Sexuality: A Geopolitics of Digital Sexual Cultures in Estonia, Sweden and Finland* (2020–2022, grant number 1035-3.1.1-2019), the Strategic Research Council at the Research Council of Finland (2019–2025, grant numbers 327391 and 352520) for the consortium *Intimacy in Data-Driven Culture* (IDA), as well as Sydney Social Sciences and Humanities Advanced Research Center (SSSHARC), University of Sydney, where Susanna was Hunt-Simes Visiting Chair in Sexuality Studies in the spring of 2022.

IDA supported the work of the wonderful Maria Vihlman, who conducted the thirty-one interviews among Alastonsuomi users explored in this book. While Maria could not take on coauthoring our book due to their other commitments, they are the coauthor of the three journal articles roughly forming the basis for chapters 3, 4, and 5, published as: Paasonen, Susanna, Jenny Sundén, Katrin Tiidenberg, and Maria Vihlman (2023a), "About Sex, Open-mindedness and Cinnamon Buns: Exploring Sexual Social Media," *Social Media + Society* 9 (1), https://doi.org/10.1177/20563051221147324; Tiidenberg, Katrin, Susanna Paasonen, Jenny Sundén, and Maria Vihlman (2023), "Vanilla Normies and Fellow Pervs: Boundary Work on Sexual Platforms," *Sexualities*, https://doi.org/10.1177/13634607231215763; and Sundén, Jenny, Susanna Paasonen, Katrin Tiidenberg and Maria Vihlman (2024), "Locating Sex: Regional Geographies of Sexual Social Media," *Gender, Place & Culture* 31 (4): 424–440. Huge thanks, Maria, for enjoyable collaborations and your sensitive interview skills, without which this book would not have taken its current shape. Kiitos ihana!

We also would like to thank the participants in two workshops related to the *Rethinking Sexuality* project, as well as the invited speakers to our symposium "Rethinking Sexuality in Nordic and Post-Soviet Contexts" hosted at Södertörn University, September 29–30, 2022, which helped shape our thinking and collaboration toward this book: Kristina Birk-Vellemaa, Kath Browne, Charlotta Carlström, Ulrika Dahl, Tuula Juvonen, Mariah Larsson, Uku Lember, Raili Marling, Kristian Møller, Michael Nebeling Petersen, Michal Pitoňák, Rebeka Põldsam, Jens Rydström, Laura Saarenmaa, Łukasz Szulc, and Riikka Taavetti. We learned a lot from you all.

Finally, we are sincerely grateful to all of our participants who opened up to us and let us into their platformed sexual lives.

1　Sexual Social Media

My use of this platform has varied in different periods of life somehow. I've used it to pick people up. I've used it to learn more and to join different groups and networks and stuff like that. I've used it to check people out that I have a crush on and read their presentations very closely. I've used it when I've been completely heartbroken, to check out the ex's profile and trace everyone who has liked something of theirs. I've used it as, God—what haven't I used it as? [*laughs*] I use it as a form of social contact, too. Reading friends' diaries that you might know from elsewhere and seeing what their lives are like. You might be socializing with them in a professional context and then they're on Darkside and you can go in and see their kinks and read their diaries and think, "Oh yeah, this is what you do on the weekends." It's a reminder that people are complex creatures. It's quite nice. . . . It's a living room in many ways, with groups that you are part of and where you have talked and supported and encouraged each other for years. But then, in parallel, you can also just shop around and find new people to connect with sexually. So, there is this possibility of anonymity, even though it is also a social space where you respond to events. You can be an anonymous booty hunter and be in your safe forums. You can be both, in a way.

—Malin

Sharing the story of her long-term use of the digital kink platform Darkside, Malin describes it as a crucial element of both her personal social media diet and her sexual life. A device for learning, fantasizing, flirting, and hooking up, it is also a social space and a community, and it offers a sexual geography. Building on accounts like hers, this book explores three locally operating sexual platforms through an ethnographic lens. In addition to the Swedish platform Darkside, these include the Estonian Libertine.Center, used mainly by nonmonogamous people, and the Finnish Alastonsuomi used for a wide variety of nude and sexual self-expression. Based on sixty-four interviews with their users and developers, we ask what kinds of social media these platforms comprise and, conversely, what studies of social media may gain from including such sites in their realm of analysis.

The pathways to our objects of study can be all but straightforward. Some projects we arrive at for strategic reasons; it can be a timely topic, a funding possibility, or a collaborative opportunity. Others we engage in for more personal reasons; we choose them because they move close to our hearts, or to our politics. These projects tend to involve labors of love, and we do them because they matter but also because they can be highly enjoyable. We may research things we like, or dislike, sometimes very much both at the same time. We might keep falling in and out of love with our research or stick to it because there is just something there, like a persistent itch, a je ne sais quoi quality that propels us forward. And sometimes a project manages to be all the above: a timely thing, a funding opportunity, and an enjoyable collaboration involving plenty of heart on issues that matter. The *Rethinking Sexuality* project on which this book is based was one such for us.

Research ideas do not arrive fully formed, nor do they "write themselves," no matter how brilliant any initial idea may seem to the authors themselves. The first impulse for this project arrived at a small cocktail bar on a dark Helsinki night, but it was not fleshed out more fully until we let it circulate through a long and lively email thread, weaving together our separate locations in Tallinn, Stockholm, and Helsinki. Given our combined research trajectories, we knew we wanted to work on digital sexual cultures in our respective contexts as a northern counterpoint and a contribution to an "international" field of digital media research dominated by a focus on US-born platforms. We also knew that we were interested in sex-positive digital platforms and more regional or national options in a time when nudity and sexual communication are vigilantly weeded out from so-called mainstream social media.

We initially discussed using kink as an entry point for the project. We considered looking at local online forums or platforms for kinksters, combined with talking to users about how the internet shapes kink practices, possibly in combination with a fieldwork component covering local in-person kink events—even if, as Katrin put it, "I am sure many Estonians are super freaked out about going to events because they think they will run into their kids' kindergarten teachers there, which, frankly, they probably would." Scale matters, as these are small countries, especially Estonia with its 1.3 million people (Finland has 5.6 million and Sweden 10.6 million, respectively).

While kink was one opening into our joint project-in-the-planning, we quite quickly broadened the scope to include a wider range of sexual practices and identities that rub up against ideas of sexual normalcy and the presumed privacy of sex. We also wanted to add to an understanding of what sexual liberation might mean or look like in platformed contexts. Considering this starting point, it is not hard to understand why we chose to study Darkside—a Swedish platform launched in 2003 for BDSM practitioners and other kinksters that embraces a wide range of sexual expressions, identities, and practices. With its approximately two hundred thousand members, Darkside is not only the largest Swedish kink community online but also one of the few sizeable national online communities that has not only survived but continued to thrive in the era of large global social media platforms. Darkside houses everything from social and sexual networking, including members' profile pages, diaries, image galleries, and libraries of written erotica, to discussion groups and chats, event information, editorial material, and advertising. The platform traffics in nonnormative sexualities by providing, as the site states, "a social community for gender-, relational- and sexual minorities—fetishists, sadomasochists and other queer and non-normative groups" firmly set within an ethos of risk-aware consensual kink. The platform is used in different, coexisting, and sometimes conflictual ways: as a community in its own right for flirting, socializing, and building normalcy in sexual otherness; as a space for seeing and being seen through both visual and textual means; as a springboard for kinky hookups and play dates; and as a compass to help in organizing sexual lives rooted in local (or regional, or transnational) spaces of play.

Yet while our study is certainly inclusive of kink and BDSM, it is not limited to it. In Estonia, we initially planned to study a long-standing platform called Iha.ee (*iha* means desire in Estonian), as this platform is the best known and tends to be equated with the "sexual internet" in Estonia within the public discourse. This would have made it quite similar in terms of its (lack of) specific kink or sexual subculture focus to the Finnish platform under study— Alastonsuomi. However, during the early days of fieldwork, a new platform was propelled into the Estonian public attention. Its developers were open to interaction with researchers, and the opportunity to witness the process of developing and experimenting with building a platform led us to refocus our attention on Libertine.Center. It targets "swingers and open-minded singles," which means that the prevalent platform vernacular is focused on practices of nonmonogamy, including event-based group sex.[1] This expanded the repertoires of nonnormative sex we studied within the project while simultaneously creating an interesting bridge between all the platforms, as consensual nonmonogamy (and polynormativity) is prevalent also among, for example, kinksters. As opposed to Darkside, which is the oldest of the platforms, Libertine.Center, with fifty thousand users, was launched in 2018 and is rather a child of the post-Tumblr era—or to be more precise, post-Tumblr-adult-content-purge—bringing some freshness to the sample.

Our Finnish case—Alastonsuomi of circa 138,000 registered users—is thematically the most capacious of the three platforms. Its shared vernacular focuses on nudity rather than a particular sexual practice or subculture. Since its launch in 2007, the platform has housed a broad range of nude self-expressions, including those of kinksters, swingers, cross-dressers, and beyond, but it also traffics in more mundane forms of undress, the dick pic being the most common choice in male users' profile pictures, and the most shared pictorial content beyond them. Initially advertised as "IRC Gallery for adults," Alastonsuomi borrowed much of its format from IRC-Galleria, which dominated the Finnish pre-Facebook social media landscape. The overall rationale of Alastonsuomi is simple: Users can establish an account by submitting a photo showing their face or naked body, or both, to rate and comment on contributions from other users; to participate in "clubs"; write blogs; chat; and publish photos, animated GIFs, and videos. Some use the site primarily for hooking up, others for the pleasure of their bodies being seen, and possibly complimented, and yet others for mixed reasons ranging from voyeurism to sex work. Susanna had been keen to study Alastonsuomi for a decade but felt unable to tackle it as a solo project. Within this collaboration, the platform allowed us to consider kink as a borderland of sorts through more ephemeral boundaries of sexual normalcy. The site's name translating as "naked Finland" invites a questioning approach to what is considered regular or normal in registers that are quite quotidian. And, as Susanna put it, "Turns out people are pretty pervy." By bringing together local sexual platforms that both overlap and complement each other in the domains of nudity, sex, and kink, we aimed for both diversity and cohesion.

Out with It!

For us, the appeal of these sites as objects of inquiry is self-evident, not least since there is not much existing research zooming in on sexual platforms. Yet there is also contextual urgency to examine networked sexual sociability, given the extent to which nudity and sexual communication are weeded out from social media. Not so very long ago, the internet used to be spoken about and imagined as a safe space for sexual exploration and for negotiating sexual norms (Daneback 2006; Döring 2009; Tiidenberg and Gómez-Cruz 2015; Waskul 2003). The centrality of networked connections predating social media for LGBTQI+ communities has been amply documented (see Cassidy 2018, 8). During the heyday of 1990s cybercultures, mailing lists, electronic bulletin boards, newsgroups, chatrooms, and text-based virtual worlds dedicated to so-called cybersexual practices (e.g., Branwyn 1994; McRae 1996; Odzer 1997; Waskul 2003) housed lesbian bars and communities (Correll 1995; Wakeford 1996), gay male erotic spaces (Campbell 2001), furry-themed cybersex (Reid 1996), and BDSM practices (Rambukkana 2007).

With the introduction and drastic expansion of social media and hookup apps in the 2000s, online sociability has become more and more centralized on select platforms. In tandem with progressively more powerful devices, apps, and networks, this has paved way for a proliferation of digital modes of sexuality and intimacy (Andreassen et al. 2018; Dobson et al. 2018; Paasonen 2018a; Sundén 2018, 2021). Understood in this vein, networked digital media are more than conduits of desire: They are intrinsically entwined with people's sexual attachments and connections and shape how desire takes form and becomes oriented. Platforms are creatively appropriated for sexual uses, as in underage users experimenting with "pervy role-playing games" in a virtual world targeting tweens (Nielsen et al. 2015) or users routinely going against social media's content policies in their flirty and smutty backchannel exchanges. How we operate on platforms contributes to how we relate to ourselves and others sexually, what we consider sexy, and how we communicate, experiment with, or experience sex. Or, as Tiidenberg and van der Nagel (2020, 15) put it, "What happens on and with social media is as relevant as what happens on the street—and in the bedroom."

It is nevertheless a sad fact that, with the increasing centrality of social media in people's experiences of the internet—and in particular the concentration of power and users into the hands of few platforms and even fewer data giants known for their limited appreciation for, and understanding of, sexual cultures and practices—online spaces have grown less and less welcoming of sexual expression. This is evident throughout the social media ecosystem. The community standards set by Meta and ByteDance, as well as the policies mandated by the Google and Apple app stores, ban nudity; YouTube allows sex education materials only to those over eighteen, effectually blocking the main chunk of their target teen audience (see Garwood-Cross 2022). Tumblr—once a safe and vibrant space for sexual expression, particularly for sexual and gender minorities—banned depictions of sex and nudity late in the year 2018; this decision meant the effacement of archives and connections formed over years (Byron 2019; Cho 2018; Pilipets and Paasonen 2022; Tiidenberg 2019).

Coinciding with a moment of intense political populism and related intensification of Christian conservative discourse in the United States (the home of several data giants), it is not surprising that after decades of pushing for obscenity laws to censor the internet, various stakeholders managed to get two such pieces of legislation passed in both the US House of Representatives and the Senate (McDowell and Tiidenberg 2023). In April 2018, the "Allow States and Victims to Fight Online Sex Trafficking Act" and the "Stop Enabling Sex Traffickers Act" (FOSTA/SESTA) were passed with full bipartisan support.

The platforms we study have been developed by Swedish, Estonian, and Finnish companies (the Swedish platform Darkside has been single-handedly run by the same webmaster since 2003). They are hosted on servers within the European Union (EU), and they use EU-based payment processing systems (e.g., Paytrail). Thus, as they are subject to EU legislation and primarily address local users, they are not directly impacted by FOSTA/SESTA. Why would we then care about a piece of American legislation? Well, we are happy to tell you.

US-registered social media platforms are among the most used in the world, shaping what we think social media is and should be used for as well as constraining new platforms' field of vision and possibilities. The FOSTA/SESTA law package marks the first time since 1996 that Section 230 of the Communications Decency Act (CDA230), a piece of legislation holding "the 26 words that created the internet" (Kosseff 2019), was amended. For decades the CDA230 exempted US-registered platforms from liability for what their users post. Among internet researchers, it is common to claim that CDA230 has driven innovation and protected free speech online, allowing people to organize around activist causes and post content that speaks back to power (Kosseff 2019; Lingel 2020). At the same time, platform governance scholars have been keenly aware of CDA230 as a double-edged sword (Gillespie 2018) in that its protections have created a system where content moderation is driven by corporate interest rather than social responsibility and where the mechanisms that foster free speech also afford harassment, hate speech, and manipulation (Marwick 2017).

FOSTA/SESTA made it possible to hold internet intermediaries responsible for some content that users post despite the CDA230 protections, namely when "websites . . . promote or facilitate prostitution" (Allow States and Victims to Fight Online Sex Trafficking Act 2018, 1253), or when they are "knowingly assisting, facilitating or supporting" sex trafficking (Allow States and Victims to Fight Online Sex Trafficking Act 2018, 1255). While few would argue against fighting sex trafficking, the moral and legal status of prostitution is much less clear, given decades-long debates on where sex work begins or ends and what it encompasses. According to some critics, porn performers engage in prostitution; according to others, porn comprises a distinct field of labor. However, the laws' vague wording makes censoring sexual expression the pragmatic choice for platform companies (Blunt et al. 2021; Bronstein 2021). Instead of investing time, effort, and money into figuring out how to differentiate between various kinds of content—to ban that which "knowingly facilitates sex trafficking" while keeping content that educates, informs, entertains, crafts bonds, and delights—even platforms that had thus far allowed for sexual expression decided to summarily ban it, throwing out the baby with the bathwater (in particular, Tumblr and Craigslist have been discussed in this context; cf. Lingel 2021; Pilipets and Paasonen 2022; Reynolds 2021; Tiidenberg 2021).

Since their content policies are horizontal, and their moderation practices are largely (albeit hardly only) automated, large social media platforms are not primed to consider the contextual specificities of photos featuring nudity, even as their community standards allow for some exceptions. The notion of community standards builds on US obscenity legislation, centrally the 1957 court ruling *Roth v. the United States* concerned with "whether to the average person, applying contemporary community standards, the dominant theme taken as a whole appeals to the prurient interest" (Hudson 2018). Yet when a platform such as Facebook has three billion active users globally, it is obviously impossible to pinpoint "the average person" among them. The current solution is then to ban nudity in a blanket manner "because some people in our community may be sensitive to this type of content" (Meta 2024). In this vein, Meta turns a blind eye to the cultural and regional diversity of its users and their different understandings of what may or may not be considered sensitive (see Paasonen and Sundén 2024; Spišák et al. 2021), hiding culturally specific tendencies behind a rhetoric of a global, networked community.

Since FOSTA/SESTA passed, platforms already inhospitable to sexual content, such as Facebook, Instagram, and TikTok, have operated with increasingly tight content policies on visual content and sexual communication. In this equation, there is little for these platforms to lose since sexual content is difficult to monetize. While such content may attract clicks and views, advertisers are generally unwilling to have their commercial messages appear next to posts that risk being deemed offensive or obscene—and it is, of course, fully understandable how a company like McDonald's would not want to promote their novelty burgers next to photos of rimming, for example. There are further risks to a social media platform's brand image and stock market value if it is labeled as a site for smut: In other words, there is the reputational risk to consider. Combined with the further potential risk of legal repercussions connected to sexual posts, courtesy of FOSTA/SESTA, the overmoderation of sexual content may simply come across as commonsensical. As companies operating in the US need to comply with these law packages, they hold considerable power internationally, no matter how vague and problematic they may be.

All this has resulted in what Stephen Molldrem (2018) aptly identifies as a wave of deplatforming of sex. Because of this, and speaking to Tumblr's sex ban, the shuttering of Craigslist's personals, and the weeding out of sex worker subreddits in particular, FOSTA/SESTA is credited with creating direct harms to sex workers, LGBTQI+ internet users, artists, activists, sexual subcultural communities, academics studying them, and other communities beyond (Blunt and Stardust 2021; Blunt and Wolf 2020; Engelberg and Needham 2019; Musto et al. 2021). In addition, the laws have also proven useless in what they set out to do. Given that sex trafficking was already illegal in the US, it was not protected under CDA230 to start with, making FOSTA/SESTA basically unnecessary (McDowell and Tiidenberg 2023). This probably explains why FOSTA/SESTA has not been widely employed in legal disputes (Goodwin et al. 2021).

From the perspective of the argument at hand, the deplatforming of sex on social media reverberates loudly through the entire ecosystem of online expression and, as such, offers important analytical insight. On the one hand, as we will go on to show shortly, it has directly shaped the emergence and governance choices of new sexual platforms. On the other, it has elevated sexual social media into a prime case study of governance and established it as a mainstay of platform governance studies. Our own and colleagues' work exploring the banning, shadowbanning, demonetizing, and suppressing of sexual expression on a variety of platforms (Are and Paasonen 2021; Paasonen and Sundén 2024; Pilipets and Paasonen 2022; Reynolds 2021; Stardust 2024; Tiidenberg 2021) highlights the opacity and arbitrary moralizing involved in governance practices often positioned by platforms as a means of saving us from ourselves.

We argue that what the processes of the "deplatforming of sex" accomplish is not a safer space, but rather a categorical dismissal of the fact that human sociality is inclusive of sexuality, that sexuality is deeply social and builds social ties and attachments. The deplatforming of sex further entails a rejection of expressions of curiosity, desire, libidinous longing, need for information, support, and community, not least among those already marginalized—that is, within queer, gender-nonconforming, and kink communities that are particularly reliant on digital networks. It is thus crucial to point out that a respect for sexual rights—such as the rights to bodily integrity, sexual knowledge and self-expression, and pleasurable sexual experiences free from discrimination and violence, as outlined by the World Health Organization among other institutions—cannot be reconciled with a moral platform economy ruled by conservative (US as well as Chinese) notions of appropriate content. Networked connections allow for access to sexual information, pleasure, and community. Curbing this kind of self-expression, sociality, and knowledge is detrimental to sexual rights on and beyond the internet (Berlant and Warner 1998; Dobson et al. 2018; Plummer 2003; Spišák et al. 2021). Or, to reiterate, the deplatforming of sex constitutes a direct threat to any version of sexual and intimate citizenship encompassing sexual rights, responsibilities, and needs for recognition, as well as a broader understanding of the importance of sexual desires and pleasures for our ways of being in the world (see Plummer 2003; 2007).

In contrast, sexual platforms of the kind we study afford forms of relating where the (relative and controlled, rather than all out there) publicness of sex is not understood as inappropriate but rather as a mode of sociability

(McGlotten 2013, 30). At the same time, only allowing sex on specialty sites tends to further marginalize it in ways that do not reflect many people's experiences of sociality—or those of a meaningful, fulfilling life. This relegates sexual connections as if into semi-hidden, dark corners of everyday life, deeming them as something that can only exist in some kind of secrecy. The degrees to, the ways in, and the limitations within which the platforms we study open up spaces for sexual expression and communication present a complex question that we explore in the chapters to follow.

Replatforming Sex?

Online sociability most certainly predates platforms such as Myspace and Facebook, yet it was only through their broad popular appeal that the term "social media" became commonly used. In interrogating how "the social" is reconfigured in social media, Nick Couldry and José van Dijck (2015) argue that these platforms have come to appropriate the social (also Mejias 2013) so as to redefine not only how people connect online but also what it means to be social in the first place. They call for studying platforms "as if the social mattered" when social relatedness becomes reduced to computational connectivity within corporate infrastructures. Taking a more specific spin on this call, we attend to how sociability is crafted, maintained, and disrupted in sexual social media to register "the fractured spaces from where alternative proposals of 'the social' might be built" (Couldry and van Dijck 2015, 2). To incorporate the sexual into this equation of building and rebuilding the social, from which it is mainly excluded, we argue, is a matter of political urgency.

The sociability offered by the mainstream social media economy privileges popularity, visibility, reach, and connectivity connected to both voluntary and involuntary sharing of user data. It is rooted in an arguably egocentric outlook built on user profiles and networks clustered around those, leading to imaginaries of social media as affording individualism—or plain antisociality—instead of mutual connection and interest-based communication (Tiidenberg et al. 2021). This version of sociality also prescribes a strikingly retrograde understanding of the sexual, relegating it from networked publics to more private realms as something risky, unsafe, and sort of dirty. Even as increasingly diverse options are available for users to identify their gender on social media platforms, they are not designed to prompt the presentation of sexual selves—quite the very contrary (Bivens 2017).

By contrast, sexual platforms offer forms of sociability revolving around the centrality of sexual desire. They are also grounded in modes of sexual relating that do not necessitate affective ties or a particular sense of belonging, even as they may afford these. Here, sexuality is not understood as surplus or excess to social lives but rather as something that drives and shapes connections and, hence, builds sociability in meaningful ways. Addressing sex as intrinsic to the formation of social bonds, Juana María Rodríguez (2011, 339) poses the rhetorical question, "For what is sex if not sociality of the most intense order—a place where bodies not only touch but are pushed and pulled into one another, a coming undone predicated on a coming together?" Indeed! On the platforms we study, this intense sociality of sex becomes a kind of social aphrodisiac and an energy that interlinks bodies, makes and shapes sociability, and invites people to connect. At the same time, what inspires some users to come together may rub others very much the wrong way. While providing vital spaces for sexual self-expression—and hot connections—platform connectivity can also be full of friction as expectations, wishes, and desires clash and collide.

In creating a rhythm for this book, we move from discussions of methods and research ethics to more thematically oriented chapters that allow us to tackle user perceptions of safety and risk, proximity and distance, visibility and invisibility, and privacy and publicness in other than binary ways. In chapter 2, "Studying Sexual Platforms," we unpack our research methodology, its ethical underpinnings, and legal frameworks with the idea that this can be useful for those wishing to study platformed sexual sociability in the future (in the very near future, we hope!). This hands-on approach continues in chapter 3, "Governing from the Margins," exploring the three platforms' functionalities and governance practices so as to uncouple sexual content from ephemeral notions of risk and danger used to delimit its presence in most social media. Moving into a more thematic mode, chapter 4, "Sexual Sociability and Spaces to Breathe," examines social connections on the three sites as inclusive of, yet not simply limited to, the sexual, and it discusses how users move promiscuously between platforms that are more or less accommodating of sexual expression. Chapter 5, "Sense of the Local," asks what makes these sites local, whom they may exclude, and how users imagine and engage with location in ways that challenge the common presumption that digital and social media help to overcome distance. Chapter 6, "Vanilla Normies and Proud Pervs," inquires after what our interviewees understand as enjoyable sex and how these articulations connect to normative notions of "good" and "less good" sex, while chapter 7, "When Sex and Intimacy Are Not the Same Thing," looks at how they draw the boundaries around things considered intimate, and how sex may not come across as very intimate as such. Our concluding chapter 8, "Apprehension, Friction, and Mundane Pleasures," zooms in on the question of ambiguities and tensions involved in the uses of the three platforms studied where users both connect and disconnect from one another, are both agitated and excited, and keep logging in.

A key rationale of this book is to consider sexual platforms as social media with the aim of creating an understanding of sexuality as something that makes sociability rather than something that poses some kind of a threat to it and, hence, needs to be curbed. We ask what we can learn from including sexual platforms in definitions of social media and, by extension, from including sex in definitions of "the social" at play. What avenues do our three platforms open up for understanding the role that sexuality plays in people's networked routines, social bonds, and forms of relating? And what can such a framing add to our understanding of social media, or the social more generally? On the three sites studied in this book, sexual expression, learning, fantasy, and desire become forces binding users to the sites and fueling diverse engagements between them. In this sense they explicitly *replatform* sex within the social media ecology.

Studying local platforms that may seem marginal (not to mention rather vintage in their designs), we suggest, allows for new ways of understanding sexual cultures and digital sexual geographies as well as networked sociability more broadly. These platforms exist on both sexual and geographic margins in a number of ways: They are less bound by Google's and Apple's app store prudishness (yet, as we will see, they are bound in other ways by, for example, notions of "good taste"), they trouble sexual norms and ideas of normalcy, and they inhabit geographically marginal spaces of sorts by virtue of their Nordic and Baltic situatedness within social media ecologies and economies dominated by data giants. By studying alternative digital platforms where sexual content is not only allowed but forms the foundation for social connecting, our case studies are, in a sense, "edge cases" that trouble binary divisions between, for example, oppression and liberation or "East" and "West" and make space for both contradiction and dissonance in doing so.

There is a profound significance to sexual social media as spaces where people have a sense of freedom of sexual self-expression, where they make sense, and have a right to exist. Yet they inescapably do this within specific constraints, designs, and platform vernaculars, as explored in this book. Our aim is not to track a realm of sexual freedom as a rhetorical means of critiquing puritan data policies (although we certainly disagree with them), but rather to address the pleasures, tensions, and frictions involved in platformed sexual sociality and to create an empirically grounded analysis of the complexities involved. In exploring why and how sexual platforms matter, and for whom, we set out to make an intervention in debates on the value of social media, one mindful of the granularities of lived experience and the deep ambiguities that sexual networked lives entail.

2 Studying Sexual Platforms

Studying social media—making sense of platforms, their users, cultures, economies, norms, and practices—involves many moving parts and often opaquely motivated actors. There are global generalities and extreme specificities involved that do not align neatly with national borders, language groups, or subcultures. In other words, this is a profoundly dynamic object of analysis. Studying sex is a similarly complicated affair, given the added weight of loaded discourses, public anxieties, and (presumed) vulnerabilities connected to sex that shape what people think they are doing when they are doing or studying it, as well as how they are willing or able to talk and write about it. Studies of digital sexual cultures are further complicated by how platforms are built and governed, what policymakers presume online risks to be, and how academic institutions empower or constrain scholarly quests for knowledge.

Because of the complexity of studying sex and sexual platforms, we use this chapter to unpack our research methodology and its ethical underpinnings, hoping this will be a helpful resource for current and future colleagues entering this space, navigating its complexities, and negotiating with various bodies of oversight. This includes our interview design, the considerations addressed when submitting our project for ethical evaluation in our respective institutions, recruitment tactics, and best practices emerging from our inquiry. Unpacking both our methodology and the particularities involved in doing research on sexual sites, the chapter also covers reflections on studying such sites during the peak of the COVID-19 pandemic and its aftermath, as well as the ethics involved in researching networked sex "at a distance." As "work" and "home" have become increasingly entangled, and as personal devices are used for occupational tasks and libidinal thrills alike, what does this mean for research on sexual cultures? Is home a comfortable, safe space for conversations about private matters, or is it a more fraught place with little to no privacy? Both of the above?

This allows us to bring nuance to the question of safety, which here expands to include not only safe modes of relating and connecting on sexual platforms but also ways of creating safe encounters between participants and researchers. Part of this discussion of safety and risk involves reflections on what it means to study sex and sexuality when data about one's sex life or sexual orientation is understood as sensitive by default, as is the case under the European Union's General Data Protection Regulation (GDPR), which forms a legal framework for our study. Such an understanding of sex as a sensitive matter resonates with psychoanalytical notions of sexuality as a site of trauma. While sexual trauma certainly is a real thing, we argue that talking about sex does not automatically render one vulnerable, nor is trauma part of the equation in any straightforward or causal manner. Counter to this standpoint, it is our conviction that researching sexual cultures is important in destigmatizing and detraumatizing them and in foregrounding the importance and value of sexual lives on both individual and societal levels. Sex talk can, after all, be a source of empowerment and worldmaking (cf. Plummer 1995).

Let's Talk About Sex? Our Methods, in a Nutshell

Our book builds on a three-year collaborative project involving platform walkthroughs to make sense of the platforms' design, terms of use, ethos, and engagement options; participant observation on the platforms; analysis of user-posted content; and in-depth interviews with administrators and developers of Darkside and Libertine.Center (n = 4) and with the users of all three platforms (n = 60). The central, project-wide research questions guiding our research design were as follows:

- How do these platforms shape marginalized or nonnormative sexualities, practices, and communities?

- How are notions of sexual liberation and oppression; egalitarianism and domination; normalcy and deviance; privacy and publicness; pleasure and play embodied and imagined on these platforms and in the sexual cultures they mediate?

- How are these sexual cultures experienced in relation to national self-understandings, as outlined by interviewees?

We approach social media platforms as microsystems consisting of interconnected elements: technologies, users, practices of use, content, ownership and business models, and modes of governance (see van Dijck 2013). In order to further understand what these platforms allow for—what their affordances in terms of sexual expression and communication might be—we relied on platform walkthroughs, which are a widely used method in practical user experience (UX) and software development, and which have been adapted for critical platform studies by Ben Light, Jean Burgess, and Stefanie Duguay (2018). They recommend slowing down the process of engaging with the platform studied in order to render its technological functionality observable and analyzable, to make sense of the cultural values embedded in it, and to examine how interface design nudges users toward particular kinds of use.

Light et al. (2018) write of two phases of platform walkthroughs, both of which come with specific steps: the exploration of intended use and the technical walkthrough. We conducted both. On the level of intended use, we analyzed platform visions (how site descriptions, marketing texts, and the developers themselves articulate their target audiences and goals), business models (ambitions and strategies of monetization, and how these were addressed in the developer interviews), and their approaches to governance and moderation (explicit rules as stated in Community Guidelines and Terms of Service agreements, as well as moderation practices as discussed in the interviews and observed in fieldwork). We also conducted technical walkthroughs by documenting the process of moving through the interface, starting from setting up the account to everyday use to leaving the platform.

Walkthroughs have allowed us to focus on platform politics, as unpacked in the Terms of Service and modes of governance; their business models and positions within the broader social media ecology; and their socio-technical conditions apparent in features and intended affordances, patterns of content, and user interactions. In incorporating walkthrough data in our analysis, we build on the premise that social media platforms afford rather than facilitate social acts (van Dijck 2013). By synthesizing existing work on perceived and imagined platform affordances (i.e., Nagy and Neff 2015; Rice et al. 2017), we understand these as perceived possibilities for action.

Following best practices, as described by scholars using and developing ethnographic methods of, on, and with the internet (Boellstorff et al. 2012; Markham 2017), we spent a few months at the beginning of the project on participant observation on the platforms. Rather than being a method of data collection as such, we treated this initial fieldwork as a form of immersion pointing us toward better ethical decision-making, as information guiding our interview protocols, and as sensitization of our interpretative filters for later analyzing them.

We prepared our interview guides collaboratively, relying on what we had learned from the participant observation and platform analyses. We started from an interview guide for the developers, and after having conducted these interviews, informed by what we found in those interactions, we created the interview guide for users. We also revised the interview guide after having used it in a couple of test interviews in each country. Our interviews were semi-structured and in depth, which means that we followed the guide loosely, making sure to cover all the topics while not being overly invested in their specific order, or in the precise formulation of questions. This allowed for the conversations to revolve around aspects and experiences relevant to our interlocutors. The interviews among Alastonsuomi users were conducted by Maria Vihlman, who builds on this material for their doctoral research, and the interviews in Sweden and Estonia by Jenny and Katrin, respectively.

Broadly, the themes in our interview guide focused on situating the studied platform within the social media ecosystem and our participants' social media practices, covering their personal background in terms of their site use trajectory, their experiences of using sexual sites, and the value that all this holds. We then moved to the interviewees' experiences with the platform's design, features, functionality, and rules, inquiring after the digital sexual identities and social relations (as well as hierarchies between those) that they saw the platforms as affording. We asked how they considered platformed sexual cultures in connection to local contexts and, finally, how they perceived vulnerabilities and risks, on the one hand, and sexual pleasure, on the other, as being at play on the sites. Within the context of ethnographic and walkthrough data, our interviews offered deep insights into how platform affordances are perceived by users, how these shape and constrain practices of use, and how they afford sexual communities and cultures.

The interviews were conducted during the COVID-19 pandemic in 2020–2022, the methodological and ethical implications of which we will return to shortly. To find our participants, we combined snowballing with reaching out to specific users and posting calls for participation on-platform. On Alastonsuomi, where the admin did not respond to our interview request, recruitment was done off-platform through calls on websites focusing on sexual cultures.

We recruited participants in several stages, in part using a methodology developed in previous research on digital sexual cultures (Tiidenberg 2019) where the preliminary contact is pseudonymous (the researcher can also be pseudonymous, but Jenny and Maria were not). If there was initial interest, we provided additional information (describing, among other things, how the interview would be conducted and informed consent negotiated). In the case of continued interest, we asked for the prospective participants' email addresses, to which we forwarded a formal information sheet including a detailed description of the research's rationale, process, and data management. An informed consent document was sent when setting up the interview.

Our recruitment tactics were site-specific and tailored to best fit each context. The case study of Darkside, for example, started out with a firm focus on queer women, trans and non-binary participants, strategically composed to address not only sexual expressions at social margins but also the kinds of sexual norms that are created when moving beyond "vanilla" tastes. These interviewees spoke at length about the dominance of straight cismen in the world of kink and on the platform, which then led us to more purposefully recruit men.

The question of community is both valuable and complicated as a methodological concept. Continuing with the example of Darkside, participants both feel and do not feel that they belong to the same kink community. Depending on gender identities and sexual orientations, their primary belonging may be in a separatist community of queer women and trans and non-binary people, a community of gay men, or one catering to the pansexual, straight-leaning crowd more broadly. While there are some overlaps between these contexts, given that some people have multiple and fluid belongings, they are also rather distinct (cf. Simula 2019, 10). Then again, as the interviewees circled around their uses of the platform, they did mark it as an overarching Swedish kink community. For many, this is a community riddled with tension, depending on their proximity to straight, cis-male norms, but it is also a place where they feel at home, as well as where they feel a camaraderie of sorts with fellow Darksiders vis-à-vis the outside world.

We conducted online audio(visual) interviews, each from forty minutes to two hours in length, mostly via Zoom (although participants were offered the choice of platform), which were then transcribed, open-coded, and pseudonymized. We then created analytic memos (Tracy 2013) and, after discussing these, collaboratively designed pattern codes (Saldana 2009). After coding all data for patterns, we conducted cross-platform thematic analysis. Beyond the shared and systematic analysis, the process has nevertheless been essentially iterative and intuitive in us turning back, and back again, to the interviews in search of insights that we did not initially plan to focus on, or that we would not have recognized at the start of the fieldwork. Over the years that we have spent working on this project, we have done much revisiting that has opened our eyes to new questions and lines of inquiry. This is how it became apparent that we had more to say or, more precisely, that our material needed to be allowed to speak more than is possible within a fixed-length article format, leading us to write this book.

Who Were We Talking To? Our Participants

Our participants are, for the most part, not casual lurkers but invested users, some of whom have been site members for over a decade. As is the case with any self-selected group of participants, their contributions to our research have, in many cases, been motivated by their active engagement with the sites in question, as well as by the value that these hold in their sexual and social lives, even as some of our interviewees had already opted out from the platforms, and even as many voiced degrees of disillusionment with them. On the one hand, our participants wanted to describe their own experiences and showcase their value—to make their perspectives heard. On the other hand, they articulated a desire to understand the platforms' sociality and function more fully and accurately, beyond the merely sexual that they felt these are easily reduced to. Ville elaborated on the matter: "I know that research is important and you gain important knowledge through it, so if I can help with research, I'm glad to. And, on the other hand, that community is close to my heart on some level that if it can somehow gain visibility, or people talk about it somewhere else as well, then I'm also gladly part of that, too." For her part, Julia appreciated the research project for "making visible all else that Alastonsuomi is than those, flash dicks [dick pics taken with a flash] and sort of hookup culture." Noora went on to consider the potential participants' representativeness, so that our study could grasp what makes the site special for her: "I hope that people of as many genders and sexualities as possible participate in the study as I think that one of the nicest aspects of the site is that you get to see and meet people who have an entirely different world than I do, and it teaches really a lot. It's absolutely a good place to be."

Motivations of participation further expanded to broader questions of platformed sexuality and self-development. Tapio addressed the meta-level of humanity when articulating Alastonsuomi's potential importance, suggesting that

> different sites and the sexuality of social media have maybe shaped and impacted humankind, not just Finnish society, but humanity in general. I think this is an interesting reflection and it's one of the reasons why I'm quite happy to take part in this kind of study. I hope to maybe grow a little bit wiser when talking about these topics, and this presumed wisdom can, in different situations, either in private or in work life, be maybe useful.

Our participants are diversely connected, using the most popular generic social media platforms (e.g., Facebook, Instagram, TikTok), dating apps (e.g., Tinder, Grindr), porn sites (Pornhub being a recurrent referent), and other sexual social media platforms (e.g., FetLife, GROWLr, Recon, Scruff, BDSM-baari, SDC, Xperience United). All in all, the internet plays an important role in our participants' (sexual) lives. While our participants were all born between the 1960s and the early 1990s, the majority of them were born in the late 1970s and the 1980s, thus sexually coming of age when the Web was young, but definitely present. Sara, for example, used her parents' desktop computer to search for spanking videos that resonated deeply with her. She did this with the help of Altavista—a market leader in search engines before Google, launched in 1995—and discovered Darkside long before she had the courage to sign up:

> I think I was quite early in understanding this about myself. I think that this interest in BDSM was sparked at the same time as my interest in sexuality in general, in middle school. When you start thinking about what you like and don't like, and so on. I think I searched the way you did in the early days of the internet on your parents' home computer. So I googled, it's the kind of thing you only do when you're a teenager and have no sense of actions having consequences. I probably knew that Darkside existed long before I created an account there, or I know I came in contact with it because I googled. Or whatever it is you did back then, altavisted! [*laughs*]. . . . Maybe I wasn't quite ready to google a lot of weird stuff on the internet when I was like thirteen or fourteen years old. But it was this desire that led me somehow. I remember that I was going to start high school, and I was going to move away from home when I started high school, and I remember writing in my diary that "I've been going to these weird spanking websites all summer, and I don't

actually think it's anything strange, I'm going to keep doing it." I remember that I wrote like a defense speech to myself. Well, this is how it will be now, that I somehow understood that this is the kind of dignity this will have. Of course, there are also stories where people have struggled a lot with feelings of shame, but I was just too stupid to feel that way. Somewhere in my teens, the desire took over in some way. . . . And there is also a kind of safety in numbers. I think that Darkside was like that. Most of the people who have been, who are my BDSM friends are pretty tidy, well-functioning people who have socially responsible professions, so it seems to have worked out pretty well for them.

For many of our participants, their discovery of kink (or a vocabulary to articulate the impulses, curiosities, and desires that had always accompanied their relating to other people) and of themselves as being drawn to sexual practices and expressions beyond the prescribed bounds of normalcy coincided with a more general sexual awakening. This, as explained by Sara, had at one point made sexuality, nonnormative sexual practices, and online connections to some extent inseparable from one another.

Most of our participants are cisgender, but they include one trans man and a few identifying as both female and non-binary. Their sexual self-identifications include straight, gay, lesbian, bisexual, bi-curious, pansexual, and queer—as well as gradations such as "mainly straight"—while their kinks and relationship practices span from BDSM and fetishism (including things from shibari, age play, needle play, and puppy play, to bondage, spanking, mental dominance, and discipline, and to leather culture, latex clothing, and diaper fetishism), swinging, ethical nonmonogamy, exhibitionism, cross-dressing, and watersports. It is however important to note that tentative, complex, and reflexive self-identifications did abound throughout, as in "I'm a straight man, but I also have feminine sides. . . . I'm only interested in women, but I really enjoy dressing and wearing makeup as a woman. That's how I define my sexuality" (Juhani) and "relationship-anarchist polyamorous kinky" (Julia[1]). For Teemu, self-definition required situational contextualization: "I usually self-define as just a man. But then, in certain situations I clarify, I use the term man with a trans background. . . . I don't usually define [my sexuality], but if I do, then a little depending on the situation, as either bisexual or queer." Aleksi, again, explains that "it's kind of developed over the years, so that previously I lived the life of a bi-man, trying to force myself into that façade." He continues to explain that he has since "basically blossomed and I've lived years as a gay man, but the boundaries are nevertheless so blurry that nothing's straightforward."

While educational background or socioeconomic status were not something that we inquired after, it is not surprising for many of our self-selected participants to have a middle-class bent, considering their investment of time and their overall motivation to contribute to a research project. And, echoing the ethnic makeup of the three platforms, together with the avenues we used for recruitment off-platform, our informants tend to be white and speak Estonian, Finnish, or Swedish as their first language, even as occasional immigrants living in the three countries also made the sample. Such privileged positions are reflective of the compositions of kink communities in a number of other studies, showing how marginalization and risk-taking in kink may be mitigated by race and class privilege (Bauer 2014; Carlström 2018; Weiss 2011).

Most of the Swedish participants have remained in contact with Jenny since the interviews, first in discussions of the interview transcripts where things needed to be clarified and later in relation to publications. The webmaster has been particularly interested in our project progression and even came to our closing conference in Stockholm in Fall 2022. About half of the Alastonsuomi participants remained in contact with Maria in order to both hear about the uses of the interview material and to share their more recent discoveries and thoughts about the platform in a reflexive manner; many also checked the transcriptions and participated in their additional anonymization. Similarly, some of the Estonian interviewees have remained in contact after the interviews and Katrin has interviewed the Estonian developers multiple times.

Continuing contact with participants serves many functions in terms of research ethics, reflexivity, and rigor. It provides important insights referred to as "member checks" of researcher interpretations in the ethnographic tradition (Tiidenberg 2018) and "temperature checks" in particular when it comes to dialogical informed consent and other principles of ethics of care (Tiidenberg 2019). In other words, keeping in touch allows for checking in with participants to make better choices regarding keeping or obscuring certain aspects about their identities or practices in print, and making sure they continue to be comfortable with particular information about them being shared. This is not always necessary but is sometimes incredibly helpful, and keeping an open line of communication after the interview gives researchers access to this valuable resource.

We are grateful for their participation and for what they shared with us in pandemic times of partial self-isolation, which forced many to distance themselves from physical encounters and search for other ways to keep the flame alive.

(Not) Having Sex in a Pandemic

DAVID: Well, rubber is not the most insulating material!

JENNY: No, it neither breathes, nor does it warm you.

DAVID: It's very impractical, and it gets ruined by water, air, oil. It gets ruined by everything and it's crazy impractical. But at the same time, no pain no gain.

JENNY: You look fantastic!

DAVID: Thank you!

It was cold out that day. As the pandemic had turned physical intimacy and closeness into physical distance, our interviews had to be conducted on screen instead of face to face. For the interview that Jenny did with the founder of Darkside and its longtime webmaster, David Jatko (who due to his public role has asked to appear in this book under his real name), they both made an effort to look nice. He was in full fetish wear, head to toe in a gorgeous black, shiny bodysuit of rubber. Given his consistent rubber presence in social media and on the streets of Stockholm, we expected as much from him. In an attempt to somehow match his vibe, yet remain in the domain of scholarly respectability, Jenny was wearing a black silk shirt for the occasion. The black silk had a deep shimmer in the Zoom window, accentuating and propping up David's lively, lacquered presence. It was one of the first interviews we did for the project, and we felt we were off to a good start.

It may seem like a digital platform would be the ideal object of study in the midst of a pandemic. But being screened off, as much as being on screen, can also take something important out of the encounter, making digital spaces rather anemic. Of course, this depends on platform affordances and platform vernaculars. It matters what users think a platform is *for*. Is it primarily a digital sexual space that does not serve as a springboard toward meeting up? Or is it a digital place that, while enjoyable in and of itself, is always ripe with the potential for differently or more embodied encounters? These different motivations may also coexist and shift over time. Taking pleasure in flirting, or learning, or socializing on these platforms does not preclude using them as a catalyst for hookups. And conversely, grounding one's sexual practices in play dates and play parties does not drain the networked dimension of one's sexual life of meaning, either.

Our point here is that something can happen to this interplay, or layer-ing, of digital and more obviously physical modes of connecting and relating when social distancing is mandated and physical proximity cut short. On the one hand, digital connectivity may grow increasingly intense as one of the few safe ways to enjoy, flirt, and desire (see Sundén 2021). On the other hand (and as we discuss at length in chapter 5), digital communities and platforms in general—and sexual platforms in particular—are deeply interlaced with physical bodies and locations. As club nights and play parties came to a stand-still (at least formally), it was almost as if our platforms, too, held their breath for a moment. No matter how tailored for digital existence and experiences they may be, such spaces still need flesh and blood and skin and warmth. And nobody seemed particularly inspired to socially distance, perhaps especially because these communities are more used to sexual safety measures than many others. In kink and BDSM communities, for example, safety measures around risky sexual practices, such as routines for disinfecting tools and sur-faces, are well developed. There is a decent supply of not only face masks but full-on gas masks. There are also habits of engaging in erotic powerplay from a relatively safe physical distance. After all, a bullwhip can easily be six meters long, while public health officials only recommended two for safety.

It was precisely such inventive sexual practices that made an official set of unusually candid safe sex and COVID-19 guidelines from the New York City Department of Health go viral—from Twitter, to *The New York Times*, to *Vogue*, and beyond. "You are your safest sex partner," the guidelines informed us, and advised to wash both your hands and your sex toys with soap and water for twenty seconds before and after sex. The short document went on to acknowledge safe practices in sex work, digital sex, oral sex, and anal sex—even glory hole action that uses a wall as that extra layer of protection—all things that are not usually part of governmental public health communica-tion. But no matter how inventive sex in a pandemic might be, many par-ticipants longed to reach the tail end of the virus, or at least better vaccine coverage. Björn elaborates, "I am looking forward to the big orgies that will occur later on, once the vaccine has been released and proven to work. It will be like after the Black Death!"

Context-wise, COVID-19 policies were different across the three countries involved in this study, ranging from Sweden's (in)famous laxness in keeping restaurants and other businesses open even during transmission peaks, to the closing of schools, universities, bars, libraries, cinemas, and theaters, and the banning of public meetings in Finland and Estonia. Estonia also mandated asking for proof of vaccination to be able to participate in certain events (e.g., to see a movie) and asking for masking in supermarkets; both regulations had a deeply polarizing effect on the society, and their lawfulness has been much debated. Yet none of these countries had extensive firm lockdowns comparable to those in place in Italy or the UK delimiting people's mobility outside the home. It was recommended that people not socialize beyond their key social circles and that they should self-isolate when diagnosed with COVID-19, yet none of this was monitored or otherwise controlled. Some of our participants discussed not hooking up during the pandemic, and others spoke of still doing so. Tiina unpacks some of the ambivalence:

> The past year, that I've been on Alastonsuomi, it's exactly enabled social connections. Since in the midst of COVID we've been pretty much in our own foxholes and I'd just broken up, but I had kind of a need to get it out of myself as I'd been in a really dry relationship. So, I needed closeness and specifically sex. I felt that Alastonsuomi is a really good platform for finding company, and I was really active to meet people there, roughly from last Midsummer till October or so. I somehow thought that, well, it's maybe better to meet one person at a time in your own home than go into a mass of people in the midst of COVID. So yes, it absolutely brought closeness within that COVID year and, basically, 95 percent of the men I've met through there have been exceedingly nice and, well, I've had a really fine sieve, too, I haven't gone to meet just anyone. But I admit that without Alastonsuomi it would've been a pretty lonely year.

Others, like Elin, used sexual platforms to feel less lonely during a time when all major kink events were put on hold:

> I think Darkside has meant even a bit more now during the pandemic, when you haven't actually been able to go to events or meet people that way. Plus, all the big events I was going to go to this year have been canceled. So, I think it has meant a lot to just be able to check in and see that you are not alone. To be able to see that there is a larger context, it has meant quite a lot.

Hookup app companies further played into the sexual ambiguity of the (early) pandemic, at a time when people craved connection but may have been reluctant or unable to meet up, issuing sensible in-app public service announcements at odds with their business mission to, instead, promote dating at a distance (see Duguay et al. 2024; Sundén 2021). Tinder was claiming, "Your wellbeing is our #1 priority," Bumble urged people to take their dates virtual, and Grindr's tagline read "Stay home, stay connected," which quickly changed to "Staying safe at home can still be sexy. You are your own best sex partner, so take some time to practice self-care☺." While some of our participants defied government recommendations to socially distance, many cut down on their hookup habits in ways that recharged their platformed sex lives.

In the context of the pandemic, sexual platforms thus grew in importance as people (mainly white-collar workers and students) began to work remotely, spending much time at home and being online for most of it. Uses of online porn, too, peaked in the spring of 2020 as different parts of the world went into lockdowns and as people self-quarantined (e.g., Böthe 2022; Grubbs et al. 2022; Sundén 2021; Zattoni et al. 2020). Similarly, people returned to virtual environments they had previously frequented but had since abandoned (Barreda-Àngeles and Hartmann 2022; Paul et al. 2022). Basically, *all* online traffic peaked, making explicit the extent to which networked connections have grown infrastructural to everyday lives, as well as the centrality of social media platforms—sexual ones included—in the making and maintaining of social connections and belongings.

Our project began in January 2020 with the intent of preferably meeting up with the participants, yet things shifted quickly, and, by the time the interviews were set up, we were working from our bedrooms, kitchens, living rooms, and home offices. On the one hand, it may have been easier for us to recruit interviewees under pandemic conditions than otherwise, given that many had grown bored of the spatial limitations and the monotony of socially distanced lives (Paasonen 2022) and a scholar reaching out could have felt like a diversion. This was largely before Zoom fatigue set in, and when the possibility to connect through screens still felt like something like a lifeline. Yet COVID-19 forms something of a tacit background for our research in that we did not explicitly inquire after people's experiences of the pandemic, even as we were all living through it (albeit in obviously different ways), trying to measure risks and navigate safety.

Safe Sex, Safe Interviewing?

Quite independent of pandemic contexts, the question of safety is vital not only in sexual practices but also in researching them. Many of our interviewees engage in sexual practices that are marginal or even stigmatized in ways that render encounters with a researcher potentially problematic for them. Our own (non)belonging to the communities we study connected to this in various ways. Sometimes belonging to the group (either in terms of the sexual subculture or in terms of participating on the platform) helped in establishing trust as it signaled that we approached what our participants were doing from a position of empathy, or at least from a position of withholding judgment.

For example, Jenny's belonging to a queer BDSM community helped with trust, as did the fact that while she used to be part of the more public scene, she had over time become more of a private practitioner. The participants could then take comfort in knowing that she was one of them, even though not currently coexisting with them in public, physical venues. There is just something not overly sexy about sharing play spaces with research participants (or students, for that matter, which is bound to happen when you have taught gender studies for a decade and a half). It can also be ethically complex, perhaps in particular if erotic power exchange is a core practice, as there is a different form of power at play in research (and teaching). The downside of being a (partial) insider is of course that things may remain unarticulated, as mutual understanding and shared experiences are expected, when in fact they might not be there. Further, some of our other credentials helped. Maria, who conducted all the Finnish interviews, is a clinical sexologist and an accredited sex therapist who was at the time working for Sexpo, a well-known Finnish NGO specialized in sexual training, counseling, therapy, and consultation. Their decade-long professional experience added a particular tone to the interviews they conducted. At the time of the interviews, Katrin's coauthored book with Emily van der Nagel on sex and social media had just been translated to Estonian and had received some media attention—this, too, in some situations, helped.

Assumed belonging also involved some complications, ones intensified by the ongoing pandemic and people's different ideological stances connected to following (or not following) governmental recommendations for social distancing. The nonmonogamists interviewed by Katrin tend to move rather quickly from initial conversation on platform to dates in cafés, and then further to events, or bedrooms. Some continued doing so when many others were avoiding contact to prevent the spread of COVID-19. There were a couple of instances when Katrin asked for an interview and received an invitation for a face-to-face date, or, memorably, to accompany the participant to a group sex event. While "be my date for an orgy" does have a lot of potential as an opening for an ethnographic vignette, it does also introduce additional calculus over risk and safety into one's work. This situation created a need for the researcher to occupy conflicting positionalities when concurrently asking someone for their time and opening up on a potentially sensitive topic, but also when negotiating possibly conflicting attitudes toward the pandemic and its regulation measures and making good choices about one's own health and safety. Further, while being invited on a date or an orgy in a good-natured, unconditional way after an interview may feel like evidence of well-established rapport, having one's request for an interview be met with an invitation for sex framed as kind of a precondition of, or payment for, one's participation in the project can in fact come across as threatening, or creepy.

It was up to the participants to pick an interview setup that, given the circumstance, had the right balance of safety, disclosure, and partial anonymity. All interviews were conducted in Estonian, Swedish, and Finnish, and the direct quotes in this book are translated by us. One of the interviews was conducted face to face in Stockholm before the second viral wave hit, but the others were held online. We mostly used Zoom, both with and without video (Maria turned off the cameras and changed the interviewees' usernames to date tags while recording for an added level of anonymity), as well as on the phone with audio alone. The audio conversations were particularly intimate, as the absence of the visual made for an exceedingly focused exchange and cloaked the conversations in a blanket of presumed, faceless similarity.

Zoom has very particular methodological affordances in encouraging particular ways of relating, while making others difficult, or plain impossible. For example, the impossibility of eye contact, and the sometimes-distracting feature of staring at oneself (even if this function can be disabled), tends to entail a certain sense of distance, or even a kind of social numbness. At the same time, this being the white-collar pandemic modus operandi, lots of people—including ourselves and many of our interviewees—quickly got used to it. There is nevertheless a certain trepidation connected to what one will see when switching on the camera, perhaps even more so for the researchers than for the participants. In a September 2020 entry of her researcher diary, Katrin has written the following fieldnote: "I did not expect having to say hello to toddlers. I did not expect screaming kids on laps. I was somewhat worried to opening the call to see someone wanking; it was oddly disconcerting to see a kid instead." A couple of interviews later, the binary between the explicitly sexual and the parental got further complicated: "Well, today I was first greeted with view of a naked torso of a man, next to him his wife in a tank top and tiny panties. Visually very much a 'we have come here to seduce you' aesthetic. Then a moment later, suddenly, a baby. It had a strange impact in terms of me choosing a voice, or a vibe for the conversation."

It should however be noted that most of our video conversation participants were *not* scantily clad or sporting fetish gear, but rather wore loose hoodies and t-shirts at home and work attire at their offices—during or after work hours. The video could also be turned off entirely as they went on a walk that took them through surroundings unbeknownst to us. During the strictest lockdown in Estonia, when most everyone was directed to stay at home, we even conducted one typed chat-based interview, as the participant was not forthcoming about their use of the platform to their partner and both of them were home. Such layers of people revealing and concealing things, showing particular facets of themselves without displaying everything, or much at all, are in line with how the three platforms studied allow for users to decide what to show, how, and to whom. The intimacy of the conversations was often aligned with the level of privacy of the chosen spaces—but not always. One particularly open and candid interview interlinked the researcher's bedroom with a small conference room discretely booked by the interviewee for this very purpose. In another case, an interviewee was speaking from their office, interrupted at one point by an entering assistant, who, according to the unperturbed interviewee, "knows about my lifestyle anyway."

Talking About Sex Ethically

Our project received approval from the ethics review boards of each of our respective universities in Finland and Estonia, as well as from The Swedish Ethical Review Authority (a national government agency). We used the gold standard of research ethics (explicit informed consent, confidentiality, carefully deidentifying the data) as our point of departure, but we also went a step further to incorporate an ethics of care to mitigate things that might feel intrusive or problematic to our participants. An ethics of care does not start from a distance (from the field, from those "we" research, and in writing), but from closeness and complicity (Rooke 2009; Sundén 2012; Sundén and Sveningsson 2012). Further, a care approach to ethics is relational in going beyond avoiding harm and by aspiring to beneficence achieved through empathy and trust (Ellis 2007; Held 2006; Noddings 1984, 2003; Preissle and

Han 2012). This kind of care is concurrently a value and a practice, affective inasmuch as cognitive, and typically practiced by "adopting a particular attitude toward participants (mindful of power relationships, deeply engaged); toward representing them (trying to give voice to participants' own perspectives and represent them in emancipatory ways); and in an ambition of giving back to, or being useful for, the communities" (Tiidenberg 2019, 7). We accomplished this through contextual knowledge brought forth through ethnographic immersion. While some of us have been on these platforms for years, something certainly shifts through the change of perspective from user to researcher—a shift that makes you see things in a different light, even if you hardly see these things for the first time. This change of roles is of course not unproblematic, as these platforms are strung together by intimate connectivity and, at least in part, community formations that are experienced as deeply valuable. These collective formations of vulnerability and trust strike a fragile balance that the presence of a researcher may quite easily disrupt. We tried to remain mindful of this, especially in our choices of what to analyze and reproduce as data.

We enacted our ethics via several small tweaks, such as being cautious in what we represent about the platforms and their content, conducting pseudonymous interviews, negotiating pseudonymous informed consent, and re-pseudonymizing participants' on-platform usernames. We did not ask for their real names (first names were often volunteered by participants but not recorded in data), and the interviews have been recorded, transcribed, analyzed, and presented in using only research-specific pseudonyms: To make it clear, Tapio, Juhani, Mari, Anna, Klara, and other names we refer to our participants by in this book are their research-specific pseudonyms. We have chosen to not analyze or reproduce any visuals from the platforms. In our ethics, sensitivity is key, but it is operationalized as sensitivity to the context and our participant's experiences, rather than as a wholesale categorization of everything they tell us as sensitive data.

Sexuality as Sensitive Data by Default

Within the European Union, research ethics is significantly shaped by the General Data Protection Regulation, introduced in 2016 and passed into law in 2018. In GDPR, data relating to a person's sex life or sexual orientation falls directly into the category of "sensitive personal data" (also known a "special categories of personal data"). The special protection afforded to sensitive personal data aligns with EU's intent of fighting discrimination based on sexual identities, sexual practices, and other acts that may reveal sexual orientation (as established in Article 21 of the EU Charter of Fundamental Rights). Hence, under GDPR, the processing of special categories of personal data is generally prohibited, encompassing "the processing of personal data revealing racial or ethnic origin, political opinions, religious or philosophical beliefs, or trade union membership, and the processing of genetic data, biometric data for the purpose of uniquely identifying a natural person, data concerning health or data concerning a natural person's sex life or sexual orientation" (EU 2018). Such data can only be collected if specific exceptions apply, and, in such instances, it must be "be handled with extra care and security." This legislative shift marked a drastic change in ethics review processes in many EU countries. In Finland, for example, humanities and social science research into sexuality, pre-GDPR, necessitated a review process only if dealing with vulnerable subjects, such as minors or pregnant women, or if subjecting study participants to sexually explicit materials—the topic of sexuality itself was (and still is) not, according to the National Board of Research Integrity, deemed a particular risk. In Estonia, there were no ethics committees for social science and humanities projects at most universities, which relied on researchers' self-regulation instead. Post-GDPR, there are increased mandates for procedural research ethics, according to which all researchers of sexual practices and cultures are treading on sensitive, and hence inherently risky, terrain.

Ethics committees' guidelines make seeking ethics review mandatory in projects that collect and analyze sensitive data. This needs to be done before any fieldwork has started, adding logistical factors to the project. This, we suggest, presents specific problems for critical sexuality studies: first, from the perspective of destigmatization and the acknowledgment of the importance of sexuality as that which makes the self and the social alike and, second, because there is ample evidence that subjects and populations deemed vulnerable by regulatory mechanisms are understudied since researching them requires more effort and resources (Lai et al. 2006; Markham and Buchanan 2012; Yan and Munir 2004). While we in no way advocate for a laissez faire approach to research ethics within critical sexuality studies, we do want to highlight the implications that categorical assumptions of sensitivity and vulnerability have.

To explore these implications, we now discuss a particularly poignant case in our project—ethics regulation in Sweden. Sweden is one of few countries in the world that regulates ethical review of research by law (Eldén 2020; Johansson et al. 2023), and it is a criminal offense to initiate research projects that, for example, involve the processing of sensitive personal data without first obtaining approval from The Swedish Ethical Review Authority (Etik-prövningsmyndigheten, EPM). EPM is a national government agency with the explicit aim of protecting participants involved in research. The basic principle of their ethics review is that research may be approved only if it can be carried out with respect for human dignity in ways that take human rights and fundamental freedoms into consideration by prioritizing human well-being over the needs of society and scientific research. Moreover, "research may be approved only if its scientific value outweighs the risks it may entail for the research participants' health, safety and personal data privacy" (Etik-prövningsmyndigheten n.d.).

Originally developed to regulate research ethics in biomedicine, the Swedish ethical review system is, first and foremost, concerned with protecting "research subjects" from risk and harm, both physically and mentally. Research ethics is here primarily a form of risk management and less the kind of reflexive research practice more commonly used in the humanities and the social sciences (Quennerstedt et al. 2014). The Swedish ethical review system has, for this very reason, been criticized because the institutionalized ethics review prevents many researchers from describing their ethical dilemmas in ways that resonate with their views on ethical research practices (e.g., Thor Tureby 2019). In a biomedi-cal discourse, research subjects are perceived as vulnerable and in need of protection. In the extensive form, which is the basis of the EPM ethical review, there are multiple sections on risk, harm, and perceived benefits, which require descriptions of the risks involved for research participants (directly building on The Helsinki Declaration, a statement of ethical principles for medical research involving human subjects). This includes prompts such as "Describe how the project has been designed to mini-mize the risks for the research subjects" and "Describe the contingency plan for dealing with unexpected incidental findings or events during the research process that may jeopardize the safety of the research sub-jects." The risks involved include physical or mental harm, pain, or dis-comfort, as well as short-term or long-term invasion of privacy. When it comes to the processing of personal data, this may involve the possibility of identification despite pseudonymization.

To protect research participants from being exposed to exploitative research—to, for example, circumvent their explicit consent or expose their sensitive personal data—is of course crucial. But what risks or harms are imagined to arise or become amplified when participants are invited to talk about their sexual practices or experiences? What does it mean to research sexuality when sexual lives and orientations are understood as sensitive by default, and when sex—precisely by being understood as this sensitive thing—is intimately coupled with notions of risk and harm? These questions, we suggest, scale well beyond the legal particularities of the Swedish context, as they influence ethics review processes across the EU, and elsewhere.

Swedish scholars have developed vernaculars for articulating risk and harm, as well as ways of doing ethical research in a particular way in response to how the topic is operationalized by EPM. To safeguard against being rejected by EPM, we included information about where to turn to for counseling, should the need arise, and we specified the type of "sensitive" questions or themes involved in our study. By letting the participants' uses of sexual platforms be the focus of the study, more direct questions about sexual practices were avoided and merely entered the conversations on their initiative. Such tiptoeing around questions regarding sexual practices and experiences, however, made little sense to the interviewees, who were more than happy to share.

We argue that to treat sex and sexuality as sensitive matters by default takes something important away from the participants' sense of agency, their ownership of their stories, and their ability to decide what they feel comfortable sharing. To feel *safe* as a participant, to have one's data kept safe, and to have it processed safely is essential; this becomes particularly clear with participants who experience stigmatization due to their sexual identities or practices. But this does not mean that talking about such practices in and of itself puts someone at risk—on the contrary, this can be a life-affirming instance of being seen and heard. The tacit stigmatization of kink as something that might need counseling when talked about can arguably be much more triggering than talking about it.

Sex Talk and Trauma

Understanding sex as a sensitive matter also ties in with psychological approaches, broadly building on Freud's understanding of sexual fantasies as being bound up with trauma as kind of a playback, or that which Martin Barker (2014, 145) discusses as a "distorted management of childhood problems and traumas, almost always family generated"—as well as something deeply embedded within the dynamics of heterosexual nuclear families. As critical feminists, we are not prone to downplay the burden and power of sexual trauma, yet we do find it necessary to consider sex and trauma on open-ended terms void of causality. The marking of sexuality as a realm of trauma, be it actualized or potential, echoes the labeling of sex as sensitive, objectionable, offensive, obscene, or risky on social media platforms, and hence something regulated and effaced in the overall name of user safety (as in "NSFW," see Paasonen et al. 2019). Basically, all of it becomes a terrain of possible harm.

Here, our participant Julia's narrative is particularly noteworthy as something to think with and through. Having been on Alastonsuomi since becoming a legal adult, she had acquired all her "friendships and social relations" on-platform, so that:

> It's basically enabled everything that there is, in terms of social relations. I'm the kind of person for whom Alastonsuomi has shaped my whole life, in a good way. I've always been sort of very uninhibited and open and sort of a naturist person who doesn't very much worry about nudity, for example, so as an eighteen-year-old young woman I didn't fit in very well with the people who do, and I never really have. But then I found Alastonsuomi and started to meet people and found my way through chat to summer cottage meets and, so, I've found the most important friends and people in my life there. It's given shape, in a certain way, to our large family where everyone looks after one another. I have a huge and really important support network there, and a huge number of lovely friends and just lovely people and contacts.

Against preconceptions of a young woman joining a sexual platform to potential harm and predation, Julia's story is manifestly celebratory. She told us about how Alastonsuomi has enabled her to live and craft her life, from the initial seeking of affirmation while being a young woman insecure of her body, and getting positive feedback on the platform "on how gorgeous and great and sexy you are . . . in such a total and radical way," to her establishing lasting social ties. She basically narrates this as a journey from (desired) sexual objecthood to sexual subjecthood. This is not, however, merely a narrative of fun and laughs, as "pretty shit experiences" have also played a part: "Once I had to face the kind of thing that I got raped on [a meetup] trip. And it's something that we've dealt with [in her Alastonsuomi meet family] for a very long time. The person in question has done that to many people through the site, and they haven't been caught yet. It's been kind of a grief within our Alastonsuomi community for many years." Explaining that the man in question is manipulative and that it often takes the victims a while to realize that sexual violence has in fact taken place, Julia discusses the predatory behavior as difficult to prevent, even when foregrounding that she has received "really a lot of support" both from her "meet family"—the group of people with whom she meets up for sex parties—and individual people she's met through the site.

This is a gruesome story of sexual predation, both past and ongoing, yet one that Julia does not frame as a problem intrinsic to the site itself. Rather, it is posed as an issue of the man's opaque and imperceptible modes of operation. The interview obviously offers no access to Julia's experience beyond what she wishes to disclose to us, and how, and it is precisely that which occupies us here: the recounting of sexual assault as something of an illustrative anecdote, "a pretty shit experience," that she does not dwell on, or particularly elaborate on, in terms of personal harm. There is no indication in the interview that revisiting the experience is a source of pain, as Julia remains in control of her narrative. Importantly, too, this interview was conducted by Maria, someone with extensive specialist training and professional experience in sex counseling and therapy.

Moving on to discuss potential vulnerabilities connected to the uses of the site, Julia associates these with outsider perceptions rather than on-platform experiences, explicitly renouncing the coupling of sexual communication with potential harm. Julia associates potential vulnerabilities with open expressions of sexuality in contexts where these may become stigmatized:

> My job is such that my sexual orientation could be pretty heavily used against me, if need be. There've been situations in the kink scene, for example, where in court they have shown photos of the other partner being like submissive in bed and sustaining violence when discussing whether they'll be given custody or not. So this kind of sexuality can be used against you—"If you're like this in the bedroom, you're not capable of these things in your life"—which I find really horrible.

Vulnerability is here associated with the risk of unwanted exposure and the operations of sexual normativity in situations of context collapse, when content shared within the (relatively) safe space of the sexual platform leaks to other milieus. Yet, Alastonsuomi is hardly simply safe for Julia, either, despite her notable attachments to the site. Its gendered social vernaculars can also be a source of irritation and hurt for her, as she explains:

> Just a few days ago, one male person approached me on Alastonsuomi in like a very sexualizing and kind of fetishizing way. But, like, addressing me as his biggest fantasy who's surely totally ready to discuss just how I could fulfill his biggest fantasies after having just said "hi." And I'm like, *jeez* [in English], buy me flowers first [*laughs*], or something. And then I gave him public feedback on his profile, like "Hey, even though I'm here, and I express my sexuality very openly, I'm still a real person." That I'm not some walking *fetish factory* [in English], but I kind of said that sharply. But, anyway, my point was that I'm here for me and not as some always-ready sex object. And then a couple of days later an eighteen-year-old woman messaged me, saying that she'd seen my comment on the man's profile and that she wanted to thank me for setting a good example on how to respond to men with no manners who are objectifying women there. So, you have to stand up for yourself, on that platform, as the flipside of the openminded community is that you get tasteless and thoughtless comments since some people don't have enough blood for both ends of their body at the same time.

Defining herself as a "wild rubber perv," Julia discusses Alastonsuomi as her place "where I can be myself," it having impacted her body image and sexual selfhood "beyond words." Using the platform has also been a learning experience in the course of which she has become better equipped to deal with unwanted attention by drawing personal boundaries. Julia's account is markedly one of sexual agency where her boundaries have previously been breached, but where she is now the one to draw the line, and where the "shit" experienced through the platform does not cancel out its importance for her ways of being in the world.

We are lingering on this specific interview, not by virtue of it being the only example recounting sexual violence occurring via the platforms we study, but rather due to how Julia makes sense of it when addressing the value that she attaches to Alastonsuomi, and due to the situation of the interview itself. Despite its equalitarian reputation, Finland has high degrees of violence against women. According to recent nationally representative studies, 34 percent of Finnish women aged eighteen to seventy-four have experienced physical violence in their relationships, 9 percent reported having been raped in them, and 54 percent of all women have been otherwise sexually harassed (Attila et al. 2022; Tilastokeskus 2023). Julia's account thus has to be interpreted in this framework where the risk of sexual aggression remains a constant. This also means that online platforms are not necessarily perceived of as particularly risky as such, given the anonymity and distance that they allow for, even as they necessarily reflect the gender dynamics within the society at large.

We suggest that Julia's self-narration of moving from sexual objecthood to subjecthood is of importance to her and to how she wants to be perceived. Us framing the account in terms of sexual trauma would not do justice to how she sets the parameters of importance in what she wishes to disclose and fore-ground. An ethics review board preemptively diagnosing Julia as vulnerable and mandating counseling after the interview would take away from, rather than add to, her sense of safety and agency. It is indeed the value of being able to recount this personal trajectory leading up to the point where she is occupationally moving into sexology, and where her on-platform engage-ments can help younger women navigate its gendered sexual dynamics, that Julia wished to highlight.

Situational Ethics

This chapter set out to offer a practical blueprint of designing a transna-tional, nuanced, and rigorous qualitative research design for studying digi-tal sexual cultures, for navigating ethics review processes, and for reflecting on implicit assumptions of the connections drawn between sex, sensitivity, vulnerability, trauma, and research. Contrary to the premises of data protec-tion legislation and ethics guidelines, we argue that sex talk does not render one automatically vulnerable. Event talking about what are, for most intents and purposes, awful experiences may involve therapeutic, agential, and self-aware acts of empowered communication. There is importance to studying networked sexual cultures that, as our research participants make clear, can be sites of discovery, learning, stigma reduction, and self-expression. We also believe that doing research on online sexual cultures during the pandemic helped highlight interesting moments of negotiating the agency of research-ers and participants by bringing into focus dynamics that might otherwise remain opaque even to seasoned sex and social media researchers. Should it be up to the participant to choose the setting for an interview (on chat, on the phone, on Zoom, at a café, during an orgy?), or should this, from the start, be approached as a negotiation between two individuals with their own boundaries of (dis)comfort? Is the home automatically the safest space to speak about sex?

Rigorous and detailed planning, auditing, and negotiation toward the best course of action is of course vital at each methodological juncture. All ethical questions are, after all, questions of method, and vice versa (Markham 2006). But we do think that good research—both methodologically good as in being rigorous and ethically good as in being beneficent to the participants and the society at large—comes from sensitivity to particular contexts, people, and stories, rather than from casting all sexual data as sensitive or its subjects as vulnerable by default. Our methodological approach, deeply informed by feminist ethics of care, builds on the understanding of ethics as situational and sensitive to the moment and context to remain respectful of and to convey the agency of the participants. This means listening with a keen ear to how participants make sense of sensitivities and vulnerabilities, remaining aware that these may come about in ways and in contexts impossible for us to predict beforehand.

There is default unpredictability to research processes, which for us necessitates a situational, context-sensitive approach to the ethics of care that always tries to be mindful of the power that researchers hold by virtue of their professional status. There are, however, also cases when researchers need to be able to protect themselves, lest the participants empower themselves on their account—as in Alastonsuomi users sending Maria unsolicited, graphic descriptions of the sexual acts they would want to do to them during the platform walkthroughs. An ethics of care in studies of sexual platforms also encompasses self-care (Korn 2017, 105), and the politics and ethics of consent cut both ways.

As we have argued in this chapter, to treat sexual lives as sensitive by default takes something critical from our participants' sense of sexual self and agency, their ability to own their stories and decide for themselves whether they feel comfortable sharing them, and how. To feel safe when you participate in a study—in the sense that your data is stored and processed safely so that you do not risk involuntary outing—is critical. But there is an important difference between such risks of exposure and the risks involved in talking about sexual preferences and experiences. For our participants, prejudice and discrimination in the society at large is the problem, not a research project interested in their views and perspectives. For many of them, participation on sexual platforms is nothing short of empowering, and to share their experiences with researchers something equally affirmative and valuable.

At the very least, our context-sensitive approach allowing for participants to map out the realms of vulnerability, rather than proscribing them from the outside, makes it strikingly clear that casting sexual content and communication as inherently risky and unsafe—as articulated in GDPR and many social media platforms' community standards—bears no connection to how they make sense of and valorize things. These are people into showing off their own bodies, having a look at others, chatting about sexual lives, and getting it on with one another. As discussed in the following chapter, this does not however mean that anything goes. In addition to moderation practices and content policies—to which we will turn next—users also attend to on-platform safety among themselves.

3   Governing from the Margins

Sexual platforms not only allow for but also structure and govern expressions of sexuality. They shape and constrain which cultures emerge, which practices flourish or perish, and how this all unfolds. Platform governance is a matter of how users perceive platform affordances and how these connect with possibilities for action. Yet this is also a matter of how platforms are built, what rules developers set for using them, and what in turn are matters of law, regulation, and the interpretation of cultural norms (Gillespie 2018; Gorwa 2019; Klonick 2018; Suzor et al. 2018; Tiidenberg 2021). Here, sexual platforms and general-purpose social media platforms are often set strictly apart, given how it is increasingly the norm to ban sexual expression on more mainstream sites (as discussed in chapter 1). Most generic social media platforms draw the line of unwanted content at explicit sexual content and pornography, representations of violence and obscenity, harassment of other users, hate speech, representations of or promotion of self-harm, and representations of or promotion of illegal activity, particularly drug use (Gillespie 2018; Tiidenberg and van der Nagel 2020, 54–58). But if sexual platforms are approached and understood as social media instead, the norms attached to the sexual are bound to shift. Or, perhaps more to the point, the governance practices of the platforms we studied render evident the fundamental sociality of the sexual.

This chapter explores the affordances and governance of the three platforms, focusing on how sexual content and communication are articulated and imagined in business models, content policies, and moderation practices. We suggest that *value* offers a useful concept in platform governance, one separate from notions of safety that dominate global discussions on the topic to date. When nudity and sex are detached from notions of risk and harm, and considered as the stuff that build sociality instead, an intriguing model for platform governance emerges.

To discuss how the notion of safety becomes uncoupled, even if not entirely removed, from sexual content, we start by analyzing both explicit and tacit assumptions of intended platform use, asking how gender and desire play into content policies and moderation principles as well as what role purchased participation plays in user practices and experiences (cf. Light et al. 2018). We then move to discussing how the risks and hazards connected to socio-sexual exchanges are framed, imagined, and experienced on the platforms as being much less about sex, nudity, or "obscenity" than about consent, authenticity, and the avoidance of harassment.

Imitation Is the Greatest Form of Flattery

In the most obvious sense, sexual platforms are social media by virtue of having been designed as such. Their developers emulate and remix elements from established mainstream platforms and their functionalities while also expanding their affordances to better serve sexual ends. The sites we study share many of the same features, functionalities, governance principles, and moderation solutions as their local predecessors, generic global social media platforms, and, occasionally, even one another—yet they have also come up with alternatives of their own. Rather than downright copying, emulation indicates a use of external models as a basis for building solutions (Rudmark 2021). This means that emulating generic social media services does not require compliance with their content policies as these can well emulate other, more suitable models. How platforms become spaces encouraging the kinds of sociality that they do is then a matter or both citation and remix.

The platforms we study have been inspired by others in a number of ways. The emulation they have undertaken is sometimes straightforward yet can also entail rejection when building a site that in some ways resembles another. For its part, Alastonsuomi was launched as an adult version of IRC-Galleria (est. 2000), a Finnish image gallery once popular among teens with a strict content policy on nudity and sex (Lehtinen 2007; Suominen et al. 2013): In a drastic flip of community standards, nudity is the main rationale of Alastonsuomi. It retains much of IRC-Galleria's functionalities and has gone through only one design overhaul to date, hence representing a vintage approach to platform design. Joonas describes it as "frankly—fucking awful," identifying it as a relic "that should be framed and put in a museum of tech-nology." Juhana elaborates:

> It's made in such a way that that it's not hugely user-friendly. . . . I think it was
> made about fifteen years ago and they've only once had a larger update. It's a very
> basic, even a very old-fashioned site and it lacks—everything—certain sociability,
> and more. It's just a platform for publishing photos and videos, which is very
> simple. . . . I find it very old-fashioned; it doesn't meet today's needs anymore.
> That's why my use has decreased, as it lacks options for sociability. That's really
> a shame; I waited for a long time for it to update, but then I realized that it's not
> going to change, and Instagram and other sites surpass it, at least from my per-
> spective, yeah.

Darkside is one of the few Swedish early 2000s platforms that continues to flourish in the era of big social media. Helgon.net (est. 2002)—an online community for musical subcultures significantly overlapping with alterna-tive sexual cultures and an affinity for latex, rubber, and leather—and Qruiser (est. 2000)—the largest Nordic web community for LGBTQ+ people—served as inspiration for Darkside, creating an infrastructure of sociality recognizable to those already belonging to subcultural domains. Further, the webmaster David (who created Darkside and has run it for over two decades) describes how the site has gone through a series of upgrades, with some of its function-ality emulating, and some pre-dating, features of generic social media like Facebook. For example, you have been able to add people as friends all along, but a personalized media stream or news feed is a more recent addition (and something that Alastonsuomi lacks). "It's difficult to keep up with global tech giants," David says, yet he hopes to strike a balance between the individual-ized feeds and profile-centric sociality of mainstream platforms and the sense of community afforded by shared spaces:

> It's about doing the best you can to offer similar things in a feed. But I think that
> because Darkside isn't aimed at everyone in the society, it also gives you an oppor-
> tunity to have shared spaces and an overview in a way that you can't have on Face-
> book, for example. Here, you can have shared libraries, pictures, contests, and news
> that concern people and create a sense of community. Instead, on Facebook there
> is no community, just a billion individual profiles clustered together in different
> ways. So Darkside has something of both worlds, I'd think.

Libertine.Center is the newest of the three sites and the only one established in the platform era, so it is not surprising for its features, functionality, and design to directly quote the current social media ecosystem. For example, its developers, who were Tumblr users, wanted to build something "like

Tumblr" in terms of a platform that affords vibrant sexual cultures and meta-communicative use of hashtags, but with additional functionalities to compensate for what they thought "sucked" on Tumblr (e.g., Search, Messenger). They also wanted to add Tinderesque functionality as they presumed that the intended users—swingers and group sex enthusiasts—needed it. And, since Libertine.Center was launched about two weeks prior to Tumblr's infamous NSFW ban in December 2018, the consequent shift within the ecosystem of sexual cultures online directly shaped it. According to the Libertine.Center developers, their brand new, still-in-beta platform was included in some of the widely circulated lists of alternative spaces for "Tumblr refugees" to go to. One of the developers said, "We were brand new, we knew nothing, and then we had thousands of new accounts set up every day and everything was glitching. I mean, it was good, too, we got everything fixed and beta tested really fast, but it was like a storm." The avalanche of platform governance "refugees" who tried to use every new site exactly as they had used Tumblr also directly shaped the moderation principles of Libertine.Center. The platform responded to the sudden influx of users and content by incorporating user verification and a freemium model to pre-moderate users rather than the content they post (Tiidenberg 2021). As with Alastonsuomi, here too developers enacted emulation through rejection, by envisioning and building their site to stand apart from the already established Estonian sexual site, iha. ee. That site is nearly identical to Alastonsuomi, having probably emulated it, as well as the photo rating logic à la hotornot.com that was all the rage in the early 2000s. The developers of Libertine.Center claimed that "no younger couple would go on iha.ee" because they are used to and expect features like newsfeeds, timelines, and functionalities such as verification. To imitative and rejective emulation, we can then also add the practice of contextualized emulation, where site developers presume that users accustomed to the current social media ecosystem will not accept previously popular platform designs and features, at least not without added or altered functionality.

Platform Rules and Platform Values

To state the obvious, the platforms we study are not only sex positive but sex-centric: Images, videos, and verbal exchanges of the kind plain banned on Facebook, Instagram, and TikTok form the bulk of content shared on them. From the perspective of platform governance this means that the notion of user safety has pretty much been uncoupled from sexual content. Whereas many leading social media platforms flag sexually suggestive and explicit content as risky or harmful (Paasonen et al. 2019), on these platforms, sex fuels engagements between users, making room for alternate kinds of sociability, even if frictions remain present, and even as obscure content moderation standards still apply (Gorwa et al. 2020; Roberts 2018).

Moderation on social media platforms can be loosely divided into three categories based on: who is moderated (rules about who gets to participate), what is moderated (rules set for content; what is allowed or not), and how moderation is performed (the application of rules and the tactics for checking compliance and noncompliance, usually by combining human and algorithmic actions) (Tiidenberg et al. 2021). Starting from the top—who is being moderated—all three sites rely on age-gating and stipulate that users should be over eighteen years old, and by joining acknowledge the platforms' sexual nature. The platforms vary in terms of the broader imaginaries of intended users and use: Darkside houses a wide range of sexual expressions, embracing almost anything when it comes to (legal) kinks and forms of fetishism. It prioritizes openness, kink outness, and destigmatization in the name of sexual justice, thus siding with BDSM activists, but is careful not to impose openness on members in ways that would compromise their safety. Alastonsuomi does not address any specific sexual subculture or community, taking a rather horizontal approach to sexual visibility instead. As we discuss in the following chapters, sexual communities on Alastonsuomi result from self-organization rather than targeted address or profiling done by the platform: The site simply invites naked self-presentation. Finally, Libertine.Center has gone through a number of interface, features, and functionality adjustments, including tweaks to their self-identification and name (currently LC Dating). Mostly, as articulated by both the developers and the platform itself, the tweaking has happened at the intersection of "dating app (for swingers)" and "sexual social media platform."

Moving to what content is being moderated, all three platforms have specific rules regarding photos. Alastonsuomi and Libertine.Center both stipulate that users should be present in the images they publish, that they hold the copyright, and that everyone else appearing in them do so consensually and are legal adults. Alastonsuomi's rules further add that photos should not feature any animals, violence, or racism, or incite violence or racism, in accordance with Finnish law. Darkside sets specific rules for profile pictures, which should represent the user, or something they think suitably stands in for them, but avoid focusing on "the lower body." The site also stipulates that the material posted by users (images, videos, texts) must not be copyrighted by someone other than themselves.

Finally, platform rules governing what is allowed and what is not are first and foremost linked to economic reasoning, even if this is often articulated through the language of values (Gillespie 2018; Paasonen et al. 2019). All three sites articulate values that users should strive toward, and all list specific things as forbidden. While decoupled from sexuality, things considered "not OK" are similar to what we see in more generic platform governance in that depicting or encouraging violence (Alastonsuomi), racism (Alastonsuomi and Darkside), homophobia (Darkside), or content in any way "defaming, criticizing or otherwise damaging other users" (Libertine.Center) is forbidden. Violence has a slightly different place on Darkside as consensual violence of sorts is a core practice—and pictures of the marks such practices might leave are rather cherished—which makes the platform draw the line at "depiction of major bodily injuries." Abuse of membership (spamming, advertising, misusing features and functionality, misrepresenting oneself as someone else) is not allowed; neither is sex work. Illegal activities (attempts at sex trafficking, depictions of actual torture, depictions of incest, sex with minors or animals, drugged sex) are also forbidden, with Darkside presenting the most detailed list, including, for example, webcam shows, sex work, and trade in used panties for money.

Alastonsuomi FAQ advises that "images that are copied from the web, of poor quality or inappropriate are rejected without warning!" The "inappropriate," in this context, has nothing to do with the sexually explicit, but rather with the ambiguous and ephemeral boundaries of what counts as "good taste," so, for example, "analwhore666 or bigcock1337 kinds of usernames are generally rejected." These articulations of acceptability aim to set the overall tone for user sociability that is, on the one hand, visually and textually very much in your face (as close-ups of genitalia do abound), yet on the other hand still loosely controlled and with techniques of reporting and blocking in place. On Darkside, again, the standard of appropriateness (in Swedish *städad*, which also means clean or proper) is linked to profile images not focusing on "the lower body" (*underkroppen*). While there is plenty of visual material that does focus on the nether regions on the platform, we associate this policy with a platform ethos of consent and mutual respect.

In terms of values and principles that are elevated as important on each platform, both Darkside and Libertine.Center explicitly emphasize consent. While on Libertine.Center this is rather laconic—number 5 on the Libertine. Center list of rules simply reads, "No means NO! The Users who ignore this rule will be blocked by the Administrator or by the other users"—on Darkside, users can "opt in" to see sexually explicit material of the genital kind. Here, politeness, consent, and respect for others and what others might be looking for is key, including respect for others' wishes for contact (or the lack thereof).

Presumptions of Gender and Desire

On our platforms, registered users come in a broad age range, within a whole spectrum of gender identities, and with diverse sexual likes, identities, desires, and kinks. This heterogeneity implies a default lack of boundary-building around sexual preferences. However, platform walkthroughs soon revealed limitations to the representation of diversity, starting with the limited gender options on both Alastonsuomi and Libertine.Center. "Male," "female," and "couple" are the proffered gender options on both sites, and users' profiles are visualized through a color-coded gender binary (red/pink vs. blue). Libertine.Center also allows "trans" as a gender identification, whereas on Alastonsuomi people with non-binary identifications need to opt for either male or female, with the pending administrative threat of suspension if this is somehow deemed to be the wrong one.

In the binary yet horizontal space of Alastonsuomi, sexual orientations or nonconforming gender identities remain unmarked on the level of platform structure, yet they are articulated in the content that users post—as in usernames marked with "tv" or "cd" to imply cross-dressing, or in men inviting male-only attention to their bodies. The binary content policy is actively discriminatory in making it possible for people to flag bodies as "not appropriately gendered." Teemu, a trans man, has had his photos removed: "I've even had to have this [laughs] email discussion with some moderator who also didn't seem to understand anything about what it was about." How adherence to such categories is upheld often takes the form of "subtle cultural privilege at work" (Gillespie 2018, 8), even on platforms frequented by marginalized and minoritarian communities. As in Teemu's experiences of getting flagged, this becomes particularly visible in how both platforms and users react to the presumed veracity of gender identifications (Del-Teso-Craviotto 2008; Zolides 2021).

Within these rather limited trans taxonomies, Darkside represents an enlightened outlier. Choices of gender identities and sexual preferences are both multiple and nuanced beyond the binary of male/female. Nonetheless, according to site statistics, Darkside is male dominated (68 percent), as well as dominated by straight forms of sexual self-identification (63 percent), formulated as "attracted to other genders" (84 percent) as opposed to "attracted to similar genders" (24 percent). Besides further categorizations, such as bisexual (16 percent) and pansexual (4 percent), there is also the option of "experimental/questioning" (10 percent), which Erik struggles with as a gay male user: "Something I've been thinking about, there's like this category [on the profile pages] called 'experimental.' You can be that on Darkside. I've been wondering what that means. Because there're quite a few guys who mark themselves as experimental, but they're still straight. So, then, I've been wondering about that." "Questioning" as a sexual orientation usually indicates some uncertainty in sexual self-understandings, signaling an openness to experiment, to find out, or to learn more about oneself. But what at first sight appears to provide such an expansion of the field of possibilities of same-sex desires is here rather cut short by a kind of straightness leaving limited room for doubt.

Beyond identifying one's gender and relational status, all three sites offer ways of signaling what one desires, or is looking for. In some cases, this is offered as a selection of self-referential categories. As a site dedicated to kink and BDSM, Darkside presents a broad palette of sexual preferences, expressions, and roles. In terms of BDSM practices, the most popular ones include bondage, spanking, mental dominance, discipline, and pain, whereas site statistics places, for example, gimp, bootblacking, and pony play at the very end of the extensive list (which users may supplement if something is missing). There is also a more recent addition marking one's relational identities, from monogamy to polyamory to relationship anarchy, and beyond. The male-dominated, straight-leaning crowd aside, the multitude of options makes for movement within and between categories of gender, sexuality, and relationality in ways not limited to neat taxonomies.

Our Darkside interviewees gave ample evidence of the value of an extensive kink list while also pointing at its limitations. For Malin, the importance of the kink list has shifted over time, since quantifying desire is not always helpful, or even possible:

I think the kink list was probably more important in the beginning. Back then, it was much more like I sat and weighed each kink: "Is it one plus? Or is it two? What will it say about me when someone looks at my profile if I put two pluses or one?" I worried a lot about whether I would be chosen or rejected based on what was written there. But the longer you've been doing it, at least for me depending on who [you want to do something with], you can get pretty excited about pretty much anything that's on that list. Those who I want to meet might actually want us to have the same settings on that list, but for me it gives more of an indication and not something that needs to be taken so literally. Today, I think it feels a bit boring if they come to me with an expected list of seven things that should happen.

Emma further elaborates on how kinks and preferences may be context specific in ways not reflected by the design of the kink list:

Some things I like to do with one person but can't imagine doing with someone else. Should I write those in my kink list or no? Because I don't want someone to be like, "Oh, I saw that you're into"—now I can't think of anything—"that you're into electricity, should we play with electricity?" Yes, but I only do that with this specific person. So, is that something to put in, or something not to put in?

The kink list read as an indication of a possible starting point is different from one that understands it as more of a set wish list. These accounts show how set categories, labels, and scales, while useful for communicating certain likes and appetites, may put too much emphasis on certainty and clarity, leaving little space for desire to move and alter between partners and across scenes of sexual play in more ambiguous ways.

On Libertine.Center, the dropdown menu of categories involves a mixed bag of sexual identities, sexual subcultures, preferences, personality traits, and even activities/occupations, which are presented as mutually exclusive—that is, users can (and must, to set up an account) only choose one. Further, these categories are linked to one's chosen gender identity. If one has identified as female, the category options are, for example: "Libertine," "Tantric," "Exhibitionist," "BDSM," "Sugar Baby," "Cuckqueen," "Cuckcake," "Cougar," "Lesbian," "Model," "Naturist," "Nymphomaniac," "Exotic Dancer," "Photographer," "Masseuse," "Mistress," "Submissive," "Slave," "Slut," and "Curious." If one identified as male, they also get to be a "Bull," "Dominant," "Master," "Sissy," or "Sugar Daddy." The categories seem to rely on a number of presumptions regarding gendered preferences for sexual subcultural roles (a female cannot be a Dominant, for example, only a Mistress).

While on Darkside and Libertine.Center it is possible to search for sexual preferences and to mark one's interests, Alastonsuomi does not allow such nuanced labeling. Its image galleries are filtered according to thirteen content categories ("tits," "asses," "bodies," "faces," "group pics," "tattoos," "shoes," "vaginas," "penises," "intercourse pics," "fetish," "art pics," and "piercings") instead. When compared to the elaborate categorizations on porn aggregator sites and kink networking sites such as FetLife, these come across as rather paltry—both overtly general and sort of random, or ad hoc—in missing the specifics of what people may be into, or search for. This results in a logic and rhythm of use reminiscent of online porn use preceding the era of tube sites as people browsed through photo albums and image gallery selections in search of something to catch their attention—something to grab them. Zabet Patterson (2004, 109) described this dynamic as involving both the titillating promise of abundant content and the inevitable frustration involved in finding things of interest—two decades later, there is similar friction to searching for specific poses and scenarios within the circa 1,500,000 images uploaded on Alastonsuomi to date.

Darkside and Libertine.Center users, in turn, have rich search functions at their disposal that allow for matchmaking recommendations, especially if you provide ample information about yourself—the more information you provide, the sharper the search tools. You may sort content by, for example, age, gender identity, and geographic location. On Darkside, there is also an intricate system of tagging and categorization of not only pictures but also diary entries and other textual content. The users value these search systems and tagging practices highly, and perhaps in particular when it comes to the diaries where such labeling and searchability is not expected. As Thomas recounts:

> I think this is a great feature on Darkside! I don't know how Facebook could provide the same thing, the fact that you can tag your diary entry on Darkside and mark what it's about. So that people can find it, even those you don't know. It would be a huge list on Facebook of course, but it's a great feature on Darkside that would be pretty cool if it was on Facebook. Let's say I would like to find people who have created a diary entry about tennis balls, that could be exciting. You can do that on Darkside, maybe not about tennis balls exactly, but you get my drift.

Understandably due to its focus on nonmonogamy, Libertine.Center allows for nuance across swinger-specific categories. Further, the platform developers have a vested interest in educating people and popularizing the term "Libertine," which is envisioned as a cooler, sexier, and more inclusive alternative to "swinger," applicable also to single individuals interested in having sex with nonmonogamous couples. On the platform, Libertine is rather arbitrarily defined as "an extreme form of hedonism. Sexually almost everything goes. Libertines care very little about social, moral, or common values. They may practice open marriage/relationship, swinging, flashing, voyeurism, cuckolding, or any other less traditional sexual behaviors." Oddly enough, the definition ends with a caveat that "this doesn't mean they don't have any boundaries," yet the boundaries of Libertines have not been detailed.

What Money Can Buy

All three platforms offer both free and paid memberships, with a variety of perks becoming available for a fee. They also offer or demand user verification, both to make sure that images of someone else's (naked) body are not used to set up an account and to create a sense of safety for sexual communities (van der Nagel 2020). On all three, new users need to be approved by admins.

Given the site's default publicness, participation on Alastonsuomi necessitates publishing a profile photo showing one's naked body or one's face, or both, making membership both pseudonymous and highly embodied. To convince the admin of the photo's authenticity, new users are urged to write the site's name on their body—a piece of advice long common on amateur photo sites committed to original content (Paasonen 2011, 91)—albeit not many do. The site's publicness results in the factual impossibility of controlling potential audiences. Nonregistered visitors cannot comment on or rate the content, yet they can freely view large chunks of it. The site's front page includes a random selection of photos and menus for new, best, archived, and the most popular images, the top twenty-five images of the week, as well as submissions from those currently online. Within these shots, people pose at home, while away on holiday, in nature, at summer cottages, and in cars and bathrooms of different kinds. One can observe furniture and bedding designs, laundry baskets, and all sorts of mundane flotsam in quotidian and often playful sexual displays, even as dick pics remain the primary visual trope.

While anyone can browse (some, but not all) photos and blogs, only registered users have access to videos, discussions, and clubs operating as interest groups. Full participation, including private messaging, requires VIP membership that can be gained through credits either purchased or donated by other users as signs of appreciation (a one-month VIP membership costs a few euros; the price of credits depends on their volume of purchase). Gifted credits tend to be unevenly distributed along the axes of gender, age, and perceived attractiveness—keeping in mind that the majority of the site's users are straight men—in terms of the attention, support, and visibility afforded to individual users. Some end up paying for VIP membership without this leading to any interaction with others, whereas others are gifted with VIP membership without putting in much more effort than a few published photos deemed hot.

Users can also openly ask for sponsorship, which, according to side admins, indicates the exchange of photos, videos, used underwear, or Zoom sessions for money (Oksanen 2018). Given the Finnish law banning the procurement and advertising of sexual services, the admins detach sponsorship from the selling of sex, yet there is little they can do, or know, about what users agree on among themselves—not least since one-on-one communication tends to happen off-platform. There are limited options for sex workers to advertise their services, this being illegal in the country even as sex work itself is not, and it is not surprising for them to make use of Alastonsuomi to boost their visibility and to connect with potential clients. This entails many a gray zone in terms of where the advertising of sexual services begins or ends, also since there are complexities to interpreting the legislation itself.

Many of our interviewees interpret sponsorships straightforwardly as entailing sex work. Sanna speaks of her dislike for men suggesting sponsorships "and direct questions of whether you come over and have sex with me for money." Sponsorships are a divisive topic, and, according to Timo, they seem to irritate male users in particular. Joonas points to a drastic increase in requests for sponsorship. Whereas some years ago women would mostly "beg for VIP membership and credits from men," it now seems that "every other profile is, like, only sponsored company or sponsor me, or buy knickers, or buy socks, or buy anything, really." Julia sees this as a longer development connected to the 2019 closure of the site Sihteeriopisto, a site for advertising sex work (established in 2000, it was the hub of the local sex trade and run from servers outside the country to circumvent Finnish legislation; see Paasonen 2007, 60), after which queries for sponsorships began to increase on Alastonsuomi. For Marko, sponsorships connect to unwanted transformations in the site's user base, to the point that it had begun to feel like a "pimping site," with the recent influx of young women frequenting it for business. This broader development can be seen as connected to the relative public acceptance of sugar daddies and sexual entrepreneurship on OnlyFans while also entailing commercialization fitting ill with what many perceive as Alastonsuomi's DIY, homemade feel. Acknowledging the irritation that sponsorships evoke, the admin has made it possible to opt out from seeing them.

Darkside membership is free, which gives you good access to the platform and its functionalities, but there is a VIP option that significantly expands your storage space for messages and pictures, along with unlimited searches and sharper matching tools with other members. More storage space also means that VIP members can post pictures of higher quality, as these do not need to be compressed. Users can opt for everything from two weeks for approximately 2,5 EUR and up to one year for about 32 EUR. Membership fees also support the maintenance and development of Darkside. Awareness of this is a recurring theme in the interviews, as many testify to purchasing the VIP membership not because they need the extra storage space but because they want to support the site and show their appreciation. As Malin puts it:

> I buy VIP membership, not because I need the extra space in my inbox, but mostly because this place exists. It's so fantastic, that you can just hang out here and be your normal self and just exist. It is a kind of respite in so many ways. I mean in the sense of the marginal things one does, so it's absolutely fantastic, because you suddenly find twenty other people doing the same thing. It's a watering hole and a breathing space in so many ways. You don't have to pretend to be something else. But you are there for your sexuality. Because you're sexual. So, you don't have to hide anything. Everyone is there because they do things that are not considered mainstream. It doesn't matter how small, or unusual, or odd things you put on your kink list, there's always someone else who has put the same thing. You don't have to hide the fact that the things you have there are for your own appreciation and excitement. You don't have to pretend. That's quite nice.

Others—like Thomas—more explicitly point to the pivotal role of the founder and webmaster in creating and maintaining Darkside, and how buying a VIP membership is a way of supporting his work to sustain and develop the platform:

> I trust Darkside and David more [than Facebook] in that it's created by an enthusiast for other enthusiasts as this meeting place. Yes, he's trying to make a living out of it, I don't know how well he's doing. But if he's making a good living from Darkside, good on him! I feel joy when I pay. Yes, it's quite expensive with a full-year VIP on Darkside, you can feel it in your wallet, but it gives me so much that I pay it with joy. It feels great. Of course, the boy should be paid; he has created something fantastic!

However, the idea of earning a decent income from developing and running a fringe site in Sweden is not quite in touch with reality: "If the ambition was to get rich, then Darkside is not the place to be," David told us. He can just about make ends meet with what he earns from it, and he needs to do some tech freelancing on the side. This of course stands in stark contrast to the financial muscle of large-scale social media platforms.

For its part, Libertine.Center has a tiered system of paid and free accounts, which they have continued to experiment with over the course of the period of our fieldwork, and which they see as playing an important role in how the platform moderates both content and users. For most of the duration of our project, when the platform was named Libertine.Center, there was a one-off verification fee (forty-nine euros), which gave the user a green tick mark next to their profile name and a "lifetime" membership. The verification fee was arrived at via trial and error (starting from three euros), when the developers were purposefully trying to fine-tune the filter of acceptance and stem the influx of users from sites such as Tumblr, who were less interested in creating original sexual content, interacting with others, and meeting up, and more into posting miscellaneous sexual imagery found online, referred to by developers as "random crap." Other account options included a "fan account" that allowed for viewing the newsfeed, but not posting on it, and came with a monthly fee. This account type was articulated by owners as designed for single men not interested in participating in the lifestyle, but in watching, whose fees were intended to "sponsor" those using the platform as intended. Finally, there was a limited-functionality newbie guest user account intended as a transitional step from finding the site to a verified account.[1]

On Good Taste and Flagging Fluids

The specific kind of networked sociality that takes shape on platforms hinges on how any given platform governs and moderates users, interactions, and content. Looking at the Terms of Service and Community Guidelines of the three platforms, focusing particularly on violations that content and community moderation is intended to deal with, we see that risks and hazards are framed distinctly differently than on generic social media platforms (Gillespie 2018). Three notable violations emerge, each pointing to things valued that can then be considered as criteria for safety: shaming as a violation of respect, harassment as a violation of consent, and fakeness as a violation of authenticity.

First, harassing or insulting other users, primarily in the sense of judging their sexual lifestyle, is considered not only a social no-no, but a rule violation on all platforms. What is valued, in contrast, is openness, respect, and destigmatization of sexual diversity and sexual lifestyles in ways aligning with the general "open-mindedness" that our interviewees identify as being key to the platforms' sociality (see chapter 4). Many of our participants foreground a broadly accepting culture of body positivity and sexual openness. This applies especially to female users, who often speak of positive commenting cultures, and it is surely common knowledge on all three platforms that it is easy to get attention as a female user by posting revealing images. Yet Emilia sees this positivity as equally extending to photos of small and micro penises: "Maybe it's a little like, 'Oh, cute,' so there's a little of that tone, but, in any case, all kinds of bodies and all kinds of penises, they get positive feedback and admiration on Alastonsuomi." The narrative of mostly positive feedback is corroborated by Juhani and Lauri, who estimate that all or 95 percent of the feedback they have received has been positive. In ways aligning with Katrin's earlier research on naked self-presentation on Tumblr (Tiidenberg 2014), our platforms' commenting and feedback cultures are often contrasted with those of Facebook, Instagram, and YouTube, seen as running rife with negativity and toxicity.

This does not mean that harassment would simply be absent, since it can well be "the flip side of the positive processes of community management" (Taylor 2018, 221). Staying with the example of Alastonsuomi, Jari speaks of rigid platform hierarchies and aggressive dynamics: "Trans people and crossdressers probably get most of the shit all the time. . . . And of course, gays and, well, it's also pretty racist, and you don't see many foreigners there. . . . Users kind of spar with and trash each other; there are sometimes pretty fiery fights." Noora notes that some men start behaving badly when their sexual advances are not welcomed:

> As a representative of the female gender I have a pretty low threshold for that sort of thing, so a no is a no, and then if you don't get it, then it's a block and bye-bye. But at some point, I had been too kind to the trolls for too long. There was no other option than to start afresh, because my profile had become kind of contaminated [*laughs*] from them having too much information about me and the means of contacting me, for example, and they wouldn't believe that I don't want to. So, I had to shut it down and start a new one.

Noora's narrative suggests that she did not reach out to admins when dealing with trolls and harassers—rather, she resigned to the hassle involved in closing down and starting a new account. While this can be attributed to Alastonsuomi only having two moderators dealing with reported content, it may also be a personal preference of just not being bothered. In contrast, Anna points out that the admin has much more power to deal with those not respecting the site's social codes, as she had once reported a user for posting "filth" and the admin promptly dealt with the issue.

However, a DIY culture of moderation via self-governance and community governance (Caplan 2018; Matias and Mou 2018) came up often in our participants' accounts of the platforms. Jari spoke of this as collective self-defense of sorts:

> So, for example, there's been some photographer who's been convicted, he actively looked for new people to take pictures of there [on Alastonsuomi]. And he got several years for some abuse, and suddenly all his social media accounts just disappeared. Then there have been some known violent criminals, who've been looking for company, so we find them fairly quickly. And, of course, admin probably gets a lot of reports; I also reported this bully guy with my friend, we even took screenshots directly to the owner, so it only took minutes for the profile to disappear. These kinds of things still work pretty well. . . . But there are some, including myself, who also kind of look out for that.

Despite these positive characterizations and the platforms' emphases on tolerance, respect for the wishes and preferences of others, and community-led forms of governance, shaming does occur. Alastonsuomi's insistence on the content posted confining to "good taste" entails a particular source of friction. Users feel that their content can be removed without good reason, or because the taste criteria are opaque. Among the interviewees, such unclarity applied especially, albeit not exclusively, to watersports, which again pointed to a much deeper friction among certain kinksters and more mainstream tastes. According to Juhani, "piss pics" were not allowed during the platform's early years: "It lasted very long, it was four or five years at least. And then they were suddenly allowed." As one sharing the fetish himself, Marko has been equally puzzled by the content policy, trying to figure out what was allowed:

> The piss-play part I don't understand, especially since today there's such a squirting fad, they probably put it in one category or another according to some [volume criterion of] deciliters; one gets flagged and the other one doesn't. But maybe it's the assumption of what kind of material could drive people away. . . . I guess they think from the vantage point of average users.

Here, the ephemeral figure of the "average person" evoked in community standards when drawing the boundaries of the obscenity and pornography in the US (Hudson 2018; see also chapter 1) makes an unexpected entrance into how sexual content is flagged as deviating from the norms of good taste as "questionable." Hannele is critical of the policy:

> In the videos there may be something, like, you have to put a warning in the begin-
> ning that it contains questionable material, if people piss in it, which is an interest-
> ing discussion, what makes that material questionable. But maybe it speaks of that
> very, very, rather conservative undertone. There are really diverse people on the
> site, and it's interesting, too, what kinds of counteractions you get, [it's] 2021 and
> you can still bump into people who're clearly made anxious or angry by things like
> kinky sex or gay men [*laughs*].

The interviewees addressing the policy had difficulties in remembering how the tagging and flagging of questionable content works exactly: Is it done by the users uploading photos and videos, by the admin, or by fellow users? Their sense of how things work varied, and since the admin did not want to participate in our study, such opacity of governance carries through to what we can know about it.

In the bigger picture of social media, it may seem counterintuitive to identify a platform trading in explicit sexual content as having a "rather conservative undertone," yet this becomes understandable when consider-ing the ephemeral inasmuch as tenacious, and possibly hurtful, drawing of boundaries between what goes and what does not, what remains within the realm of "good taste" and what is flagged as questionable instead. This makes explicit that sexual platforms are not free from discrimination against kinks: Even as they open up the hierarchies of "good sex" (see chapter 6), hierar-chies do remain. The opacity of content policies, combined with the ease with which some users become upset when facing visuals not of their own liking, means that governance is a tricky business, and that its actors and norms are by no means evident.

From Nonconsensual Dick Pics to Blocking Dullness

Digitally native forms of harassment, including astroturfing hashtags or conversations, and sending out mass hookup messages are frowned upon across our platform rulesets. It then follows that the values elevated, or secured, include consent, respectful interaction, and the ability to "read the room." Forms of harassment, however, can be quite specific to the platform and its vernacular culture. On Darkside, for example, sending nonconsensual dick pics is routinely reported as abuse.

In Jenny's interview with the webmaster David, it became clear that the site has a pretty good safety net that automates dealing with a lot of harassing content: "For example, someone posts a picture of a cock in a public feed and doesn't mark it as 'this is a cock appearing in a public feed.' Handling such a case is pretty standard and it's done with a single click." He even wants to take this content regulation automation one step further to, just with a simple keystroke, compress the picture, attach a description of what happened and how, and file a report to the police. "It would be epic" he says, "if Darkside gets this reputation that no one dares to send juicy dick pics to strangers, because they get all sensitive and PC about it." Such zero tolerance for sexual harassment on a BDSM site is understandable, given that consent is the backbone of the community.

But even with automated content moderation, as well as assigned moderators, this is also very much a user-driven endeavor (Fiesler et al. 2018; Seering et al. 2019). As on Alastonsuomi, especially Darkside's female users are quick to block others in order to reduce unwelcome advances. Eli, a queer female and gender-fluid user, has a diary entry titled "Can I block all heteronormative cis men?" When her gender identity is set to "female," her inbox is flooded with sexual propositions from men who disregard her sexual orientation as well as her self-presentation, but when she switches to "androgynous," these advances stop completely. Others, like Linda, rely heavily on the block function for minimizing drama and setting a good tone:

LINDA: I fly under the radar all the time. If there is a drama, I'm the first one out the door. I'm not the least bit curious, so I just walk away. And I'm extremely fond of the block button. I block several users a week. Preemptively.

JENNY: What are you blocking then? Are they similar blocks, or can they apply to a range of things?

LINDA: The bottom line is that I don't need this person in my life. It's not worth the risk of having this person in my life. But it can be anything from them posting things on their presentation page that I think, these are disgusting values, thank you very much, goodbye, or that they have written to my friends in a way that I don't think we need in our lives, or that they express opinions in the forums that I think we don't need. I'm incredibly quick on the block button. So, I've several hundreds of blocks. . . . I think it's very nice as far as functions go, and I think it's also one of the reasons why I have quite a nice atmosphere in my comments.

Content moderation on Darkside also happens through self-regulation in anticipation of, or to avoid, being reported or outed as a harasser. In the interviews, it becomes clear that straight male users often avoid showing appreciation for female users posting nudes or semi-nudes, as they make clear that they may not be seeking positive affirmation from strangers, but merely from their friends (more on this in chapter 4). Some male users even avoid giving compliments or liking images of seemingly straight male users as this is rarely appreciated and tends to result in them being blocked—presumably as a way of safeguarding one's heterosexuality by policing its boundaries. Sexual appreciation thus rubs up against social codes and ideas of appropriate and respectful behavior, making this sex-positive space one where female users are especially exposed to undesired attention and where others tread lightly so as to not upset or come across as a harasser or a creep.

Sometimes these efforts to curb unwanted attention move one step further, as there is also a tendency to control or delimit that which is simply experienced as dull, or uninteresting. Linda continues:

> I'm thinking about this business of screen-grabbing conversations and posting them, masked or unmasked. And I think that contributes to a very strange atmosphere. Because the conversations posted in this way are far from always unpleasant. They can just be boring. Or bland. Or just not what this person wanted to hear today. But the person who is being screen-grabbed will feel exposed. I think that culture is very bad for Darkside in the long run. That this is a normalized behavior and that it's okay to do so. I understand sometimes when people have been obviously assholeish, of course. But when people are just boring, or a bit clumsy. It must be allowed to be like that. You don't have to respond to everything, you can just say, "Thank you very much, I don't think we are a match, have a good day." Block! This is a recurring issue and I don't know what will happen in the long run. It's getting harder and harder for people to make contact.

As part of a broader social media ecology where people are quick to take offense and redistribute hurt and discomfort by outing and shaming others (Sternberg 2012), here blandness or dullness becomes grounds for counteraction. Offense is something of an affective glue in social media as waves of aggravation become inseparable from the dynamics of shaming involved in mocking, outing, or disagreeing with others. Offense certainly occupies a sliding scale, from the downright violations of laws and social

contracts—such as the incessant unsolicited advances and sexual sugges-
tions directed at female users—to something that rather involves annoyance
or resentment toward a perceived insult. Of course, what someone finds
offensive, someone else may find silly, ridiculous, or just boring. The interesting thing to notice here is how the user moderation of unwanted attention takes a slightly different turn so as to keep in check forms of address that
do not excite or amuse, making this space for social and sexual exchange
tricky to navigate.

Can I Trust You?

Finally, fake participation, such as dummy accounts, phishing accounts,
imposter accounts, and fake content lifted from elsewhere featuring people
who are not whom the captions indicate them to be, is seen as a violation
across the platforms. This means that authenticity, in the sense of using the
platforms sincerely and representing one's preferences accurately, is highly
valued.

For example, on Libertine.Center, authentic users are valued not only
in the sense of each account belonging to one physical person or couple
but also in the sense of the user truly being interested in nonmonogamous
sex—it is important that people are *really* into it for there to be trust and
for the sociality to work. This version of people's authenticity is expressed
in their profiles, their verifications, the fact that they post images, reply to
messages, and ideally meet up with people face to face. Developers have put
a lot of thought into offering users peace of mind and a sense of safety that
would lead to such participation. The platform has always pushed for user
verification, elevating its "almost entirely verified userbase" as something
that makes them stand out from other sites in Estonia, and elsewhere. Both
users and developers are in agreement over this. Verification is argued by
both groups to lead to the platform being populated by "real users" and "real
people," as opposed to the "gray mass of weirdos and fake accounts" or "only
sex workers soliciting 'sponsorship,'" which the other main Estonian sexual
social media platform (iha.ee) is arguably "known for." They also suggest that
verification leads to the platform being used by "nice, polite people," who do
"not post random crap."

Further, on Libertine.Center, user verification and the verification fee thus
create filters that, according to the developers, take care of the vast bulk of

their need to moderate content. Flagging-based after-upload moderation of posts and blocking of users is supplemented with what is essentially preemptive user moderation through verification. Beyond verification initiated by the platform and its administrators, Libertine.Center also allows for users to authenticate each other by leaving testimonials or reviews. These are mostly based on face-to-face encounters and centered on sexual prowess, personality, and attractiveness. Thus, a male user self-identifying as a "Bull" has left a comment for a couple account saying: "a lovely, playful couple, who has a great sense of humor and a lot of passion for sex," while another couple has left a review for him as "a great fuckbuddy ;) or, more simply put, a passionate lover with whom we have enjoyed many great moments." Another couple has been complimented for the male partner's "A+ cock and personality" and the female partner for being very gorgeous and kinky.

A more vernacular version of verification happens on Darkside where openness and outness are valued and designed into the site's affordances (reflected in how the users are, for example, encouraged to show their faces in their profile pictures). In addition, there is also a more formalized system of verifications that users may get from those who have met them IRL (in real life), which signals a different kind of authenticity through their friend network. While this verification system creates a form of safety in the encounter, Klara points out that it does also add to geographical inequalities in kink communities:

> I have hundreds of verifications; others may have zero. I have it because I've been active in social BDSM contexts in larger cities for a long time. Of course, I would've had a much harder time doing that had I lived in the hinterland of Norrland [the sparsely populated Swedish north]. For many, the number of verifications affects whether and how they make contact and whether they are perceived as serious members of the culture.

Finally, on Alastonsuomi, the publicness of profile pictures is seen to weed out inappropriate users—a tactic that both does and does not work. The public visibility of the profile photos premises the sociality on the site on shared vulnerabilities—at least potentially so. This gives rise to a specific social baseline, even as the risk of harassment remains present. Despite a number of perceived shortcomings, people stay on the platform as it still allows them to talk to "fellow perverts," which holds much value to them.

Reframing Safety and Governance

It is crucial to our three platforms' existence that they are not impacted by the FOSTA/SESTA law packages in their local operations. They are also less subject to the rulings of app stores, as hegemonically run by Google and Apple, and their content policies governing and effacing the visibility of sex (more on this in chapter 4). The fact that the sites operate within the EU raises the further question of their compliance to GDPR, which regulates the collecting and transfer of all personal data within the EU and (as discussed in chapter 2) delimits the collecting of personal data pertaining to sexual identities and practices. On something like Alastonsuomi, "a natural person's sex life or sexual orientation"—to follow GDPR's parlance—is, of course, much less a sensitive issue than a basis for networked sociality. GDPR is impactful for platforms, which, to comply with the regulation, must identify data controllers, disclose their data collection practices, and specify both the lawful basis for data collection and the period for which the data will be retained. Libertine.Center's website states that it is GDPR compliant and that it does not collect identifiable user data beyond the email addresses they use to sign up. As a platform that firmly builds on consent and the protection of user privacy, Darkside was basically already GDPR compliant prior to the passing of the law. Darkside is located within Sweden's borders, and user data is not shared with third parties. But as the webmaster David points out, deleting things quickly may also come with a cost, such as when protecting user privacy coincides with protecting a potential sexual offender.

The privacy notice is a legal document, the crafting of which necessitates legal expertise and comes at a financial cost (Klonick 2018). For platforms operating with something close to shoestring budgets, such investments may be major. And while GDPR is designed to protect people's privacy and to minimize potential vulnerabilities arising from the uses of personal data— all very noble causes—such protection does not necessarily align with the risks and gains involved in the uses of sexual platforms, as articulated by our informants. By creating monetary hurdles for platforms to operate, GDPR may then delimit the options for smaller platforms to exist in the shadows of the digital giants and curb the conditions for minoritarian sexual cultures to remain online, even as such existence is key to the people comprising these cultures.

Sexual connections and expressions fuel engagements between users on our platforms and make space for alternate understandings of the value of sex on platformed sociability. As we have discussed in this chapter, this is possible because the governance principles of our sex-positive platforms differ from generic, ultimately sex-negative social media in a number of ways: First, the notion of safety is uncoupled from sexual content and the imperatives of moderating it. Secondly, safety here becomes reframed through the notions of respect, consent, and authenticity instead (Tiidenberg 2021). Finally, this particular reframing of safety invites nuanced forms of moderation, such as user moderation through verification, as well as other forms of user and community governance, such as tactics of blocking and reporting users or content.

To harass or insult others, in particular in the sense of judging their sexual preferences, is, as we have seen, considered a violation across the three platforms' rules. While our participants all have stories to tell of a garden variety of hateful speech or harassment, they report overall positive experiences distinct from those of more generic social media. That said, they had a hard time remembering how the flagging of questionable content works, which made for a volatile situation regulated by notions of "good taste" and "good behavior" both opaque and arbitrary. This was especially obvious when considering the place and limits of leaky bodies and bodily fluids in networked sexuality, be it watersports or something else. Even on platforms trading in the sexually explicit, bodily fluids and their ability to mark a line between marginal kink and more mainstream palates provide interesting limit cases of supposedly liberal sexual content moderation.

Harassment and shaming may cut both ways as those harassing others may be publicly shamed for being disappointing or plain boring. Adding further insult to injury, sexual platforms are certainly not free from internal discrimination or kink shaming: When moving beyond "vanilla," a range of other norms are established instead (more on this in chapter 6). No matter the level of sexual openness and respect for others different than oneself, the vagueness of content policies—combined with how some users are easily offended in the face of messages or images that they disapprove of—means that platform governance is a constant site of friction between user expectations, perceived levels of safety, platform rules, and social codes.

4 Sexual Sociability and Spaces to Breathe

Well, yes, for the few contacts that have extended off Alastonsuomi, we've exchanged emails, or I don't remember what chat apps there used to be. But during the past couple of years Kik app has been the one I've used. But, as I said, Alastonsuomi has become less important in terms of getting to know people. But there are a lot of people there that I know from other circles, and then we're friends also on Alastonsuomi. We're friends on Facebook and we're friends on FetLife and we chat on WhatsApp or Telegram or Signal, and then we're also in contact on Alastonsuomi.
—Tapio

Addressing his cross-platform contacts and friendships, Tapio, similarly to many of our other interviewees, situates the sexual platforms he uses in a broader personal social media ecology. While there may not be drastic differences to the kinds of sexual outness and self-expression that constitute the sociality he enjoys on Alastonsuomi and FetLife, this would obviously not apply to globally dominant social media platforms like Facebook. Social media research to date has been largely invested in analyzing individual platforms, their user cultures and affordances, yet there is also a growing interest in how people move across them in promiscuous ways, so as to give shape to complex, habitual, and contingent social media ecologies (Payne 2015; Taffel 2019; Phillips and Milner 2021). Even when looking across platforms, however, it matters where one starts. As we will see in this chapter, starting from sexual sites makes for an encompassing walkthrough, as users easily address their use of more generic platforms after having spoken about sexual ones. But when the starting point for research is their experience with Facebook or LinkedIn, they are less likely to continue to describe a personal social media ecology inclusive of sexual platforms.

Contributing to cross-platform inquiry, this chapter focuses on the question raised in the introduction as our book's *leitmotiv* of sorts: What follows from considering sexual platforms as part and parcel of social media? And, consequently, what can they tell us about the value of sexual sociality in a moment when its deplatforming tends to be the general norm? To tackle this, we discuss our platforms as infrastructures that shape and constrain sociality, paying attention to how they are built and how they connect to developer perceptions of what social media is, or what it should be. We further ask how these platforms are used and experienced as socio-sexual "silos"—a concept we will furnish shortly—connected to the users' personal social media ecosystems. In connection with this, we examine how perceived silos relate to safety and demarcate the boundaries of sexual cultures and connections on-platform. Within all this, users articulate conflicting desires to both maintain boundaries between experiential and affective silos and to have things travel across them (Tiidenberg et al. 2021, 13). Thus, we consider sexual expression as something put in motion across platforms, user cultures, content policies, and sexual norms, and the perceived silos as being leaky by default.

In attending to cross-platform traffic and silo-sociality of the users of our three sites, we also reexamine the notion of "context collapse" (Marwick and boyd 2011), broadly used to conceptualize how generic social media disallow social boundary work, highlighting how strategic audience segregation meets leaky boundaries and how both content and data bleed in social media presence. Rather than furthering a veritable collapse of contexts, we conceptualize such leakiness as "context promiscuity": a partially deliberate bleeding and blending of data and contexts.

Cross-platform connections involve situational negotiations between pseudonymity and real-name policies, and the constant motion across them involves degrees of opacity and visibility in sexual expression and exchange (Light 2014; Sundén 2023a). As Alex Cho (2018) has shown in his study of (pre-"porn ban") Tumblr, the platform held allure to queer and gender-nonconforming young people of color in the content and social contacts that it afforded, as well as in its lack of real-name policy. Whereas data giants such as Alphabet and Meta connect real-name policies with authenticity and safety while aggregating as granular user data as possible, Tumblr, in affording users to set up several accounts with the same email address without identifying one's legal name, afforded safety from outing and unwanted exposure.

Taking such nuanced negotiations of layered identities into consideration, we draw on discussions of the value of anonymity and pseudonymity in digital cultures in general (Hogan 2012; Marwick and boyd 2011; van der Nagel 2017; van der Nagel and Frith 2015) and in queer digital cultures in particular (e.g., Cassidy 2018; Dhoest and Szulc 2016; Triggs et al. 2021), considering how partly concealing oneself becomes a tactic of resistance—queer or otherwise—to social media logics of authenticity and monetization (Keilty 2024; Sundén 2023b). Yet we also recognize that there is value in real-name self-presentations as exercises in openness and outness. On a platform like Darkside, usernames also take on a life of their own as these are frequently used at community events and play parties, becoming reattached with the people "behind" them. Moving between platforms with widely different policies and politics of making oneself visible and identifiable (or not) means navigating a complicated terrain. Such navigational practices may not only be tricky or risky for individual users but sometimes also for others who—by association—can become outed against their wishes.

Social Media, or Something Like It

The sociality on our three sites is experienced on the intermeshing axes of the social and the sexual, to the point that it is impossible to pinpoint where one ends and the other starts, or how they might be plied apart—or, indeed, why one would want to do so (cf. Wignall 2022). This deceptively trivial statement needs to be unpacked in order to demonstrate the granularities involved. On the one hand, sex is fundamentally social—intensely so (Rodríguez 2011). On the other hand, the degrees to which norms governing behavior in public places (Goffman 1966) have separated the social and the sexual in most societies and relegated the sexual to private and semi-private confines (Berlant and Warner 1998; Califia 1999) cannot be underestimated. This separation is further codified and reified online (McKee et al. 2015) so that sex in social media is subject to a "trifecta of anxieties" emerging from overlaps between sexuality, publicness, and the internet (Tiidenberg and van der Nagel 2020).

On our platforms, social exchanges are framed on sexual terms by default in that users can look for hookups, for play dates, or simply at each other. For users, these platforms function as socio-sexual "silos" within their personal social (media) ecologies. Silos are experiential and imagined social spaces that emerge out of shared interests or desires—or in this case a certain open-mindedness—and are sustained "through shared practices, vernacular and sensibility" (Tiidenberg et al. 2021, 13). "Silo-sociality" is a matter of *boundary activation* and focuses our analytical attention to an experiential, recognizable basis for sociality that may, but does not have to, coincide with the boundaries of a platform, or a subculture of people with a particular kink on the platform (or across platforms), or those of sex clubs or events. Examining our platforms as socio-sexual silos highlights how they afford respites as sites of sexual expression. Here, silo-sociality is about a particular type of sexual relating that constitutes what is experienced as a social space: On these platforms, there is no need to beat around the bush. This became particularly clear in comparisons that our interviewees drew between these platforms and the kinds of sociality encouraged in most (semi)public spaces as well as on generic social media. As Liisa says of Libertine.Center:

> It's a handy platform, because it brings together people who, well—like in a nightclub—how do you get to this point as a single woman, where after I meet a guy and we decided we want to have a one-night stand, I tell him, "Hey, let's find one more guy to take with us," it's a really difficult conversation to have with a random person in the club, but really easy here, because there is some baseline of shared interest.

Sanna agrees, pointing to a sense of safety on Alastonsuomi:

> And it also makes for a relatively safe environment to think about such stuff: as in it's somehow a normal thing to say on Alastonsuomi that I'd like to have sex with two or three men at the same time. Things that are pretty taboo, or that you couldn't necessarily chat about as freely otherwise, on Alastonsuomi they're, well, I'm not sure they're "basic," but pretty much so. I haven't discovered a thing that wouldn't be allowed on Alastonsuomi. Or of course illegal things aren't allowed, but [when it comes to] legal sex and things connected to having sex, probably there's some club, or group, or some user base that likes every legally permitted thing. . . . It's a forum that makes it possible to make fantasies come true, yeah.

In addition to being able to start sexual conversations much closer to the point, the silos emerged from the fact that users felt that the friends they had made on the platform were more open-minded, and more socially and sexually active than their "other friends," pointing to the particular value that such sexually oriented silos may hold and how they can extend across different forms of sociality, both online and off. In Joonas's words, "It's a little like meeting a stranger in a café, it's a nice chat. But it may just begin with the other seeing my cock and I see the other's cunt." For him such casual sociability comes with a "specific pleasure" as the situation is "in a way reverse" to most other encounters in everyday life. Lauri describes his socio-sexual silo as a "breathing space" shared with other people who are

> similarly nerding off on sexuality and taking a liberal approach to sexuality, and having this open-minded approach. I've found lots of people who share the same values and with whom we've developed friendships over time. It's, yeah, many great people have entered my life through the site, and I'm really happy for having found them.

Lauri has a child with another Alastonsuomi user ("I'd mark that down as one of the site's achievements") and has traveled abroad with friends he has met on it. In other words, the sociality established on-platform has obviously not been confined to it, nor has it been limited to the sexual alone. Julia similarly described the platform as her key social hub in ways both sexual and not—as her "family." Our participants describe interactions with platform-sourced friends as regularly expanding to ostensibly unsexy endeavors such as going on a hike or helping a friend redo the roof of their summer cottage. In other words, friendships regularly emerge through and from sexual sociality.

One central reverberation of sexual sociality—which is possibly the most manifest among Alastonsuomi users, given the platform's image gallery format and rating options—is the impact of positive feedback on one's self-esteem and the broadening of sexual horizons as something that adds to general well-being and basically sustains people. Here, Johanna's narrative is both specific and speaks of an undercurrent of sexual sociality—of feeling seen—more broadly:

> It's raised my self-esteem incredibly. I've lived in that kind of depression hell for years and years as I became disabled when young, and became unfit for work. Then, just around the spring of 2018 I realized that, damn, I'm a woman, and got brave enough to post some photos, and I got such good comments, that raised my self-esteem. And through that I've dared to approach people and let my own sexuality loose. It's, let's say that since I got registered on Alastonsuomi in 2018, my life has been in an upward spiral all the time. They've cut down my depression meds and my self-esteem has grown and my sex life is better. It's been, let's say that if I hadn't gone on Alastonsuomi then, I'd probably be moping at home and not be ok with myself.

Our participants' experiences reinforce what our colleagues have been finding across studies of sexual apps, platforms, and sexual uses of the internet—that their felt impact on subjective well-being can be quite profound (Andalibi et al. 2018; James and Webster 2018; Nixon and Düsterhöft 2018; Tiidenberg and Gómez-Cruz 2015). As sexual self-expression can be couched in layers of privacy and shame, being able to express that part of oneself—to have it be seen and validated by others—cuts across a variety of needs, gratifications, and pleasures important for mental, physical, and social well-being. Beyond complimentary feedback on one's appearances, or accepting, curious, or libidinous reactions to one's sexual preferences, connecting based on sexual affinities that many people have otherwise limited networks in becomes a resource for relationship creation and community building. In this vein, sexual sociability can enrich and widen social worlds in direct ways, from hooking up and sexual play to all other sorts of connecting. At the same time, the sexual underpinnings of the connections taking shape add something important—something extra, a frisson of sorts—also to markedly nonsexual encounters.

Darkside users may, for example, add "nonkinky" interests—such as "choir singing" or "knitting"—to their profiles to differently approach and connect with others. Evelina elaborates on the meaning and function of inserting the nonsexual into the sexual and points out how this provides a different relational point of departure:

> I think it's quite funny actually, because I think it gives an opportunity for someone to open up about something that isn't just straight up sexual. It doesn't bother me at all if people are very straightforward, as long as they are nice, respectful, and clear. But I can imagine that it also makes it a little easier, maybe, if you like something and you see a person who likes something you like. That you both have the same kinks, but also an interest you share outside of that. For me, it can be something that works as a discussion starter, some kind of ice breaker. That's mostly how I've thought about it, I think. It's fun!

Emma, in turn, is a passionate knitter and has met others in the community for dates called "naughty knitting" held at public places like cafés. "Though there was really nothing naughty about it," she comments: "We just knitted." However, building on the tradition of munches and other casual gatherings in the world of kink and BDSM, the seemingly mundane, nonsexual—or indeed unsexy—always comes lined with the knowledge of being in the company of other kinksters. This carries the possibility of interactions growing kinky later on. Or it can just as well entail the tacit pleasure of sharing wants and desires that may remain unarticulated in a given social context, yet have a meaningful presence. The webmaster David further elaborates on the distinction and blending of kink and nonkink on the platform:

> So, there's something of a division, at least in terms of discussions of sexuality, kink, and nonnormative living on the one hand, and a civilian part of one's life on the other, where we recommend movies and engage in gardening. And then a third part for those who are into more conventional sex. You're free to choose which ones you want to participate in without being too disturbed by the others, I hope. The fact that there's this breadth fosters something of a we-feeling, I hope, of being able to socialize in a pub, for example. You go there with people from Darkside, and you know deep down that everyone you meet there is united by the fact that we can be open with our personalities and our sexualities. We can, in a sense, mirror each other. That's a basic kind of freedom. And then at that pub meeting you can spend an entire evening just talking about home decor. And nothing else. But it also has a purpose in some way, to be able to have contexts that are on the surface very ordinary. But they take place in a community to which you feel a sense of belonging and where it is safe. You feel that you can be ordinary while still being self-affirming.

The mundane has an important place in kink communities that exceeds how everyday settings and rituals in and of themselves may set the stage for BDSM practices and kink play, such as age play and its ways of feeding off of the perverse potentials and temporalities of "family" and "home" (Bengtsson 2022, 129–176). Mundane spaces like bars and cafés also provide opportunities to be out and about in public, yet discreet, and to not only take pleasure in being in the company of other open-minded people, but to feel that what makes this community special is also quite ordinary, after all (we expand our discussion on the intersections of mundane and sexual spaces in chapter 5). This sense of ordinariness can have an important normalizing function, which without softening the edge of kink can expand or accentuate its ordinariness. The mundane framing can thus help make the extraordinary feel ordinary, by virtue of people simply coming together for coffees and beers.

Infrastructures of Sexual Sociability

Experiences of these kinds of socio-sexual silos change over time, depending on how people make sense of platform designs and features in comparison to social media more broadly. In other words, the platforms' perceived socio-sexual affordances are not static. Our participants made comparisons to other platforms—as in describing Darkside, Alastonsuomi, and Libertine.Center as "Facebook for adults," "pervy Facebook," or "sex-Insta"—and highlighted both the perceived benefits and limitations of generic social media in doing so. Since metaphors, defined as "understanding and experiencing one kind of thing in terms of another," always illuminate some aspects and eclipse others (Lakoff and Johnson 1980, 5), such comparisons hint at expectations and judgments over forms of networked sociality—what one can do and where, what one would like to do, and what does not work at all. The issue does, of course, also concern the factual limitations of use. As Elina explains, she cannot present herself on Instagram as she would like, "since they have those community standards and rules. But it's also the case that I tell considerably less about myself on Alastonsuomi than in other social media, and protect my privacy differently than in other social media." Helena similarly says that in comparison to her friends on Facebook and Instagram, she does not know people on Alastonsuomi: "And I stay anonymous there, I don't want to reveal my identity." Such careful guarding of the boundaries of privacy— calculating how much to tell and how exactly to connect with others—was a common tactic in mitigating vulnerabilities (see also chapter 7).

It was, however, equally the case that participants cast the studied platforms as allowing similar connectivity as Instagram, OkCupid, or Tinder, or even encouraging more intense, "sexier," or "improved" kinds of sociability wherein users can express their sexual desires and personae. Anna, for example, sees Alastonsuomi as an "alternative to this Tinder thing where you either like the face, or don't. On Alastonsuomi I get to discuss things very directly, in an uninhibited way—and then find sexual company, or just chat, if I've been looking for different kind of company. It's possible to express my own sexuality and find a partner in a more uninhibited way." For Sofia, "Alastonsuomi is where I can most be myself, whereas Facebook is like the public image visible to everybody where you have to behave according to all social norms." Comparisons were equally drawn between the studied platforms and other sexual platforms like FetLife, SDC, OnlyFans, or Pornhub. As a heterosexual swinger-couple, Mikk and Mari said:

MARI: Well, right now we have FetLife.

MIKK: We used to have an account on the Finnish XU before Libertine.Center, but that became annoying as there weren't that many Estonians on there, and so we closed the account.

KATRIN: And what does FetLife offer you? Does it have many Estonians?

MIKK: Not necessarily, but it's just so different, it's international, but the amount and diversity and quality of content is on a different level, because the amount of users is very big, and very diverse.

MARI: They have awesome pictures, that's why we go there

MIKK: We don't have a paid account, so we can't access the videos, but the quality of photos is so so so good, so diverse, and there are these little communities and people's writing, it is just very rich.

Our interviewees' experiences were importantly constrained by the sites' functionalities, as well as by their expectations concerning the platforms' roles within their personal social media ecosystems. Many Alastonsuomi users defined it as a social media platform that nevertheless lacks key functionalities that one might expect of contemporary platforms. Darkside, too, reaches back to an era of early online communities with a distinct underground feel, while also stretching forward to a time of large social media platforms. Our participants fondly remember the smaller community of those early years consisting of a quite tightly knit group of people who took support from each other on social and sexual margins, providing a vital breathing space. But they also speak of this time when the platforms were smaller as being more extreme and possibly intimidating to newcomers. Hanna reminisces, "I thought a lot of the people there [on Darkside] seemed crazy, and I didn't really want to connect with them, but with a kind of community, I guess, which I wasn't really able to connect with. Because it was unclear to me, or scary to me, I don't really know which, how to approach a place where BDSM was practiced."

The dated designs of Alastonsuomi and Darkside further add to ambivalent user experiences. On the one hand, there is a clear sense of safety rooted in nostalgia for an era when the communities were smaller, if also more marginalized—as with Sofia, whom the retro characteristics reminded of her youth while limited interaction functionality made the site feel less hectic and busy. On the other hand, many users commented on their "ugly" design. For Tapio, Alastonsuomi is "tragically" and "shockingly old-fashioned":

It's stayed just the same, it feels that here I'm a proper veteran who's used the site for over ten years [laughs]. And it hasn't changed at all, its vibe hasn't changed much. Maybe it's just that Instagram has become more common and there's FetLife and other sites too, and perhaps people who're taken seriously, who're social, live in social media. And they give a little more of themselves, they use Instagram, they use FetLife, and they don't use Alastonsuomi. Back in the day, that was really the only alternative, so maybe people used it as nothing else was available. But it's really very old-fashioned, it frankly evokes pity when you look at it, and it can sometimes carry over to the interaction on the site. It's maybe a little—I'm not the kind of guy who feels bashful around the topic of sex, but maybe Alastonsuomi evokes a bit of cringe. Not because people show themselves off naked, but because it's an ugly site [*laughs*] that hasn't been updated for years. It's just embarrassingly old-fashioned.

The lack of updates then contributed to aesthetic cringe, which Emmi extended to a sense that the users of sexual social media are themselves undervalued: "It gives people sort of the impression that this kind of sexuality, and open-mindedness, and the people interested in this stuff, that they're like a little seedy and grubby." For some, this complaint extended to the poor technical and artistic quality of the photos published by other users so that the platform comprised an aesthetic fold somehow just generally *lagging behind* and not quite cutting the mustard. A similar critique, where dated design and functionality incited judgment over content, users, and sociality alike, was evident in how the developers and users of Libertine.Centre addressed the older Estonian site, iha.ee, which all of them had previous or current experience with. Yet, to Lauri, the unpolished feel of Alastonsuomi was also a positive marker of distinction: "It's a little aged, the design and the look, which probably adds its own edge to it, so that we're not on some polished Facebook or Instagram. It's, like, a little edgier and a little rougher." For Erik, who's a gay man using a big bouquet of apps and platforms, the do-it-yourself vibe of Darkside is similarly a welcome contrast to the shiny feel of corporate platforms, but something that also extends to a view of sexuality as not ready-made, but always in process:

It feels like homemade in a nice way. Compared to for example Recon which I also like a lot, which is commercially driven and very nicely designed. So Darkside is a bit homemade instead, and it's a bit nerdy in a nice way. . . . Sex is a process [on Darkside] and you can learn and explore. I've done that quite a lot, and I think that's very nice, that you can do that here with others, and that there's openness around it. You don't have to be perfect in any way. I think that's also different from these gay sites where there's probably a harder armor on the surface. When you're out talking to people, you can talk about a lot of things very openly, but this public image on gay sites is probably more of "I'm complete. I have no doubts. I can deliver." . . . I don't know, I feel some kind of safety in the slightly more idealistic, the not so finished, not so well-packaged. There is something there that is very compassionate. I think that this nonprofit-ness provides spaces that are not so finished, there are still possibilities there.

While enjoying well-designed and good-looking apps and platforms catering to gay men into fetish and kink, Erik also points at how a smooth surface may get caught up in or reinforce an equally polished and finished idea of sexual selves with little room for vulnerability, insecurity, or growth. At fifty-three, he is the oldest participant in the Swedish sample. For him, Darkside is a valuable addition to his personal sexual social media use, which, even if it does not more narrowly address a gay male contingent, has the benefit of providing room for collaborative experimentation and continuous self-discovery.

Finally, users' experiences of on-platform sociability are shaped by the highly limited app-based functionality across the studied platforms. To circumvent Apple's and Google's app store rules regulating sexual displays, but even more so due to lack of resources, all three platforms are available as websites rather than apps (even as, at the time of writing, Libertine.Center has pivoted toward a more dating app–like iteration of itself). In this sense, they sit at the edges of the social media ecology. Yet, according to Libertine.Center's developer, "If you don't have a mobile messenger app—that's it, you're done with the younger users," which is why even during the fieldwork, when their primary use was via a browser site, they had a workaround in the form of a messaging-only mobile app. Alastonsuomi and Darkside have no mobile apps whatsoever, but their users spoke of incorporating various other messaging apps into their socio-sexual silos. The reduced smartphone functionality, however, is a distinct source of frustration particularly among gay male users used to a plethora of connective tools tailored for swift hookups.

All in all, our participants spoke of the platforms as affording finding, meeting, and hanging out with other people who are similarly sexually open-minded. The platforms were further spoken of as unconstrained by mainstream norms of propriety, as sites for hooking up (although the platforms enable that with varying ease and comfort), for presenting oneself in ways that are seen as "more authentic," and as blending the sexual and nonsexual aspects of everyday life in ways discouraged or plain banned by generic social media. For some, it is enough to be merely seen, so that connecting socially on-platform is no priority. This was the case with Juhani, for whom sociality on Alastonsuomi "is practically zero," even as the platform matters to him in terms of cross-dressing visibility.

While our participants complained of the platforms' technical and aesthetic limitations, sometimes at length, they also worked around them, so these did not, for the most part, curb user interest. Their use was often situational and fluctuating, rather than something constant: Months without spending time on a site could be followed by periods of extensive engagement, and routine browsing could be intercepted by peaks of acute interest bordering on the obsessive. Across all this, friendships established through the three sites were not necessarily confined to them only.

Silos of Safety and the Politics of Appreciation

Alastonsuomi, Darkside, and Libertine.Center are experienced as silos separated by permeable yet distinct boundaries from other platforms, social ties, and expressive modes within users' lives. Since experiential silos emerge from and are defined by shared interests and sustained by shared practices, vernaculars, and sensibilities, it follows that any singular platform can accommodate any number of them: Boundary work in and around silos is a constant (Tiidenberg et al. 2021). Therefore, we see different users of the same platform having distinct understandings of their social codes, user base, or vernaculars. This then results in users having varying understandings of what these platforms are like, or what they are for—highly social; asocial; rude; encouraging; normative; heterogeneous; embracing differences; actively discriminatory. Platforms further scale internally so that they function as silos of sorts enveloping their registered users. Then there are silos of sexual taste communities—of, for example, gay men, cross-dressers, kinksters, or swingers—as well as a plethora of smaller silos comprising "meet families" and other connections formed in accordance to sexual likes and desires, occupational interests, and friendships formed over time.

On our platforms, experiential silos emerged and diverged most notably due to differences in use, sexual expectations, and experiences of safety. Some spoke of there being less trolling, more acceptance, and little judgment as per sexual tastes on Alastonsuomi in comparison to mainstream social media so that the site makes it possible for people to sexually exist. Jaakko addresses its ethos of open-mindedness as "not judging others in terms of their desires and being pretty open to experiment and talk about it. If you know that you don't like it, then you don't like it, but, like, otherwise not judging any kind of sexuality and being able to talk about it." The kink ethos "Your kink is not my kink, but your kink is ok," may foster support of sexual diversity and difference and safeguard a community from stigmatization and shaming. Meanwhile, others disagreed. Antti talked of the ease of "shouting behind a username," and Hannele pointed out that Alastonsuomi's moderation practices had not improved since its launch: "This site like just drifts, which is part of its charm, but it's probably also a pretty horrible place if, dunno, you're somehow particularly vulnerable a person." However, as we discussed in chapter 3, individual users have personal preferences in how they deal with problematic interactions and involve moderators in self- and community preservation.

Such differences in how the platforms are experienced as being safe (or not) may riddle social encounters with tension. As we go on to discuss in chapter 5, such tensions are connected to exclusionist uses of language and boundary work over who is seen to belong, or be "one of us," which many interviewees associate with the presence of racism on Alastonsuomi in particular. On Darkside, a perceived sense of safety often becomes a question of one's proximity to straight, cis-male norms. While clearly sex-positive at its core, Darkside is construed as a social space where safety takes shape through consent. As Daniel told us, consent-based safe spaces are also constructed through self-censorship by male users particularly, so as to not be rejected in the first place:

DANIEL: I'm a heterosexual cis man, and somehow there's a jargon on Darkside where heterosexual cis men may not be the most popular. I'm incredibly aware of my privilege, and all this stuff that I have, so I'm very careful not to somehow make sweeping generalizations or talk like I know a lot of stuff or to mansplain. Even if I know something very well, I tone it down, because I don't want to get that aura. Because there are so many older, dominant men who still do that. . . . I want to stay out of that, so that's why I don't post on certain issues, because just belonging to this group somehow makes it too sensitive. It gets too risky, someone could misinterpret what I was saying, there could be a backlash. You know how Darkside works sometimes. You can have all the right intentions, and be super humble and all that, but there's a clear risk in it. I then refrain from certain discussions. As a middle-aged cis man who's dominant and into ropes.

JENNY: What is it that you feel gets too risky to do? Does it become risky to give compliments to women, or—?

DANIEL: Yeah, that's typically one of those things. Because I've seen it happen so many times, so I know it's a big no-no to write, "Oh, nice pic" to some girl who posts a scantily clad picture. Or wait, with people I know well, I could do that. I know they won't misunderstand. But maybe people I only "half know," or have met a bit, if they don't remember who I am, it could turn ugly, and I know news travel quickly. People share a lot of nicks that have been blocked, people who are stupid and that you shouldn't deal with. Why would I even risk it? It becomes incredibly rational for me then not to even write something like that. . . . I don't know. This is really interesting stuff. I haven't actively thought about this, I've just had a feeling that maybe you shouldn't do that. And that it ties in with questions of women's vulnerability, safety issues, and all these predator debates that flare up all the time. Be a lurker, so you don't stir up any shit storms. It's a shame it has to be like this. But I learned pretty quickly just by observing what the jargon is like.

In anticipation of, or to avoid, being reported or publicly outed as a harasser, straight male Darkside users then often avoid giving what they consider to be a compliment to female users posting nudes or semi-nudes. For Daniel, it becomes matter of careful deliberation to safeguard other users' well-being, even if that comes at the cost of being less free in how he approaches or expresses his appreciation for women whom he does not know well. Respect for others, their wishes and desires, cuts across our platforms as a fundamental social rule elevated as a governance principle. Such respectful ways of communicating and relating may then come with certain amounts of restraint on the part of male users to protect the safety of women who are differently vulnerable, or simply more exposed when it comes to unwanted attention. Female users, in turn, detail how posting nudes or semi-nudes may not be a matter of seeking positive validation from strangers, but merely from their friends. Nudity here is something intimately entwined with social codes and relational dynamics. As Klara puts it,

Something that I find striking is that when people post pictures or write diary entries—there is a certain conversational climate with people you know in some way that can be very sexualizing or affirming. But then some outsider comes in, often a man who has misunderstood that what goes on in this comment field is some kind of internal jargon between people who know each other. And then he says something quite similar, but that is objectifying, and then gets a lot of backlash from the person who posted the picture and their friends and then gets totally confused. Because he then thinks, "Oh someone has posted a picture of their breasts, and then everyone has written these sexualizing comments, I'll throw one in too," and then it was not okay. . . . Some use [the platform] as a dating site, others more as a kind of pervy Facebook. You have it for your friend circle. These are very different approaches, which also becomes clear through clashes and misunderstandings. If you post a picture of your breasts, then you surely want someone to write something objectifying? But perhaps you don't want that at all.

The freedom to post, to reveal, and to express oneself sexually is unevenly distributed across the axes of gender and sexual identities. Some male users may take great liberties in how they approach women whereas others self-censor; some women openly call out what they deem harassment while others resort to tactics of blocking and reporting. One user's restrained or limited freedom to move and engage translates into another's protection and safety. This dance with the sexual in relation to a sense of safety on highly gendered terms, combined with the effects that a misstep might have, shows clearly how sex-positive spaces also come embedded in both cis-heteronormative male privilege and internal, often opaque boundary dynamics (more on these in chapter 6).

The Work of Distinction

Similar tensions extend to questions of social class. Many of our interviewees expressed with more or less colorful metaphors that while they have a lovely network of friends on-platform, the users external to that network tends to be quite "common." Petteri elaborates how responses to surveys—an Alastonsuomi staple—in particular make evident the platform's political and class dynamics:

The level of education is below average and it's kind of, how would I describe it, a little True Finn-centered [persukeskeinen, in reference to the major far-right national populist party, previously known as True Finns] and has a kind of petrolhead vibe [bensalenkkarimeinki, a creative expression translating as "gas-pedal-sneaker-vibe" and pointing to non-urban male cultures of car tuning] . . . Maybe some sexual minorities are starting to be pretty common. But gender minorities get really strongly—critiqued there. And if someone has something more special, like some fetish or such, [the platform] is pretty judgmental. But in a bigger picture of course there's a lot of different people there. So, you do find then, something for everyone here, suitable groups of friends. But like thinking of what kinds of comments you get there it's pretty much a yokel place [junttipaikka]. Of course, you shape

your own circle of friends. . . . But based on my pretty long [history of] use, I think
that the majority of users are fairly—it may not represent the society, the levels of
income and education of the users are very low.

While Petteri explicitly describes the emergence of social silos ("something for everyone there, suitable groups of friends") as spaces of more
friction-fee and pleasurable exchange, his comments also highlight differences in levels of education, social status, income, taste, as well as the
political stances connected to them. This illustrates the inseparability of
sexuality from broader social fabrics: how one wants to connect, with
whom, and who are certainly not considered members of one's in-crowd,
or who one might have sex with. In a particularly poignant example,
Taavi told Katrin that during the COVID-19 pandemic, vaccination status
became an additional criterion of choosing whom to connect with on
Libertine.Center. "Some couples actually said, 'We won't allow a vacci-
nated cock inside.'"

Mikk and Mari add further nuance to questions of class and cultural
capital in how safe spaces take shape on the basis of presumed similarity on
Libertine.Center.

MIKK: Well, this is a very bold statement, but I don't think there are many people
on the platform who are EKRE voters (the populist, right-wing, conservative party
in Estonia), although—although—although, everyone tends to assume that kinky
people are not conservative, but conservatives have their own kinks, they just
move in somewhat different circles, not so much on LC, but elsewhere they are
very much present, and they have their own sexual portals and spaces.

KATRIN: So where do they go then?

MARI (MIKK'S WIFE), LAUGHING: Yeah, and how do *you* know where they go?

MIKK, LAUGHING: Well, I think you'll find more of them on FetLife than on
Libertine.Center, for example. Conservatives just have different ways of expressing their kinks; they might be into straight on battering women, I'm not kid-
ding. But beyond this, as I already said, it's not like there are only one kind of
people on Libertine.Center. A conventional image is that it is all people who're
wealthy, manage their lives well, middle-class people who have a ton of time
and nothing else to do, but to spend it on sexual perversions. But it is actually
all kinds of people, some are cashiers in grocery stores during the day; I haven't
really seen people who are on welfare, but on the other site, iha.ee there are
lots of people who say in their profile that they live in assisted-living facilities,
so that group is even more diverse. But it is also somewhat diverse on Libertine
Center. And so then—yes, everyone tries to find the people who are a bit like
them, who mesh with their lifestyle, ways of living, personality, and everything

else. I mean this is what we have done. We've collected people around ourselves, who are a bit like us. So, when we have thrown parties, it's really important to invite people who have the potential to get along well. We've had a couple of failures; there was this one party where we invited a—how to say it—a simpler gentleman, who wasn't very talkative—and his presence stood out so sharply, he was so uncomfortable, he didn't know how to contribute to the conversation, he didn't understand what others were talking about, so Mari finally said to him, "You know, it's OK to just be quiet and focus on what you were invited to do here," which was of course said in a very humorous, jokey way. And I am sure that there are equally party groups for more simple people who like to drink a lot of beer and go to sauna, as there are for very fancy people, who go to very fancy beach resorts together.

We see here that a certain cultural and socioeconomic similarity is attributed to users of Libertine.Center, but it is cast as less homogenous than what the public discourse on the sexually adventurous groups, more specifically swingers, is. Further, even within this presumed similarity, patterns of affinity emerge that still include references to preferences based on cultural capital, education, or what is wrapped in a multifaceted diagnosis of "simplicity."

Yet ideological differences or the porosity of one's social silos were not seen merely as disturbances. For Hannele, the fact that Alastonsuomi is used by people from diverse walks of life involves a welcome broadening of horizons as "you get politically really different kinds of people with different backgrounds in a completely different way than in one's friendship circle, for example." The question of class differences reemerges in Marko juxtaposing vanilla people—"the straightest and the cleanest, the people who live [in] a kind of—standard decency"—with the main bulk of Alastonsuomi's userbase:

Success and how they kind of show it, success in terms of the standards of a status society, I don't think there are many people like that on those sites [sexual platforms]. Sure, they exist, too, but the basic middle-class high-flyer, those are fairly few, I think, it's rather sort of an alternative crowd, or then it's like, how to say it. The people whom you don't necessarily think of as open-minded in Finland, there's a bit of a, kind of *white trash* [in English] vibe, how to say it nicely. It's kind of divided, but the crowd who's middle-class successful according to common standards, I think they're fairly few. But you get everything there. At some point when I was thinking of participating in this [interview], I recalled that I've also met people from the university. Well, I've ran into a couple professors even, or at least highly educated people. There've been medical doctors and, can't remember anymore, but in principle I've ran into [people ranging from] professors and doctors and all kinds of things.

Marko's description of Alastonsuomi as having a "white trash" vibe while being frequented by professors and doctors speaks of ambiguity in identifying class distinctions on the basis of what fellow users post, yet it also entails an aesthetic assessment similar to Petteri's account of a "yokel place" where friendship and hookup silos nevertheless allow for a sense of insulation. Marko's discussion of the largely absent norm of middle-class meritocracy and vanilla decency—that which he identifies as "the straightest and the cleanest"—further evokes Sara Ahmed's (2006, 16) discussion of straightness as aligned with and progressing to goals without detours, as well as being metaphorically tied to notions of the right and the proper. Such bodies are, in short, "in line" with normative understandings of embodied spaces for action (Ahmed 2006, 66). Such alignment, again, is connected to how sexualized bodies take up space, echoing Alastonsuomi users' critiques of how heterosexual desires are foregrounded at the expense of other inclinations and orientations. Contra to such diagnoses of vanilla dominance, Marko describes Alastonsuomi as frequented by "an alternative crowd" who, following Ahmed (2006, 20), deviate "from the straight line" in their kinks and likes, whether these are straight or not, and craft spaces for being differently oriented.

Context Promiscuity

Mainstream social media platforms are heteronormative in how they are built and the kinds of sociality they support (Monea 2022), yet they can also be seen as queer in how they propel networked promiscuity, multiple intimacies, parallel connections, and fleeting attachments (Haber 2017; Payne 2015; Sundén 2018). Such fluid, or slutty, forms of relating and connecting are nevertheless consistently troubled by how both content and audiences are distributed within and between platforms and their respective normative frames.

In their influential discussion of context collapse on Twitter, Alice E. Marwick and danah boyd (2011) address the conflation of multiple audiences into single contexts—as in, say, one's user account being simultaneously followed by friends, family members, colleagues, sexual partners, and random strangers. Such collapse necessitates boundary work especially in how personal or intimate information is revealed (Light 2014). This boundary work is not merely an individual endeavor since it can involve considerations of overlapping social circles: Someone posting something reverberates across these circles in ways possibly rubbing against other people's boundaries. If someone is open about their belonging to kink communities in mainstream social media, others may inadvertently be outed by means of "guilt by association." As Sara expressed it:

> The people who are both my Darkside friends and my Facebook friends also have different boundaries about how visible they want to be, or what they think is appropriate in different forums. There may be some people and discussions that can be a bit more fluid between these different sites and contexts, but with others it may well be the case that certain things simply cannot be posted on Facebook.

The need for boundary maintenance is further accelerated when having an identifiable presence on multiple platforms. Elina explains that she has told of her Alastonsuomi presence on Instagram, and that people have then been able to find her profile. On Facebook, where her friends are relatives and coworkers, no such disclosure has taken place. The labeling of sexual content as "sensitive" or "objectionable" in mainstream social media feeds a tactic of siloed self-presentation and sociality across platforms, so that someone with a visible kink presence on a sexual site may choose to disclose no details concerning their sexual identities, experiences, or preferences on something like Instagram, even if their friendship circles on the platforms overlap. This, however, does not entail complete silence as differences remain between signaling belonging to sexual communities and being detailed about the specificities and directions of one's desires (see Sundén 2023b). It is also the case that sexual communities exist as closed groups on platforms with prohibitive community standards, as in Maarit's discussion of her simultaneous existence on Alastonsuomi, FetLife, Xperience Unlimited, and Facebook, so that her presence is to a degree recognizable across them. In fact, many of our participants found out about the study through a closed Facebook group for Alastonsuomi users.

For a minority of users whose social circles are well aware (and part) of their sexual self-expression, or who are activists, sex educators, or visible kinksters in public spaces and occasions such as Pride parades, there is little managing of contexts as the "collapse" between them is quite intentional. Most of our interviewees, however, experienced sexual sites as silos in the sense of having no or limited overlap with their social networks on Instagram, Facebook, LinkedIn, or in hookup apps. The question was primarily one of sexual outness (Fox and Warber 2015), as in Tiina's discussion of boundary work: "Although I've been long on the site, and in BDSM scenes, I'm fully closeted about this stuff. I somehow feel that my sexuality is nobody's business except mine and those with whom I want to be. I have no need to announce to my family that I use this sort of site." Conversely, such boundary maintenance worked both ways and could include keeping "those boundaries pretty strictly so that people from Alastonsuomi wouldn't come to my other social media" (Anniina) and the platform becomes "a completely separate isle" (Emilia). Yet such boundary work is by necessity leaky, and ultimately uncontrollable. For many, content bleed—and both intentional and unintentional data bleed (Duguay 2016)—occurs across sexual and generic social media platforms. Rather than context collapse, we identify this as "context promiscuity"—*a partially but not entirely deliberate blending of contexts that can involve subtle ways of outness*. If context collapse implicates an inadvertent breakdown of contexts, context promiscuity, while not being entirely intentional (since platforms, silos, and their boundaries are leaky well beyond the control of their users), provides an opening for considering strategic modes of understated visibility. In other words, sometimes you might *want* a bit of context collapse. Or more to the point, you might wish for things to bleed and leak in promiscuous ways. Darkside users, for example, may imply their interests on Facebook by replying to kink event invitations or by belonging to secret or closed kink-themed groups. In many cases, cues of sexual lives remain and can be traced across platforms and user profiles. People may pose with a subtle choker or combine a heart emoji with a fist in their status updates, ripe for interpretation for those who know how to read the signals. There is thus a range of kink visibility to mainstream social media, from being out and proud (which only a few can afford) to barely visible signs and traces that nonetheless build a sense of normalcy in sexual otherness by signaling alternate ways of living and existing.

For some of our participants, the optimal—even if not possible—solution would be to do away with social (media) silos altogether and expand the shame-free sociality of sexual platforms well beyond them. Joonas describes his dream society where I have an Alastonsuomi profile showing my cock and my body and my sex life and my face. And even if my boss knows about it, it's fine, and not only is it fine, it's in no way awkward. So, it'd be ok to find you with a nick there and if someone wants to check out your equipment or your ass, go ahead, it's there. I'd so enjoy if the world could be like that one day.

Even though such openness remains utopian and is hardly desirable for all, sexual sociality is a joining force that moves across and interlinks people, groups, events, meetups, platforms, and apps, and gives shape to both local and networked sexual cultures extending across diverse platforms in ways both explicit and tacit. Our participants speak of how their online presences form a continuum crafted in accordance with platform content policies and social vernaculars. For some, their presence expands from Instagram and Facebook to Tinder and Grindr, and further to Xperience United, SDC, FetLife, and OnlyFans, and their accounts can be followed in connection with one another. There is also more bilateral platform traffic, as in hearing about Alastonsuomi on Tinder or sharing links to Alaston-suomi profiles on Tinder in order to disclose sexual preferences in ways not afforded by the dating app's terms of use. Some Libertine.Center users have set up chat groups where those interested can share their profiles on "other adult sites," and for Darksiders, it is very common to use the site's acronym DS on Tinder profiles to discretely signal belonging to kink communities.

Yet others connect apps and platforms based on practical needs or in accordance with degrees of trust. Given Alastonsuomi's limited messaging options, the default intermediary for many users is Kik, an anonymous messenger app that necessitates no sharing of phone numbers. It was however typical on all three platforms to turn to non-anonymous general-purpose apps like WhatsApp, Messenger, Instagram, and Facebook as trust between users becomes established. "Transitioning to Facebook" can be considered a relationship stage as people either become online friends or hook up with one another in enjoyable ways—in any case, it was described as very much a controlled one-way street from one platform to another. The sharing of Facebook profiles was further interpreted as indicative of trustworthiness that can speed up the development of sexual relationships (exchanging photos, arranging a date).

Content and contacts do not merely bleed from sexual platforms to mainstream ones, but there is also traffic in the other direction. This can become a point of contention. As Eli says, there are plenty of Darkside members who use the platform almost the same way as they use Facebook:

> They may post that they're pregnant, for example. And not even pregnancy-kink, but that they actually got pregnant! And then I think, well, if you think that's fine, good for you, but for me it's the wrong platform. For me, these kink platforms, even if they are social, they are also sexualized. So, if someone posts that they've been out jogging, that's just so boring. When people post things like that, these worlds collide for me. I find it very strange when people use their kinky social media for such things. . . . Knowing that someone likes to do puzzles, I don't know how that enters the picture. For me, it's a kinky, sexual place to find friends, connect with friends, find kink events, and hit on hot queers.

Our interviewees are rather protective of this remaining a special place you can seek out to get horny, to feel your kink side come alive, and to check in on your friends and their diaries covering recent play sessions, their pictures of fresh bruises proudly displayed as trophies. They take great pleasure in logging in to see that "so and so has made cinnamon buns, and so and so got a good spanking" (Emma). While wishing for destigmatization and more openness of sexual expression, they also want to protect that which makes this place distinctive. Or, as Emma puts it:

> I think it's really about the fact that for me it's two completely different worlds. And it has to be. Because I think I don't want to bring too much of my everyday life into my kink practice, because then I imagine that some of the magic will be lost. Or maybe it's not really everyday life that destroys the magic, but more that I'm not turned on by everything. Maybe it's more that. Knitting is a huge interest for me, but it has nothing to do with eroticism, it has nothing to do with my BDSM persona. . . . I really don't want to bring in too much of my everyday life, because I don't want to kill the magic. I don't want Darkside to become Facebook. I think that's it. Darkside should be that place for kink, sex and I want to get a bit horny when I go in there. That's why I go in there, because I want to read someone's lovely diary, admire bruises and things like that. I use Darkside because I want to get a bit horny and I think that's lovely. Not to read about people's everyday lives.

There may then be a limit to how much everydayness a sexual platform can accommodate before it becomes unsexy, too Facebook-like, and hence boring. The boundaries between the sexy and the unsexy—or between the magical and the mundane—are however differently experienced. As we have discussed, the mundane may in one instance offer a sense of normalcy in sexual otherness, whereas it may also present a distinct limit to what is considered sexy and exciting in the first place.

On Sex, Sociality, and Cinnamon Buns

Intimate lives are increasingly made public on social media platforms (Dobson et al. 2018), yet sexual displays, expressions, and communication involved in this are actively policed and pushed back into presumably private domains. In a contentious social media landscape where sex and sexuality are simultaneously rendered visible, commodified, and plain banned, sexual platforms are important loci for advancing sexual sociality and queer bonds through tactically planned online presences and deliberated shifts from pseudonymous to non-anonymous connections, and from one platform to another.

Queer, in this context, does not only pertain to sexual identities (as these platforms house significant "straight" contingents), but to the bending and challenging of heteronormative, "SFW" social media sociality. Queering social media is also a matter of twisting understandings of sexual likes and practices through promiscuous, kinky, and nonmonogamous means, pushing beyond the bounds of normative heterosexuality—that is, forms of straightness considered desirable, regular, healthy, or generally "ok" (cf. Jackson 2006). As Joshua Weiner and Damon Young (2011, 223) ask, "When we speak of queer bonds, what sociality does this 'we' speak of? In what ways do our erotic lives constitute legible forms of sociability? And how is sociality both driven and riven by (our) sexual being?" They discuss how queer bonds certainly are social bonds, while their very queerness puts pressure on, or questions, the meaning of the social and its perceived legitimacy.

Our interviewees speak of the felt value of sexual social media platforms as sites of seeing and being seen, learning about the sexual selves and tastes of others. They speak of the value of the social inclusive of sexuality—of the importance of sites "where we can, in one moment, talk about last night's sex experiences and, in another, ask if someone has a good recipe for cinnamon buns" (Julia), even if they also feel the need to protect the sexual from some of the blandness of more generical sociality. Even as attempts at boundary work around platforms and social circles are a constant, and often an issue of concern, the participants see sexuality as fundamental to how social bonds take shape and develop, speaking of the importance, gravity, pleasure, and ease of connecting with others similarly attuned.

All this yields very particular types of sexual sociability—ones experienced as more social than those of sex-only platforms, as both more sexual and more intensely social than those of generic social media platforms, and possibly as not social at all. This points to silo-social experiences within the social media ecosystem where technologies, corporate interests, individual and group practices, norms, and ideas converge in ways accommodating certain degrees and types of sexual display and exchange (and not others). The boundaries between such silos can be perceived as either firm or highly porous, and users may disagree over which platforms are best suited for which purposes. While the term "silo" may imply firmness and the capacity to isolate exchanges so that things just do not leak, the default ooziness of stuff is well acknowledged as something that the participants recognize with varying degrees of unease. Social silos are porous and, to a degree, ephemeral in their makeup, even as they are also experienced as clearly bound and providing safety in being so. Data and content leak, strangers visit one's profile and possibly try to get in contact, and social connections formed on sexual platforms extend beyond them.

Learning from the users of sexual platforms makes it possible to understand the value of networked sexual sociality, its risks and possibilities. In our study, people of different ages, genders, sexual orientations, bodily abilities, and sizes address safety and unsafety as connected to the creation of social and content silos—no matter how porous these may be in practice—as nuanced negotiations over consent, and as both tactical and unpredicted platform promiscuity. Contexts may indeed collide and collapse, resulting in more or less involuntary forms of sexual outness. But there is also more subtle context bleed in what we called "context promiscuity" as a partly purposeful blending of content and contexts involving subtle signs or traces of sexual lives, identities, and practices. As a form of selective boundary opening, context promiscuity may be a way to flirt with the limits of community standards, and to signal things without being too obvious, literal, or explicit. Context promiscuity then involves the creation of continuity across platforms that injects the sexual into sex-negative platforms, or uses sexual "double-speak" making it possible for things to fly under the radar of content moderation. To move promiscuously across platforms creates a sexual undercurrent of sorts that affords a sense of normalcy and comforting mundanity in sexual otherness (even though, for some, such everydayness very much tempers that which they consider sexy, or even magical).

Our interviews also open up alternative analytical approaches to the perceived risks and harms of social media, ones expanding to the things lost when sex is ousted from networked forms of sociality in a blanket manner à la Meta. For what kinds of experiences, contacts, and explorations then become zoned out, and at what expense? Consider, for example, Tapio's account of how Alastonsuomi has been a means of documenting his presence on social media for over a decade "also as a sexual creature": "That's a quarter of my life, and—about half of my adulthood. So, I do feel that it's been a much more rewarding half of my adulthood, the one where I've been sexually able to express, or where I've been able to express my sexual identity and being." The removal of sex from social media delimits sexual sociality for all and truncates ways of understanding what makes the self and what interests, forces, and attachments drive people on levels both individual and collective. As discussed in chapter 1, such truncation disproportionally targets sexual cultures, practices, and identities already deemed marginal, such as the self-proclaimed "perverts," kinksters, swingers, cross-dressers, and exhibitionists on whose voices this book is built. All in all, our participants speak of the importance of sexual expression, learning, and enjoyment, even as it is cut through by frictions between contexts and platforms, or the kinds of inconveniences and frustrations that are part and parcel of sociality, whether on-platform or off.

5 Sense of the Local

Oh, well, it's really Finnish. . . . Its premise is that people speak Finnish and users are from Finland, and so on—since the hookup or search functions there are so useless, regional groups have emerged—people don't really discuss anything in them but they're there in the profile as a sign that I'm from there, or that I'm looking for company over there. . . . And, then I find it kind of interesting that there are people from all across Finland, in some really small town, somewhere in Lapland—all over Finland.

—Teemu

Addressing the "localness" of Alastonsuomi, Teemu discusses it as ranging from the national to the more narrowly local, also mentioning how some users mark their location by using telephone area codes—an anachronistic practice in a country where landlines are no longer in operation due to the long-term ubiquity of cell phone use; the practice also only makes sense to people old enough to have once dialed them. Alastonsuomi, Darkside, and Libertine.Center are all markedly local in ways leading us to questions concerning physical locations, user cultures, and ambiguous, contested belongings. In their different functionalities, our platforms include uses and features similar to those of hookup apps, social media platforms, and messaging apps. Their users, as we discussed in the previous chapter, integrate them into their personal social media ecosystems and use them for self-expression, finding sex partners, performing, and information-gathering. These platforms allow for, and collapse, multiple layers of locative sense-making, such as placing oneself on a sexual map, making oneself visible and accessible for sexual relating, and reconfiguring places and locations on sexual terms.

Writing a while back now, Paul Dourish (2006, 301) argued that a conceptual distinction between spaces (seen as abstract) and places (seen as embedded in cultural and social meaning) does not hold when discussing virtual spaces that, as design objects, condition and shape possible uses so that things are at once abstract and very much concrete. Dourish further points out that virtual spaces invite people to re-encounter everyday spaces by transforming how they relate to and understand them. Following this line of thought, we ask how our three platforms, designed to afford certain uses and not others, work with and through mundane locations, spaces, and places in a context where divisions drawn between the online and the offline, the digital and the everyday, have become pretty much blurred within the ubiquitous connectivity afforded by smartphones.

Historically speaking, networked media and its entanglements with sexual identities and communities involve a default spatial dimension. As online platforms grew key to sexual communities and the formation of sexual identities in the course of the 1990s, Usenet newgroups and chatrooms promised to free users from geographical constraints. Such presumed "placelessness," however, proved time and again to be an illusion, as one of the most common questions among users was "Where are you?," anchoring anonymous and pseudonymous digital spaces in specific geographic locations, bodies, and imaginaries (Sundén 2003, 91). The standard chatroom request of "A/S/L" similarly demanded people to disclose their "age, sex, location" up front in ways conflicting with the ideal of the internet as a realm of identity play "where nobody knows you're a dog" and, consequently, where it does not matter who you are, or where you are from, or where you can be just about anything you like (Nakamura 2002, 35). Such sexual spaces predated more fluid and mobile forms of digital connectivity—this was, after all, an era of desktop computers, clunky laptops, unstable and sonorous dial-up modems, and narrow bandwidth. At the same time, the sexual imaginaries that took shape on them were catalysts for physical encounters (Campbell 2004), affording the pleasure of knowing where the other was located so as to meet up in the flesh.

The spatial properties of how sex and sexuality entwine with digital technologies have become explicit with mobile and locative media. Research on dating and hookup apps has traced the practices of men who have sex with men through location-based apps like Grindr (e.g., Blackwell et al. 2015; Bonner-Thompson 2017; Miles 2017; Mowlabocus 2016; Race 2015) while also expanding to apps like Tinder primarily targeting straight users (e.g., David and Cambre 2016; Duguay 2017; Krüger and Spilde 2020; Ranzini and Lutz 2017). Hookup apps are per definition geosocial, building on the swiftness of the swipe and the geographical proximity between bodies in ways that reconfigure spaces and locations—not least for queer, sexually subcultural, and gender nonconforming communities, the members of which, depending on where they are, can find themselves among dozens of potential contacts, or as numbingly alone (Rawlings et al. 2023). Finally, even as generic social media have grown unwelcoming of sexual expression, their direct messaging functions are commonly used for sexting.

In what follows, we address the local and linguistic boundaries of our three platforms and ask how our participants articulate a comfort and investment in these sites of sexual display and exchange. We first focus on them as a means of digital wayfinding: connecting sexually to others and possibly hooking up. We then move to consider how they operate as sexual places in their own right, how they help to reimagine physical locations as ones of sexual play, and how this transforms ways of moving through and inhabiting such spaces. Finally, we offer a discussion of how our participants address the sites' local and linguistic specificities, and how these connect to the sense of proximity and distance, risk, and safety. The linguistic and regional specificity of these sites—while not excluding cross-national connections— evokes the question of belonging and membership in the socio-sexual silos and communities that they offer. It is crucial to note that there is striking whiteness to these platforms suggesting that their local sexual publics are not equally open for all. Inquiring after their localness then also means asking how they contribute to understandings of "Swedishness," "Finnishness," and "Estonianness," respectively, and what boundary work this involves in sexual relating.

The "local" is here very much a moving target. It signifies that which is close at hand—a language, a culture, a sense of proximity—in ways that map onto nation-bound boundaries, imaginaries, and perceived meanings. Yet the local also plays out on much smaller and specific scales when used to concretely designate things going on in one's immediate physical surroundings—a neighborhood, city, or province—whether this means belonging to locally grounded sexual communities, attending play parties, hooking up, or fantasizing about what might be going on down at the corner store. The "regional," in turn, sits between the local and the national, while also much more expansively designating the transnational Baltic Sea region inclusive of our three respective national contexts, and connected by frequent ferry and flight connections. The regionality of our platforms offers a contradistinction, or a counterpoint to internationally operating social media services, allowing us to address their experiences and meanings jointly.

Searching, Connecting, Hooking Up

"To locate" is a matter of wayfinding; the orientation involved in identifying or discovering the location of something, or someone. The platforms we investigate are spatialized tools for digital wayfinding, or wayfaring, in helping to locate partners and sites of sexual play—from Libertine.Center's explicit hookup functionality, to Alastonsuomi's implicit yet routine hookup possibilities, to Darkside's modest hookup affordances. This lack of functionality in orchestrating swift sexual encounters led Leo to describe the site as a jumping-off point where additional apps and platforms have to be incorporated in order to fulfill one's needs:

> Other tools are just better suited. There are some possibilities on Darkside, but others are more efficiently tailored for a quick response. You can write messages, but the site doesn't even have a chat function, for example, which would facilitate communication. For many people I know, when you're horny you want a date within half an hour, and then it's difficult to get a quick response through the slow messaging system.

Building on Tim Ingold's (2009) notion of wayfaring, Larissa Hjorth and Sarah Pink (2014) write of digital wayfaring as a means of conceptualizing the interweaving of the physical and the digital in mobile media use that produces new social spaces (see also Hjorth and Richardson 2017). In our study, platforms become orientation devices for actualizing encounters in the flesh and putting bodies in motion, sometimes in ways necessitating local, national, or even transnational travels—as in Estonian swingers hooking up with Finnish ones, or people partying together on the large ferries on the Baltic Sea sailing from Finland to Sweden, and back again (a tradition with much gay history). These movements and encounters in turn leave traces in, and feed back into, platformed sociability. While our three sexual sites afford more and less wayfinding, this is not merely an issue of their functionality.

Wayfinding is explicitly encouraged on Libertine.Center as its users are interested in finding, screening, selecting, and getting together with others. The founders describe the site as geared toward "meeting people." Because of this, users' geographical locations are important functional and meaning-making categories. Reporting one's location is mandatory when setting up a profile, and when a location is entered, the system attempts to translate it into GPS data. If successful, it communicates a relative location (e.g., five kilometers away) to all viewing the profile. The default distance is 50 km, although options expand up to 10,000 km and users can be searched by distance. Events cannot be sorted by location, but distance from each user is shown in the event preview (as in "Naughty List Christmas Party, 5 km"). While our interviewees spoke of the platform as serving a variety of purposes, straightforward wayfinding in terms of seeking people to meet up with and identifying lifestyle-compatible places were recurrently mentioned.

> Yes, I guess it's a tool for meeting people, for me. And on Libertine.Center it's certain, or—well, you know what people are there for—you don't have to be very careful about asking what they're into, it's quite straightforward, people are there for these types of acquaintanceships, people are looking for a libertine way of life, for meeting other libertines and enjoying life together. (Kaspar)

In contrast, Darkside and Alastonsuomi are more imprecise in their geo-locative search functions, only allowing searches by county (Darkside), city, or region (Alastonsuomi). Nonetheless, many participants use the sites as a springboards for play dates with strangers. Darkside users appreciate the clear kink framing offered by the platform and the fact that the context is given since most of them are not interested in vanilla (nonkinky) encounters. Klara, a female queer user, compared Darkside to Tinder, which, due to its normative heterosexual framing, forced her to be very explicit about her desires and preferences in ways that made her feel uneasy, even if the direction or orientation of her sexual desire was not exactly a secret. She recounts how kink and BDSM have always been an intimate part of her, as has her queerness, and how this interconnectedness does not translate smoothly into Tinder's dating and hookup choreographies:

> For me, my BDSM interest is so much an integral part of me and my sexuality and my identity. I haven't had a relationship that wasn't characterized by BDSM since I was fifteen, and have no interest in having one. BDSM intertwined with queerness is my sexual orientation. It is not something that can happen alongside, or be placed on top of something else. So, for me, it would probably feel strange to think that I could separate those parts completely. . . .
>
> For a while, I tried Tinder. But I found it very difficult to know how to use it. After all, I am very uninterested in meeting someone if I'm not compatible with them in terms of BDSM. And that, in turn, means that I sort of need to spell that out

on Tinder. Because otherwise there will be such pointless discussions. Of course, I may think that people are good looking on Tinder, but I sort of don't know what to use it for. And anyone who googles my name will quickly understand that I'm into BDSM, so, it's not a secret in that way. But I still found it difficult to spell that out on Tinder, the fact that I have no interest in meeting someone who doesn't want to dominate me. Because it suddenly felt too offensive, too vulgar, too sexual somehow. But if someone googles my name, these things still come up, and that doesn't bother me. So, there is some sort of tension between privacy and openness for me as well, even if it's not always that clear.

Tinder's superior wayfinding affordances could not compensate for the sense of vulnerability that its explicit normative sexuality generated for a user of minoritarian sexual preferences (we discuss the gradients and inversions of sexual norms in more detail in chapter 6). The geosocial affordances of apps do not emerge unproblematically from their wayfinding affordances but are, rather, negotiated through personal, normative, and cultural lenses.

Alastonsuomi users interested in hooking up often move to a messaging app and sort out the locations for themselves. Emmi explains that her impetus for joining Alastonsuomi had to do with "getting to have group sex, and maybe getting into some parties and events." When asked whether she can estimate how many meets there are, and how many groups organize live meets, Julia gladly elaborates:

> Oh, there are so many of those. And they've completely exploded during the past years so that we've already had to, kind of limit them, because there started to be so much interest that meetup people's budgets couldn't handle that, joining everything. Since it's like, we always divide the payments equally among everyone, it costs money. And then there are different meets with different starting points. . . . So, they happen all the time. When you start looking on Alastonsuomi with that kind of an eye of what kinds of [on-platform] clubs there are you'll see that some organizers always put info on their meetups first and, knowing how to find the right people, you start finding them. That cottage meet thing is kind of, like, you've got to get into that bubble. You've got to find some channel to find your way into those. But there are so many of them, all the time [*laughs*].

Antti further unpacks the regional dynamics at play:

> Of course, people concentrate in big cities, and then there are these summer cottage meetups that I've been to and, some meets can be 200–300 kilometers away, and some even drive 400 kilometers, so, come from far away. Of course, in the bigger cities there's more to do and maybe the threshold of going to some meetup when it's a long journey is high for someone there in the countryside. . . . But, yes, there have been these meetups all over the place, mainly in Southern Finland but—in

fact I met, I'm from the south myself and in one meet near Jyväskylä [in Central Finland] I met a guy from Oulu [Northern Finland]. So yes then, people even travel long distances.

Such sexual wayfinding, while occasionally involving long distances, reso-nates in obvious ways with the uses of hookup apps. An app such as Grindr builds on a "zero feet away" geolocative logic of instant gratification (Batiste 2013), fostering a spatiotemporal sense of immediacy and proximity of the kind often imagined as being closely aligned with urban gay male desires. The uses encouraged by app design do not, however, necessarily equate to the practices and experiences of actual users. Stefanie Duguay (2019) argues that queer female Tinder users experience a scarcity of dating options even in urban contexts, calling into question the idea that apps unproblemati-cally link people and places by bridging geographical constraints. Similarly, Jed Brubaker, Mike Ananny, and Kate Crawford (2014, 5) show how the use of hookup apps in sparsely populated rural areas may in fact emphasize an "absence of connection." If there is a lack of people to choose from to begin with, an app will obviously not be of much help. In addition, it is not uncommon for queer dating app users to insert false locations in order not to be outed in rural areas and smaller towns, but to opt for a nearby city instead. Whether on a hookup app or on a sexual social media platform, incongruences between reported and factual places of residence are used to strategically strengthen anonymity and safety (Breitschuh and Göretz 2019; Albury and Byron 2016)—a practice present on all three of our platforms.

Kinky Takeovers and Overwriting the Grocery Store

In addition to operating as devices for sexual wayfinding, our platforms help to sexualize and reimagine physical spaces, reshaping how these feel and what they mean—from sexualizing a particular beach as a site of play, to re-signifying a category of places such as spas and saunas, to reshaping geo-graphical imaginaries in intimate and national registers.

Darkside offers a both imaginary and tangible geography, or a gateway to a community firmly grounded in physical spaces of play. The plat-form's calendar function comes across as a key feature in the interviews in that it opens up a world where kink is the norm. As Linda puts it, "I use the calendar a lot, to meet people in real life. Otherwise, I could just as easily have used FetLife, if it was just for the forum discussions. But it is about actually meeting people." The calendar provides users with a kink compass of sorts to guide them within their local scene and give them the coordinates for clubs and events that are otherwise difficult to find. Darkside is then less of a tool for locating unknown others than one for place-making and community-building: It is an event finder and a kink map unlocking more or less hidden physical locations reminiscent of what Dominique Pierre Batiste (2013) identifies as a queer cartography mapped onto both familiar and strange spaces.

The calendar presents a concrete timeline marking upcoming events, yet it is equally a tool of the imagination outlining the contours of a community always larger than what the participants call their own. As a link to this nationally scaling community, the calendar provides a window not only into local spaces of play but to kink activities all over Sweden. This dynamic map of Swedish kink events highlights an (unsurprising) urban concentration while also offering ample evidence of, for example, countryside rope gatherings and discreet BDSM get-togethers for "fika"—a nice cup of coffee accompanied by something sweet—on the second floor of a small-town pastry shop. From the urban participants' point of view, this imagery of a small gathering of kinksters in broad daylight over coffee and cinnamon buns portrays the rural locations that some of them left behind in a very different light. While the urban focus of kink communities is undeniable, the calendar makes visible traces of kink in everyday rural contexts, showing how these are not, after all, void of options and connections. The calendar also affords a sense of normalcy, as Darkside allows for people to not only connect with those they already know but to also connect on a national scale, making things feel less lonely, and less weird. The calendar basically provides a direct link to a national kink community with a population equivalent to a mid-sized Swedish city.

The overwriting of places as kinky can also happen imaginatively in ways that further a sense of safe resonance based on recognizability. Emma recounts how BDSM literature published in the US never spoke to her directly, and it was not until she came across a series of diary entries on Darkside chronicling secret play sessions at Ica (a Swedish chain of cooperative grocery stores with roots in the 1930s) that something shifted in her:

JENNY: Do you feel that Darkside has contributed to your sexual self-understanding?

EMMA: Yes, absolutely, one hundred percent. Especially in the beginning, especially with my first account. Then it was very important for me to be able to log in, to check things out, to understand things, to read discussion threads. I went to a meetup with others too, but then I felt so insecure. So, to be able to go and read stuff and be part of an online forum, that meant a lot to me then. To be able to read about peoples' different feelings and thoughts. Because I had read these Dossie Easton and Janet Hardy books, *The Bottoming Book* and *The Topping Book* and so on, and they're great books, I really think they're fantastic. But at the same time, reading them, they are set in an American context. And being able to read about BDSM in a Swedish context like I was able to do on Darkside, that meant a lot. And also, just being able to read diary entries from people who are at Ica and play at Ica and stuff like that, it made me open my eyes to a completely different kind of way of being in my sexuality. Which meant a lot to me.

JENNY: A parallel world, sort of?

EMMA: Exactly, this parallel world that I share with others.

She details how these scenes concretely gave her a new way of relating to her sexuality, a new way of being sexual. They afforded an opening that made it possible to reimagine the most mundane of spaces as ones involving kink potential. The cultural proximity of the event—the fact that it could literally take place around the corner—not only opened up the possibility to imagine the exceedingly familiar space of a grocery store differently within a kink cartography; it rendered her desire intelligible. Swedish kink geographies and such desire for intelligibility need to be understood against the background of sexual marginalization and stigmatization. Even if consensual BDSM is legal, the law does not recognize it as a form of sexual orientation, so it remains unprotected by anti-discrimination laws. The participants speak of how their sexual desires and practices would be virtually unintelligible in their wider circles of social media friends and followers, making clear how—even in relation to a supposedly sexually liberated nation like Sweden—there are distinct limits to what constitutes intelligible desires and lives (cf. Kulick 2005).

On Libertine.Center, too, the reimagining of locations as sexual is related to the need for finding and creating "community friendly locations." Users are incentivized (i.e., they receive platform-specific tokens for doing so) to submit these into a menu item on the site. At the time of our fieldwork, the list of kinky locations included seventy-seven entries from twenty countries, most of them sex clubs and nude beaches. The platform thus invites users to imagine places as "kinky" but in some cases also to *overwrite* less sexual places so as to make them "community friendly." This connects to a material practice known as "takeovers," where resorts and hotels are rented and used in lifestyle-specific ways, usually including a temporary suspension of rules regarding public nudity and sex. However, ways of imagining locations as kinky on Libertine.Center extend the site-specific feature as users continue casting places as sexual in personal ads and chat group themes. Thus, "in the nature"—a common Estonian spatial imaginary for the summer season—takes on a sexual overtone and becomes kinky, as do spas and saunas.

Alastonsuomi similarly affords the sexualization of bars, rented manors, public saunas, and whatever locations have you. Julia explains that this happens at such impressive scales that the challenge involves the difficulty of choice, rather than available supply:

> For example, those kinds of bar-meets Alastonsuomi has, or we've kind of more generally organized those so that, for example, we book some bar for a certain period of time and then you have to know to tell at the door that you know where you're coming to. There are bar meets, then there are also sauna meets where we book some kind of public sauna space where we then have a one-night sauna meet. And then there are cottage meets, where I've been, there were eight people. But at the largest meet I've been to there were almost sixty people playing in a large mansion together for four days. That sounded wrong. I meant to say spending time [*laughs*] together. . . . So, then everyone started to organize those in different parts of Finland.

Of the three platforms, Alastonsuomi is most explicitly rooted in the local through its name ("Naked Finland") gesturing toward a nation-state. If, in terms of geopolitical imaginaries, a nation-state's territory can be considered a "container" that becomes filled with specific meanings that accumulate over time in processes of nation-building (Häkli 1999, 124; Paasi 1990), Alastonsuomi both builds on existing national imaginaries and reshapes them in its ample graphic displays of naked bodies, bodily fluids, and fetishes. Both the visual landscape and the uses of Alastonsuomi are tightly connected to the physical locations that they simultaneously transcend. In acts of sexual placemaking, people pose in city parks, in forests, at summer cottages, and by the lakeside, transforming mundane, both recognizable and generically local spaces into sites of exhibitionism, cross-dressing, group sex, and play. Through the marker of "Finland," the site performs territorial, linguistic, and cultural boundary work concerning both its presumed members and users; through the marker of nudity, it defines undress as the default mode of social relating. As an "imagined community" (Anderson 1983) of sorts, it joins users into a nation exposed, or a nation where belonging is defined through naked displays and exchanges, making room for unclothed self-expression in a region where, as one of our participants pointed out, showing skin in public is complicated due to the frigid climate alone.

It Could Be Someone Next Door!

Negotiations over proximity and distance, availability and scarcity are prevalent across the three platforms, although with different material and symbolic emphases. In addition to geographical or physical closeness, proximity points to more ephemeral things, indicating a sense of closeness, or even intimacy. And how physical distance feels, or what a certain distance means varies, and possibly shifts over time. Above, Antti described people driving 400 km as part of their sexual wayfinding. However, while distance from others is a key criterion of wayfinding, it also often involves interpretative distance. Kilometers, users' levels of experience in a lifestyle, the intensity of their desires, population density where they live, and questions of privacy, deviance, and vulnerability all converge. Thus, Libertine.Center users describe Estonia as both *too small and not small enough* for their sexual practices. Liisa points out that after an initial phase of enthusiastically participating in events near and far, she no longer considers herself to be "available for dates," because "I live—I think probably there aren't people in my town, who are LC users, or there might be, but I probably don't really want to meet them, because it's a small place, where I live." For Liisa, then, her town is too small since socio-sexual proximity carries a variety of risks that she is not willing to take. At the same time, Estonia has also become not small enough; as now that Liisa has sated her initial appetites, the capital Tallinn where most events take place has started to seem too far for her to travel: "I don't live in Tallinn, which means that I cannot go on random dates."

Elaborating on this intersection of desire and distance, swinger couple Mikk and Mari recount, "When we entered this world, we would interact a lot—now we have our circle, so we meet no more than ten to twelve new people or couples a year. But in the beginning—we might've met one hundred to two hundred people within the first six months." This sexual abundance was possible both because they had not yet met most of the eligible playmates in closer proximity, and because their curiosity and desires motivated them to travel more. By the time of the interview, Mikk and Mari had settled into a routine, and found a core group of partners, pointing out that the popular axiom of Estonia being "small enough to drive across" is simply not true:

> For newcomers it is very typical to say, "What, c'mon, we live in Estonia, it is tiny, distance is no problem!" But distance is a problem. Even fifty km, if someone lives in Rakvere, and someone else lives in Tallinn, that's it—real interaction is very much constrained by distance. And if we talk about foreign countries, then you have to do all kinds of gymnastics and put in a huge effort to create a relationship, to start something and keep it alive and then you end up meeting once a year or once every two years and the question of "Why?" inevitably arises. It is much easier to interact, not even just for sex, but even as friends and acquaintances, with people who are close to you. Distance matters.

Mikk and Mari's experience of distance has been structured by gradients of desire, enthusiasm, and a slowly growing network of recurring partners increasingly accessible without the help of the platform. Experiences of distance then depend on how you practice a sexual lifestyle: whether you are just starting out and dating more indiscriminately or you are more established and prefer steady partners and have a regular group to play with. Seen through this lens, the meaning of fifty kilometers can change radically over the course of a single year. This sense of interpretive distance also tends to shape user experiences of the placeness of the platform itself. Those who live outside of the two biggest towns (Tallinn and Tartu) imagine and use the platform as more place-like (to hang out, to play with images), while those who live in the urban centers experience Libertine.Center more as a tool for sexually organizing and inhabiting a geographic area.

In the geo-sexual imaginary of Estonia as too small and yet not small enough, the size of the country's population, the area of the country, and the functions and features of Libertine.Center form a locational assemblage of sorts. The size of Estonia's population (1.3 million) introduces particular risks pertaining to privacy and sexual normativity into how the platform is used both as a place and as a tool. The limited number of "lifestylers" increases the likelihood of running into an acquaintance or being recognized when one would prefer not to. This motivates people to avoid context promiscuity where sexual lifestyle bleeds into their other networked presence (see chapter 4). The country's small population also shapes users' on-platform practices (e.g., what kinds of photos and information is shared in profiles, which group chats are popular) and sexual practices (e.g., the process of moving from initial contact to a date or screening potential contacts). Using one's real name, including one's face in photos, and sharing information about one's job are—for reasons understandable enough—generally avoided.

The dynamics of proximity and distance are similar, albeit not identical, on Alastonsuomi where a generic dick pic can become unintentionally locally recognizable when its framing offers glimpses through the bedroom window. More broadly, local cultural markers allow for a sense of familiarity without compromising user anonymity. Several of our interviewees discuss this combination of local recognizability and anonymity as adding to voyeuristic pleasures in the titillating thought that "it could be anyone"—or, more precisely, "it could be someone next door." Whereas our Estonian participants spoke of recognizing a neighbor with trepidation and abhorrence, Mikael identified the possibility of peeping on one's neighbor as a particular kind of fantasy realization. And, comparing Alastonsuomi to the international sexual platforms he uses, Timo described it as both similar and distinct: "Since it's Finnish and people speak Finnish, and your neighbor can be there, for example."

The platform's "homely" familiarity and the titillation of just maybe spotting one's neighbors is balanced with privacy measures for managing the risks of unwanted exposure—one can, after all, very well be the very neighbor spotted. Some of our interviewees have been recognized on Alastonsuomi. Aleksi describes "kind of funny or nice discussions" with a friend after they had recognized each other on-site but says that "there wasn't anything special to it." Johanna, again, was quite upset over people contacting her after recognizing her without explaining who they themselves might be, to the degree that she removed all potentially recognizable photos. Noora relies on a presumption of shared secrecy: "If someone recognizes me from my Alastonsuomi pics, then that's saying that they're there, too, in which case it's kind of, like, *don't ask, don't tell*" [in English]. Anna sums up some of the ambivalence:

> It's usually been kind of a private discussion where they point out that, I guess I recognize that gym or I guess I recognize that tattoo, do you know who this is? One person who recognized me happened to be my friend from work. We ended up having a very fun conversation about it, a relaxed conversation, and we both

understood that neither of us wanted to be outed on this site so actually this didn't need to be talked about. So, we said hi and hello and ignored whether the other one goes to peep or not. And then the other experience I had was—I still don't know who this person is, and I got the impression that I don't want to know either, that it's not necessarily in any way beneficial that this kind of person knows I'm there. I made them swear to keep it to themselves, what they found out.

While some users are willing to take the risk of being recognized and many post photos showing their faces, most Alastonsuomi users try to protect their anonymity in at least their publicly shared content. In other words, platform sociality both bridges physical distance (that may or may not be considerable, considering the site's local character and the scope of local sexual scenes) and, intersecting with vulnerability and anonymity, gives rise to imaginaries of proximity and distance resulting in tactical forms of self-presentation and platform use.

Localized Play and Exclusionary Dynamics of Sex and Race

"To localize" is a matter of confining or restricting to a particular place or location, to place something locally, to make local, or to orient locally. Sexual social media platforms are not mere mediators in the sense of facilitating hooking up and reimagining physical locations: They equally assemble localized online places for flirtation, imagination, visibility, and appreciation that interlink bodies, visual pleasures, risks, and vulnerabilities. Put differently, sexual platforms are places of their own in that some users communicate on-platform only, without any aim of extending beyond networked connectivity. Platforms operate as sites for seeing and being seen, whether the user in question takes pleasure in testing out their sexual attractiveness through rating systems and listings of top pictures, or whether they enjoy the outness of unorthodox sexual preferences on them. There is a sense of safety and control to relating through networked means and displaying oneself, even as all this is necessarily conditioned, structured, and limited by the functionalities of the platform in question, and hence not something for users to fully control.

How sex becomes localized is also tied to how national belonging in our local contexts is contoured by whiteness, and how norms regulating gender and sexuality take shape in communities supposedly unmoored by heteronormalcy. All three platforms traffic heavily in visual markers of whiteness, as well as in specific forms of female sexiness and sluttiness, although the bodies and desires featured do cover a broad spectrum of things. Explaining that her body is not "conventionally somehow covetable, although it may sort of be," Elina notes that, as "a non-disabled straight person, I can be there in whatever way I want. But immediately if you differ from the norm, then you have to be more careful." Emma further elaborates on Darkside's body normativity:

> I have quite a few nice pictures of me bound and suspended in ropes. I don't post them, now I've lost some weight, but then there were quite a lot of bumps and folds and fat and such. That body, I don't want to show it off, because it's a forum where the people who hang in ropes are thin. And I can also really feel that with Darkside, that it's the good looking and polished that gets to be seen there in some way, or that's what comes up anyway, because that's what gets a lot of likes.

Photos that gain the most likes are often conventionally sexy pictures of young, attractive, skinny, white women, which makes other kinds of bodies less visible. Kink, BDSM, and libertine scenes are generally diverse, but the popular visuality of platforms (formalized into "top rated" galleries or aggregated from the number of likes) also reinforces the idea of Swedishness, Finnishness, and Estonianness—and by extension (aspirational) Nordicness—as something that coincides with whiteness (see Lundström and Teitelbaum 2017). As Hanna points out, "Whiteness is the norm—not only because the community is largely white but also Darkside's front banner, which bothers me every time I log in, which as far as I can see depicts five white, good-looking, slim people."[1]

Indeed, BDSM as a form of risk-taking has been argued to presuppose gendered and racial privilege (cf. Weiss 2011, 190–201), while swinging as a practice is often critiqued for both heteronormativity and homophobia (Frank 2008; Serina et al. 2013), and the users of Alastonsuomi critically comment on the platform's underlying straight male dominance in how attention clusters to certain bodies. Participants on all three platforms spoke of these spaces as challenging normative frameworks and making space for other bodily expressions and ways of relating than those seen in mainstream, commercially produced sexual and pornographic content. It is nevertheless also clear that efforts to move beyond, play with, and trouble the visual galleries of fitness, whiteness, and hetero-normalcy can well reiterate these very same regulatory frameworks. The fact that our self-selected participants are themselves white (as far as we know, as we did a few interviews with audio alone) further reflects the platforms' user demographics. It also adds difficulty to considering the broader ethnic and racial dynamics at play—there are, after all, things that white users will not experience, or even notice happening.

Further, while participation in English is included in the studied sites' palette of sociality, their specificity was often articulated on cultural and linguistic, rather than simply regional terms. Stephen, a non-Estonian Libertine. Center user told us that while in his everyday life, he had a sense that Estonians speak pretty good English and are happy to use it, then on the site and when trying to meet people for sexual encounters, the willingness to interact across a linguistic divide diminishes. Although Stephen was not sure if people saying they don't speak good enough English reflected their level of competency, or just functioned as a convenient excuse to not talk to him. Mona, the female partner in a swinger couple, said that while they often go to Riga (capital of Latvia), which is closer to where they live than Tallinn, meeting up with Latvians has so far "only remained an idea, because it seems so much more comfortable to speak in your own language." The Finnishness of Alastonsuomi was for most participants also bound up with Finnish language and culture. For many, both (relative) physical proximity and a shared first language emerged as very much practical concerns connected to the ease of connecting, as in Emmi's account:

> It's nice in a way that, if you want to meet up, it's at least kind of closer. And of course, the language then, that you can speak Finnish here. On sites where you have [people] from all over the world you need language skills. Of course, there are some with whom you can talk in Swedish or English, for example. But here it's—it's kind of a common identity denominator that—like, it's even called Alastonsuomi [*Naked Finland*], so we're Finnish, and we like to be naked [*laughs*].

This sense of proximity also translated into a sense of realness, or authenticity, in terms of both self-expression and how one relates to others on-site:

> It's kind of a down-to-earth platform. If you compare it to the porn you find online, for example, like Pornhub or such, people are clearly looking at content from some producer. On Alastonsuomi, it's like this person could be my neighbor, users are real people, and they're Finnish. People mainly speak Finnish. So, people approach it from two directions maybe, those who like to make that material, exactly from those starting points [i.e., realness and localness, intertwined], and those who like to watch that material from those starting points. It's maybe a unifying thing, as the name also says Naked Finland [*laughs*], so it's Finnish and somehow homely. (Anniina)

Localness then blends into a "home-grown" feel as the site caters much amateur content shot in domestic settings without extensive mise-en-scène involved. For Hannele, the marked Finnishness of "Naked Finland" as a national nude image gallery of sorts (Vihlman 2022) was something that she had never thought about during her years of use, yet that she equally associated with relatability and familiarity:

> Yes, Fatherland, [*laughs*]. I've never thought about that, but yes it probably makes it very specific in comparison to international sites, where you might have a Finnish subdivision. Its accessibility is much better like this, as it's really homemade and everything is in Finnish. The English version is still not entirely available, so you can't use the site normally. . . . Probably the fact that it's in Finnish makes it feel closer to you. And if this were some international site, it would [create more] distance—[in the sense that I'd wonder if] I'm performing there and who are these people. On Alastonsuomi you know that they're probably from somewhere in Finland and so it becomes—it's hard to put into words but, "more real" is a bad word, but it's easier to imagine the reality of these people in comparison to having users from all corners of the world.

When inquired about the presence of non-Finnish-speaking users on the linguistically bound Alastonsuomi, Juhani defined the ratio as thousands of Finns versus a few foreigners, the latter being approached with interest "as a nice extra spice and stimulant," while Teemu argued that nonwhite bodies are easily fetishized. Pointing to the same issue, Julia noted that people with darker skin gain both very positive and negative public comments due to being hypervisible against all the bare pink flesh displayed across the site. Or, as Mikael put it, the only dark-skinned woman he had seen on the platform over the years stuck out "like a comet in the sky." Many participants also spoke of the users' aversion to transgender and cross-dressing users, as well as its homophobic undertones occasionally growing into overtones.

When asked about how people react to messages written in English, Emilia spoke of racist reactions, such as responding with "Write in fucking Finnish, we're in Finland now"—although, technically, the users of the platform can of course be anywhere in the world. This view was echoed by Petteri who saw anti-immigration rhetoric as running rife on the site. In contrast, Maarit argued that there is no racism, and that non-Finnish users are warmly received. Tapio offered a more hesitant reflection of the dynamic:

> It's my sense that, on Alastonsuomi, there's kind of—like a pretty white culture, especially if you're good looking, young, and white, then you have a certain status—but

if you're a lonely immigrant man who doesn't speak Finnish or speaks bad Finnish, and then if you have darker skin or such, for example—I'm guessing that it can be more difficult to operate and socialize there to a degree. But this is just my sense.

For Lauri, linguistic divisions were recognizable, but he saw no real difference between how people communicate or become acquainted across them, even as he recognized the tendency to exoticize nonwhite bodies:

I'd claim that you get just the same kinds of comments, well, how to phrase that? Just as good or just as catastrophically bad comments you get from Finns and Finnish speakers and people identifying as Finnish and from whatever other people. I'd say that they're pretty much on the same level in terms of communication. And I'd say that there is some kind of exoticism, or some users seek exoticism and seek it, or can seek those qualities in other people. Sure, there are also those negative aspects to this, like anywhere else, for example if you took a cross-section of Finland then you're sure to find those negative bits. But I'd say that, as a rule, we're moving pretty much on par with these [nonnative] Finnish speakers.

There is, in sum, considerable range and diversity to accounts of linguistic, national, and racialized dynamics on Alastonsuomi among our self-selected, white, and Finnish-speaking participants. That the one and the same site can be defined as racist and nonracist further speaks to how othering and hateful speech become recognized as such, if and when they are encountered, and, consequently, how they matter differently to different users. In the Finnish context, as elsewhere, social media are key engines of racist and xenophobic discourse (Horsti and Saresma 2021). It was a general theme in our interviews that discrimination along racial and linguistic lines was discussed from a distance as something that occurs without our participants playing any part in it themselves. In this vein, racism became articulated as an external issue rather than a social dynamic within which Finns, Swedes, and Estonians by necessity operate—whether by supporting, ignoring, or resisting it (e.g., Hervik 2019). All this involves a certain color blindness, be it intentional or not.

This, again, speaks of unequally distributed visibilities where racism may simply not be visible in one's social media bubble due to its homophilic makeup—that which Wendy Chun (2021, 24, 82) identifies as a founding logic of racial segregation in so far as there is an urban history of racism to the algorithms that underpin social media networks. Within this logic, similarity breeds similarity and sameness attracts sameness. Such homophily is true of how socio-sexual silos function as bubbles, one example being the "meetup families" where people gather together to share similar likes and kinks. Yet there is a very real sense in which homophily connects to the localness of the three platforms, breeding a perceived sense of safety-in-sameness. All this points to how there can be no "us" without a postulated "them," or any inside without an imagined outside, any inclusion without exclusion, even as all kinds of gradations occur in between.

Safety Bubbles?

Physical locations are necessarily connected to the possibilities of sexual expression and relationship-making—for example, there tends to be less room for alternative sexualities in rural areas, and in regions dominated by conservative Christianity (e.g., Gray 2009). This means that for someone whose sexuality is in conflict with the norms of their immediate local community—and the users of all of our platforms can be considered to violate some norms of "appropriate" sexual behavior—a sex-positive site can function as a lifeline allowing for knowledge, peer support, self-expression, and the possibility of getting together in a safer space. This has been abundantly demonstrated in previous work on sexual platforms and sexual uses of the internet (Muise 2011; Rak 2005; Tiidenberg 2016; Waskul and Martin 2010). At the same time, being able to speak to like-minded others in one's native language and sharing certain cultural understandings creates an additional experience of safety unavailable on international platforms—one also exclusive of international users.

Some Alastonsuomi users explicitly connected the platform's homely Finnishness to a perceived sense of safety and trustworthiness drawn along national lines: They felt that they could trust the site more by virtue of it being Finnish. While our participants were regularly critical of the forms of sociality that the platform fosters—the fact being that many users behave badly—they maintained that, as a socio-sexual space, it feels different from international ones.

> Yes, there are also people who message in English, but I don't know if it's about them not speaking Finnish, or if they aren't in Finland, dunno. But most are, of course, Finnish and everything is in Finnish. I think it brings somehow a kind of safety that, well, not sure how to explain this, that it's not, if something should happen there, then at least it's your fellow countryman. And if we think of some crimes and such, the police—still has some sort of power in Finland. Often if it's something, some foreigner scams, then the police don't have much power to do

anything here, and maybe they don't know about such foreign phenomena. Then again there's more knowledge of Finnish phenomena and more power to intervene, and so on. And also, somehow on a psychological level I feel that there's kind of communal spirit—even as you of course get negative comments and all that. But we're much more accepting—I feel. And just that it's in Finnish and in Finland and Finns so, I feel that it somewhat influences the positive spirit that there is. But mainly maybe just the safeness, safety, and that, of course there are all kinds of bad Finnish people, too, and all this, what dark web and blah blah blah, there are Finns there, too, and those photos may end up there also through Finnish hands. But maybe, I'm more afraid when I have photos on foreign sites—and I've had more problems on those sites, that those photos have ended up somewhere else. (Kristiina)

There is much to unpack from Kristiina's articulation of safety and risk and how it plays out. Context-wise, Kristiina has had an Alastonsuomi business account since 2016 (similar in its functionalities to a VIP account but also allowing her to promote her shows and online presence). Her concern over how personal content becomes ripped, recycled, and repurposed across international platforms, or, indeed, on the dark web, is then also a question of occupational risk for those trading in commercial sex. Her discussion of the possibilities to turn to the police in case something goes awry, while not necessarily reflecting the factual possibilities, or willingness, of Finnish officials to investigate copyright infringements and image theft in social media, especially when it comes to sexual content, connects to generally high levels of social trust—including trust in public institutions such as the police—in Finnish society (cf. Kääriäinen 2008; Pirkkalainen et al. 2024). It however points even more to a sense of safety rooted in national specificity premised on divisions between the Finnish and the not. The Finnishness, or "spirit," of Alastonsuomi becomes tied in with shared cultural codes, trust, and degrees of safety, while also being connected to liberation from social norms and hierarchies delimiting sexual expression, bodily visibility, and the articulation of desires. For Kristiina, Alastonsuomi *feels* more manageable than international platforms, and Finnish users more trustworthy than international ones, so that the site's spirit translates as a particular kind of affective charge, or resonance.

The ways in which Alastonsuomi fosters both belonging and ostracism is also an issue of the contemporary Finnish political climate where anti-immigration activism and the success of nationalist populist politicians with extreme right tendencies have fed definitions of Finnishness drawn according to exclusive, even ethno-nationalist notions of belonging, especially so during the past decade (Pantti et al. 2019). According to Mikael, there is support for such views on the site, as shown in on-platform surveys, and nonwhite users with lacking language skills are openly discriminated against. In its horizontal display of user profiles, Alastonsuomi is, on the one hand, inclusive in the range of bodies it features, while, on the other hand, it enables segregation similarly to any other social media platform (Chun 2021) and involves the outright hierarchization of bodies through its ranking systems. The site's local vernaculars then arguably feed racism, making it necessary to ask who is seen to belong among the Finnish, who are trusted, and who may be excluded from networks of sociability and exchange dependent on cultural codes and conventions that the platform's users are presumed to share (Pirkkalainen et al. 2024).

However, Mikk, the husband in the Estonian swinger couple using Libertine.Center, offered an alternative link between safety and language. For him, like for the Alastonsuomi users quoted above, shared language makes for easier communication and thus more satisfying sexual encounters. But in some situations, a sense of safety comes from anonymity provided by sexual encounters with people not from (the too-small in this case) Estonia, which makes people seek out foreigners instead.

> MIKK: We've enjoyed exotic fruit, sure, but both our own and our friends' experiences point to most people preferring to interact with people in their own language; even within Estonia, Russians hang out more with other Russian speakers and Estonians with Estonians, so even within one country, we have a language barrier. When we just started out, one of our first dates were a Russian couple who had just moved to Estonia, and the husband actually spoke pretty good Estonian considering he had lived here only for a year or two, but we quickly realized that the language barrier is a major issue for us. We like to be able to have a conversation. And the more time we have been in the lifestyle, the more we think that. We keep trying, but we keep finding out the same thing. So, the couples who specifically seek out foreigners are definitely a minority, although there can be specific reasons for it; a member of the Parliament might be interested in meeting with Latvian couples just in case (laughs). For example, we once dated a Latvian couple and the wife was top brass at a big Latvian company, and they had this principle that they don't hunt on their own territory, so to speak, to avoid possible issues.

Just as Alastonsuomi operates through cultural and linguistic codes of Finnishness, and Libertine.Center with negotiations of Estonianness, the sense of safety on Darkside is a combination of the site's "Swedishness"—the language, the terminology, the cultural context—and, above all, its local embeddedness, as the people you connect with are often close to you geographically. Many participants are part of an international network of kinksters, and they use FetLife for international kink travels (mainly to Berlin). There is thus a certain linguistic fluency and a habit of moving across borders and between contexts, yet things do get lost in translation. Malin spoke at length about what it means to her that the platform is in Swedish:

> MALIN: It means a lot. It's really nice. I have an account on FetLife too, but it's not nearly as user-friendly. There is so much terminology that doesn't resonate with me. When choosing a relationship, you can choose, for example, "I'm in a leather family." It took me until last year to understand what kind of concept "leather family" was in the US context. It means nothing to me. I kind of can't really express myself or relate in a way that works for me, because I don't have the correct terminology—FetLife is more of a necessary evil, while on Darkside you can express yourself in a completely different way. So, it means a lot that it is Swedish. It's my context, my language, and my expressions.
>
> JENNY: Yes, so it's about ways of expressing yourself. But is it something else too?
>
> MALIN: Yes, it's a slightly easier way in [to the community]. Both to meet people, to pick people up, because those who are on Darkside are sort of nearby. It's also culturally easier. I can relate in a different way. I know how to write and how to approach others. We speak the same language. But it's not the language itself. I mean, I work in English, English is not a language barrier. But it can be a cultural obstacle.

There is, thus, an obvious linguistic dimension of a freedom and fluency of expression and understanding of oneself and of others tied to one's native language as a carrier of cultural proximity. No matter how good your English is, it simply is not the same as having the possibility to express yourself and relate to others in your first language. In addition to platforms having specific platform vernaculars (Gibbs et al. 2015), Malin here refers to a localized kink vernacular, which partly, but not entirely, overlaps with a platform vernacular.

Close By, or Not

Location and locatedness are, in sum, imagined and created in a number of ways as users make sense of geographical, normative, and cultural distances on and through the platforms. In contrast to how researchers of mobile and locative media emphasize a seamless layering, or copresence of digital and physical spaces (de Souza e Silva 2006; Hjorth and Lim 2012), our platforms show how digital sexual geographies also take shape through experiences of local scarcity, cultural proximity, and experiential distance. Distance here becomes an obstacle in geographies of hooking up, but it can equally be a protective shield against the vulnerabilities and risks linked to unwanted openness and outness.

How sex is located and localized on and beyond these platforms thus challenges the common notion that digital and social media in general, and hookup apps in particular, are primarily a means to overcome distance. Physical proximity is obviously a key factor of sex and sites of sexual play, and our platforms quite powerfully bring people together in this sense. But just as important are our participants' investments in a range of pleasurable proximities and distances across scales ranging from the geographical to the cultural and to the imaginary (it could be someone next door!). While connecting people and bringing them close, our platforms also afford a way of playing with and at a distance—as there can be safety to distance—in relation to which specifically local geographic imaginaries create their own sense of proximity, cultural intelligibility, and belonging. Networked forms of sex may not only extend spaces of sexuality beyond the immediately proximate but also intensify these encounters in ways that make them *feel* more proximate (Cockayne et al. 2017). To this we would add that the feel of our three platforms is created not only through a sense of intensified proximity but also through a distinct sense of distance, echoing Gill Valentine's (2008, 2103) understanding of how digitally mediated distance does not necessarily cut intimacy short. In order to feel seen and to feel connected, some kind of distance can also be necessary to open up spaces for playful, sexual tension, for desire to circulate, and for relational dynamics enhanced by sexual social media to emerge.

The practices of digital sexual placemaking explored in this chapter then show how proximity and distance do not form a binary, but rather involve gradients of both pleasure and apprehension. There is the sense of desired proximity in instances when the whole point of the connection is to physically meet up. There are situations where geographical proximity instead adds a layer of pleasure and excitement in knowing that an encounter *could* happen even when a desire to meet up is lacking. Geographical distance may equally function as a safety net, which leaves plenty of space for a collaboratively imagining something, secured through the improbability of the encounter. There is of course also the kind of geographical distance that provides a barrier to even imagining the contours of something when one's desires are linked to physical meetups. Finally, there is the sense of the local and the proximate that functions as an exclusionary, distancing, or downright racist tactic toward those who are not seen to be "one of us."

There is thus a range of tensions to the uses of the three platforms, ranging from uneasy negotiations of belonging and exclusion to the vulnerabilities involved in visibility, outing, and sexual relating, yet their value is equally manifest among our participants. As discussed in this chapter, the platforms help to craft out sexual maps of places to hook up, party, and play so that otherwise unextraordinary, mundane sites become reframed—and thus to a degree transformed. In doing so, they help to map out erotic, ludic topographies (Bell and Valentine 1995, 16), or geographies of digital sexualities (Nash and Gorman-Murray 2019) built on sexual relating and belonging. Our three platforms allow for wayfinding both in terms of self-discovery and making meaningful social connections in environments where diverse bodily displays and pleasures are appreciated. At the same time, on-platform power hierarchies and practices of discrimination play a central part in who is seen and appreciated, who gets to be close, and who gets to be pushed away instead.

6 Vanilla Normies and Proud Pervs

As we have been arguing throughout this book, sexual platforms revolve around sexual sociality, self-expression, learning, and connecting. But their uses are also driven by a quest for pleasure. On sexual platforms, pleasures explicitly seen as sexual and those as very much not can overlap and shift. Further, platforms play a variety of roles in explicitly sexual off-platform pleasures in that they inspire, fuel, or help people find partners for titillations predicated on physical presence. In this chapter we talk about all of this: pleasurable platform practices, pleasurable sex, but, more than anything, the conceptual and normative complications involved in delineating what one finds pleasurable and, hence, somehow "good." We explore how our interviewees describe personal, subcultural, and historical forms of sexual belonging and articulate them in relation to the perceived cultural and sexual mainstream. As we go on to argue, these articulations involve the activation of symbolic boundaries within and around the notions of pleasurable sex. Platforms are part of these negotiations, sometimes in explicit ways and, at other times, as infrastructures and spaces that make possible the feelings and experiences that necessitate an activation or a shift of a boundary.

Michèle Lamont and Virág Molnár (2002, 168) describe symbolic boundary practices as conceptual distinctions that people make to "categorize objects, people, practices, and even time and space." Further, moral boundaries—understood as a subsection of symbolic boundaries—are distinctions made specifically to deem certain behaviors deviant in some contexts but not in others (Lauderdale 1976). As much previous work has shown, boundary work is key to how both sexual normalcy (e.g., Fjær et al. 2015; Rubin 1989; Sprott et al. 2021; Warner 2000) and variations of "good," "good-enough," or even "magnificent" sex (Hargons et al. 2022; Kleinplatz and Ménard, 2020; Metz and McCarthy 2003) take shape and become regulated. We examine our participants' boundary work in terms of their perceptions of various sexual norms and ask how this plays out on the platforms studied. Such boundary work hinges on tacit value hierarchies where sexual desires and practices are deemed contextually "valid or invalid, appropriate or inappropriate" (Weeks 2017, 138).

In practice, our participants equate pleasurable sex with "liberated sex," which again regularly becomes mapped out against "vanilla normalcy." Through such boundary activation and movement, pleasurable sex becomes a tacitly normative matter, even when it does not start out as being so. To unpack this with nuance and texture, we have organized the discussion as follows: First, we explore how and why our participants find pleasure on the three studied platforms. Second, we show how our interviewees' notions of good, pleasurable sex are linked to liberation and constituted against the figure of vanilla. Third, we discuss how this boundary work taps into national imaginaries concerning sexual normativity more broadly—that is, what kinds of normativity our participants identify and map out as contexts for their own sexual exchanges, both on-platform and off. Finally, we address the complexity and occasional ambiguity of sexual norms, as well as the stakes involved in the valorization of "nonvanilla" as a heterogeneous yet not necessarily altogether coherent category of desires, practices, and orientations.

Pleasure-Platforms and Platform Pleasures

When asked about the pleasures that sexual platforms make possible, some of our participants were quick to downplay them or, like Hanna, imagined others as having more pleasurable attachments to them:

> I assume that there are a lot of people who have great sex chats, and who get a kick out of sharing a gif on Darkside of their partner being spanked. Or that there is also pleasure in writing a status update about your vibrator breaking because you've used it so much. There are lots of stories about pleasure on the site in pictures and text. I also sometimes see photos that I think are hot.

Others argued that the issue was not one of sexual pleasure exactly, but of a different enjoyable, possibly contingent thing. Aleksi discusses the pleasures of taking selfies as overshadowing those connected to sharing the outcome, even though he considers the experiences and possibilities of sharing as an important source of pleasure as such: "I don't feel—that I get any immense pleasure from sharing my own things there [Alastonsuomi]. . . . It's however fun to share experiences and then have good discussions on the platform and meet like-minded people. It comes from that maybe, my own pleasure too, on the site."

For Teemu, the site's attraction is similarly connected to discussing sexual likes and fantasies that yields "maybe not pleasure but enjoyment and fun." This view was shared by others who felt that pleasure is too strong a word for capturing their experiences and motivations of platform use as such—with Jaakko even suggesting that "displeasure" is more descriptive of his overall user experience, despite some "arresting moments" of the more positive kind. Emmi explicitly detached the pleasure of viewing naked pictures and conversing with other users from sexual arousal, explaining that on-platform communication on Alastonsuomi "isn't for me in any way a thing that gives sexual pleasure." Tuisku describes this rather as "social pleasure" deriving from being accepted by others, having similar interests, and having a sense of belonging. Peeter, a Libertine.Center user similarly mused, "I'm sure it is very personal, but I don't get a special pleasure from scrolling the feeds—if the goal was not to meet someone and do something together, then I don't think I would go there so often; virtual voyeurism isn't my thing. If I am after that, I would rather go on Pornhub." This seemingly paradoxical detachment of pleasures of using the sites from sexual titillation was not shared by all. Some discussed using the sites for masturbation and others very openly confessed to it being extremely pleasurable to get positive feedback on their images. As Mikk said, "You post your picture, and get your sweet hit, when everyone comes and—essentially—strokes or pets your ego." Yet even this pleasure remained connected to an overall emphasis placed on the forms of sociability that sexual social media allows for. Hannele associates on-platform pleasures with

> A kind of immediate sense of relaxation that maybe comes with that, with exposing myself. . . . Enjoyment and pleasure, at its best I think when you meet people and chat and, by default, you've already stripped off a lot, some taboo layer which in other contexts you have when talking to people—now I'm feeling like I've somehow downplayed the sexual charge that there surely obviously is, maybe I wanted to foreground that it's not the main or the only thing [laughs]. But sure, yes, generally forthright talk about sex and seeing sex as pleasurable in itself. There isn't some layer of shame or other stuff that you first need to overcome like you'd need to if you had the same conversations in many other contexts.

Hannele highlights some of the nuances and layers of pleasure involved in these platformed exchanges, ranging from the enjoyment of self-exposure and a boost of self-esteem from getting positive feedback on one's images to the more obviously carnal pleasures of sex itself, and talking about it with others. Sexual platforms offer points of entry into social connections where sexual likes and pleasures offer something of a steady backbeat, rather than comprising some dirty secret. It would be problematic to argue that sexual shame is entirely absent from sexual platforms, but the platforms we studied allow people to connect with like-minded others, to resist pressures to sexually conform, and to discover novel tastes and modes of being, so as to negotiate what is considered "good sex" on levels both personal and collective (Nixon and Düsterhöft 2017; Tiidenberg and van der Nagel 2020).

Good Sex?

As described above, finding, talking to, and meeting like-minded peers was elevated as one of the predominant pleasures on all three of the platforms we studied. But what is involved in deeming someone pleasurably like-minded, exactly? As we showed in previous chapters, plenty of distinctions are produced and reproduced about the user base along the lines of class, cultural capital, social status, language skills, and race. How do users then come to experience each other as similar instead, across such differences?

In discussing the sex that our participants and their like-minded peers find pleasurable, they delineate a sort of liberated sex against the notion of uninteresting vanilla. This involves something of a reversal of the sexual hierarchy of "good sex" that Gayle Rubin (1989) outlined in her formative article "Thinking Sex." Broadly sketching out the dynamics of the governance of sex in Western cultures and engaging with the political context of 1980s Reagan-era US in particular, Rubin posed the issue as gatekeeping wherein "good, normal, natural, blessed sexuality" is plied apart from its opposite—the "bad, abnormal, unnatural, damned." Within this, "good sex" becomes the terrain of heterosexual, married, monogamous, procreative, noncommercial exchanges practiced in pairs of individuals of the same generation, in private and without the aid of pornography, sex toys, or other paraphernalia. Such "goodness" could also be conceptualized as normative heterosexuality. The "bad," by extension, entails sex that "may be homosexual, unmarried, promiscuous, nonprocreative, or commercial. It may be masturbatory or take place in orgies, may be casual, may cross generational lines, and may take place in 'public,' or at least in the bushes or the baths. It may involve the use of pornography, fetish objects, sex toys, or unusual roles" (Rubin 1989, 281). For Rubin, the perceived goodness and badness of sex are issues of social normativity, and of boundary work wherein some exchanges became cast as aspirational, and others as very much not. Obviously, such norms change according to time and place, and there is considerable complexity to how sexual norms become recognized, articulated, and lived. Our participants valorize sexual liberation and openmindedness over the presumed tedium of vanilla to articulate an aspirational kind of sexual hierarchy that explicitly plays with the cultural, normative, and political construct of what Rubin framed as "good sex."

Broadly, our participants' understandings of pleasurable sex revolve around the notion of sexual liberation, or liberated sex. Such liberation is not necessarily synonymous with sexual freedom as such, nor is it coupled with political movements advancing sexual equality and sexual rights. Rather, it is connected to more personal forms of sexual learning, knowledge, and experimentation where sexual platforms can play a key part.

When discussing their experiences and definitions of liberated sex, our interviewees highlight it as willing, variable/diverse, and self-reflexive, more or less implicitly marking it apart from its opposite (the reluctant, the monotonous, the nonreflexive). Liberated sex is *willing* in the sense that there is a lot of it, but also in the sense that the people having it are characterized by their active and open orientation toward different sexual life-worlds—both the ones they share and those that others inhabit. When describing themselves and others like them, our interviewees rely on words signaling sincerity and lack of prejudice ("open," "honest," "curious"), but also openness as activeness ("active," "up for anything") and boundary-pushing ("self-confident," "out there," "easily bored," "thrill-seeking").

Willingness to experiment with, and to push, boundaries is central to many of our participants' kink practices, as well as to their understanding of what makes them liberated. This focus on the exploration of (bodily and mental) boundaries aligns with the dominant norms within BDSM practices that may involve very intense forms of play. Thus, on Darkside, notions of "good sex" as the practices that many users value—these not being necessarily genital in nature—often coincide with boundary-pushing practices linked to physical force. Linda explains:

The first thing that comes to mind is that soft sex is not so central. Good sex is sex with an edge of consensual violence, you might say. In a way, it's quite rough and perhaps triggers something even rougher. It's a bit like, the goal is to push your boundaries, that the best sex is pushing your own boundaries, ending up in sub space. There may be a tendency toward that anyway. At the same time, this is quite natural given the context. I think that many are open and curious and want to develop and push their own boundaries. But there's not so much talk about sex being both, hard and soft. I think it's makes sense though, given that the other, the softer side is everywhere else in society.

While set in a frame of prenegotiations and practices of consent, sexual openness and curiosity is here linked to being open to, or curious about, harder forms of sex. The boundary between normative and nonnormative sex, or between the softness and hardness of things, becomes rather firmly drawn. Malin, however, problematizes such a focus on hard edges and boundary-pushing:

Sometimes Darkside feels a bit like the person with the least resistance wins. That it somehow becomes a bit of an extreme, how can I put it, it becomes a bit of a dick measuring contest. The most advanced strokes, or knots, or bruises. I would probably say that good sex here is to be as "out there" as possible. Those who just like a bit of rough sex can be mocked. . . . On Darkside, it often goes like this: "I like to push your boundaries. I like to test where your limits are. Together we take it one step further." So, there is a lot of that on people's profiles, that you should always be ready and willing to go a little further. You have to be ready to push yourself. That's the ultimate sexuality.

Here, liberated sex hinges on norms that regulate bodies, power dynamics, and boundaries connected to skill, intensity, and a certain extremeness of practice. It is simply not enough to enjoy a bit of roughness since practices involving physical force also require a fair amount of skill and advancement. Malin's preferences and desires are different, and while intensity certainly is part of what she finds pleasurable, she also values a dynamic that does not presume high intensity as the ultimate goal. On the one hand, then, a "zone of difference" (Abbot 1995, 877) is created around willingness as characteristic to the us-group and the sex that it finds pleasurable. On the other hand, further boundary dynamics occur within that zone to specify what willingness means in particular situations and for particular people. Further still, willingness as an open and enthusiastic orientation toward the world can take on broader meanings, implying not only one's attitudes toward sexual practices, sensations, and pleasures, but rather one's general approach to life. Mikk and Mari recount:

MIKK: Well, curiosity is the main thing, if we want to create a hierarchy of people on Libertine.Center, and there is a hierarchy—the people who actually break out of the fantasy and are willing to meet up, do something—are open, curious, socially active—what else, courageous. . . . Actually, we have noticed that in the past four years our social circle has transformed. . . . And we've noticed that the main difference between our old friends and this new group we've met thanks to Libertine.Center and being in the lifestyle is that the new friends are really willing, open, and always ready for whatever.

MARI: They go with the flow.

MIKK: They go with the flow. You might need help fixing the roof and it's the "weird" friends that show up instead of making excuses. . . . The mindset isn't "I can't," it's "How can I make it happen?"

But liberated sex is not merely described as willing: It is also *diverse* and *variable*. Willing, active, open-minded people, we were repeatedly told, have diverse, imaginative, and skilled sex (cf. Harviainen and Frank 2018) unbound by taboos and traditions. Juhani explains:

In a way it means, yeah, sexually promiscuous, it means that you can have sex in many ways both physically and also, visually, it comes with the clothes and the accessories and everything else. . . . fundamentally that it's active. It's not once a month as it is in some relationships, or once a week as it is in others. But it's several times a week, or even several times a day, and in many different ways.

Circling back to our discussion of platformed socio-sexual silos in chapter 4, such boundary work was also seen as situational and contextual in being mapped out according to one's orientations and platformed connections. When asked about the sexual hierarchies at play on Alastonsuomi, the "mostly pansexual" Antti defined these as something that everybody assembles for themselves—or, more precisely, as something defined by one's specific social connection and "bubbles":

For example, [the axis of] monogamy—polygamy limits it on some level, or polyamory. Monogamy sort of marks those out, [there's] kind of a pecking [order] on some level. But I don't see it as being hierarchical in the sense of a top-down layering, but it's more about creating bubbles, just that we're in our own bubble or reference group here, so to say, from which you maybe don't see the other person's perspective sometimes, you don't understand things. I'm sometimes guilty of that myself, but then I try to understand that, okay, so, for one person monogamy works, and for another, polyamory and something such. It can be a little like that sometimes, feeling that others don't share your opinion, so it can leave the kind of impression that, okay, s/he thinks that s/he's on another level of hierarchy.

Antti speaks explicitly of ephemeral yet tangible on-platform hierarchies connected to perceived sexual liberation, describing how free-mindedness involves frictions as users fail to appreciate each other's tastes and rank them instead. As this example further illustrates, our interviewees also foreground *self-reflexivity* as a marker of liberated sex. Here, self-reflexivity concerns both one's personal sexual preferences and practices as well as the ways in which they relate to how sex is mapped out, or governed, in public discourse. In so doing, our participants articulate a symbolic boundary (Lamont and Molnár 2002) enveloping the (by necessity) amorphous "us" of the sexually liberated who are interested in sexual knowledge and sociability and less governed by taboos in how they judge their own desires and those of others, while also acknowledging that it is all about different strokes for different folks, so that one should not judge. This means understanding sexual life-worlds as rife with different desires, proclivities, and identifications, including those that one does not share. For Julia, this is a question of

how liberally I perceive other people versus how liberal I'm as an actor myself. So, of course, as a subjective human being, my own uncertainties that I've got to process and that I work through are always there in the background, and I need to be open and honest with my partners so that I can feel good, and let others around me feel good, too. But in addition to that, I also feel that I can perceive the diversity of sexual, gender, and human relations quite extensively, so I can accept people's sexuality in a very open and understanding way.

Our interviewees often connected self-reflexivity with the language of personal transformation, of having grown into a person who knows and accepts both their own desires and sexual diversity more broadly (cf. Beckmann 2009, 232, 239). Here, sexual platforms play an active role as sites of learning that broaden one's sexual horizons. Our participants are also quite aware of how values and codes connected to sex deemed pleasurable vary across the platforms' socio-sexual silos, or bubbles, formed around shared likes. For Antti, Alastonsuomi has been formative in terms of opening up and feeling less shy about—and, indeed, being okay with—his interest in men "and others—[a] nonstraight orientation and all this stuff about fetishes and such." This has made him come to terms with how "a so-called perv is not necessarily a negative, a negatively loaded term, and that there are a lot of these kinds of people, and you can express this sexuality in many different ways." Self-reflexivity was then tied in with a way of owning the struggles that it took to get to that place of acceptance and relating to sexual life-worlds in an open-minded manner.

Elusive Vanilla

Our interviewees tacitly link liberation, as well as its divergence from what they perceive as normative and vanilla, to the sex that they find pleasurable, so that pleasurable sex and sexual liberation become co-constitutive. This is sometimes explicit, but mostly it unfolds through situational and contextual boundary work encompassing practices, preferences, and ways of being, and pointing to an implicit taxonomy. Our participants create symbolic, and sometimes also moral, boundaries between "normal" people of waning sexual willingness and boring, normative vanilla tastes, and the contingent category of "us, the liberated people" that they self-identify with, or aspire to be. This collective denominator refers to the users of our sexual platforms, to specific sexual subcultures, and to groups constituted by a partial overlap between the two—Noora, for example, discusses the perceived bulk of Alastonsuomi users as "just ordinary people who want ordinary socks-on sex" to mark her own preferences apart from it, while Kaspar, a Libertine. Center user speaks of platform users as markedly more liberated, pleasure oriented, and sexually adventurous than "typical Estonians." Divisions of vanilla and nonvanilla then result from the activation of situational, nested, overlapping, and sometimes contradictory boundaries.

When discussing willingness, variability/diversity, and self-reflexivity as values and qualities key to pleasurable sex, our interviewees often rely on what we identify as the "vernaculars of vanilla." Vanilla is a popular, expansive term for conventional, unimaginative, normative sex, especially so within kink communities defining themselves against the very category (e.g., Chalkidou 2022, 571; Langdridge and Butt 2004, 42–43; Pohtinen 2019; Rehberg 2017). By associating vanilla with the sexual practices of others, our participants equate "nonvanilla" with the kind of liberated and pleasurable sex that they themselves enjoy. For our swinger-identifying participants, vanilla points to monogamy and nonvanilla to the freedoms of nonmonogamy. For our BDSM-practicing interviewees, vanilla stands for nonkinky sex while BDSM is established as its liberatory counterpart. For yet others across the three platforms, vanilla more opaquely indicates normative heterosexuality and disappointingly bland "romantic naughtiness." Nonvanilla becomes articulated as good, liberated, and valuable against the notion of vanilla that, by extension, comes to mark dull, inhibited, and pointless sexual lives. However, as we will go to show, these boundaries tend to slip and blur.

Framed expansively as an issue of the "vanilla world," vanilla marks boundaries between perceived sexual normalcy and things deviating from it. It can equally point to varieties of sexual and nonsexual relating, as in Tapio's discussion of his "vanilla" and "perv" browsers: "When I use my vanilla browser, it has for example news and kid's sports hobbies and I look at, well, different stuff, whatever comes out of such vanilla world. And then I have a separate browser, where I have, for example, been logged into my Alastonsuomi profile and FetLife profile and there's some Pornhub and different sites connected to sexuality." While Tapio articulates something of a pragmatic division within his personal technology use, for others the issue is more explicitly one of value judgments, and of avoiding the judgment of others. Daniel, for example, imagines the vanilla world and its people as sharing a particular sensitivity, so that alternative sexual likes and activities need to be delicately phrased, should they be phrased at all:

> On the platform [Darkside], you socialize around these issues in an incredibly relaxed way. I've even had these discussions with my vanilla friends I know well and who know what I do. I've asked them, how much do you really want to know about what I do? For real. Because if they ask, "But what did you do on Saturday?" what should I say? Should I say that I hung someone up and whipped them until they screamed? To exaggerate a bit, but yes. It's quite nice to have had that conversation, because then you know how much they want to know and if they are curious, I encourage them to ask further. I'll tell them if they want to know, but otherwise you don't have to shove it in their faces. You can try to be mindful of the norms and limits of how ordinary vanilla people talk about these things. . . . You don't want to become someone who's completely uninhibited but in a bad way, who doesn't understand other codes and who's too much in their own world. It's better to have one foot in each world. I like that idea, that you can have one foot in the vanilla world. You have to remember what it's like to be at an ordinary dinner party with people who don't do this sort of thing. It's just silly to forget how to do that. Because I know people who are just doing a lot of kink stuff. They don't hang out with any vanilla people anymore. It has its charm, but I don't know why you would want to voluntarily close the door to the majority society.

The comment about the helpfulness of remembering how to behave at a regular dinner party is particularly striking, as it delineates a world with kink at its center as one where—for social reasons if nothing else—it is useful to not completely lose touch with the vanilla world. To be clear, kink practitioners are by no means immune to what counts as legitimately desirable in the vanilla world. When the participants speak of internal sexual norms on Darkside, they assign high status to practices that are visually striking and "photograph well." Further, they link this visual appeal to mainstream aesthetics, and to what manages to circumvent the algorithms of generic social media platforms. Thus, of high status are artful, Instagram-compatible images of shibari, or sexy leather and latex imagery that does not get flagged and filtered out as inappropriate nudity. Such visually striking practices also overlap with the kind of images that are most likely to cross over into the mainstream:

LINDA: The latex people are among those who are absolutely at the top. That's the cool thing. And then you have people who're fond of scat, they're still very stigmatized. Things that others simply don't understand at all, like yarn and wool sweaters, are probably not very high on this list either. So, it's definitely a scale.

JENNY: But what is it that gives latex such high status?

LINDA: Because it appeals to more common forms of sexuality, I would say. Basically, any vanilla guy I meet will say that latex is hot. And I'm like, you have no idea, do you? When you touch the shit, it's slimy, you're not gonna like it. When I take it off, the top layer of my skin comes off with it, think about that. No, but I think that's it. It's hot for everyone. It's like a slice of normative sexuality.

Our three platforms are rife with visual sexual norms and hierarchies that both do and do not overlap with the ideals of vanilla. Latex can become a desirable, hot choice due to its aesthetic qualities, but also because it ties into more mainstream ideas of edgy yet not-too-out-there sexiness. The skintight and shiny material has been branded as kinky by the mainstream for decades, and thus its edges have been smoothed over. It has become a semi-normative signifier of nonnormative sexuality—something that, as Sara puts it, "mainstream society understands." Margot Weiss (2006, 105) argues that an increasing presence of BDSM imagery in popular culture allows for people "to flirt with danger and excitement" while at the same time being conditioned by sexual norms that reinforce the boundaries between vanilla and deviant sex (cf. Beckmann 2009, 4). But perhaps these boundaries between vanilla and nonvanilla may not necessarily be strengthened, but actually weakened in this process. The kind of "vanilla intelligibility" that becomes operable on Darkside seems to rather screw with norms and boundaries between kink and not-kink in ways that make them less distinct in the process. Put differently, mainstream flirtations with kink imagery and practices do not automatically lead to kink becoming further stigmatized: It may also soften the perceived boundary between sexual life-worlds as these come to overlap.[1]

Moving beyond vanilla is thus less a process of somehow moving beyond normative regulation than it is one of reimagining and reinventing sexual norms and boundaries. For example, the discourse of poly-normativity is so strong on the three platforms that our interviewees often felt the need to "explain" their more monogamous orientation (cf. Fennell 2022). Monogamy, thus, is cast as very vanilla. Yet our nonmonogamous interviewees position cheating monogamists lower in the hierarchy of liberation than faithful ones while rating nonmonogamous couples as the most liberated (cf. Conley et al., 2019). Consistently with that, experienced nonmonogamist couples self-identify, and are often portrayed by others in the community, as having ascended to a higher level of sexual liberation. This has less to do with the sex they practice than it does with the presumption that practicing liberated sex transforms a person, a couple, and their relationship, for the better. Peeter, a self-identified "veteran-lifestyler" describes the impact that practicing non-monogamy has had on himself and his relationship:

> It has improved and strengthened our relationship very much, not that there was anything wrong with us before. . . . I just can't imagine the situation where I'd cheat on my wife today. It's just—it just doesn't exist. . . . And it's exactly the same for her—but this kind of relational confidence, or this kind of trust in each other—and one that's based on desire—because you could be loyal through gritted teeth, but that you really want your woman the most, and she'd always choose you, because we know what we're capable of with each other—you can't get it without experience. To have that freedom to trust each other, it's an awfully nice feeling, but you have to earn it.

Arguably, we see here again an instance of "vanilla intelligibility" where the discourse of transformation validates a nonnormative sexual practice (e.g., nonmonogamy) through its legibility within normative discourse (e.g., for the sake of strengthening the marriage). At the same time, the argument is very much an ethical one connected to openness and consent as laudable values in any sexual arrangements.

Scales and Limitations of Liberation

For the most part, our interviewees define their sexual practices and preferences as liberated, free-minded, or open-minded: Our Estonian and Finnish participants use the terms *vabameelne* and *vapaamielinen* (the languages are related, so the word is etymologically the same) that have a long history of being used for the sexually open-minded, and also those who have frequent sex or many sexual partners. Many of our Finnish and Swedish participants further self-identify as "pervs" (from *pervertikko/perverssi* and *pervers*, respectively) which, in its vernacular uses, flexibly and humorously refers to sexual tastes and outlooks of the nonnormative sort. "Perv" (*pervo*) was also introduced in 1990s academia as a Finnish translation for "queer" in a similar move of recuperating a term used to classify and injure (Juvonen 1993; Kekki 2006; Rossi and Sudenkaarne 2021)—something that younger generations of scholars have resisted exactly due to the baggage that the notion of perviness packs.

Our participants invoke further boundary work within sexual liberation through comparative contextualization as a work in progress: Libertine.Center user Taavi defines himself as "definitely liberal compared to other men my age," while Kaspar says that he wants to change his on-platform label to "Libertine," yet he feels that this would be false advertising, and that he needs to gain more experience to justify the title. Such scales and limitations of liberation are further articulated against the kinds of diversity that interviewees' struggle to understand or accept. Or, as Anna puts it:

> Let's say that I'm pretty open-minded. Previously I considered myself very liberal but during my sex therapy studies I realized that, oopsy daisy [*laughs*], I've been pretty liberal, but I've had difficulties understanding non-binary gender for example, or the need for young people to change their gender, or this strong outcry of homosexual families and rainbow families and the drumming up of their rights to the point where—the rights of heterosexuals kind of become trampled on. . . . Let's say that I'm constantly becoming more liberal—[but] I'm still a little underdeveloped for these [*laughs*], much freer themes.

Finally, our participants probe the limitations of liberation within their own sexual subcultures, communities, and on-platform connections. While there are many queer libertines, it appears that—alongside and layered into the boundary work on vanilla and its opposites—heteronormativity remains a tacit value among Libertine.Center users. It was, for example, common for women (both single users and as part of couple accounts) to be portrayed as more sexually fluid and open to same-sex play partners, while the men's heterosexuality was often explicitly emphasized—even as some questioned the genuineness of this. Kaspar, a single man who has sex with couples and groups commented:

> I think it's a bit weird that it's such a liberated platform and everyone's so, well—I'm surprised that I've had a couple of experiences where someone claims to be straight on the platform, but then when you talk, they seem to have quite a bit of bi-interest, and I wonder why they're so, to some extent they're still, I don't know what they're afraid of, or why they don't want to say it openly. Some of the couples do put down "bi" for both of them. I'm not a homophobe, but it's easier to arrange play when everything is clear.

Chris Haywood (2022, 117) describes a similar hierarchy within UK sex clubs where even on bi-nights bi-sex is only visible between women and where, in contrast, sexual activity between men is relegated to the invisible and liminal spaces of darkrooms. Jaan offers more insight into the heteronormativity of ostensibly liberated spaces that both he and Kaspar inhabit:

> I have in the last, say, half a year, maybe a year, I've just discovered this bi interest in myself, but I have not added it to our profile yet, because—and probably a lot of people might feel the same way, that other people's opinions matter. This is very Estonian. Estonia is this small, tiny, lovely country, but you say you're a bi man and some people will refuse to meet you, so I guess people don't add it to their profile, but will try to introduce the idea of it in the beginning of the date.

These self-critical reflections on heteronormativity within spaces that otherwise pride themselves on being nonvanilla, open-minded, and sexually liberal, were offered freely without being prompted by us. We interpret this conditional and contextual articulation of liberation as having to do with the importance of *variability/diversity*, as discussed above, but now in the sense of self-identity and self-categorization. This points to how sexual liberation is not merely co-constitutive with the kind of sex one finds pleasurable, but also something articulated as dependent on aspirational, if not necessarily accomplished capacities to shift from "*an* admitted *fact*" to "*an* accepted *norm* of sexual diversity" (Weeks 2017, 135). In other words, our interviewees value sexual liberation even if this is not necessarily something that they feel they can fully live up to.

Willing, Reluctant, Yuck

Our interviewees evoke, and activate, symbolic and moral boundaries to make nonvanilla cohere into a shared and meaningful category. Not only is vanilla bracketed off from nonvanilla, but there are internal politics to non-vanilla. In other words, there are right, wrong, and so-so ways of practicing nonvanilla. This is particularly poignant in the case of consent within BDSM cultures.

Explicit negotiations of consent are often one of the first things brought up when delineating vanilla from nonvanilla. Outspoken consent negotiations are a key ingredient of nonvanilla, precisely because it is nonvanilla, meaning what will happen cannot safely be presumed and needs to be explicitly negotiated instead. In general, discussions of consent have moved from a "no means no" (as an emphasis on the right not to be abused or violated as a basic sexual right) to a freely given, affirmative, and enthusiastic "yes means yes" approach understood to accentuate active and engaged pleasurable sex (Albury 2002; Friedman 2008). It is nevertheless the case that dominant discourses of consent remain largely based on a heteronormative framework where gender figures in predictable ways when it comes to who is expected to be the one asking for consent and who is expected to do the consenting (Corinna 2008). This then takes something away from the kind of sexual agency that an emphasis on enthusiastic affirmation aims or claims to embrace. Consent vocabularies further tend to address it as something temporary and possible to revoke at any time, adding a dimension of contextual or situational awareness into the mix.

In BDSM, an understanding of consent as provisional and negotiable is strong to the point of being constitutive. Consent is not here understood as a one-off event that would give the more dominant party a free pass of sorts but, as Robin Bauer (2014, 79, 84–85) argues, as something ongoing and collaborative. This may, for example, figure in prenegotiations, as part of checking in, in safe wording during play sessions, as well as a part of after-care. In general, there is the idea that the vanilla world has a lot to learn from BDSM and kink practitioners in allowing consent to not be a bottom-line item of negation, or a linear mode of enthusiastically saying "yes," inasmuch as embodying a fickle temporal dimension and a capacity to move and shift. However, taking a deeper look into our participants' perceptions of consent negotiation allows us to see how it is not only an instrument of boundary work between vanilla and nonvanilla, but also between right and wrong ways of doing nonvanilla.

Many of our female kink participants (both queer and less so) are quite critical of how consent plays out in practice. Hanna points to the complexity of boundary work within and around it:

> I think consent is a very interesting and very complex question. It manifests itself in any random male profile over forty on Darkside writing, "It's of course consensual," but the very wording assumes my consent before any desire has been realized. . . . There's something about the whole concept of consent that almost shifts the conversation away from, for example, pleasure, or listening, or community in sexuality. Which I think is sad. . . . You quite often see claims that the vanilla world should take after BDSM, you should become better at negotiating, better at consent, and so on. And that is of course true in many ways. But it is also a question of how it's done. It's not enough to copy and paste these scales, which are also built into Darkside, where you have to rate on a scale from 1 to 5 if you like sploshing not at all, moderately, or if it's your lifestyle. It takes the focus away from what's happening in the moment between practitioners.

As Hanna and others explain, they are mindful of how conversations on Darkside tend to disconnect consent from matters of desire, pleasure, or even actually listening. If consent is a pregiven and reduced to a checkbox, things quickly get much less complex than advertised. As Malin points out, even if the submissive gets to set the limits, knowing one's limits is not an easy thing to figure out in the first place, and neither is finding the ways to express them: "As if it's the easiest thing in the world to do. To both know where your limits are, but also be able to stand by them and have a relationship where you feel you can express them and where you are listened to." She moves into discussing how it feels getting a "no," and how this not merely marks a limit but also entails an edge of rejection:

> I've been to queer BDSM workshops where you just sit and practice saying "no" to each other. "We honor our noes in this community." Okay, that's good, but of course it's still hard to get a "no." You can't get away from the fact that it's also hard when someone says "no" to you, that they don't want you, even though you should of course protect each other's "noes" and all the things you should do and all the nice words. But of course, it's hard to get a "no." To not feel desired. . . . If we make it so banal that it's only about "no," we can never talk about consent in a more reasonable way. It's just saying no. Yes, but how do you take it then, a no? It needs a little more context, perhaps, it's not possible to speed up the process.

Becoming even more complex, the contractual nature of consent can sometimes be in conflict with how things *feel* in that it values legal evidence over sexual experience and desire as this fairly elusive thing (see Novack 2017). Indeed, as Joseph Fischel (2019, 2–4) argues, such reconciliation may be impossible within the legal constraints of consent, as consent in its affirmative form also excludes or rejects more pleasure-driven sexual politics. Klara proposes:

> I think [the idea of] good sex can sometimes be about dominants not really listening to the submissive, but doing what they think is best, if it ultimately results in a positive experience for the submissive. It's interesting how, for example, people write diary entries about their own sexual experiences along the lines of "I protested and I screamed no, and then he did it anyway, and it was so damn hot, it was so fantastic," which is met with encouraging and supportive comments. While if the same story results in a bad feeling for the submissive, then the dominant is instead perceived as a perpetrator. So, discussions about consent often appear very clear and simple, but when you look at how consent is negotiated in practice, it becomes much more blurred.

Our participants highlight that while BDSM cultures are ground zero of consent negotiations, the symbolic and moral boundaries of consent as a constitutive value of liberated nonvanilla sex are, in fact, not at all that obvious. Understood as always situational, provisional, and negotiable, consent is also by necessity tentative, given that you consent to that which is yet to happen, and within nuances that no one can really predict. It is thus unclear whether it is even possible to consent beforehand, "or whether consent can actually only be given in the moment of action or even in retrospect, once one can actually feel in the body whether a certain action is desired in this situation or not" (Bauer 2014, 83). People's sexual practices may involve things that they do not want, or that they do not really know they want, or that they are only in the process of realizing they want, or something that they, in retrospect, realize they would or would not have wanted. Some of our participants discuss enjoying taking risks (as in showing up in someone's office naked) or being turned on by a power dynamic that temporarily strips them of active agency. This all involves sidestepping explicit consent, moving from the zone of "safe, sane, and consensual" to "risk-aware consensual kink." Or, as Avki Saketopoulou (2023) argues, this makes for a queer form of consent—a consent at the limit of consent itself that is not about safeguarding the boundaries of the self but about risking experience as such. Here, sexual platforms become unique spaces of discussion and education, allowing people unprecedented access to community knowledge of the nuances and dynamics of how pleasure links to consent.

Norms, Norms, Norms

Our interviewees also use the vernaculars of vanilla as rhetorical coordinates for boundary work tapping into context-specific, culturally and regionally bound sexual imaginaries (Grigoropoulos 2022; Harviainen and Frank 2018) that help them further define and delineate the kinds of sex that they take pleasure in. Their comments on so-called typical Estonian, Finnish, or Swedish sexual attitudes bookend boundary statements that allow for casting their own preferred forms and practices of sex as liberated. Here, articulations of liberated sex evoke vanilla as a point of comparison, just as articulations of sexual diversity and fluidity require postulating other forms of sexuality as rigid and fixed (cf. Ahmed 2000, 84; Paasonen 2018b, 141). Even if, empirically, vanilla hardly comprises a monolithic category, there is a tendency among our participants to typecast typical sex lives and attitudes within their countries of residence as conservative, introverted, tepid, and dull. These statements indicate that those having hot liberated sex and those not are separated by a symbolic, if not a moral, boundary. Consider Klara's description of "typical good Swedish sex":

> It's of course heterosexual, and then it's equal. Sex which can be separated from life in general. There are very clear sexual scripts about what is included, what comes first, with foreplay and some kind of main act and so on. Good sex is consensual, but it's not explicitly consensual, it's about just being able to read and understand each other in a wordless way. Because as soon as you have to be verbal about sex, there is a norm that says that everything that's exciting and romantic and interesting disappears. These are some examples of what good sex is. It should also be a little innovative and a little exciting, and you can definitely do things that border on BDSM, but it shouldn't be too much, because then it suddenly becomes threatening and perverse.

Yet, this boundary, like others that we have presented so far, also becomes complicated. For example, our interviewees tend to make references to the presumed shared sexual "relaxedness" or "peasant pragmatism" that they attribute to Nordic and Baltic cultures, particularly when comparing these to the puritan tightness associated with Anglophone ones. Peasant pragmatism here stands for a set of more or less vague ideas linked to the sauna and skinny-dipping traditions prevalent in our three national contexts. These are seen to involve and build on historically looser attitudes toward social nudity and, by extension, also toward sex, so that this northern region becomes marked apart as distinct. Teemu argues that:

Finns have a certain kind of relaxedness about sex and treat sex as ordinary. You can kind of just take other people's sexuality with humor instead of condemning it. But many of them will still have a really moral—really, they may have really rigid ideas about their own sexuality. So, they may tolerate others and be like "hee hee hee, he's such a perv" and "what the hell, let them do what they want to do," but then they themselves may implement their own sexuality in a very traditional and rigid way.

Annina chimes in, explicitly referring to the power of cultural sexual norms on both international social media platforms, and within Finland:

If you compare [Finland] to like the US and consider that Instagram and Facebook and those American social media tighten and ban the expression of and discussions on sexuality more and more. So, in this respect, I feel that in Finland we're quite open and accepting, and sexuality is mundane for many. But, on the other hand, it may be fairly narrow, I think. There's a certain norm that's familiar to many and people act according to it, and within those limits it's pretty open. But if we go a little beyond the norm then that's a different thing altogether, then we're maybe not that tolerant and open. . . . I see that heteronormative, monogamous relationship sex is the thing, or an acceptable and desirable ideal.

Evident in Klara's, Teemu's, and Annina's statements is complex situational boundary work where the sexually liberated "us" is marked apart from their imagined compatriots who are then further set apart from the members of other cultures. Further, these national imaginaries entail boundary dynamics hinging on whether liberal attitudes—or the lack thereof—have to do with one's own sexual practices or with the liberty of others to do what they wish. The boundary work around liberated sex then entails a dynamic dance around what one does and desires, as well as how tolerant one is toward that which others are into. This further connects to what other Swedes, Finns, or Estonians are imagined to sexually do and desire, as well as to the cultural norms of "good sex" both in one's country and elsewhere, such as Puritan North America (the national cultures we address have a mostly Lutheran bent while being notably secular). This allows for ignoring contradictions so that one's own sexuality can be mapped out as liberated at least through some of the available comparisons.

Sexual platforms play an important role in how our interviewees map their preferred forms of sex against national imaginaries. Here, too, we see multiple, situational, and oftentimes contradictory, boundary dynamics. Our participants describe the users of sexual platforms as more liberated than Estonians, Finns, and Swedes on average while also pushing back against such simplifications; for some of them, the platforms simply make visible sexual diversity that has always been there. For some, the platforms offer "only a surface scratch" (Aleksi) into the sex that all kinds of people are having in any case, while for others they afford the pleasure of discovering and witnessing unexpected kinkiness among one's compatriots. Many Alastonsuomi users discuss their appreciation for the site as one where they can find, talk to, and support their "fellow pervs." Toomas and Pille feel similarly about Libertine.Center:

> I mean the surprise—people using this site are so open-minded, friendly, courageous, active—Estonians are typically very modest, but we've found that once an Estonian gets over their initial shyness, they go all in. The first time we went to Cap d'Agde in France we were asked where we're from, and people were like, "Oh, Estonia, we have had a few Estonians here, and they are completely wild, they do things we don't even have words for in French!" Can you believe that? Estonians! On this site, we're constantly surprised at how open-minded people are.

It is important to point out that, even though our participants tend to position themselves as personally liberated across all the intersecting boundaries addressed above—and, more often than not, articulate a positively valued "us" against heteronormative, mono-normative, body-normative, trans- and kinkphobic national vanilla imaginaries—they do remain mindful of the generalizations involved.

By representing oneself as liberated and open-minded, our interviewees position themselves as standing out from dominant cultural sexual imaginaries (Gatens 1996, viii). Moira Gatens argues that (individual and collective) bodies are imagined and that "those ready-made images and symbols through which we make sense of social bodies and which determine, in part, their value, their status and what will be deemed their appropriate treatment." For Gatens, such imaginaries shape embodied subjectivity and influence the potential for various kinds of sociability. By acknowledging the relationship between imaginary bodies and social imaginaries, or how social imaginaries produce certain embodied subjects, she offers helpful ways of conceptualizing the importance of collective ways of imagining embodiment and sexuality. Within this, subjects also have the power, or at least the potential, to collectively shape the social imaginaries they invest in, and to which they conform (Gatens 2019). We see this in how our participants imagine and describe themselves in order to feel differently in relation to others and the normative sexual imaginaries that they see as being at play in the society at large.

Good, Bad, and Stuff In Between

When thinking through and defining enjoyable sex, our participants do not perform a full inversion of Rubin's schema of good sex. Rather, they determinedly dislodge vanilla (as monogamous, nonkinky, heteronormative, and just boring) from the top of the sexual value pyramid. In so doing, they mark vanilla as a place where hot things do not happen. A similar dislodging is arguably at play in Rubin's mapping of sexual hierarchy, which not only points out the narrowness of the terrain of "good sex" but equally shows how the very "goodness" of vanilla, as devoid of unruly fantasies or titillations of improvisational play, ultimately presents something of a void—a blank nothingness of sorts—in ways that question its attraction as a point of sexual self-identification (Paasonen 2018b, 4–5). In this sense, there is no "there there" in vanilla worth getting excited about, and it may in fact be plain impossible to live according to the norm when it promises no sudden shudders of sexual desire. Rubin (1989, 283) nevertheless argues against drawing hierarchies (moral, ethical, or other) between sexual acts, suggesting that these should be judged instead in terms of how "partners treat each another, the level of mutual consideration, the presence or absence of coercion, and the quantity and quality of pleasures they provide. Whether sex acts are gay or straight, coupled or in groups, naked or in underwear, commercial or free, with or without video should not be ethical concerns." On the one hand, this maps onto how our interviewees speak of liberated sex as independent from any particular preferences (nonmonogamy, BDSM, fetishism, exhibitionism): Instead, it is seen as revolving around willingness, variability/diversity in both one's own practices and tolerance of others, self-reflexivity regarding the role of sex in one's life and sense of self, and in the challenges involved in becoming sexually liberated so as to fully embrace diversity (Weeks 2017). At the same time, as we have seen, while the sex they find pleasurable and sex they describe as liberated is explicitly unmoored from vanilla—it still often remains tacitly heteronormative, especially so when it comes to sex between men. Further, the ability to embrace and enact the kind of sexual diversity that our participants' articulations of liberated sex is predicated on is admittedly aspirational, yet not always lived out.

Rubin (1989, 283) goes on to argue for the centrality of detaching ethical considerations from sexual shaming and one's personal likes from normative value judgments, suggesting that it "is just as objectionable to insist that everyone should be lesbian, nonmonogamous, or kinky, as to believe that everyone should be heterosexual, married, or vanilla." Kristiina, a sex worker, similarly resists such a tendency to judge, as well as being cast as judgmental herself in the face of some scenarios, explaining that she is open-minded but holds onto her own boundaries, which se defines as "very classic":

> I accept everything, like, whatever it is that you like, I'll accept it. I don't think that anything is, how to say, condemnable. So, some fetishes or some things might be to me like, wow, how can you like that, like I don't see anything sexually fun there. But at the same time, I understand that, well, for the other one it's just the thing or that, well, s/he [*Finnish, like Estonian, lacks gender pronouns*] likes that, that's their thing. So is it judging if I find something a little strange or, like, wow, I don't see anything fun in that, but I'm glad that they do, that this person has found their own thing. But I'm, like, how to say, accepting but then I'm also kind of classic myself. [*pause*] I have very classic boundaries, for example, I don't do any swinging stuff, it's not my thing at all, and I grow kind of anxious and irritated when people ask me, and then they're very much, like, we're a free-minded, open-minded couple, or something. It just makes me feel that, are they trying to say that if it's not my thing, that I'm then somehow close-minded? But if so, then be it. Doesn't bother me. If it's not my thing then let me be close-minded [*laughs*]. But, at the same time, I fully understand and recognize that it's someone's thing and they can do it, and express themselves, and so forth. But I'm like, yes, it's all good, all's allowed, as long as you don't push that on anyone else.

According to Kristiina, there is then a certain friction, or paradox, to how Alastonsuomi users deem one another as open-minded, or deem them as the opposite when their boundaries are differently drawn, and when they do not consent to things that others find highly desirable. Somehow then, our participants' definitions of "liberated sex" target vanilla as an issue of sexual taste rather than as one of morals, but there is nevertheless an explicit valorization of nonvanilla as that which allows for richer, more complex, and interesting sexual subjecthood in ways amounting to an evaluative hierarchy.

The conceptual division of non/vanilla, as it emerges in the interviews, helps to construct a sexual hierarchy to where it may be difficult to draw one, given the range of sexual practices and bents that can be included in such flexible categories, and which are on proud display on the three platforms. Rather than being seen as a (tasteless, bland, unhot, blah) monolith necessary for outlining its (savory, spicy, hot, oh-oh-oh) counterpart, vanilla—like sexual tastes more generally—can be considered as involving gradations, nuances, and experimentations wherein, say, elements of power-play intersect with missionary sex, where role-play may spice up relationships marked with familiarity, and where a water sports session may liven up a stay-at-home evening. The boundaries of sexual norms are elastic and on the move. It then follows that boundary work reliant on the binary of non/vanilla helps to make visible, and thus give shape to, sexual tastes excluded from or fitting ill with the perceived sexual mainstream.

When framed against the expansive notion of the "vanilla world," non-vanilla comes to mark spaces of sexual relating that hold value as enclaves for the similarly minded—especially so on sexual platforms that are designed to support and encourage this. This sense of expansiveness has to do with the power of sexual normativity and how it impresses itself on people whose interests are of the more unruly sort. Seen in this vein, vanilla is actually a suffocating thing: a bland, lukewarm, unsavory pudding that one is nevertheless supposed to desire, lap up, and enjoy. Yet, as we argue, this valuation cannot be an analytical starting point, or let alone a concluding one, for studying sexual cultures, whether on-platform or not. The issue is not, after all, a clear-cut one, but rather one involving slips and improvisations where sexual tastes are tested out, and possibly discovered. Although our three platforms cater to different sexual cultures—and Alastonsuomi basically tries to cater to everyone, with varying results, as in us facing a lacuna of lesbian users—there is striking similarity to how their users discuss enjoyable sex and the presence of sexual norms to the point that it does not analytically matter who is the user of which site. When considering these three sites as replatforming sex, as is the starting point of this book, it is obvious that they thrive from the kind of content squarely banned on Instagram or TikTok, and that their users explicitly value the sexual sociability following from this. Yet they also make evident contentious distinctions within and across sexual cultures as people mark out and make sense of their own tastes and craft spaces for not just sexually existing but thriving.

7 When Sex and Intimacy Are Not the Same Thing

For me at least, what I post is something of my—it's my essence, my innermost, my core in some way. If that gets mistreated, it's much worse than if something else is. It's so damn fragile in a way. But it's probably about losing control, because if someone, if we were in a club and someone said something, then I have control, then I can respond to it. But being online is a bit scary. I don't really know why, because it's nothing I'm ashamed of really. I think it's something beautiful. I just don't know. But sharing a lot of things with people, without having any idea who they are. It may not be a question of lacking integrity, but it will be, well, I don't know, maybe it loses some of its beauty? My core is for those I love, for those closest to me, and not for everyone.

—Stina

Discussing her experiences of sharing content on Darkside, Stina talks about how her felt innermost core becomes part of her online presence in uneasy ways, since the boundaries of intimacy grow fuzzy when matters of great personal importance meet the platform's sociality. She further suggests that a sense of intimacy involves a tangible edge of fragility and vulnerability—that there is something at stake when sharing things that she considers as being core to her being (cf. Paasonen et al. 2023b). In all this, intimacy entails boundary work between one's close ones and the people beyond as something of a safety measure, it being hard to maintain a sense of control on-platform. For Stina, intimacy takes shape through the attachments and shared vulnerabilities afforded by the platform. At the same time, there is no generalizing as to who the users of sexual social media are, or who they feel intimate with: After all, there can be intense intimacy to connections of all sorts.

Her take on intimacy is echoed in thesaurus definitions equating it with the closeness of friendships, relationships, and kinship—with attachments and felt affinities. The term's Latin root, *intimus*, signifies the inmost, innermost, and deepest, suggesting deeply personal things shielded from outsiders' eyes. It is also connected to knowledge and intimate ways of knowing, from the Latin word *intimare*—to make known, to impress, or make familiar. The state of being intimate, in this sense, is to be intimately familiar with someone, or to know them intimately.

In its quotidian uses, intimacy is a common euphemism for things connected to sex, sexual connections, and regions of the body marked as sexual, as in such more or less circular expressions as "intimate relations," "intimate others," and "intimate body parts." Through such associations, intimacy as if zones off attachments and bits of bodies as the stuff not intended for public viewing, expression, or connecting. The intimate can then be "too much information" for others to witness or, alternatively, something that grows intensely titillating when private things become revealed, witnessed, and shared. Things experienced as "a bit too intimate" can move well beyond anyone's zones of comfort—and hold distinct appeal in doing so. Stuff may be too close for comfort and, at the same time, just close enough.

This chapter makes sense of the unstable meanings of intimacy from two perspectives. First, it examines how our participants evoke—or, in many instances, do not evoke—the notion of intimacy when discussing their engagements with sexual platforms and their fellow users: what they understand as intimate and how this connects to sexuality. Second, working with an understanding of intimacy as connections and attachments that make and unmake us—as the stuff that we depend on and that matter to us in terms living (Berlant 1998)—we set out to push discussions on digital intimacies beyond the sexual, posing the interconnection of sex and intimacy as an open question instead. Both the term's "lack of fixed meaning" (Wilson 2016, 265) and the diverse ways in which it is deployed in academic work render intimacy slippery in ways that can feel both inviting and frustrating. We nevertheless argue that intimacy can do much critical work in understanding how networked connections matter. To make this argument, we start with a dive into studies of intimacy.

Studying Digital Intimacy

Addressing the term's unbounded nature, Ara Wilson (2016, 249) points out that it is used synonymously with "proximate, close relations: local, microlevel, private, embodied, involving the psyche" in feminist and queer scholarship in particular. And, indeed, intimacy has long been explored in feminist work on domestic labor and sex work to discuss how boundaries are drawn and transgressed between private and public life-spheres (e.g., Bernstein 2010; Boris and Parreñas 2010; Gregg 2013; Zelizer 2009). Such inquiries have consistently shown that the separation of the public from the private is messy business to start with.

The cultural theorist Lauren Berlant (1998) suggests as much when arguing that the confinement of intimacy within the private sphere—its literal domestication within the home and the family as realms of feeling—is an ideological fallacy that has allowed for casting the public sphere on rational terms in return. Yet feelings are equally key to social organization and belonging—be it in terms of nationality, religion, or other connections making up the public sphere—so that intimacies push and shape the social. Berlant (1998, 284) addresses intimacy as *connections that people depend on for living*: as attachments that we rely on, and which are not confined to the private realm. Seen in this way, the innermost is very much social since intimacies craft attachment between people, groups, and collectives, these being the connections that make (and unmake) us, and that we depend on. Such making and unmaking of the self certainly takes place on and through digital platforms as spaces of intimate connectivity and sociality. Understood as affective attachments or critical connections, intimacy does not necessarily take conventional forms (as something propped up by particular social fantasies or formations such as friendship, the couple, or the family). It can take shape through a range of relations and spaces instead:

> What if we saw it emerge from much more mobile processes of attachment? While the fantasies associated with intimacy usually end up occupying the space of convention, in practice the drive toward it is a kind of wild thing that is not necessarily organized that way, or any way. It can be portable, unattached to a concrete space: a drive that creates spaces around it through practices. (Berlant 1998, 284)

While Berlant's thinking in the late 1990s had little to do with digital connectivity—or, indeed, with media and technology—her ways of theorizing intimate and wild attachments as unbound by yet occupying concrete spaces has come to resonate with studies of digital intimacy and mobility (e.g., Hjorth and Lim 2012; Lasén 2015). In the contemporary moment, devices, apps, and platforms are default parts of the equation when considering intimate connections as ones that we depend on for living. On our three platforms, the drive toward intimacy and meaningful connectivity is part of the glue holding these spaces together.

During the past decade or so, an emphasis on networked relations and connections, on the one hand, and an interest in the blurry boundaries of the private and the public, on the other, have given rise to digital and mediated intimacies as a field of research (Andreassen et al. 2018; Attwood et al. 2017; Dobson et al. 2018). Some scholars use digital intimacy broadly to address all kinds of mediated connections and attachments (Rambukkana and Wang 2020) from online hate to social media activism, ASMR videos, and music streaming (e.g., Krijnen et al. 2023; Sadowski 2016; Zappavigna 2023). Although seemingly disconnected from one another, and not commonly understood as intimate per se, such practices all involve the crafting of connections through networked means where things deemed intimate become shared either willingly or due to the platforms' data practices. In other words, intimate stuff leaks by design, both by users and platforms, while not being entirely for users to control. Whether it be the tipping of webcam performers or the constant automated generation of user data, digital intimacies operates as a blanket term for exploring mediated relations that make the self and sociality in datafied contexts. An obvious question connected to this has to do with expansive uses of intimacy where the notion becomes detached from the sets of meanings that it is most commonly associated with—the private, the sexual, the familial, the approximate.

While this risks conceptual ephemerality or draining of meaning, we also argue that it is equally problematic to define sexuality as a realm of intimacy on blanket terms, let alone to use the concepts as synonymous with one another. For scholars also define digital intimacies more narrowly as descriptive of networked sexual connections including "'sexting'; selfies; making, viewing and circulating sexual content; using hookup apps; and searching online for advice about sex" (Smith et al. 2019, 2). For many, although hardly for everyone, smart devices and networked connections are infrastructural in building and maintaining sexual connections—a development that grew strikingly visible during the COVID-19 pandemic when our interviews were conducted and when many of us were stuck behind our screens at home. Here, Anniina's description of how "many things that there previously were, or social contacts that I previously had somewhere in-person with people, have moved to Discord, to remote socializing" is then hardly exceptional.

Research on digital intimacy also extends to decidedly queer connections and disconnections across private/public boundaries, from how direct messaging shapes relations, desires, and intensities (Sundén 2018) to how gay men navigate online sex publics, game cultures, DIY porn, and streaming media (McGlotten 2013; Ruberg and Brewer 2022; Wang 2020; Wang 2021). Operationalized in this vein, the notion of digital intimacies describes networked forms of sexuality and the centrality of smart devices in and for sexual lives, encompassing a plethora of things from teenage sexual self-discovery to webcamming, Zoom sex parties, and OnlyFans content creation (Cardoso et al. 2023; Lopes et al. 2020; Martins 2019). Here, as in much quotidian discourse, intimacy becomes something of a euphemism for sexual relations and acts. Such paraphrasing can be highly strategic, given that many research funders feel more comfortable dealing with projects addressing "intimacy" than "sex," or let alone "porn."

It should be noted that a surprisingly large bulk of research operating with the notion of intimacy gives limited attention to the concept itself, as if implying that there is an easy shared understanding that it refers closeness, care, entanglement, trust, sexuality, or love (e.g., Giddens 1993; Khubchandani 2020; Rojek 2016; Wolf and Nusser 2022). In broadly connotating "good feeling—warmth of a kind" (Strong 2021, 381) or "a positive affection" (Lopes et al. 2020, 2736), intimacy then becomes coded on happy terms as something enjoyable and pleasant by default. Meanwhile, critical sexuality studies, in exploring vulnerabilities and risks associated with intimacy, suggests that it is not all about cuddles, hugs, and sunshine. Building on the gay porn director Paul Morris's discussion of barebacking as "unlimited intimacy" that is both unsafe and involves radical openness, Tim Dean (2009, 45), for example, defines it as an issue of relationality: "The term *intimacy* sometimes stands as a euphemism for fucking, but it also signals the emotional experiences that accompany sex." While Dean does not linger on definitions of the term, he, like many other sexuality studies scholars, foregrounds vulnerability, relationality, connectedness, and proximity as key to intimacies cutting in and out of considerations of risks and pleasures (Khubchandani 2020; Martin 2023). As an issue of being touched, moved, and impacted, intimacy then concerns both openness and the edge of vulnerability.

As a matter of proximities and connections, intimacies can be brought forth by circumstance. They can be acutely desired, of the fleeting kind, or rather tenacious attachments that hold up one's very life. Intimacies are highly personal and collective, also extending to nonhuman entities such as devices and platforms, spaces and regions (Dawson and Dennis 2020). Within all this, the meanings of intimacy are shifty: As a *sense* of things, it is a matter of perception and experience, and therefore subjective stuff by default.

We find studies of digital intimacies productive in considering the stakes involved in networked sexual connections, yet our research also points to conceptual gaps between how scholars, on the one hand, and our research participants, on the other, verbalize their practices and experiences, bringing us back to the interviews. As we go on to show, our participants evoke intimacy to address felt connections and proximities, but equally to discuss degrees of disconnection and distance. Intimacy here becomes a question of both safety and unsafety, as well as descriptive of being comfortably or uncomfortably close to others. It comes with what we consider as an edge—or risk—of vulnerability that becomes heightened as bodies, feelings, and connections come to circulate and stretch across the unsteady boundaries of privacy and publicness, as tends to happen online.

Intimacy and the Edge of Vulnerability

It is noteworthy that none of our interviewees who regularly participate in play parties and hook up with fellow users frame these activities as intimate as such. Even as these practices were described as ones of great personal importance, intimacy was not a go-to term for discussing them. Rather, our participants deployed the term intimacy (or locally/linguistically suitable vernacular variants like "delicate topic," "sensitive matter," or "a personal thing") when addressing the risks and degrees of vulnerability involved in participating on sexual platforms, publishing content on them, rendering oneself accessible to the eyes and comments of others, and possibly being exposed or outed without one's consent. Several interviewees recounted how they had been subject to unwanted attention in the past and how this had made them rethink their presence on the platforms. As Linda puts it, "I have no need to talk about sensitive things with 350 people with whom I'll have no other interaction."

Many evoked the notion of intimacy in connection with the uneasiness, or the plain risks involved in how their content becomes received. This riskiness was particularly pronounced among queer female users trying to carve out their own community within the straight-leaning Darkside community:

> **EMMA:** I have no control over how my content is received. I have no control over who reads or looks at it and what they think. And that doesn't feel good, because it feels in some way like you're exposing a very intimate and close part of yourself, and you don't know who will read it. For many people, it might feel like a freedom to be able to share this, but I've never really felt that way when it comes to sharing—I've probably never shared too much super intimate stuff like that. I wouldn't feel safe sharing too intimate things.
>
> **JENNY:** No, and especially because, as you say, because you have no control over who is looking or reading?
>
> **EMMA:** Yes, and then also like, I know those times when I have posted a picture, or updated the kink list, and a cisman always writes an email. It happens every time, and I find that so very sad. Then it doesn't feel safe or fun to do anything. So, if I were to write something that was really intimate and important for me, I don't want some fucking cis dude texting me about it. "Oh, I read your diary, so hot!" It wasn't for your eyes. It wasn't for your dick. It was for my queer friends, for the ones who are part of my world in all of this.

Darkside, in this case, does not comprise one but several overlapping contexts experienced at various proximities and distances. This finding in fact scales in that all our three platforms afford different sexual ecologies—ones that our participants discuss as bubbles, circles, and islands, and which we have above conceptualized as factually leaky yet experimentally meaningful silos. In other words, any one platform is bound to mean and afford distinct things for different people depending on the connections and content they assemble.

For Emma, Darkside's queer circle is the one close at hand, whereas the platform at large constitutes a more volatile and unpredictable context over which she has very little control. In many cases, the vulnerabilities imagined by users remained hypothetical as things that could occur, as ones that they had heard of, or as ones that they knew had happened to others but which they had not experienced themselves. For example, Johanna evokes the notion of "intimate moments" in connection with the hypothetical scenario of tension-filled breakups where Alastonsuomi users could share photos and videos without their former partners' consent out of sheer spite and revenge, resulting in hurt and damage. For Noora, the boundaries of intimacy have much more broadly to do with what content people share and what modalities of communication this involves. She sees visual means of expression as differently intimate than textual ones:

> It's, like, sometimes I get messages like, hey, you should post more revealing shots so, I never do because I don't, I feel that that part of my sexuality is too intimate to be there. So, I save it, I save myself for these kinds of face-to-face [*laughs*] encounters. But all this, all that's important to me, like fantasizing through text and such, that I can well realize and express myself there.

Noora saw not only explicit forms of nudity but equally the sharing of intimate things as the platform's main premise, or rationale, while continuing that this was interesting since nudity and sex are not the same thing—after all, as kinksters well know, "you can also have sex with your clothes on." She could have continued to argue that intimacy is similarly detachable from both nudity and sex, as is our argument, yet her overall point had to do with maintaining personal boundaries, the breeching of which involves a risk of vulnerability. This articulation was similar to Sanna's:

> Well, yes, it's kind of like really intimate things show up there. And depending of course on the kinds of photos and videos you post, sure, these are things that other people don't usually see. There's this risk of vulnerability but of course everybody chooses it for themselves, like how recognizable [they are] or if they for example show their faces in the photos; or if they have tattoos, are they hidden, and how many recognizable factors the author censors. Everyone decides that for themselves.

Intimacy is here connected to the level of exposure and the degrees to which people are recognizable or identifiable. This means that a naked body or depictions of sex are not in themselves perceived as intimate, but that intimacy becomes activated when this or that body is identified as being particular, specific, and identifiable as such. In this sense, intimacy was seen to mark the boundary of the kinds of personal disclosures and engagements that users are willing to have with one another in ways harking all the way back to the term's Latin etymology (the inmost, the personal, and shielded from others). Such boundary work around intimacy involves the sharing of photos and videos of bodies and sexual acts, but also disclosing sexual experiences, desires, and fantasies of the kind that are, generally speaking, excluded from mundane sociality among virtual strangers. In Sanna's account, intimacy was bound up with vulnerability, or the risk thereof, in ways exceeding the straightforwardly sexual. Liisa, a Libertine.Center user, gestured even more explicitly to a hierarchy of vulnerability where online nudity is experienced differently than whatever it is that occurs face to face:

It's a matter of taste, but I don't want there to be material like that of me out there or in other people's possession. . . . . I can share my experiences and excitements—for me today, when I am having fun, then—well, today sex for me is just—pleasure, or a practice in and of itself, it's not linked to love, or I don't think it needs to presume living with someone, or dating someone. I can have sex with five different men over the course of the weekend, depending on the situation, if I feel like it and I am in the mood and it happens according to my preferences in different situations, but I won't, for example—I can do the acts, but I won't put a buck-naked full-frontal image of myself up online for everyone to look at.

A distinction of intimacy is here drawn between sex as physical acts of pleasure ("I can do the acts") and nudity as involving images shared for the viewing pleasures of others. The detachment of the photo from sex as act or action is mirrored by a distancing, or detachment, from the image itself—as in "I won't put a buck-naked full-frontal image of myself up online for everyone to look at." Intimacy was then explicitly articulated as an issue of boundary work—of distancing, detaching, and disconnecting—in the face of unwanted commentary, contact, evaluation, and potential hurt and not at all about "intimate" body parts touching. As Anna explains:

Yes, the amount of sort of filth messages is incredible, when they ask you to send panties for money, or whatever. And, it's like—there's something connected to vulnerability—when people say in the comments that they'd fuck or wouldn't fuck [you]. So, it's also a little like you post a pic of yourself and thirty-seven go click that they'd fuck, and thirteen go to write that they wouldn't fuck, so that not-fucking, unwillingness to fuck, doesn't necessarily have to do anything with the actual person, or even the photo. It may just be that, I see, she's wearing panties, she doesn't have anything more explicit, well, I wouldn't fuck. But it's the kind of thing that for some people may involve the risk of vulnerability if you dare to publish something very intimate about yourself and then you get "wouldn't fuck, wouldn't fuck" types of comments and that kind of endless clicking.

Such disturbance of unpleasant social noise involving the risk of hurt was particularly pronounced among female-identifying respondents, independent of their sexual or gender preferences or tactics of use. Consider Kristiina's description of "weeding out" trolls and creeps as someone who uses the platform for occupational purposes:

My so-called survival strategy is that when I go on social media, or to Alastonsuomi, or anywhere, how do you say it, I pluck out the weeds and choose, it's kind of weeding out of what I focus on and what goes directly into trash [*laughs*]. It's a little like that. And as it's just a job for me, and they comment on that character, that online persona of mine and that figure that I play online and at work, and it's not necessarily even me [*laughs*]. It's kind of *detached* [in English] from me. I feel, of course I want everyone to love this character I've created but no, those comments may move me but if I feel they're moving me too much then I can always be a little like, okay, *detach* [in English] from that figure that they're critiquing now, it's not me. And I think that if you're just as yourself on that site, or online, and something as intimate as your body and looks and sexuality is commented on, then I think it can be much harder than it's for me.

As someone using Alastonsuomi in strategic ways so that the connections she makes are occupational as part of the business, Kristiina distanced herself from users engaging in identity work and rendering themselves more directly open and vulnerable:

It's exactly this question [*laughs*] that I wonder about, people just post photos there and it's such a vulnerable and intimate and *sensitive* [in English] thing, and just, I've somehow interpreted that they're expressly studying themselves and may not be fully ok with themselves yet, so it's really brave of them, and I'm glad they've found this way to do something better than just get stuck in their own heads about stuff, so that's good that there's something where you can express and explore yourself, some kind of an active thing you can do rather than just think about things inside your own head. But, at the same time, I also think about whether it is smart to put pics online. For me, everything I put there is for work. And what if, after some twenty years, the photos pop up from somewhere, then it's always clear to me that, well, that was my job, and it was my career that I had. There's nothing to be ashamed of there. . . . I did it for work and it was a good career and still is. But then, your average Jane, what if the pics pop up from somewhere, I've wondered, what then, how does that feel [*laughs*]?

In Kristiina's narration, online sexual self-expression entails the kind of vulnerability that she does not herself experience but recognizes among other users. And, indeed, our interviewees spoke recurrently of the vulnerabilities involved in being seen, figuring out their sexual selves, and articulating their desires. For the non-binary, nonstraight Tuisku, this is somewhat categorical in that "people and people's sexuality are vulnerable things, and people's bodies are vulnerable" in ways that add a particular sting to personal comments and critiques, and render people "subject to social maltreatment." Such an edge of vulnerability, whether seen as a constant or not, is something that our participants balance and try to shield themselves from, to the degree that this can ever be possible. Various modes of refusing intimacy, detaching oneself, or building a protective shield toward unwanted attention, take shape in similar yet also different ways across and between platforms, given their divergent foci and modes of operation. Hanna, for example, has a bondage persona on an open Instagram account, enjoying the idea that random strangers can see her there, whereas she feels much more exposed—and hence more vulnerable—on Darkside, a platform entangled with her intimate connections to her local kink community:

> In the local kink community in [this city], there are many who've seen me in sensitive play situations and maybe also in situations where I have very little control, as a bottom. While what's visible on Insta is perhaps above all a craftsmanship, where I've tied up someone else—and then there are pictures that are very, well, I don't know, where I look strong and hot and cool. Whereas if you share a physical play space, then people will see you when you are vulnerable and open and not in control of your face. It feels like that part of my stage persona is more visible on Darkside. I don't mean mainly in pictures, but perhaps in the form of experienced memories that live in the relationships that are represented there.

In contrast to Liisa, who felt that photos online render people more vulnerable than participating in something like an orgy, Hanna sees physical play spaces as involving more vulnerability than carefully edited images published in social media. On her "rope Insta," she has a sense of being in control, both in terms of playing the more obvious active part of the one binding someone else, and in displaying a skill. In photos where she is being bound, she still maintains editorial control and merely posts pictures showing strength and where she thinks she looks good. Darkside is a different story in the sense that the platform is intimately entangled with and has traces of play sessions that involve a loss of control on the part of the submissive. In these scenarios, a sense of having control—or not—coincides with the sexual dynamics of dominance and submission.

Across the bulk of our interviews, intimacy emerges as risky by involving potential vulnerability in ways that may—but do not need to—coincide with the sexual. Intimacy is connected to situations where something is at stake, be this about disclosing one's innermost feelings and fantasies or being seen and commented on so that others can get under one's skin in unpleasant or plain painful ways. Dealing with intimacy becomes a sort of risk management moving between social connections, engagements, senses of belonging, and investments. This also means that disconnections emerge as tactical measures of protection so that random strangers, for example, do not have free rein to peek into or evaluate stuff considered personal. Disconnection, or detachment, is then not an opposite of intimate attachments or connections, but rather a vital dimension in how things are felt, assessed, and valued—a point elaborated on in chapter 8. If intimacy, following Berlant, entails those connections that we depend on for living, it follows that disconnections are equally vital to making lives liveable.

In an ontological sense, connections necessitate disconnections, as without a disconnect there would be no way of connecting (Karppi 2018; Karppi et al. 2021). Detachments similarly enable attachments, meaning that without disconnection, or some form of break in connectivity and ways of relating, connections would matter much less. To say that disconnections build on and afford connections is to consider how the disconnect, or the possibility of it, lends connections with both affective charge and social weight (Light 2014). Breaks and interruptions reveal the premises and promises of digital connectivity, what these connections mean, and how they feel. Disconnection, then, does not comprise either a negation or a lack, but is rather productive in bringing together supposedly separate things as a generative force underpinning digital connectivity (Sundén 2018, 2021).

When, for example, Kristiina "detaches" a bit from her online (sex work) persona as comments get too close for comfort, this is a way of fine-tuning and regulating an attachment by stepping back so as to dull or preempt the edge of vulnerability. It is not a question of just quitting or detaching completely from the platform. Even though that too is a possibility, it is not preferable for occupational reasons. Rather, she works across the scales of risk and vulnerability to connect more selectively. Linking her ability to tactically detach or disconnect to her professional capacity also forms the assumption that for those who engage in more personal self-exploration, such connections would be both intimate and difficult to detach oneself from. Ben Light (2014) discusses the power of disconnective practices such as unfriending, untagging, backchanneling, or hiding to create breaks with how platforms feed on public visibility and sharing. What we have observed is something slightly different, yet our participants equally speak of partial disconnection and selective connections as constants. Connections are, in a sense, always partial, always at risk of being disrupted. As a conscious strategy, selective connectivity is nevertheless a matter of seeking out those connections that temper unwanted networked vulnerability and intensify connections that feel good.

Physical Proximities and Felt Affinities

While Hanna speaks of experiences in specific physical spaces as lending her Darkside presence a particular intimacy, our participants also spoke of more ephemeral and broad shared spaces as giving rise to a sense of belonging that some of them identify as intimate. This brings us back to the themes of local modes of belonging, as in the platforms being of relatively small size and operating in Finnish, Swedish, and Estonian languages and as such involve shared cultural codes, locations, norms, and expressions:

> Yes, it does bring sort of intimacy to it. Or, like, we're all here in the same country and in the same language, we encounter the same cultural expectations, for example. And it also sort of brings with it this lovely excitement and exhilaration, like, hey, that person could live next to me, and I've seen their piss equipment [*laughs*]. So, it's wonderfully titillating like that. But I think that mostly we speak the same language. Everyone who can speak Finnish or English can discuss all the burning topics and those—that all Finns encounter in our everyday life, for example, expectations and pressures about sexuality. And then when you can talk about local sex shops or sex, well, yes. Sort of, being able to talk about the same things. It brings people closer to one another. You get more of a communal aspect. (Julia)

For Julia, intimacy emerges from a sense of shared things—of communality and possibly even a sense of community. Anniina, her fellow Alastonsuomi user, further addressed the platform's local specificity and modest size as entailing intimacy as a sense of safety:

> For me also it's the approachability and somehow, like, you don't have to consider everything so much. So, what you put up there, is this pic really good now or not, I can put it up there. And it's still fine. And there seems to be safety there somehow perhaps just since it's Finnish, even as it may have many users of foreign origin, those who write in English, but it's still Naked Finland. So, it feels like a cozy community of a small circle even as it actually has pretty many users and pretty different users, too. Still, it has this feeling of being fairly intimate. Compared to some equal international thing.

As discussed in chapter 5, the platform's local focus, in combination with its language, evokes something of an imagined community connected to cultural intelligibility, which here becomes articulated as intimate. As Anniina explains, this is much more a matter of impression than a fact, given Alastonsuomi's factual size and user base, even as this impression is something that matters a great deal in how she orients and situates herself on the platform. However, local specificity affording a sense of safe intimacy also comes with a flipside in the vulnerabilities that it can give rise to. As Evelina details:

> Darkside is a very large community, but it's still quite local. If something goes wrong on, for example, FetLife, it's not as close; there are so many people who are so far away and have no way of finding out who you are. It might be rare that someone does that on Darkside, but the chance is still greater that someone is in your close proximity. So, if you want to meet someone, that person is then in your proximity and in your proximity on Darkside. This can be both good and bad in terms of vulnerability. So, in that way, this localness, on the one hand it can feel like home, but sometimes it can also be full of drama in ways I find difficult.

The relative anonymity afforded by a large transnational sexual platform like FetLife and the freedom this affords is here contrasted with the local feel of Darkside. The intimacy of proximity (we also discussed this in chapter 5), or that which is within reach both geographically, culturally, and emotionally, is here synonymous with a sense of home. And as a "home," it also comes riddled with certain tension and drama. Among Libertine.Center users, this notion of unsafe or risky proximity was even more pronounced, perhaps unsurprisingly given that Estonia is the smallest of the three countries involved in our study. Peeter, when comparing Libertine.Center to the global platform SDC that he and his wife use when traveling, said,

> As for Libertine.Center, well the Estonian community is very different from the international one, Estonians are very closed and well, those who have been meeting up with people and have been to a couple of events, well these, I think can be broken into two categories—some will become full of themselves, like they now have a secret and they have done stuff and are just so cool. It's a bit weird, I think. Like when someone becomes rich suddenly, and will go kind of stupid with it, while other people will not. And then on the other hand there is a lot of anxiety in Estonia, that oh my lord, what if someone finds out. Because the country is small and everyone knows everyone and so everyone wants to be very careful, people are also very tentative about exchanging pictures, usually when we want to meet someone—and we don't do blind dates—so we'll just send a picture of ourselves first, because then the others will be also be brave enough to do so.

The intimate size of the country comes with many default connections and attachments, which breeds an anxiety of exposure, which in turn fosters cautious image-sharing practices as a necessary safety measure in the process of turning digital connections into physical ones. However, a further inversion of the relationship between intimacy and (un)safety can equally occur. Mikk, the male partner in the interviewed couple Mikk and Mari, explains that while Libertine.Center has a small user base, this, together with the platform's user verification policy, creates a more intimate atmosphere and a sense of transparency that he equates with safety, comparing it to another local sexual platform, Iha.ee:

> Both the benefit and the drawback of Iha.ee is that it has more traffic. Libertine. Center doesn't have a lot of traffic, their number of users is limited, and nothing much happens, it can become a bit boring. But the benefit of Libertine.Center is that the group that does use it have all been verified, and you don't have to wonder if a couple is a couple and a woman is a woman. On Iha.ee it is quite typical that a man will be writing from a woman's account, and will tell you that they're a couple. As Mari just said, Iha.ee is overwhelmingly horny, lonely dudes, and it is just awfully tiresome.

Intimacy as a question of the scale or size of platforms is interesting, as these are platforms possible to relate to "as a whole" in everyday use, as opposed to how users on Facebook, Instagram, or TikTok, for example, have little sense of the totality of platforms housing users in the billions, relating to a very limited subset through the context of followers and friends instead. This is of course not to say that large platforms cannot afford a sense of intimacy. Avid TikTok users, for example, testify to how the algorithmic curation of news feeds and safe spaces of like-minded people fosters a particular kind of intimacy distinct from platforms where users feel they have less algorithmic control (Şot 2022); the libidinal economies of Black Twitter (resistant to being renamed "Black X") come equally steeped in intimacies (Brock 2020). But having a feel for the whole platform is a thing apart. Whether our participants use friends lists or want their content to be private, available to their friends only, or something for the entire platform to appreciate, the entirety of the platform can be experienced as both tangible and intimate.

Bringing together the two modes of intimacy evoked by our participants, Timo, the only male-identified Alastonsuomi interviewee to explicitly evoke the notion of intimacy, associates it first with the disclosure of personal details, and secondly with the platform's scale:

> Let's say that if I have 350,000 views on PornHub, here my videos have hundreds of views. And for my profile pic, which I've had the longest, there are 20,000. So, quite a big difference. And then I also noticed that I've been on PornHub for a much shorter time, the mass is much bigger there. But since they're foreigners whom I'll never meet, it doesn't feel intimate. With Alastonsuomi that feeling is much more intimate.

In addition to the question of scale and potential audience, the intimate feel of platforms may be connected to their visual economies. For Hanna, there is a distinct sense of intimacy to Darkside as a platform due to the lack of image rating systems of the kind seen on Alastonsuomi and Libertine.Center, combined with a quality of pictures being less than perfect (compared to something seen on Instagram). She continues:

> [Image rating systems] makes me angry, because I don't think you should score and rate things that have to do with desire. It ultimately creates systems that only motivate people to post more attractive pictures, people who might otherwise share something that was cute, or intimate, and so on. Now they will start thinking that they look ugly there, or that the focus was not so good in that picture. So, I think it would be counterproductive in relation to what I think the platform should be used for.

Large, image-driven social media platforms certainly influence and shape the visual cultures on our platforms too, even as there is much ambiguity to this (considering, for example, the explicit nature of much image content, or the ubiquity of low-fi dick pics on Alastonsuomi). And yet, there is something to say about how platforms that are less technically up to speed and use inferior tools for image compression, rendering, and resolution create, as a result, their own sense of intimacy. Similar to how Instagram users create and maintain "finstas" (secondary Instagram accounts) for sharing more vulnerable, low-quality, or "decorous" content with close friends as a way of negotiating dominating platform norms and expectations (Xiao et al. 2020), the less than ideal image quality on Darkside and Alastonsuomi may help to peel off the glossy, filtered ideals of a social media mainstream, and add a dimension of rawness and imperfection that moves closer to the skin (although, as we argue in chapter 4, this sense of intimacy can be both something delightful and something grubby). Here, Tuisku evokes the Finnish idiom of photos taken with a "potato" referring to low-fi, amateurish, technically inept, and aesthetically lacking pictures as also having their own fan-base.

As articulated and experienced by our interviewees, intimacy is a deeply ambivalent thing: Something that moves close may feel good to someone, too close to someone else, and sometimes these two modalities may be experienced simultaneously in dynamic tension. Considered as interconnected to vulnerability, intimacy is moreover impossible to pin down within a logic where it becomes associated with proximity, comfort, and safety in the sense of being distinct from distance, discomfort, or unsafety. On the contrary, certain forms of discomfort may mark the contours of intimacy in signaling that something, or very much indeed, is at stake. Someone, or something, may move too close for comfort; one may disclose too much; there can be a connection that leaves a resonant or dissonant impression—all this can feel highly intimate. And certain forms of comfort, or a sense of being at ease, may well lack the frisson of risk, making close familiarity feel less intimate— and hot—in its lack of intensity. Being "too close" can then also mean lacking the ability to stir something up, to actually feel an intimate attachment or connection. Too close, yet not close enough—an intimacy paradox.

What's in a Word?

It is certainly warranted to consider the specificities of language just here. In Finnish, Estonian, and Swedish alike, "intimate" (*intiimi, intiimne, intim*) entails proximity but also that which is delicately, disturbingly, bodily, and often embarrassingly close—hence Finnish media's privacy regulation being named "intimacy protection law" established in the mid-1970s when the notion of "intimacy" was (and still is) broadly used in marketing genital and anal health products (Saarenmaa 2010; 2012). In fact, none of the Estonian interviewees used the word intimacy or intimate *at all* (in vernacular setting the word is used for hygiene products, but also for an atmosphere of a space of a social gathering; it may be used as a noun for closeness or sexual relations in a relationship, but that is less common). Instead, they would use words like closeness and connectedness to talk about the "comfortably close," variety of relational intimacy, and the word "personal" to talk about boundary work around things seen as being "uncomfortably close." It is also possible that our Finnish participants referred to intimacy by virtue of the interviews being conducted in connection with the research project, "Intimacy in Data-Driven Culture," mentioned in the call for participation.

The Swedish interviewees, in turn, used the terms intimacy and the intimate in a few instances to describe certain content, moments, or parts of one's inner self, but also as a way of distinguishing intimate nonsexual topics (such as mental health) from less than intimate sexual ones. More commonly used terms were "close," "personal," "sensitive," and "vulnerable" to describe the risks and pleasures involved in revealing rather than concealing oneself. The vocabulary was notably similar on Alastonsuomi, despite the language differences. This is not to argue that the contextual connotations would be radically different from those at play in English, but that, within the linguistic and cultural context where our research is situated, intimacy has for decades been used in outlining the boundaries of privacy and (dis)comfort, in contexts both sexual and not. This makes the question of intimacy's recognizability—and viability—as a marker no less pressing, considering how the field of digital intimacies transgresses language boundaries as an international amalgamation of research interests.

We argue that our interview material suggests something of the limitations of the notion of digital intimacy as a general term, or a roundabout way of discussing networked displays of nudity and sexual communication, as well as studies thereof. This brings us back to the problem of expansiveness, vague meanings, and gaps between academic and quotidian uses of language, as already raised above. Our concern is that when used as a descriptive concept, or marker, for a range of phenomena, and as an analytical concept for making sense of these, intimacy does not necessarily connect or coincide with how people experience and label things—there can well be a glaring disconnection. In some interviews, when we asked about whether they make themselves vulnerable on the platform, and if so, in which ways, there is a telling pause. Some interviewees did not even understand the question:

> MARTIN: What do you mean by vulnerability? Vulnerable to whom and in what way?
>
> JENNY: Yes, that was sort of the question!
>
> MARTIN: Well, both me and my girlfriend have a clear exhibitionist vein, which Darkside is a great outlet for. So, it's rather, I don't feel vulnerable in connection with things I post. I get a kick out of it!

For dominant, male participants (be they straight, bi, or gay), the disconnect between the intimate, or the vulnerable, and the sexual was particularly pronounced. Leo explained:

> My level of vulnerability on the Darkside, I would say, is very low. I am open and comfortable with who I am. And I don't really know how much I open up otherwise. I enjoy control to a high degree. If we only focus on the physical aspects of the sexual, there isn't a whole lot of vulnerability there either, because I like to be in control primarily. Although I can appreciate if someone else takes the initiative, starts touching me or going down to suck me off or things like that. So, sexually, I'm probably not particularly vulnerable. It's about other things for me, like the power in dominance.

At the same time, Leo experienced more casual, less than sexual contexts as ones holding considerable intimacy, as in his puppy play and cuddles with other puppies:

> In more intimate contexts that may not have anything to do with sex and such, I'm not as clearly dominant and in control. If I hang out with my pups, for example, when I'm in a group with other puppies, it might be seven, or even ten of us, when we hang out at night. Then I have no problem lying down, lying next to another pup and hugging and cuddling or sort of buffing the other and giving that kind of response. During nights out with my pups, I've also have no problem with hugging or being a sissy, or how should I put it.

Using digital intimacy as a euphemism for networked sexualities is then not very helpful in understanding such disconnects between intimacy and sexuality on the one hand, and a reconnect between intimacy and other forms of comfortable (or uncomfortable) closeness, on the other. There is a risk of the field of digital intimacies being detached from how both sexuality and intimacy are enacted and understood in everyday practices, to the point of only making sense to an academic crowd sharing similar semantic codes internationally. This then begs the question of how well the marker communicates and how analytically productive it may be.

As Susanna has previously proposed, considering the notion of digital intimacies in a literal sense, it can well be asked whether, or how, or to whom, something like a webcam show, a porn clip, or a dick pic shared through Instagram's Direct Messenger comes across as *intimate* (Paasonen 2024, 88). A dick pic can be shared with a potential partner as a form of flirtation, invitation to sex, and advert for one's physical goods and comes embedded in mutual dynamics of desires—and be intimate in this sense. Alternatively, the very same photo can be sent to a complete stranger alongside rape and death threats as a tool of harassment and sexualized violence (e.g., Amundsen 2021; Paasonen et al. 2019; Waling and Pym 2019). While the aim here would be to get under the recipient's skin, the overall dynamic is not best characterized as intimate in the sense of closeness and connection—or let alone as connections that we depend on for living. An interconnection may momentarily take place, and vulnerabilities may emerge, but the notion of intimacy does little analytical work in unpacking the things at play: It lacks focus.

Semantics matter, we suggest, as there is much blurriness to data economy, and beyond, in how the notions of privacy, sensitivity, intimacy, and the personal are used (we discussed some of these semantics around the notion of safety and sensitive data in chapter 3). These terms are sometimes used as distinct from one another, other times as near-synonyms, and at yet other times intimacy is understood as an area, or subset, of privacy. Within the data economy, user data is expansively mined, analyzed, sold, and aggregated for the purposes of targeted advertising (Srnicek 2018). The activities of users are tracked from one site to another, giving rise to amalgamations of data that can include very intimate details indeed. People use apps to track their menstrual cycles and generate data on their sexual preferences on OnlyFans, porn sites, and hook-apps, while this data routinely leaks to third parties without users' explicit knowledge or permission, despite regulatory attempts (Maris et al. 2020; Rama et al. 2023; Saunders 2023 Sundén 2023). The Norwegian data protection watchdog fining the gay male hookup app Grindr over six million US dollars in 2021 for sharing users' personal data with third-party advertisers without their permission can then be seen less as an isolated incident than as illustrative of the broader patterns of contemporary data economy at play, of which sexual connections form a part.

The Analytical Value of Intimacy

The question then remains: If intimacy does not emerge as a concept in empirical inquiry as something that people spontaneously use to make sense of their sexual activities and engagements, as was the case in the interviews conducted for this study, what is the analytical value of framing these activities and engagements on intimate terms? It is our argument that a routine conflation of sex with intimacy requires critical questioning. To state the obvious: Sex is not automatically experienced as intimate in the sense of involving attachments that matter (Rosa 2023). Sex can be an issue of work, whether entailing intimacy, or not; sex in partnership may lack intimacy; a random hookup can be intensely intimate, or anything but. Attaching the label of intimacy to everything sexual also comes with an uncomfortably normative bent, a presumption that all things sexual should, rightfully, be deeply personal, hidden from view, revolving around a life-sustaining connection.

Conversely, intimacy entails proximities and connections well beyond the sexual—as in practices of care and friendship. The intimate can be something deeply personal, but it is not necessarily sexual by default. Sexuality, again, is also an issue of human rights, equal civic rights, occupation, public visibility, social organization, well-being, and activism: It is by necessity a public and social issue and the rights connected to it are continuously, albeit differently, contested from one political, national, and commercial context to another. This was also the point that Berlant (1998) made when writing about the fallacy of considering intimacy as simply a domestic, personal, or private concern, foregrounding its role in the building of life-worlds instead.

In sum, and across our interviews, intimacy was much less connected to sexual displays, communication, or contact than it was to a sense of proximity: to who or what is experienced as being comfortably or uncomfortably close, to the kinds of closenesses that were desired, and what chafed against one's sense of comfort or safety instead. Within this, proximity and distance, safety and unsafety involved gradations and negotiations within which the one could quickly and unpredictably flip into the other. Intimacy then emerged as an issue of constant boundary work and tactical disclosures vis-à-vis vulnerability, on the one hand, and as connected to the platforms' locations and scales, on the other.

As we have discussed in this chapter, digital connections can be intensely intimate in involving the risk of vulnerability, or then again not at all. Living with smart devices within ubiquitous connectivity further means that networked media are not simply external factors, instruments, or aides for everyday lives, but rather infrastructural to how they are managed. Our mundane dependencies on devices and platforms mean that considerations of intimacy as connections that matter need to extend to the infrastructural role of digital technologies in the functionality of personal, social, occupational, and collective lives (Paasonen 2018a; Paasonen 2021, 50–54; Sundén 2021; Wilson 2016). Or, to rephrase, personal devices mediate intimacies while also involving intimacies themselves.

Such dependencies may be banal, yet they are also deeply meaningful as part of the stuff that makes everyday life and the connections that sustain us. We argue that it is in this infrastructural sense—in how lives operate, how various mundane routines are maintained, and how various human and nonhuman bodies become tied up with one another—that the notion of intimacy does the most critical work in cultural and social inquiry. Wilson (2016, 215) similarly identifies intimacy as a "placeholder," a "flexible, provisional reference that emphasizes linkages across what are understood to be distinct realms, scales or entities" that "allows analysts to look at relational life, including the feelings and acts that comprise it." Network connectivity, together with the interoperability of platforms and personal devices, functions as a mundane infrastructure for the building and maintenance of intimacies so that such connections are at once social, affective, and technological. As connections that we depend on for living (Berlant 1998), intimate relations are the stuff that makes and unmakes us: Without them we, and our world, would not be the same.

Intimacies are situational, and there needs to be sensitivity involved when casting networked media practices on these terms, given the gaps emerging between how things become classified (whether to protect individual rights or to identify a field of research) and how things are experienced, lived, and made sense of. As we have shown in this chapter—even within the realm of the sexually explicit—that which is considered intimate, what is articulated as intimate, and what is experienced as allowing for connections needed to sustain life, do not cleanly overlap. The stuff is complex.

8 Apprehension, Friction, and Mundane Pleasures

> I think it's incredibly great that there's such a platform, even if I hate the logic of use, and usability, and the site's age, and admin, and everything else on there. Since I've, I don't even know how many user names I've had there. I've probably joined it tens of times, been there, lost my patience with the people there, left it, and then gone back. Me losing my patience has mostly been [about] my ignore-list starting to become so long that I've been: "Fuck you people, I'm off now."
> —Joonas

Prompted to share any further thoughts he might have at the end of his interview with Maria, Joonas discusses his attachment to Alastonsuomi as fundamentally ambiguous in him enjoying a platform that he also actively dislikes. When it becomes too much, he tends to leave and cut all ties with other users and then at some point come back again as the site's sexual openness holds value to him. Joonas is hardly alone in this ambiguity where sharp affective peaks of irritation constantly rupture enjoyable interactions, be it on the sexual platforms studied in this book or in social media more generally. In his research on Australian gay men's uses of hookup apps and social media, Elija Cassidy (2016) identifies them as cut through by "participatory reluctance" as a mode of engagement "when we would actually prefer not to or would rather do so under altered circumstances" (2614)—as "participation in a state of discontent, neither fully active or absent" (Cassidy 2018, 6). He goes on to discuss participatory reluctance as part and parcel of social media engagement:

> The begrudging use of SNSs (or parts thereof) that people don't ideologically agree with, or which lack genuine alternatives, for example, is relatively commonplace. In particular, through its capacity to contribute to analyses of the many tensions

associated with maintaining a social media presence, the concept offers an additional avenue through which research on participation in SNSs can continue to develop beyond binaries of use and nonuse and, thus, further nuance our understandings of (dis)engagement and (dis)connection in these environments. (Cassidy 2016, 2626)

A situation where "large numbers of users engage with a digital platform in a state of discontent" (Cassidy 2018, 148) is recognizable among those of our interviewees who have misgivings about the sites' designs, other users, commenting cultures, and much more; yet they, for the most part, continue to use them. Indeed, many of our interviews are rife with accounts of friction, irritation, and frustration. This can be conceptualized as a ubiquitous sense of inconvenience, which Lauren Berlant (2022, 2) identifies as an unpleasant sense of over-closeness with the world: "the affective sense of the familiar friction of being in relation." For Berlant (2022, 6), such a sense of inconvenience is a constant in social connections to the point of being something akin to an ontological condition. Deeply ambiguous, inconvenience can be draining inasmuch as animating, and the "mere existence of other people can be a positive fact or a negative irritant." She elaborates:

> The sense of it can come from nothing you remember noticing or from a small adjustment you made or couldn't make, generating an episode bleed that might take on all kinds of mood or tone, from irritation and enjoyment to fake not-caring or genuine light neutrality. In other words, the minimal experience of inconvenience does not require incidents or face-to-faceness: the mere idea of situations or other people can also jolt into awareness the feel of their inconvenience. . . . The important thing is that we are inescapably in relation with other beings and the world and are continuously adjusting to them. (Berlant 2022, 2)

Her discussion of "the inconvenience paradox of dependency"—of "needing people or a situation and hating to have that need" (Berlant 2022, 36)—further speaks to the frictions that networked lives entail. Online connections are marked by irritations both minor and major, as well as conditioned by platform policies, interface designs, and social codes that may not sit well with users. This resonates with Taina Bucher's (2021, 104) discussion of how "Facebook's deep ambivalence" creeps up "in various blog posts and comments, in the many disparate attempts to leave and disconnect, in research findings and everyday encounters" so that the platform is "both time thief and lifeline, a tool for self-promotion and a conduit for self-deprecation, both friend and enemy, and much more."

The frictious dynamic of needing and hating—or at least being wary of—this very need is manifest in how our participants rely on platforms for sexual expression and relating while also wishing that things could be different. As is most likely the case with any examples of networked lives, our participants discuss their platformed engagements as messy, complex, and often ambivalent in terms of how they navigate their visibilities and invisibilities, proximities and distances.

Disconnecting, Reconnecting

This brings us back to the question of disconnection, as already raised in prior chapters. For obvious reasons, internet research has focused on forms of connecting ever since the field became established as such. This has paved the way for studies focusing on the ubiquity of disconnections—distancing, muting, blocking, and avoidance—in networked lives (John and Dvir-Gvirsman 2015; Light 2014; Karppi 2018; Karppi et al. 2021), given that connections and disconnections by necessity encompass a dynamic wherein there cannot be the one without the other (Sundén 2018; Sundén and Blagojevic 2019). Together with Ben Light, Cassidy has conceptualized "the disconnective strategies of suspension and prevention" as not merely resistant tactics, but also as socioeconomic lubricants that orient and fuel online exchanges (Light and Cassidy 2014, 1169). In such a framework, disconnections can happen within and between platforms, in relation to other users, as well as in relation to physical places and locations of use. It can entail opting out from joining a platform, leaving it, or momentarily suspending one's participation (Light and Cassidy 2014, 1173).

This all rings familiar. Among our participants, disconnective strategies range from editing photos to render faces unrecognizable and hide distinguishable tattoos, listing a location where one does not actually live, and choosing *not* to hook up or otherwise connect with other users. Disconnective tactics further include, but are not limited to, controlling to whom the content posted is visible on-site (the possibilities for delimiting audiences vary across the three sites); how other users are ignored, blocked, and reported; how identifiable presences and social connections carry over from one platform to another, or not; how locations and personal identifiers are muted or hidden (even as they can certainly also be highlighted), and how participation varies across time so that intense periods of platform use can be followed by intervals of disinterest. As Joonas pointed out above, this may oscillate as a persistent on/off dynamic, which is also picked up by Noora:

> Really, kind of on–off. I've had my account there hidden many times and then I've always made a comeback. . . . Very strongly according to the menstrual cycle, so that when it's ovulation and one is really horny all the time, Alastonsuomi is kind of a substitute for porn [*laughs*]. And if there's less sex in my own relationship, as there occasionally is, then I'm clearly more active there.

While Noora's (dis)connective relationship with the platform echoes the ebb and flow of her libido, Estonian swingers Toomas and Pille describe an intermittent sense of fear that is described as both a function of increasing self-revelation on the platform, on the one hand, and a function of people's changing personal life and relationship dynamics, on the other. Toomas, describing his early years of using sexual platforms, says:

> I think the younger you are, the more likely you are to create an account, upload some photos, poke around a bit, and then you get scared—I for example used to get these panics, "What if someone will recognize me, what if someone will see." And then I would delete my account. At some point the fear passed and I would create a new account, then the panic returned and I deleted again. Or, another reason for why it's typical on these sites for people to kind of keep disappearing and reappearing, is when their relationship status changes. When you break up, it's polite to delete the account you had with your ex.

Sofia, linked her fluctuating use of Alastonsuomi to more momentary or fleeting senses of anger, or irritation, evoked by other users and their ways of interacting with her, as well as by the platform as a mediator of such communication that holds addictive, overly seductive appeal:

> I then occasionally get these periods when I can for example momentarily freeze my account completely, that I'm really gone from there. As a baseline, I'm irritated by how easily the site itself hooks me, and then again from there, as counterbalance to all the good conversations, you sometimes get such horrible texts from male users in particular, that you just lose the patience for all people.

For Marko, the question is more one of regularly getting fed up: "It's usually like—you're there for a while so you can get excited for a while and then it starts to badly piss you off and then you leave." This oscillation between excitement and being "badly pissed off" speaks of the persistent and acute presence of negative affective intensities within siloed sociality. For example, queer participants in both Andre Cavalcante's (2019) and Tiidenberg, Hendry and Abidin's (2021, 150) studies on queer silos (Cavalcante called them vortexes) on Tumblr speak of a similar movement where excitement, even a sense of a delightful utopia, spills over into some kind of negative affect and an almost mandatory "cooling-off stage" (Cavalcante 2019). This results in affective oscillations that draw users onto and into the platforms, and push them away again.

As discussed throughout the preceding chapters, our participants constantly draw boundaries between what goes: whom they want to connect with and who is better left ignored, what is considered intimate in the sense of involving an edge of vulnerability, and what proximities are actively desired. For some, these platforms offer anonymity for expressing forms of sexuality that they do not—for a range of reasons—otherwise share with the world. For others, sexual self-expression forms much more of a continuum that bleeds across platforms, and does not remain on-platform only.

On the one hand, disconnections involve tactics knowingly practiced by users to guard their own boundaries, as discussed in chapter 7. On the other hand, people get cut off against their will when they are ghosted and blocked, or when they do not receive feedback or likes to start with. People sometimes describe ghosting as the politest possible way to express one's lack of interest in others. Mona, who shares a couples' account with her male partner on Libertine.Center and identifies as a swinger, describes their search for best practices of disconnection.

> **MONA:** We've been thinking about how to politely turn people down. It's a problem for us, because we don't want to hurt people's feelings—like saying "You're not right for us" would. So we tend to quietly kind of slip away, we stop communicating. We don't get into a fight, but we just quietly move on.
>
> **KATRIN:** Yes, I can see how that is difficult, because on the one hand, people tend to claim that they want to be told in a straightforward way that they are not wanted, but then they do get offended and you may end up with trolls, like that couple you described, who just went out of their way to speak ill of you to others.
>
> **MONA:** Yeah. Actually, I don't know if I'd even want someone to honestly tell me, "You're ugly and I don't want to communicate with you anymore"; it is much easier if people just stop communicating to you. And we've met a lot of people with whom we've just stopped communicating or who have stopped communicating with us. And we've come to the realization that well, if they stopped talking to us, then that's your answer, we weren't right for them. Neither of us get in touch—that means that it's been decided that we're not a match.

There are, however, differences in disconnective tactics based on ghosting between single users and couples, between swinger cultures and other kinksters, and between heterosexual and queer logics. Existing literature on ghosting among adolescent and young adult users of dating apps has highlighted the negative impact it may have on the ghostee's self-esteem, in particular in terms of their self-perceived sexual and romantic appeal, and thus it is mostly positioned as a practice harmful to the well-being of the people ghosted (Campaioli et al. 2022). At the same time, the experiences and motivations of ghosters have been found to vary, as ghosting is not necessarily acted out consciously or with malicious intent (Timmermans et al. 2021). Within a heterosexual logic that, to a large extent, regulates our platforms, many women discussed their constant deliberation over which men to respond to, and how, as the volume of messages can be overwhelming, and as their tone often leaves many things to be desired. Ghosting, in these cases, can be the only sustainable tactic of ignoring the unmanageable flood of irritating messages. Addressing on-platform frictions, Emmi points out that:

> The kinds of comments from men you get there perhaps irritate women in particular. For example, just getting directly to the point to suggest—sex or, then, otherwise commenting in a slimy way, or just writing out some of their own, some fantasy with no invitation or introduction, just that I'd do this and this to you.

How the studied platforms are experienced varies clearly along the axes of gender—as well as those of ethnicity, age, body size, sexual likes, and kinks—so that things causing persistent irritation to some users may remain fairly invisible to others. For his part, Björn got a sneak peek into the world of female-identified users and how such waves of attention may unfold in real time:

> BJÖRN: I sat next to a friend who signed up and started receiving messages before she even finished her presentation, because she had identified herself as a woman. They've tried to add functionality on Darkside so that you can't just send messages willy-nilly, which I think is good. But it's not enough. And it's not possible to solve the fact that people are idiots through writing better code. It's a larger societal problem. In the same way that it's difficult to have a pub where guys won't hit on girls. As long as it's not completely separatist, it happens. Unfortunately, it does.
>
> JENNY: Yes, that is of course annoying. But shouldn't there be some room for flirting or connecting with strangers?
>
> BJÖRN: Yes, of course, there is room and openness for flirting and contacts and all kinds of—but there's a difference between a healthy level of mutual contact, and the impossibility of presenting yourself as a woman because that means immediately receiving one hundred messages. That's just unreasonable.

The added functionality Björn refers to consists of how you can specify the type of contact you are interested in (general social contact; friendship; company for clubs and parties; flirt; sex chat; BDSM play; "traditional sex"; relationship; and so on), which then pops up when someone who is not on your friends' list starts crafting a message. "When dealing with strangers, it's important to do so with style and respect," the message page pleads, but, as Björn points out, this does not stop people from acting the opposite.

Apprehension and Anticipation

Connecting and engaging with platforms involves ambiguity and, to some extent, nervousness or edginess in the face of the fact that past disappointments may well repeat themselves. This, again, can result in pre-emptive tactics concerning one's visibility, recognizability, and modes of interaction. But, as we have seen, there is also optimism, hopeful expectation, and excitement to all this that fuel and drive people to remain on-platform, and to engage with others. This time, things might be different! If there was no hope, people would be less inclined to return to platforms that they have previously turned away from. In other words, there is an interesting tendency to user engagements with platforms, one that balances apprehension and anticipation with practices of connecting and disconnecting.

This can be conceptualized through Berlant's (2022, 7) discussion of inconvenient attachments as an ambiguous ontological condition, since "we cannot know each other without being inconvenient to each other. We cannot be in any relation without being inconvenient to each other." In other words, there is no way of doing away with friction in social existence. There is no proximity without some kind of inconvenience—or, as Berlant (2022, 28) puts it, things can be at the same time both diminishing and world-sustaining. Optimism and pessimism are not mutually exclusive: Both can be flattening and enlivening, and the one may come as folded into the other (Coleman 2017).

Such oscillations between anticipation and apprehension—between hope of sorts and shivers of irritation and dismay—play out differently on different social media platforms, due to variations in how they reveal and conceal the presence of users, but also due to the rhythms and forms of networked exchanges more generally. For our participants, this ambiguous networked dynamic between hope and dismay played out in a number of ways. One common tactic was to temper future disappointments with the platform and its users by selective engagement and sharing. For Evelina, who, when we decided on an interview, had already made clear her reluctant relationship with platforms, such selectiveness means having a rather instrumental approach:

> I'm very much a lurker on social media. I don't like to engage much there, and I don't spend much time there either. This applies to all platforms really. For me, social media is something extremely instrumental. I have a Facebook page, but if you look at it, I haven't written anything there during about the last three years. So, it's just other people linking to me. I use it for events, I use Messenger, so I use it very instrumentally in that I use it for things I need to do. Or people I need to connect with, people I know. I'm not on Instagram, or yes, I'm in a small private group with my nephews. And I have two reasons for being on Twitter: One is porn and the other is ice hockey! And I'm kind of the same way on Darkside and on FetLife. They're very instrumental for me in that I'm there to connect with people I know.

When digging a bit deeper into this practical and minimalist use of platforms, it becomes clear that this instrumentality can be a distancing mechanism and a way of protecting herself:

> Sometimes I think that one of the reasons I'm on social media so little is because I don't like to make myself vulnerable online. I find it extremely uncomfortable. I don't like discussing politics on the internet either. For one thing, I have to think for a long time before I write anything, because then it's always gonna be there, and then someone comes along and gets annoyed. And that's one of the reasons why I don't like to discuss things online, because I don't like to contact people online. I think it's the same on Darkside, I find it very difficult, even if I sometimes push myself. But overall, I pretty much stay in my comfort zone. Because it's also easier. Some people put a lot on the line on Darkside, and I don't think I'm one of them. Just contacting someone because you think they're hot, or because you think they have kinks that are cool, or because you'd like them to do something to you, that's still a very big deal for me. I still find that difficult, even on platforms like this. (Evelina)

To not engage here becomes a way of not opening oneself up to the risk of being disappointed, let down, or plain visible to others, accompanied by the nerves involved in attempts to break a familiar pattern. It might then be useful to ask why sexual platforms can disappoint, excite, and exhilarate in ways described by our participants. We suggest that this has to do with the affective intensities involved in connecting and relating to others from a libidinous place at a distance. Contextually, this ties in with the scarcity of contexts in which to have sexual conversations (as not ones to be had in most social situations or social groups) and the overall trend of deplatforming sex on social media platforms. If people feel like they do not have many other people or settings wherein to form sexual connections, relations, and conversations, platforms like Darkside, Libertine.Center, and Alastonsuomi will inevitably start seeming more crucial.

While lurking is a common tactic of self-protection and a means of pre-emptive disconnecting, or rather making it difficult for others to disconnect, empty or minimalist profiles and accounts that do not post anything are also read by others as suspicious—or, as Maarit points out, as plain irritating, given the intimate things that others willingly share on these platforms. This tendency to dismiss or consider as suspicious outsiders those users whose profiles are not filled out according to community standards (as including some personal information or a profile pic, for example) is a long-standing tradition on hookup sites and social media platforms alike. Liisa says that while her Libertine.Center profile is perhaps a bit more anemic than the community's gold standard, echoing her current phase of being less interested in unbridled experimentation, she always clicks on the profiles of the people who have messaged her.

> Before I reply, I look at their profile, even if new names have left likes on my pictures, I might go look at their profile. Often, if the profile of the person who has messaged me is empty, that's an immediate "no." Also, and this might be wrong, but I'm forty-one, and if this is a man who says he is twenty-eight years old and 170 cm tall, and his profile picture is of his dick, that is also a "no." I just can't be bothered with that; I don't want to be mean, but he will most definitely not interest me. Although now I added to my profile this sentence, that others in the community recommended, or I saw it somewhere, which is: "If my profile looked like your profile, would you respond to my message?" Because the messages from those empty profiles also tend to be empty. Very rarely will they say who they are or introduce themselves. They'll just say, "Hi," or "Let's get acquainted?" [in Estonian you can say "Let's get acquainted?" in a laconic one-word sentence "Tutvume?"] And since I currently do not feel the need for new acquaintances, and I guess I am a bit old fashioned, I like it when guys put in an effort, so the "Acquaintance?" message does not really spur me into action if I can't see their pictures and they haven't said anything about themselves and never post anything. So it's really important for the profile to be at least somewhat filled out, and at least somewhat populated by pictures, they don't even have to be very risqué pictures, in fact, if the pictures are like close ups of genitalia, then that's

also not my style, just aesthetically I don't like it, they might be lovely people, or a lovely couple, but if it's all pictures of zoomed in penises entering vaginas, then I don't like that, it just makes me apprehensive.

While the term apprehension has numerous meanings, such as in perceiving or understanding something, we consider here primarily its nervous edge as anxiety, suspicion, unease, or worry connected to something unpleasant maybe happening in the future. Apprehension and anticipation are some-times used synonymously, but generally, anticipation holds more openness and hope in terms of a future yet to arrive: It comes with a sense of excite-ment. Algorithmic logics of platform economies are certainly anticipatory as well in how their data practices build on past actions so as to predict users' future interests and, to an extent, to shape their actions. The issue of antici-pation in data economies is centrally one of algorithmic agency in that social media platforms feed users content that they are presumed to like based on its similarity with their previously expressed preferences and engagements—and, centrally, with those emerging from data aggregated at scale from users deemed similar. (Cheney-Lippold 2017; Lury and Day 2019; Paasonen 2023). While such anticipatory logics have enormous power and reach, our sites are cases apart, occupying minoritarian positions even within local social media economies.

Darkside, for example, collects as little data as possible, and deletes it as quickly as possible, to protect the privacy and integrity of its users. The data practices of Alastonsuomi are not precisely transparent, but, as an old-school website with a DIY feel, it is unlikely to be at the forefront of data brokering. Thus, anticipation and apprehension, as discussed here, are less about the power of platforms to shape their futures and more about user tendencies and orientations toward platforms, as well as about deep ambiv-alences at the heart of user experiences and practices (Koivunen et al. 2024; Paasonen et al. 2023b).

In a Sea of Dicks

In her examination of digital media connectivity, Jodi Dean (2015) argues that when connections intensify, so do anxieties over networked engage-ment: The more you open yourself up to platforms and networks, the more there is to worry about. As messages are sent, updates posted, pictures shared, and comments and likes set in motion, people may eagerly wait for, but also worry about responses and reactions (see also Papacharissi 2015; Sundén 2018; 2021). When you open yourself up to someone—or something—there is always the risk of letdown or failure. Dean follows Jacques Lacan's psychoanalytical understanding of anxiety as a form of excess or surplus enjoyment: "Anxiety about networked media is, in this view, anxiety about enjoyment." (Dean, 2015, 89). But within such modes of relating and connecting where worry and enjoyment entwine, it is not only disappointing platforms or fellow users that can be worrying. What interrupts joy and excitement, or heightens a sense of apprehension, also has to do with the absence of contact and connection; the failures to engage with others; a sense of loneliness in a crowd of the presumedly like-minded.

Contra the sense of an overwhelming oversupply of options and offers that many female users of sexual platforms have to navigate, some male-identifying straight users struggle with connecting in the first place, possibly with anyone at all. Antti describes how getting repetitively rebuffed on Alastonsuomi when he wants to be sexually seen and connect with others can amplify a broader sense of disconnection, loneliness, and isolation. He nevertheless remains apprehensively glued to the site:

> At least I've used it very much as a cure to this loneliness, so it's hard there sometimes, creating contacts is occasionally a little challenging. And then, at least for me, it's occasionally been a little too addictive. I spend quite a lot of time, maybe read too many texts of all sorts—whether it's social media or else, there's sometimes the problem that if one reveals too much and gets no response then it can feel a little—it can be kind of sort of harrowing. It can pretty easily add to depression or—even amplify loneliness. . . . Maybe I have the habit of being quite a lot on social media and so those certain kinds of learned manners can also enter my live-life [*live-elämä* signifying the offline; the face to face; the live] so that I can't necessarily get any kind of response from some contacts, I've noticed that for me it's added a little to, in live-life, it's caused more shyness. That I don't necessarily get into contact with people so easily then, in certain things.

Such rebuffing would be constant, given the gender imbalances on this particular platform. Sanna identifies Alastonsuomi as a "heaven for women" precisely due to its overwhelming male majority that basically makes it possible for straight women to just pick and choose (Vihlman 2023). Then, of course, what is heaven for some is something quite different for others. The sheer volume of straight male users interested in sexual company leads Julia to describe the platform as a "a sea of dicks" (see also Paasonen forthcoming). Julia elaborates:

There are so many of those lonely men there who put up pretty creepy pics as you need to have some photo—those people define the main population on the site, so to speak. And then as a subgenre in people you have everyone else. . . . But, like, mostly it's like, well we've already discussed the so-called sea of dicks that everyone on Alastonsuomi just tries to scramble forward in, as there are so many of them that you occasionally drown in it. And then you try to swim in it. . . . And then again, I notice that since I've been on there for years, I start to censor that kind of everyday panting by the sea of dicks there from my realm of vision.

Reflecting on this oversupply of possibilities, Sanna agrees that "when considering the basic principles of social interaction, it's kind of mean and a little bitchy to be, kind of, that I just pick—and respond to those who're interesting and others can message how they like and won't get a reply. But that's the situation in the number of men and women, so." Combined with both the persistent presence of norms casting certain sexual likes and orientations as lesser-than on-platform and the awareness of others not desiring new connections, the unbalanced gender ratio feeds a mode of apprehension that may well curb attempts at connecting even when such desire very much exists: "Just a few times I've put a comment somewhere, I tried to sort of create interaction, but it's really a fluke that someone there would actually start discussing anything at all, really" (Mikael). Joonas sees the issue as a lack of courtesy on the part of straight women with a tendency to ghost:

Either they don't answer the comments in any way, check your profile. Or we've been talking for a while and then they stop responding and when you inquire after them a few times they suddenly block your profile. So, then you can't see or hear the other person at all. . . . Yes, it always hurts if someone just suddenly stops communicating—shuts the door in your face without saying anything.

Kaspar, a single male Libertine.Center user who elsewhere in the interview reflected on his relative popularity among couples, saying that he seems to be liked well enough to often get invites into "couples and single women only" spaces and events, still echoes the frustrations of other straight male users:

My best experiences of starting to connect to people on the platform tend to be where I've first been at the same event with them, because just cold calling on the platform, I mean, I am sure it's the single man thing, but when you start talking to someone—I think women get so many messages, so you never know if they'll even bother to reply to you. Often, they don't. Which, frankly, I find a bit weird, that you—I mean "I am not interested," is also a reply, so it's a bit silly to not say anything. Like why did you even create an account on a site like this then.

On the one hand, Antti, Joonas, and Kaspar express frustrations over having to compete for female users' attention and the mental toll that constant ghosting takes on them; both are concerns that our female interviewees also recognize, even as they do not share them. On the other hand, Kaspar's quote above indicates a lack of reflexivity in terms of potential risks that a woman online faces when saying to a horny heterosexual man that she is "not interested." As is evident in our heterosexual female participants' comments, as well as in the existing literature on gendered sexual harassment online (e.g., Ging and Siaspera 2019; Massanari 2017), there are structural differences to participatory cultures that imbue ghosting with a variety of different meanings for single male, single female, and couple user accounts. While many of our participants, their gendered and sexual identities notwithstanding, highlighted the practicalities and pleasures involved in being able to start conversations from a place of sexual affinity, this sentiment also came steeped in a sense of entitlement when disgruntled male users discussed women ghosting them. Thus, similarly to Kaspar's question of "Why are you even on this site if you are not answering messages?" Marko, below, gestures to a sort of presumed consent where women, merely because of their presence on-platform—but especially so if they have posted explicit photos of themselves—are supposed to welcome sexual advances, at least within certain limits:

> I guess it's like if you're there with pics, where you can see everything, and if you indicate in your profile that you're looking for company, then that boundary has gone, in a way; communication can—you don't need to be wary of—how would I say this so that it doesn't come across as harassment. Boundaries are different than in normal life. But, on the other hand, boundaries exist here, too, of course, and then there are many people, who don't understand the boundaries that there are.

Marko's quote indicates an ambivalence of sorts, or an internal friction involved in choosing how to interpret the site as a both sexual and social space, as well as how to relate to others on it and recognizing their boundaries. On the one hand, he advocates for a lowered-by-default threshold for the acceptability of unsolicited sexual advances, which he justifies by indicating that sexuality forms a fundamental part, or even the core, of sociability on a sexual platform like Alastonsuomi. On the other hand, he is wary of his sentiment coming across as one condoning harassment and points to a respect for boundaries still being relevant on a sexual platform. Further, not everyone experiences these frictions as ones primarily connected to sexual relating. Jari addresses the issue as one of awkwardness on behalf of people who have formed, or tried to form, most of their personal connections online and who then basically lack social skills and manners: "They sort of don't even get it that other people really are real people, and I've wondered with a few of my friends, like what's this, how do these people hope that anyone answers their shouts in any other way than by completely ignoring them?" These are, indeed, examples of sociality-in-friction pointing to the persistent inconvenience of other people as ones that can be brought into sharp focus in platformed exchanges. Given this constant friction, affect management involved in dealing with annoying fellow users is routine as the platforms and their social vernaculars are navigated on a daily basis, and over several years—as in Julia's account of learning how to swim in "the sea of dicks," as quoted above. But friction can also build up from petty annoyances toward something more anxiety-inducing since excessive, repetitive, and layering acts of disrespect make for everything but enjoyable experiences, leading some to withdraw from the platform (even as they may, of course, be back sooner or later). In his work on intimate digital publics of Black queer men, Shaka McGlotten (2013, 13) understands the affective structures of anxiety as heightened and speculative forms of attention, and as anticipatory aware-ness oriented toward indeterminacy and protection against future race-based harm. There are similar tendencies among our participants as they move to protect themselves from sexist harassers and other constantly reoccurring disappointments on-platform.

User engagements, interruptions, and disconnections can be activated by or transformed into worry, while at the same time allowing for a kind of enjoy-ment. In a paradoxical blend of apprehension, anticipation, and hope, ways of worrying, critiquing, or feeling disappointed can become ways to recon-nect and enjoy. Following Berlant (2022, 18), such ambiguous attachments would in fact be something of a constant, in that social lives are "strongly mixed, drawn in many directions, positively and negatively charged."

In addition, some users are of course enticed by the friction of drama and find enjoyment in critiquing others or complaining about this and that. This is not to argue that everybody forms apprehensive attachments to and on digital platforms. We suggest that both the affordances of social media platforms and their relational registers for reaching out to others invite and reward apprehensive ways of connecting and enjoying. As argued above, such connecting involves an edge of vulnerability in what counts as intimate.

No matter how conflicted the users of sexual platforms might feel, they keep coming back, often for the lack of better options. Such apprehensive and strikingly ambiguous forms of relating and connecting also point to them offering something essential to their user base. Independent of how vintage their designs, how disrespectful their users are, or how wanting their moderation practices might be, they stand out in sanitized, sex-negative social media ecologies as spaces based on sexual connections and expressions, fueled by libidinous energies, wants, and desires. It is no accident, then, that several of our interviewees describe them as breathing spaces. Rather, this speaks of their value within people's lives and social media practices.

Lessons from Studying Sexual Social Media

Friction may, literally, start a fire—and be very hot in this sense. Friction emerges as resistance to the motion of bodies and surfaces trying to slide against one another, so as to result in things chafing and abrading instead. Friction can be pleasurable (or then not) since such sliding, rubbing, and chafing between surfaces can be key to sexual experiences. Friction can, of course, also more figuratively point to disagreement and discord, as when dissenting ideas, wishes, and desires rub up against each other, or rub some people the wrong way. As mapped out in these terms, friction can range from the intensities of open conflict, clash, and contention to the more subtle disturbances of mutual annoyance and irritation. In Anna Tsing's (2005, 4) ethnography of global connection, the metaphor of friction is used for getting a grip of worldly encounters: "the awkward, unequal, unstable, and creative qualities of interconnection across difference." For Berlant (2022, 11), friction's energy similarly entails "frisson, the intensity that fuels us even while the fatigue of the inconvenience of world-receptivity is pretty wearing."

Some of the frictious platform engagements discussed in this book can be framed in terms of what Oliver Davis (2009) identifies as "irritable attachments," building on the (rather surprising!) queer potentials in the work of the philosopher Jacques Rancière. Any encounter between Rancière and queer theory will, as Davis argues, be fraught with mutual irritation. And yet, he finds that Rancière's way of thinking about irritable attachment (such as that between a teacher and their student) offers queer theory an interesting response to ambient heteronormativity. There is no escaping or detaching from how relations and sexual practices are normatively valued, even in lives lived against the grain. But not being able to detach completely from hetero norms is, of course, not the same thing as being at ease, as there will be considerable irritation and friction. Within such irritable attachment, the very distance and friction between the parties forms part of their bond. No matter how irritating such connections, relations and, indeed, dependencies may be, irritable attachments also become a productive and unmistakably queer way of thinking about people's inclinations, or abilities to form attachments also when it comes to the most problematic of systems and norms. While Berlant discusses friction as default part and parcel of sociality, Davis points more specifically to the frictions involved in heteronormativity that queer people cannot escape. The same can be said for the diverse sexual norms that our participants comment on: both those coming about on-platform and those marginalizing nonmonogamous, kinky, and queer sexualities in the society at large.

It is the overarching argument of this book that sexual sociability, and the platforms allowing for it, hold great value and importance in how people make sense of their own desires and likes, and how they learn about the desires and likes of others. As we have nevertheless foregrounded throughout the preceding chapters, and in this concluding one in particular, sociability on sexual platforms involves inconveniences of their own so that these do not simply form sites of amazing liberated sex, happy coexistence, and friction-free connecting. There are frictions between users and user groups as boundaries are breeched and as social codes are put aside in ways unwanted by others. Our participants vent frustrations toward platforms, their functionalities, designs, content policies, and moderation practices under the conditions of more or less reluctant participation.

Drawing on the work of Cassidy, Light, and Bucher, we argue that sexual platforms do not form islands of exception from other social media in the frictions that they entail, nor should they be approached and analyzed through a lens of exceptionalism. To include sexual connections in considerations of networked sociality then simply means making fuller sense of what drives people, what matters, what counts as intimate, and where personal boundaries may be drawn.

Mundane inconveniences, frictions, and apprehensions involved in connecting through networked means, as well as in the flesh, mean that the contingent and leaky social silos established on platforms are, on the one hand, formations sheltering users from things becoming "too much." On the other hand, tensions occur within such silos—be they open conflicts or more of a persistent sense of there being something, or someone, irritating just there. Our interviewees speak of constant boundary work within and across social media platforms as the management of proximities and potential vulnerabilities concerning safety. At the same time, it is important to note that safety and the risk of harm are not simple opposites, nor are they mutually exclusive, and nor are they something to be controlled or preemptively managed as there can ultimately be no telling as to what gets under your skin, where, how, or why. Rather, this is an issue of degrees of safety and calculated risks as people post photos showing potentially identifying markers, disclose their sexual fantasies and experiences in blogs, hook up with others, and take a leap of faith in establishing a sexual and/or intimate connection. Disconnective tactics cut through all such connecting, just as the boundaries of social silos are leaky by default in their contextual bleeds and promiscuities.

It is equally the case that proximities and distances, as experienced and articulated by our participants when describing their connections, physical locations, and social media uses, are matters of gradations and of occasionally overlapping registers in how people not in their immediate vicinity feel close in their on-platform presence, as well as in how distances are crafted vis-à-vis everyday surroundings in networked connections. We find it crucial to both hold on to, and to highlight, such ambiguity and complexity as the stuff that makes networked lives as ones entailing pressing frustrations, yet equally sharp twinges of pleasure, and dulling boredoms inasmuch as captivating titillations.

It has been our premise that the platforms we study allow for the replatforming of sex in social media—even as Darkside, Libertine.Center, and Alastonsuomi enjoy a marginal existence in their local social media ecologies. As we have shown in this book, these sexual sites are rife with tension in how people negotiate the dynamics of gender, sexuality, social class, nationality, race, and vaccination status; in how sexual bents are valorized, and not; and in what basically makes a meaningful—or hot—connection. Yet, we have also wanted to highlight the centrality of such sites as ones of sexual visibility, desiring, learning, and acceptance that are as pedagogical as they are libidinal. It is exceedingly easy for studies of social media to bypass, or plain ignore, the importance of sexuality as something that makes the self and the social, given the degree to which none of this is encouraged in the content policies of leading platforms. Bringing the sexual (or, indeed, bringing sexy) back into the picture is then a necessary task if we are to more fully understand what makes people tick, what creates apprehension, what drives (dis) connections, and what may just be plain hot.

There is also something to say about the importance of context in studying sexual social media. It has been our argument that studying local platforms that may seem marginal—both geographically and culturally—allows for new ways of understanding digital sexual cultures and networked sociability more generally. To refocus the discussion of digital sexuality in Nordic and Baltic perspectives serves to challenge the Anglocentrism that cuts through much state-of-the-art inquiry on this topic. To this end, we have explored ideas of sexual freedom and liberation by moving between and interlinking Estonia, Finland, and Sweden. We have followed how our participants articulate a sense of sexual "relaxedness" by virtue of their geographical and cultural situatedness, especially when compared to the puritan restraints and ways of policing and regulating sex on social media platforms on a global scale. This sexual relaxedness can be thought of as an attitude loosely assembled by sauna bathing and skinny-dipping traditions, a sexual imaginary that pulls our contexts together around acceptable forms of social nudity so that the region of "the North" becomes distinctly different compared to Anglo-American contexts. The situatedness of our platforms thus offers an important counterpoint to internationally operating social media services: It makes a difference to how safety and risk are experienced and attuned in connection with sex and nudity, what enjoying a sense of sexual freedom means, and how it feels.

What we can then learn from studying sexual social media is that calibrations of safety and risk are always present in how people connect—whether online or not—and in how they want to be visible, identifiable, and accessible to one another. This is certainly not exceptional for or limited to sexual content or platforms. But it is our argument that sexual platforms provide an illuminating case for social media studies in which negotiations of risk and safety, proximity and distance, visibility and opacity become particularly clear. That, for some, the social visibility and reach afforded by sexual platforms basically makes for a fuller and more fulfilling life in ways pointing to how leading social media platforms, in contrast, curb possible ways of being in the world so that the sexual does not even get to enter the picture (even as it can be monetized in something like Facebook Dating following different content policies than the site more generally).

It is not our argument that all social media platforms should be rife with cocks, tits, and asses galore—In your face! More is more!—or that porn bots should be allowed as broad a reach as possible for sharing their messages. What we are arguing is that explicitly opting into seeing, sharing, and enjoying sexual content is key for many users, not least for those whose sexual tastes are seen as falling outside the normative bounds of "good sex," such as the kinksters, swingers, and self-identified pervs populating our study. We have, hopefully, shown that risk to one's (sense) of safety does rarely stem from the sexually explicit nature of images and utterances, but rather from the investments in and discomforts of connections, intimacies, and vulnerabilities. We further argue that ignoring the role that sexuality plays in the making of social bonds leads to inevitable blindness and bias that ultimately make it impossible to see what makes people tick, what they invest in, and what risks they are willing to take in order to lead an enjoyable life.

The replatforming of sex on social media as an issue of consensual opting in is, then, key to making platforms more equitable and more deeply social. Treating sexuality as an issue of obscenity, disturbance, and a problem, again, is basically not helping anyone beyond those willing to confuse sexual prudism with laudable moral values, the effacement of nudity with good taste, and the lack of sexual sociality with safety (of women in particular). Such policing hurts sexual rights by limiting how people can be seen, how they can connect, and what kinds of content they can access in the first place. Understanding that sexual content and communication do not pose a risk and that they are not inherently harmful—and that they can in fact be just the very opposite—is a useful place to start.

It is also perhaps a good place for us to end. To think of sex and sexuality as fundamentally social, rather than exclusively belonging to a domain of trauma, hurt, and harm, has consequences for a number of things discussed in this book, such as research ethics, platform governance, and the field of social media studies more generally. We have discussed what it means to be invested in sexuality studies in a time when the sexual is not only ousted from generic social media platforms, but when data about one's sex life or sexual orientation is understood as a category of sensitive personal data by default (as per the GDPR). Such default sensitivity delimits and defines beforehand what would be considered sensitive, and by whom, and it takes something important away from people's sense of agency and sexual self-determination. To think of sexuality as sensitive in and of itself also impedes on the interview situation. Tiptoeing around sexual matters, as was done in the Swedish context especially due to legal constraints, does not help in building trust. Then again, it became abundantly clear that discrimination and stigmatization in society at large is the issue, not an interest in our participants' ways of leading sexual lives on platforms.

We have also discussed how thinking of sociality as inclusive of the sexual offers a productive—and hopeful—model for platform governance. An important aspect of how sociality becomes networked depends, of course, on how platforms govern and moderate users, their communication and content. When we explored the Terms of Service and Community Guidelines of our three platforms, focusing especially on the kinds of violations that community and content moderation is anticipated to tackle, we found that the risks at stake are framed on starkly different terms than on generic, sex-negative social media platforms. In brief, three significant violations emerged, each being tied to something ascribed value, and which thus could be considered a core element of user safety: shaming as a violation of respect, harassment as a violation of consent, and fakeness as a violation of authenticity.

When the sexual is an intrinsic part of social media, safety is thus reframed in ways that both uncouple it from sex and nudity and link it to respect, consent, and authenticity instead. Here, alternative forms of platform governance emerge, where decisions of what, when, and how to moderate need not rely on categorical exclusion of certain topics that leads to victimizing already marginalized groups. Rather, moderation is articulated as a set of questions along the axes of how heterogenous or homogenous the users and their aims for using the platforms are, and whether preemptive, retroactive, or combinatory moderation might lead to the best outcomes. We are not saying that the platforms we studied are exemplary forms of governance. They do, however, help in imagining a way out of what otherwise feels like a governance impasse. Sometimes users can be moderated (e.g., verified) alongside their utterances, and almost always users and communities deserve more controls and opportunities for self-labeling, community moderation, and vernacular governance. More than anything—as it is unlikely that social media will be dethroned from its current position as the central communication infrastructure and dominant public space—finding ways to govern and moderate well is a question of central importance to our collective well-being. To do this in evidence-based ways respectful of human rights, we need to both include analyses of moderation on sexual platforms in broader conversations of platform governance and keep problematizing the deplatforming of sex from generic social media.

It has been our argument throughout that if sexuality is seen as intensely social—as intrinsically connected with sociality itself—it follows that social media studies cannot afford to ignore the role that sex plays in the formation of platform sociality. By working with examples of what may seem like limit cases in a social media landscape, sexual platforms may, in fact, provide prime examples for rethinking the social in social media. Looking at sexual platforms specifically, we found that these cultivate a particular kind of sexual sociability, one often experienced as *more intensely social* than that of generic social media platforms. This intensity stems from the sociality of sex and a sense of community afforded by shared spaces beyond the logic of individualized feeds and profile-centrism. Such communities may be leaky and rife with tension, as expectations, contexts, and sexual politics clash and collide, but there is a sense of community, nonetheless, which builds a form of normalcy in sexual otherness. This social intensity, or energy, also shows in no uncertain terms how social bonds and dynamics are central to how people make sense of themselves and others sexually, a vibratory tension that just may make a world in friction slightly more livable.

Notes

Chapter 1

1. That said, most of the Estonian participants also have experience with using Iha. ee, something that was discussed in the interviews. We therefore conducted additional interviews: one with Iha.ee moderators and four with Iha.ee users who are not Libertine.Center users for the purpose of grounding the interpretation within the context of Estonian sexual platforms.

Chapter 2

1. The participant we call Julia in this book has in articles published based on this study been referred to as Jenni. However, as this is very similar to the author Jenny, we have renamed her Julia for ease of reading. For similar reasons we have renamed Karin Malin.

Chapter 3

1. On LC Dating, the current version of the site, verification is free and based on a short video rather than a photo. The interface further articulates verification as now having specifically to do with gender: "A verified badge is a check that appears next to the username," the pop-up window reads: "It means LC Dating has confirmed the account gender." Thus, like on Alastonsuomi, misrepresenting one's gender is seen as an offense. There are two options for getting verified "remotely," via the video upload or "in real life," for example at events. The subscription model is no longer articulated as a fan account, but rather as a premium account (EUR 6,90 a month) that offers the ability to choose whether one wants to see sensitive content and access content in all albums, whereas in the free account both are blurred by default. While paid membership allows for greater access and superior functionality, users across our platforms rather frame this payment as access to a shared experience and as support of a community.

Chapter 5

1. The site has recently started to use a more diverse visual approach on its front page with some twenty images randomly fading in and out of each other. Compared to the previous visual profile, that dominated for years, these images represent a much wider range of racial, sexual, and gender identities, as well as kink practices, signaling greater openness and inclusion.

Chapter 6

1. A recent rebranding of Darkside further adds to the softening of this boundary in an interesting way. After our fieldwork was completed, Darkside has become Diversia (with the domain name Diversia.Social to maintain continuity with its established acronym DS). The site is thus partly moving away from a sexual imaginary of dark, forbidden desires and hidden spaces. While there was always a tension between the allure of sexualities and desires in the shadows of society and a more activist embrace of openness and destigmatization on the site, this accentuates the tricky balance between ideas of secrecy and outness. In an entry in the news section (dated May 5, 2025), this change is explained by the webmaster David as a way of carving out a space in a world quite different from that of the early 2000s when Darkside was founded: "Today, DS exists in a new reality, in a multiplicity of perspectives: some take pride in indulging in the dark and understand themselves in the context of darkness and shadows. Others understand and think about their sexualities and identities beyond—or in contrast to—images of darkness. . . . DS is for both those who live openly and those who live in secret; both for those who see freedom in dark basements and romance in the forbidden, and for those who feel that darkness and taboos conflict with their inner sense of pride and openness about their sexuality and identity. . . . Furthermore, DS aims to make diversity visible: although DS accommodates a wide range of norm-challenging interests and orientations, the greatest emphasis is placed on the marginalized minorities."

References

Abbot, Andrew. 1995. "Things of Boundaries." *Social Research* 62 (4): 857–882.

Ahmed, Sara. 2000. *Strange Encounters: Embodied Others in Post-Coloniality*. Routledge.

Ahmed, Sara. 2006. *Queer Phenomenology: Orientations, Objects, Others*. Duke University Press.

Albury, Kath. 2002. *Yes Means Yes: Getting Explicit About Heterosex*. Allen & Unwin.

Albury, Kath, and Paul Byron. 2016. "Safe on My Phone? Same-Sex Attracted Young People's Negotiations of Intimacy, Visibility, and Risk on Digital Hook-Up Apps." *Social Media + Society* 2 (4): 1–10.

Andalibi, Nazanin, Oliver L. Haimson, Munmun De Choudhury, and Andrea Forte. 2018. "Social Support, Reciprocity, and Anonymity in Responses to Sexual Abuse Disclosures on Social Media." *ACM Transactions on Computer-Human Interaction* 25 (5): 1–35. https://doi.org/10.1145/3234942.

Amundsen, Rikke. 2021. "'A Male Dominance Kind of Vibe': Approaching Unsolicited Dick Pics as Sexism." *New Media & Society* 23 (6): 1465–80.

Anderson, Benedict. 1983. *Imagined Communities: Reflections on the Origin and Spread of Nationalism*. Verso.

Andreassen, Rikke, Michael Nebeling Petersen, Katherine Harrison, and Tobias Raun, eds. 2018. *Mediated Intimacies: Connectivities, Relationalities and Proximities*. Routledge.

Are, Carolina, and Susanna Paasonen. 2021. "Sex in the Shadows of Celebrity." *Porn Studies* 8 (4): 411–419.

Attwood, Feona, Jamie Hakim, and Alison Winch. 2017. "Mediated Intimacies: Bodies, Technologies and Relationship." *Journal of Gender Studies* 26 (3): 249–253.

Attila, Henna, Miina Keski-Petäjä, Marjut Pietiläinen, Laura Lipasti, Juhani Saari, and Kimmo Haapakangas. 2022. *Sukupuolittunut Väkivalta ja Lähisuhdeväkivalta Suomessa*

2021. Loppuraportti. Tilastokeskus. https://stat.fi/media/uploads/sukupuolistunut_vaki valta_teemasivu/sukupuolistunut_v%C3%A4kivalta_ja_l%C3%A4hisuhdev%C3%A4 kivalta_suomessa_2021_-loppuraportti.pdf.

Barker, Martin. 2014. "The 'Problem' of Sexual Fantasies." *Porn Studies* 1 (1–2): 143–160.

Barreda-Ángeles, Miguel, and Tilo Hartmann. 2022, "Psychological Benefits of Using Social Virtual Reality Platforms During the Covid-19 Pandemic: The Role of Social and Spatial Presence." *Computers in Human Behavior* 127:107047.

Batiste, Dominique Pierre. 2013. "'0 Feet Away': The Queer Cartography of French Gay Men's Geo-Social Media Use." *Anthropological Journal of European Cultures* 22:111–132.

Bauer, Robin. 2014. *Queer BDSM Intimacies: Critical Consent and Pushing Boundaries.* Palgrave Macmillan.

Beckmann, Andrea. 2009. *The Social Construction of Sexuality and Perversion: Deconstructing Sadomasochism.* Palgrave Macmillan.

Bell, David, and Gill Valentine. 1995. "Introduction: Orientations." In *Mapping Desire: Geographies of Sexualities,* edited by David Bell and Gill Valentine, 1–27. Routledge.

Bengtsson, Elin. 2022. "Perversa tidsligheter: Ageplay och litenhet ur ett queertemporalt perspektiv" [The perverse temporalities of ageplay and littleness]. PhD diss., Stockholm University. Ellerströms.

Berlant, Lauren. 1998. "Intimacy: A Special Issue." *Critical Inquiry* 24 (2): 281–288.

Berlant, Lauren. 2022. *On the Inconvenience of Other People.* Duke University Press.

Berlant, Lauren, and Michael Warner. 1998. "Sex in Public." *Critical Inquiry* 24 (2): 547–566.

Bernstein, Elizabeth. 2010. *Temporarily Yours: Intimacy, Authenticity, and the Commerce of Sex.* University of Chicago Press.

Bivens, Rena. 2017. "The Gender Binary Will Not Be Deprogrammed: Ten Years of Coding Gender on Facebook." *New Media & Society* 19 (6): 880–898.

Blackwell, Courtney, Jeremy Birnholtz, and Charles Abbott. 2015. "Seeing and Being Seen: Co-Situation and Impression Formation Using Grindr, a Location-Aware Gay Dating App." *New Media & Society* 17 (7): 1117–1136.

Blunt, Danielle, and Ariel Wolf. 2020. "Erased: The Impact of FOSTA/SESTA and the Removal of Backpage on Sex Workers." *Anti-Trafficking Review* 14:117–121.

Blunt, Danielle, and Zahra Stardust. 2021. "Automating Whorephobia: Sex, Technology and the Violence of Deplatforming: An Interview with Hacking//Hustling." *Porn Studies* 8 (4): 350–366.

Blunt, Danielle, Stefanie Duguay, Tarleton Gillespie, Sinnamon Love, and Clarissa Smith. 2021. "Deplatforming Sex: A Roundtable Conversation." *Porn Studies* 8 (4): 420–438.

Boellstorff, Tom, Bonnie Nardi, Celia Pearce, and T. L. Taylor. 2012. *Ethnography and Virtual Worlds: A Handbook of Method*. Princeton University Press.

Bonner-Thompson, Carl. 2017. "'The Meat Market': Production and Regulation of Masculinities on the Grindr Grid in Newcastle-upon-Tyne, UK." *Gender, Place & Culture* 24 (11): 1611–1625.

Boris, Eileen, and Rhacel Salazar Parreñas, eds. 2010. *Intimate Labors: Cultures, Technologies, and the Politics of Care*. Stanford University Press.

Böthe, Beáta, Marie-Pier Vaillancourt-Morel, Jacinthe Dion, et al. 2022. "A Longitudinal Study of Adolescents' Pornography Use Frequency, Motivations, and Problematic Use Before and During the COVID-19 Pandemic." *Archives of Sexual Behavior* 51 (1): 139–156.

Branwyn, Gareth. 1994. "Compu-Sex: Erotica for Cybernauts." In *Flame Wars: The Discourse of Cyberculture*, edited by Mark Dery, 396–402. Duke University Press.

Breitschuh, Vanessa, and Julia Göretz. 2019. "User Motivation and Personal Safety on a Mobile Dating App." In *Social Computing and Social Media: Design, Human Behavior and Analytics*, edited by Gabriele Meiselwitz, 278–292. Springer.

Brock, André, Jr. 2020. *Distributed Blackness: African American Cybercultures*. NYU Press.

Bronstein, Carolyn. 2021. "Deplatforming Sexual Speech in the Age of FOSTA/SESTA." *Porn Studies* 8 (4): 367–380.

Brubaker, Jed R., Mike Ananny, and Kate Crawford. 2014. "Departing Glances: A Sociotechnical Account of 'Leaving' Grindr." *New Media & Society* 18:373–390.

Bucher, Taina. 2021. *Facebook*. Polity.

Byron, Paul. 2019. "'How Could You Write Your Name Below That?' The Queer Life and Death of Tumblr." *Porn Studies* 6 (3): 336–349.

Califia, Pat. 1999. *Public Sex: The Culture of Radical Sex*. 2nd ed. Cleis Press.

Campaioli, Giulia, Ines Testoni, and Adriano Zamperini. 2022. "Double Blue Ticks: Reframing Ghosting as Ostracism Through an Abductive Study on Affordances." *Cyberpsychology: Journal of Psychosocial Research on Cyberspace* 16 (5): Article 10. https://doi.org/10.5817/CP2022-5-10.

Campbell, John Edward. 2001. "Guts and Muscles and Bears, Oh My! The Body, Embodied Identity, and Queer Erotic Spaces Online." Master's thesis, University of Massachusetts Amherst.

Campbell, John Edward. 2004. *Getting It On Online: Cyberspace, Gay Male Sexuality, and Embodied Identity*. Routledge.

Caplan, Robyn. 2018. "Content or Context Moderation? Artisanal, Community-Reliant, and Industrial Approaches." Data & Society, November 14, 1–36. https://datasociety.net/output/content-or-context-moderation.

Cardoso, Daniel, Despina Chronaki, and Cosimo Marco Scarcelli. 2023. "Digital Sex Work? Creating and Selling Explicit Content in OnlyFans." In *Identities and Intimacies on Social Media. Transnational Perspectives*, 169–184. Routledge.

Carlström, Charlotta. 2018. "BDSM: The Antithesis of Good Swedish Sex?" *Sexualities* 22 (7–8): 1164–1181.

Cassidy, Elija. 2016. "Social Networking Sites and Participatory Reluctance: A Case Study of Gaydar, User Resistance and Interface Rejection." *New Media & Society* 18 (11): 2613–2628.

Cassidy, Elija. 2018. *Gay Men, Identity and Social Media: A Culture of Participatory Reluctance*. Routledge.

Cavalcante, Andre. 2019. "Tumbling into Queer Utopias and Vortexes: Experiences of LGBTQ Social Media Users on Tumblr." *Journal of Homosexuality* 66 (12): 1715–1735. https://doi.org/10.1080/00918369.2018.1511131.

Chalkidou, Aspa. 2022. "Vanilla Democracy: Sexuality, Parenthood, and Kinship in Greece." *Sexualities* 25 (5/6): 563–580.

Cheney-Lippold, John. 2017. *We Are Data: Algorithms and the Making of Our Digital Selves*. New York University Press.

Cho, Alexander. 2018. "Default Publicness: Queer Youth of Color, Social Media, and Being Outed by the Machine." *New Media & Society* 20 (9): 3183–3200.

Chun, Wendy Hui Kyong. 2021. *Discriminating Data: Correlation, Neighborhoods, and the New Politics of Recognition*. MIT Press.

Cockayne, Daniel, Agnieszka Leszczynski, and Matthew Zook. 2017. "#HotForBots: Sex, the Non-Human and Digitally Mediated Spaces of Intimate Encounter." *Environment and Planning D: Society and Space* 35 (6): 1115–1133.

Coleman, Rebecca. 2017. "Austerity Futures: Debt, Temporality and (Hopeful) Pessimism as an Austerity Mood." *New Formations* 87:83–101.

Conley Terri, Morgan Perry, Staci Gusakova, and Jennifer L. Piemonte. 2019. "Monogamous Halo Effects: The Stigma of Non-Monogamy Within Collective Sex Environments." *Archives of Sexual Behavior* 48 (1): 31–34.

Corinna, Heather. 2008. "An Immodest Proposal." In *Yes Means Yes: Visions of Female Sexual Power and a World Without Rape*, edited by Jaclyn Friedman and Jessica Valenti, 179–192. Seal Press.

Correll, Shelley. 1995. "The Ethnography of an Electronic Bar: The Lesbian Café." *Journal of Contemporary Ethnography* 24 (3): 270–298.

Couldry, Nick, and José van Dijck. 2015. "Researching Social Media As If the Social Mattered." *Social Media + Society* 1 (2). https://doi.org/10.1177/2056305115604174.

Daneback, Kristian. 2006. *Love and Sexuality on the Internet*. PhD diss., University of Gothenburg. http://hdl.handle.net/2077/10169.

David, Gaby, and Carolina Cambre. 2016. "Screened Intimacies: Tinder and the Swipe Logic." *Social Media & Society* 2 (2):1–11.

Davis, Oliver. 2009. "Rancière and Queer Theory: On Irritable Attachment." *Borderlands* 8 (2): 1–19.

Dawson, Andrew, and Simone Dennis. 2020. "Social Intimacy." *Anthropology in Action* 27 (3): 1–8.

Dean, Jodi. 2015. "Affect and Drive." In *Networked Affect*, edited by Ken Hillis, Susanna Paasonen, and Michael Petit, 89–100. MIT Press.

Dean, Tim. 2009. *Unlimited Intimacy: Reflections on the Subculture of Barebacking*. University of Chicago Press.

Del-Teso-Craviotto, Marisol. 2008. "Gender and Sexual Identity Authentication in Language Use: The Case of Chat Rooms." *Discourse Studies* 10 (2): 251–270. https://doi.org/10.1177/1461445607087011.

Dhoest, Alexander, and Lukasz Szulc. 2016. "Navigating Online Selves: Social, Cultural, and Material Contexts of Social Media Use by Diasporic Gay Men. *Social Media + Society* 2 (4). https://doi.org/10.1177/2056305116672485.

de Souza e Silva, Adriana. 2006. "From Cyber to Hybrid: Mobile Technologies as Interfaces of Hybrid Spaces." *Space and Culture* 9 (3): 261–278.

Dobson, Amy Shields, Brady Robards, and Nicholas Carah, eds. 2018. *Digital Intimate Publics and Social Media*. Palgrave Macmillan.

Döring, Nicola M. 2009. "The Internet's Impact on Sexuality: A Critical Review of 15 Years of Research." *Computers in Human Behavior* 25:1089–1101.

Dourish, Paul. 2006. "Re-Space-ing Place: 'Place' and 'Space' Ten Years On." *Proceedings of ACM CSCW06 Conference on Computer-Supported Cooperative Work*, 299–308. https://doi.acm.org/10.1145/1180875.1180921.

Duguay, Stefanie. 2016. "'He Has a Way Gayer Facebook Than I Do': Investigating Sexual Identity Disclosure and Context Collapse on a Social Networking Site." *New Media & Society* 18:891–907.

Duguay, Stefanie. 2017. "Dressing Up Tinderella: Interrogating Authenticity Claims on the Mobile Dating App Tinder." *Information, Communication & Society* 20 (3): 351–367.

Duguay, Stefanie. 2019. "'There's No One New Around You': Queer Women's Experiences of Scarcity in Geospatial Partner-Seeking on Tinder." In *The Geographies of Digital Sexuality*, edited by Catherine J. Nash and Andrew Gorman-Murray, 93–114. Singapore: Palgrave Macmillan.

Duguay, Stefanie, Christopher Dietzel, and David Myles. 2024. "The Year of the 'Virtual Date': Reimagining Dating App Affordances During the COVID-19 Pandemic." *New Media & Society* 26 (3): 1384–1402.

Eldén, Sara. 2020. *Forskningsetik: Vägval i samhällsvetenskapliga studier* [Research ethics: Choices in social science research]. Studentlitteratur.

Ellis, Carolyn. 2007. "Telling Secrets, Revealing Lives: Relational Ethics in Research with Intimate Others." *Qualitative Inquiry* 13 (1): 3–29.

Engelberg, Jacob, and Gary Needham. 2019. "Purging the Queer Archive: Tumblr's Counterhegemonic Pornographies. *Porn Studies* 6 (3): 350–354.

Etikprövningsmyndigheten. n.d. "About the Authority." https://etikprovningsmyn digheten.se/en/about-the-authority/.

European Union (EU). 2018. "Article 9, EU GDPR, Processing of Special Categories of Personal Data." https://www.privacy-regulation.eu/en/article-9-processing-of-special -categories-of-personal-data-GDPR.htm.

Fennell, Julie. 2022. *Please Scream Quietly: A Story of Kink*. Rowman and Littlefield.

Fiesler, Casey, Jialun Jiang, Joshua McCann, Kyle Frye, and Jed Burbaker. 2018. "Reddit Rules! Characterizing an Ecosystem of Governance." *Proceedings of the International AAAI Conference on Web and Social Media* 12 (1). https://doi.org/10.1609/icwsm.v12i1.15033.

Fischel, Joseph. 2019. *Screw Consent: A Better Politics of Sexual Justice*. University of California Press.

Fjær, Eivind Grip, Willy Pedersen, and Sveinung Sandberg. 2015. "'I'm Not One of Those Girls': Boundary-Work and the Sexual Double Standard in a Liberal Hookup Context." *Gender & Society* 29 (6): 960–981.

Fox, Jesse, and Katie M. Warber. 2015. "Queer Identity Management and Political Self-Expression on Social Networking Sites: A Co-Cultural Approach to the Spiral of Silence." *Journal of Communication* 65:79–100.

Frank, Katherine. 2008. "'Not Gay, But Not Homophobic': Male Sexuality and Homophobia in the 'Lifestyle.'" *Sexualities* 11 (4): 435–454.

Friedman, Jaclyn. 2008. "In Defense of Going Wild or: How I Stopped Worrying and Learned to Love Pleasure (and How You Can, Too)." In *Yes Means Yes: Visions of Female Sexual Power and a World Without Rape*, edited by Jaclyn Friedman and Jessica Valenti, 313–320. Seal Press.

Garwood-Cross, Lisa. 2022. "Interrogating the Possibilities and Problems of YouTube Sex Edutainment Content: An Actor-Network Theory Approach." Doctoral Diss., University of Salford.

Gatens, Moira. 1996. *Imaginary Bodies: Ethics, Power, and Corporeality*. Routledge.

Gatens, Moria. 2019. "Imaginaries." In *50 Concepts for a Critical Phenomenology*, edited by Gail Weiss, Ann Murphy, and Gayle Salamon, 181–187. Northwestern University Press.

Gibbs, Martin, James Meese, Michael Arnold, Bjorn Nansen, and Marcus Carter. 2015. "# Funeral and Instagram: Death, Social Media, and Platform Vernacular." *Information, Communication & Society* 18 (3): 255–268.

Giddens, Anthony. 1993. *The Transformation of Intimacy: Sexuality, Love and Eroticism in Modern Societies*. Stanford University Press.

Gillespie, Tarleton. 2018. *Custodians of the Internet: Platforms, Content Moderation, and the Hidden Decisions That Shape Social Media*. Yale University Press.

Ging, Debbie, and Eugenia Siapera, eds. 2019. *Gender Hate Online: Understanding the New Anti-Feminism*. Palgrave.

Goffman, Erwin. 1966. *Behavior in Public Places: Notes on the Social Organization of Gatherings*. Free Press.

Goodwin, Gretta L., Joseph P. Cruz, Jeff R. Jensen, et al. 2021. "Sex Trafficking: Online Platforms and Federal Prosecutions." GAO Report 21-385. United States Government Accountability Office. https://www.gao.gov/assets/gao-21-385.pdf.

Gorwa, Robert. 2019. "What Is Platform Governance?" *Information, Communication & Society* 22 (6): 854–871.

Gorwa, Robert, Reuben Binns, and Christian Katzenbach. 2020. "Algorithmic Content Moderation: Technical and Political Challenges in the Automation of Platform Governance." *Big Data & Society* 7 (1). https://doi.org/10.1177/205395171 9897945.

Gray, Mary L. 2009 *Out in the Country: Youth, Media, and Queer Visibility in Rural America*. NYU Press.

Gregg, Melissa. 2013. *Work's Intimacy*. Polity.

Grigoropoulos, Iraklis. 2022. "Towards a Greater Integration of 'Spicier' Sexuality into Mainstream Society? Social-Psychological and Socio-Cultural Predictors of Attitudes Towards BDSM." *Sexuality & Culture* 26:2253–2273.

Grubbs, Joshua B., Samuel L. Perry, Jennifer T. Grant Weinandy, and Shane W. Kraus. 2022. "Porndemic? A Longitudinal Study of Pornography Use Before and During the COVID-19 Pandemic in a Nationally Representative Sample of Americans." *Archives of Sexual Behavior* 51:123–137.

Haber, Benjamin Parrish. 2017. "The Queer Allure of Digital Sociality." PhD diss., City University of New York. https://academicworks.cuny.edu/gc_etds/2410/.

Häkli, Jouni. 1999. "Cultures of Demarcation: Territory and National Identity in Finland." In *Nested Identities: Nationalism, Territory, and Scale*, edited by Guntram H. Herb and David H. Kaplan, 123–150. Rowman & Littlefield.

Hargons, Candice N., Shemeka Thorpe, Natalie Malone, et al. 2022. "Black People's Constructions of Good Sex: Describing Good Sex from the Margins." *Sexualities* 7 (3): 457–474.

Harviainen J. Tuomas, and Katharine Frank. 2018. "Group Sex as Play: Rules and Transgression in Shared Non-monogamy." *Games and Culture* 13 (3): 220–239.

Haywood, Chris. 2022. *Sex Clubs: Recreational Sex, Fantasies and Cultures of Desire*. Palgrave MacMillan.

Held, Virginia. 2006. *The Ethics of Care: Personal, Political, and Global*. Oxford University Press.

Hervik, Peter. 2019. "Racialization in the Nordic Countries: An Introduction." In *Racialization, Racism, and Antiracism in the Nordic Countries*, edited by Peter Hervik, 3–37. New York: Palgrave Macmillan.

Hjorth, Larissa, and Richardson, Ingrid. 2017. "*Pokémon GO*: Mobile Media Play, Place-Making, and the Digital Wayfarer." *Mobile Media & Communication* 5 (1): 3–14.

Hjorth, Larissa, and Sarah Pink. 2014. "New Visualities and the Digital Wayfarer: Reconceptualizing Phone Photography and Locative Media." *Mobile Media & Communication* 2 (1): 40–57.

Hjorth, Larissa, and Sun Sun Lim. 2012. "Mobile Intimacy in an Age of Affective Mobile Media." *Feminist Media Studies* 12 (4): 477–484.

Hogan, Bernie. 2012. "Pseudonyms and the Rise of the Real-Name Web." In *A Companion to New Media Dynamics*, edited by John Hartley, Jean Burgess, and Axel Bruns, 290–308. Blackwell.

Horsti, Karina, and Tuija Saresma. 2021. "The Role of Social Media in the Rise of Right-Wing Populism in Finland." In *The Routledge Companion to Media Disinformation and Populism*, edited by Howard Tumber and Silvio Waisbord, 376–385. Routledge.

Hudson, David L., Jr. 2018. "Obscenity and Pornography." *The First Amendment Encyclopedia*. https://mtsu.edu/first-amendment/article/1004/obscenity-and-pornography.

Ingold, Tim. 2009. *Lines: A Brief History*. Routledge.

Jackson, Stevi. 2006. "Gender, Sexuality and Heterosexuality: The Complexity (and Limits) of Heteronormativity." *Feminist Theory* 7 (1): 105–121.

James, Alexandra, and Amy Webster. 2018. "I Never Realised They Were So Different: Understanding the Impact of the Labia Library." Women's Health Victoria Knowledge Paper 2:1–19. https://www.whv.org.au/wp-content/uploads/2018/11/Knowledge-Paper_2018.11.14_Labia-Library_Nov-2018_Fulltext.pdf.

Johansson, Mats, William Bülow, Vilhelm Persson, and Lena Wahlberg. 2023. "Undantag från kravet på etikprövning av humanistisk och samhällsvetenskaplig forskning. En internationell utblick" [Exemptions from the requirement for ethical review of research in the humanities and social sciences: An international perspective]. *Statsvetenskaplig tidskrift* 125 (4): 1143–1168.

John, Nicholas A., and Shira Dvir-Gvirsman. 2015. "'I Don't Like You Any More': Facebook Unfriending by Israelis During the Israel–Gaza Conflict of 2014." *Journal of Communication* 65 (6): 953–974.

Juvonen, Tula. 1993. "Kurittomat kokemukset: Queer studies lesbotutkimuksen haasteena" [Unruly experiences: Queer studies as a challenge to lesbian research]. *Tiede & Edistys* 4:277–283.

Kääriäinen, Juha. 2008. "Why Do the Finns Trust the Police?" *Journal of Scandinavian Studies in Criminology and Crime Prevention* 9 (2): 141–159.

Karppi, Tero. 2018. *Disconnect: Facebook's Affective Bonds.* University of Minnesota Press.

Karppi, Tero, Urs Stäheli, Clara Wieghorst, and Lea P. Zierott. 2021. *Undoing Networks.* Meson Press.

Keilty, Patrick. 2024. "Introduction." In *Queer Data Studies,* edited by Patrick Keilty, 1–16. University of Washington Press.

Kekki, Lasse. 2006. "Pervon puolustus." Kulttuurintutkimus 3:3–18.

Khubchandani, Kareem. 2020. "Intimacies." *Amerasia Journal* 46 (2): 236–237.

Kleinplatz, Peggy J., and Dana A. Ménard. 2020. *Magnificent Sex: Lessons from Extraordinary Lovers.* Routledge.

Klonick, Kate. 2018. "The New Governors: The People, Rules, and Processes Governing Online Speech." *Harvard Law Review* 131:1598–undefined.

Koivunen, Anu, Kaarina Nikunen, Julius Hokkanen, et al. 2024. "Anticipation as Platform Power: The Temporal Structuring of Digital Everyday Life." *Television & New Media* 25 (2): 115–132.

Korn, Jenny Ungbha. 2017. "Expecting Penises in Chatroulette: Race, Gender, and Sexuality in Anonymous Online Spaces." *Popular Communication* 15 (2): 95–109.

Kosseff, Jeff. 2019. *The Twenty-Six Words That Created the Internet.* Cornell University Press.

Krijnen, Tonny, Paul G. Nixon, Michelle D. Ravenscroft, and Cosimo Marco Scarcelli, eds. 2023. *Identities and Intimacies on Social Media: Transnational Perspectives*. Routledge.

Krüger, Steffen, and Ane Charlotte Spilde. 2020. "Judging Books by Their Covers: Tinder Interface, Usage and Sociocultural Implications." *Information, Communication & Society* 23 (10): 1395–1410.

Kulick, Don. 2005. "Four Hundred Thousand Swedish Perverts." *GLQ: A Journal of Lesbian and Gay Studies* 11 (2): 205–235.

Lai, Roxanne, Deborah Elliott, and Hélène Ouellette-Kuntz. 2006. "Attitudes of Research Ethics Committee Members Toward Individuals with Intellectual Disabilities: The Need for More Research." *Journal of Policy and Practice in Intellectual Disabilities* 3:114–118.

Lakoff, George, and Mark Johnson. 1980. *Metaphors We Live By*. Chicago: University of Chicago Press.

Lamont, Michèle, and Virág Molnár. 2002. "The Study of Boundaries in the Social Sciences." *Annual Review of Sociology* 28 (1): 167–195.

Langdridge, Darren, and Trevor Butt. 2004. "A Hermeneutic Phenomenological Investigation of the Construction of Sadomasochistic Identities." *Sexualities* 7 (1): 31–53.

Lasén, Amparo. 2015. "Digital Self-Portraits, Exposure and the Modulation of Intimacy." In *Mobile and Digital Communication: Approaches to Public and Private*, edited by José Ricardo Carvalheiro and Anna Serrano Tellería, 61–78. Livros LabCom.

Lauderdale, Pat. 1976. "Deviance and Moral Boundaries." *American Sociological Review* 41:660–676.

Lehtinen, Vilma. 2007. "Maintaining and Extending Social Networks in IRC-Galleria." Master's thesis, University of Helsinki. https://helda.helsinki.fi/handle/10138/18148.

Light, Ben. 2014. *Disconnecting with Social Networking Sites*. Palgrave.

Light, Ben, and Elija Cassidy. 2014. "Strategies for the Suspension and Prevention of Connection: Rendering Disconnection as Socioeconomic Lubricant with Facebook." *New Media & Society* 16 (7): 1169–1184.

Light, Ben, Jean Burgess, and Stefanie Duguay. 2018. "The Walkthrough Method: An Approach to the Study of Apps." *New Media & Society* 20 (3): 881–990.

Liinason, Mia. 2017. "Sex in/and Sweden: Sexual Rights Discourses and Radical Sexual Politics in Sweden." *Cogent Social Sciences* 3 (1): 1–16.

Lingel, Jessica. 2020. *An Internet for the People: The Politics and Promise of Craigslist*. Princeton University Press.

Lingel, Jessica. 2021. *The Gentrification of the Internet: How to Reclaim Our Digital Freedom*. University of California Press.

Lopes, Gerson Pereira, Fabiene Bernardes Castro Vale, Isabela Vieira, Agnaldo Lopes da Silva Filho, Catarina Abuhid, and Selmo Geber. 2020. "COVID-19 and Sexuality: Reinventing Intimacy." *Archives of Sexual Behavior* 49:2735–2738.

Lundström, Catrin, and Benjamin R. Teitelbaum. 2017. "Nordic Whiteness: An Introduction." *Scandinavian Studies* 89 (2): 151–158.

Lury, Celia, and Sophie Day. 2019. "Algorithmic Personalization as a Mode of Individuation." *Theory, Culture & Society* 36 (2): 17–37. https://doi.org/10.1177/026327 6418818888.

Matias, Nathan J., and Merry Mou. 2018. "CivilServant: Community-Led Experiments in Platform Governance." In *CHI '18: Proceedings of the 2018 CHI Conference on Human Factors in Computing Systems*, 1–13. https://doi.org/10.1145/3173574.3173583.

Maris, Elena, Timothy Libert, and Jennifer R. Henrichsen. 2020. "Tracking Sex: The Implications of Widespread Sexual Data Leakage and Tracking on Porn Websites." *New Media & Society* 22 (11): 2018–2038.

Markham, Annette. 2006. "Method as Ethic, Ethic as Method." *Journal of Information Ethics* 15 (2): 37–55.

Markham, Annette. 2017. "Ethnography in the Digital Internet Era: From Fields to Flows, Descriptions to Interventions." In *The Sage Handbook of Qualitative Research*, edited by Norman K. Denzin and Yvonna S. Lincoln, 650–668. Sage.

Markham, Annette, and Elizabeth Buchanan. 2012. "Ethical Decision-Making and Internet Research: Recommendations from the AoIR Ethics Working Committee (Version 2.0)." https://aoir.org/reports/ethics2.pdf.

Martin, Jarred H. 2023. "Fisting Intimacy: The Sexual Scripting of Intimacy in Gay Men's Anal Fisting." *Psychology & Sexuality* 14 (2): 416–431.

Martins, Eduardo E. B. 2019. "I'm the Operator with My Pocket Vibrator: Collective Intimate Relations on Chaturbate." *Social Media + Society* 5 (4). https://doi.org/10 .1177/2056305119879989.

Marwick, Alice. 2017. "Are There Limits to Online Free Speech?" *Points*, January 7. https://medium.com/datasociety-points/are-there-limits-to-online-free-speech -14dbb7069aec.

Marwick, Alice, and danah boyd. 2011. "I Tweet Honestly, I Tweet Passionately: Twitter Users, Context Collapse, and the Imagined Audience." *New Media & Society* 13:96–113.

Massanari, Adrienne. 2017. "#Gamergate and the Fappening: How Reddit's Algorithm, Governance, and Culture Support Toxic Technocultures." *New Media & Society* 19 (3): 329–346.

McDowell, Zachary, and Katrin Tiidenberg. 2023. "The (Not So) Secret Governors of the Internet: Morality Policing and Platform Politics." *Convergence* 29 (6): 1609–1623.

McGlotten, Shaka. 2013. *Virtual Intimacies: Media, Affect, and Queer Sociality*. New York: State University of New York Press.

McKee, Alan, Brian McNair, and Anne-Frances Watson. 2015. "Sex and the Virtual Suburbs: The *Pornosphere* and Community Standards." In *(Sub)Urban Sexscapes: Geographies and Regulation of the Sex Industry*, edited by Paul Maginn and Christine Steinmetz, 159–174. Routledge.

McRae, Shannon. 1996. "Coming Apart at the Seams: Sex, Text and the Virtual Body." In *Wired Women*, edited by Lynn Cherny and Elizabeth Reba Weise, 242–263. Seal Press.

Mejias, Ulises Ali. 2013. *Off the Network: Disrupting the Digital World*. University of Minnesota Press.

Meta. 2024. "Community Standards: Adult Nudity and Sexual Activity." https:// transparency.meta.com/policies/community-standards/adult-nudity-sexual-activity/.

Metz, Michael, E., and Barry W. McCarthy. 2003. *Coping with Premature Ejaculation: How to Overcome PE, Please Your Partner & Have Great Sex*. New Harbinger Publications.

Miles, Sam. 2017. "Sex in the Digital City: Location-Based Dating Apps and Queer Urban Life." *Gender, Place & Culture* 24 (11): 1595–1610.

Molldrem, Stephen. 2018. "Tumblr's Decision to Deplatform Sex Will Harm Sexually Marginalized People." *Wussy*, December 6. https://www.wussymag.com/all/tumblrs -decision-to-deplatform-sex-will-harm-sexually-marginalized-people.

Monea, Alexander. 2022. *The Digital Closet: How the Internet Became Straight*. MIT Press.

Mowlabocus, Sharif. 2016. "Horny at the Bus Stop, Paranoid in the Cul-de-Sac: Sex, Technology and Public Space." In *The Routledge Research Companion to Geographies of Sex and Sexualities*, edited by Gavin Brown and Kath Browne, 391–398. Routledge.

Muise, Amy. 2011. "Women's Sex Blogs: Challenging Dominant Discourses of Heterosexual Desire." *Feminism & Psychology* 21:411–419.

Musto, Jennifer, Anne E. Fehrenbacher, Heidi Hoefinger, et al. 2021. "Anti-Trafficking in the Time of FOSTA/SESTA: Networked Moral Gentrification and Sexual Humanitarian Creep." *Social Sciences* 10 (2): 58. https://doi.org/10.3390/socsci10020058.

Nagy, Peter, and Gina Neff. 2015. "Imagined Affordance: Reconstructing a Keyword for Communication Theory." *Social Media + Society* 1 (2). https://doi.org/10.1177 /2056305115603385.

Nakamura, Lisa. 2002. *Cybertypes: Race, Ethnicity, and Identity on the Internet*. Routledge.

Nash, Catherine J., and Andrew Gorman-Murray, eds. 2019. *The Geographies of Digital Sexuality*. Palgrave Macmillan.

Nielsen, Silja, Susanna Paasonen, and Sanna Spišák. 2015. "Pervy Role-Play and Such": Girls' Experiences of Sexual Messaging Online." *Sex Education: Sexuality, Society and Learning* 15 (5): 472–485.

Nixon, Paul G., and Isabel K. Düsterhöft, eds. 2017. *Sex in the Digital Age*. Routledge.

Noddings, Nel. 1984. *Caring: A Feminine Approach to Ethics & Moral Education*. University of California Press.

Noddings, Nel. 2003. *Happiness and Education*. Cambridge University Press.

Novack, Stacey. 2017. "Sex Ed in Higher Ed: Should We Say Yes to 'Affirmative Consent?'" *Studies in Gender and Sexuality* 18 (4): 302–312.

Odzer, Cleo. 1997. *Virtual Spaces: Sex and the Cyber Citizen*. Berkley Publishing Group.

Oksanen, Emmi. 2018. "Nytkö sugardaddy-ilmiö yleistyy Suomessa? Suositulla alastonkuvasivustolla saa hakea sponsoria" [Is the sugardaddy phenomenon becoming more common in Finland? Popular nude photo site allows you to look for a sponsor]. *Iltalehti*. October 1. https://www.iltalehti.fi/rakkausjaseksiartikkelit/a/bc07cef1 -6785-4729-b708-8d0b9070b03e.

Paasi, Anssi. 1990. "The Rise and Fall of Finnish Geopolitics." *Political Geography Quarterly* 9 (1): 53–65.

Paasonen, Susanna. 2007. "Online Pornography, Normativity, and the Nordic Context." In *Cyberfeminism in Northern Lights: Digital Media and Gender in a Nordic Context*, edited by Malin Sveningsson-Elm and Jenny Sundén, 51–72. Cambridge Scholars Publishing.

Paasonen, Susanna. 2011. *Carnal Resonance: Affect and Online Pornography*. MIT Press.

Paasonen, Susanna. 2018a. "Infrastructures of Intimacy." In *Mediated Intimacies: Connectivities, Relationalities and Proximities*, edited by Rikke Andreassen, Michael Nebeling Petersen, Katherine Harrison, and Tobias Raun, 103–116. Routledge.

Paasonen, Susanna. 2018b. *Many Splendored Things: Thinking Sex and Play*. Goldsmiths Press.

Paasonen, Susanna. 2021. *Dependent, Distracted, Bored: Affective Formations in Networked Media*. MIT Press.

Paasonen, Susanna. 2022. "Experimentations in Pandemic Boredom." In *Methodologies of Affective Experimentation*, edited by Britta Timm Knudsen, Mads Krogh, and Carsten Stage, 139–157. Palgrave.

Paasonen, Susanna. 2023. "Ambiguous Affect: Excitements That Make the Self." In *The Affect Theory Reader II: Worldings, Tensions, Futures*, edited by Gregory J. Seigworth and Carolyn Pedwell, 85–102. Duke University Press.

Paasonen, Susanna. 2024. "Dick Pics and the Shifty Meanings of Porn." *Porn Studies* 11 (1): 83–90.

Paasonen, Susanna. Forthcoming. "'In a Sea of Dicks': On the Limits of Porn." In *Handbook of Adult Film and Media*, edited by Peter Alilunas, Patrick Keilty, and Darshana Mini. Intellect.

Paasonen, Susanna, and Jenny Sundén. 2024. "Objectionable Nipples: Puritan Data Politics and Sexual Agency in Social Media." In *Queer Data Studies*, edited by Patrick Keilty, 107–127. University of Washington Press.

Paasonen, Susanna, Jenny Sundén, Katrin Tiidenberg, and Maria Vihlman. 2023a. "About Sex, Open-Mindedness and Cinnamon Buns: Exploring Sexual Social Media." *Social Media + Society* 9 (1). https://doi.org/10.1177/20563051221147324.

Paasonen, Susanna, Kylie Jarrett, and Ben Light. 2019. *NSFW: Sex, Humor, and Risk in Social Media*. MIT Press.

Paasonen, Susanna, Vilja Jaaksi, Anu Koivunen, Kaarina Nikunen, Karoliina Talvitie-Lamberg, and Annamari Vänskä. 2023b. "Intimate Infrastructures We Depend Upon: Living with Data." *Media Theory* 7 (2): 285–308.

Pantti, Mervi, Matti Nelimarkka, Kaarina Nikunen, and Gavan Titley. 2019. "The Meanings of Racism: Public Discourses About Racism in Finnish News Media and Online Discussion Forums." *European Journal of Communication* 34 (5): 503–519.

Papacharissi, Zizi. 2015. *Affective Publics: Sentiment, Technology, Politics*. Oxford University Press.

Patterson, Zabet. 2004. "Going On-line: Consuming Pornography in the Digital Era." In *Porn Studies*, edited by Linda Williams, 104–123. Duke University Press.

Paul, Iman, Smaraki Mohanty, and Rumela Sengupta. 2022. "The Role of Social Virtual World in Increasing Psychological Resilience During the On-Going COVID-19 Pandemic." *Computers in Human Behavior* 127:107036.

Payne, Robert. 2015. *The Promiscuity of Network Culture: Queer Theory and Digital Media*. Routledge.

Phillips, Whitney, and Ryan M. Milner. 2021. *You Are Here: A Field Guide for Navigating Polarized Speech, Conspiracy Theories, and Our Polluted Media Landscape*. MIT Press.

Pilipets, Elena, and Susanna Paasonen. 2022. "Nipples, Memes, and Algorithmic Failure: NSFW Critique of Tumblr Censorship." *New Media & Society* 24 (6): 1459–1480.

Pirkkalainen, Päivi, Lena Näre, and Eveliina Lyytinen. 2024. "'I Do Not Trust Any of Them Anymore': Institutional Distrust and Corrective Practices in Pro-Asylum Activism in Finland." *Current Sociology* 72 (3): 562–580.

Plummer, Ken. 1995. *Telling Sexual Stories: Power, Change, and Social Worlds*. Routledge.

Plummer, Ken. 2003. *Intimate Citizenship: Private Decisions and Public Dialogues*. University of Washington Press.

Plummer, Ken. 2007. "The Flows of Boundaries: Gays, Queers and Intimate Citizenship." In *Crime, Social Control and Human Rights: From Moral Panics to States of Denial: Essays in Honour of Stanley Cohen*, edited by David M. Downes, Paul Rock, Christine Chinkin, and Conor Gearty, 379–393. Willan.

Pohtinen, Johanna. 2019. "From Secrecy to Pride: Negotiating the Kink Identity, Normativity, and Stigma." *Ethnologia Fennica* 46:84–108.

Preissle, Judith, and Yuri Han. 2012. "Feminist Research Ethics." In *Handbook of Feminist Research: Theory and Praxis Second Edition*, edited by Sharlene Nagy Hesse-Biber, 583–605. Sage.

Quennerstedt, Ann, Deborah Hartcourt, and Jonathon Sargeant. 2014. "Forskningsetik i forskning som involverar barn" [Research ethics in research involving children]. *Nordic Studies in Education* 34 (2): 77–93.

Race, Kane. 2015. "Speculative Pragmatism and Intimate Arrangements: Online Hook-up Devices in Gay Life." *Culture, Health & Sexuality* 17 (4): 496–511.

Rak, Julie. 2005. "The Digital Queer: Weblogs and Internet Identity." *Biography* 28 (1): 166–182.

Rama, Ilir, Lucia Bainotti, Alessandro Gandini, et al. 2023. "The Platformization of Gender and Sexual Identities: An Algorithmic Analysis of Pornhub." *Porn Studies* 10 (2): 154–173.

Rambukkana, Nathan. 2007. "Taking the Leather Out of Leather Sex: The Internet, Identity, and the Sadomasochistic Public Sphere." In *Queer Online: Media Technology & Sexuality*, edited by Kate O'Riordan and David J. Phillips, 67–80. Peter Lang.

Rambukkana, Nathan, and Keer Wang. 2020. "Digital Intimacies." Oxford Bibliographies. https://www.oxfordbibliographies.com/display/document/obo-9780199756841/obo-9780199756841-0250.xml.

Ranzini, Giulia, and Christoph Lutz. 2017. "Love at First Swipe? Explaining Tinder Self-presentation and Motives." *Mobile Media & Communication* 5 (1): 80–101.

Rawlings, Richard, Genavee Brown, Lynne Coventry, and Lisa Thomas. 2023. "Hook-Up Apps Complicate Visibility for Rural Queer People: Results of a Qualitative

Scoping Study in the United Kingdom." *AoIR Selected Papers of Internet Research.* https://doi.org/10.5210/spir.v2023i0.13482.

Rehberg, Peter. 2019. "More Than Vanilla Sex: Reading Gay Post-Pornography with Affect Theory and Psychoanalysis." *Porn Studies* 6 (1): 114–128.

Reid, Elizabeth. 1996. "Text-Based Virtual Realities: Identity and the Cyborg Body." In *High Noon on the Electronic Frontier: Conceptual Issues in Cyberspace*, edited by Peter Ludlow, 327–345. MIT Press.

Reynolds, Chelsea. 2021. "'Craigslist Is Nothing More Than an Internet Brothel': Sex Work and Sex Trafficking in US Newspaper Coverage of Craigslist Sex Forums." *The Journal of Sex Research* 58 (6): 681–693.

Rice, Ronald E., Sandra K. Evans, Katy E. Pearce, Anu Sivunen, Jessica Vitak, and Jeffrey W. Treem. 2017. "Organizational Media Affordances: Operationalization and Associations with Media Use." *Journal of Communication* 67 (1): 106–130.

Roberts, Sarah T. 2018. "Digital Detritus: 'Error' and the Logic of Opacity in Social Media Content Moderation." *First Monday* 23 (3). https://doi.org/10.5210/fm.v23i3 .8283.

Rodríguez, Juana María. 2011. "Queer Sociality and Other Sexual Fantasies." *GLQ: A Journal of Lesbian and Gay Studies* 17 (2–3): 331–348.

Rojek, Chris. 2016. *Presumed Intimacy: Parasocial Interaction in Media, Society and Celebrity Culture.* Polity.

Rooke, Alison. 2009. "Queer in the Field: On Emotions, Temporality, and Performativity in Ethnography." *Journal of Lesbian Studies* 13:149–160.

Rosa, Sopie K. 2023. *Radical Intimacy.* Pluto Press.

Rossi, Leena-Maija, and Tiia Sudenkaarne. 2021. "'Queer' kotiutui–mitä tapahtui 'pervolle'?" ["Queer" became domesticated: What happened to "pervo"?]. *SQS* 15 (1–2): 66–69.

Ruberg, Bo, and Johanna Brewer. 2022. "Digital Intimacy in Real Time: Live Streaming Gender and Sexuality." *Television & New Media* 23 (5): 443–450.

Rubin, Gayle. 1989. "Thinking Sex." In *Pleasure and Danger: Exploring Female Sexuality*, edited by Carole S. Vance, 267–319. Pandora.

Rudmark, Daniel. 2021. "Designing Platform Emulation." PhD diss., University of Gothenburg. https://www.diva-portal.org/smash/get/diva2:1818125/FULLTEXT01.pdf.

Saarenmaa, Laura. 2010. *Intiimin äänet. Julkisuuskulttuurin muutos suomalaisissa ajanvietelehdissä 1961-1975* [The sounds of intimacy: The transformation of publicity culture in Finnish entertainment magazines 1961–1975]. Tampere University Press.

Saarenmaa, Laura. 2012. "Arka paikka ja naisen intiimein raikkaus: suomalaisen hygieniamainonnan kulttuurihistoriaa" [A sensitive place and the most intimate freshness of a woman: A cultural history of Finnish hygiene advertising]. *Lähikuva* 25 (1): 33–52.

Sadowski, Helga. 2016. "Digital Intimacies: Doing Digital Media Differently." PhD diss., Linköping University. https://www.diva-portal.org/smash/record.jsf?pid=diva2%3A1047582&dswid=9589.

Saketopoulou, Avki. 2023. *Sexuality Beyond Consent: Risk, Race, Traumatophilia.* New York University Press.

Saldana, Johnny. 2009. *The Coding Manual for Qualitative Researchers.* Sage.

Saunders, Rebecca. 2023. "Sex Tech, Sexual Data and Materiality." *Porn Studies* 10 (2): 120–134.

Seering, Joseph, Tony Wang, Jina Yoon, and Geoff Kaufman. 2019. "Moderator Engagement and Community Development in the Age of Algorithms." *New Media & Society* 21 (7): 1417–1443.

Serina, Alison T., Molly Hall, Desiree Ciambrone, and Voon C. Phua. 2013. "Swinging Around Stigma: Gendered Marketing of Swingers' Websites." *Sexuality & Culture* 17:348–359.

Simula, Brandy L. 2019. "Pleasure, Power and Pain: A Review of the Literature on the Experiences of BDSM Participants. *Sociology Compass* 13 (3): e12668.

Smith, Clarissa, Feona Attwood, and Rachel Scott. 2019. *Young People and Digital Intimacies: What Is the Evidence and What Does It Mean? Where Next?* Policy Brief. University of Sunderland. https://sure.sunderland.ac.uk/id/eprint/11405/1/Young%20People%20and%20Digital%20Intimacies%20June%202019%20Final.pdf.

Şot, İrem. 2022. "Fostering Intimacy on TikTok: A Platform That 'Listens' and 'Creates a Safe Space.'" *Media, Culture & Society* 44 (8): 1490–1507.

Spišák, Sanna, Elina Pirjatanniemi, Tommi Paalanen, Susanna Paasonen, and Maria Vihlman. 2021. "Social Networking Sites' Gag Order: Commercial Content Moderation's Adverse Implications for Fundamental Sexual Rights and Wellbeing." *Social Media + Society*, 7 (2). https://doi.org/10.1177/20563051211024962.

Sprott, Richard A., Jules Vivid, Ellora Vilkin, et al. 2021. "A Queer Boundary: How Sex and BDSM Interact for People Who Identify as Kinky." *Sexualities* 24 (5–6): 708–732.

Srnicek, Nick. 2018. *Platform Capitalism.* Polity.

Stardust, Zahra. 2024. *Indie Porn: Revolution, Regulation, and Resistance.* Duke University Press.

Sternberg, Janet. 2012. *Misbehavior in Cyber Places: The Regulation of Online Conduct in Virtual Communities on the Internet.* Rowman & Littlefield.

Strong, Thomas. 2021. "The End of Intimacy." *Cultural Anthropology* 36 (3): 381–390.

Sundén, Jenny. 2003. *Material Virtualities: Approaching Online Textual Embodiment.* Peter Lang.

Sundén, Jenny. 2012. "Desires at Play: On Closeness and Epistemological Uncertainty." *Games and Culture* 7 (2): 164–184.

Sundén, Jenny. 2018. "Queer Disconnections: Affect, Break, and Delay in Digital Connectivity." *Transformations* 31. http://www.transformationsjournal.org/wp-content/uploads/2018/06/Trans31_04_sunden.pdf.

Sundén, Jenny. 2021. "Networked Intimacies: Pandemic Dis/Connections Between Anxiety, Joy, and Laughter." In *Disentangling: The Geographies of Digital Disconnection*, edited by André Jansson and Paul Adams, 273–294. Oxford University Press.

Sundén, Jenny. 2023a. "Digital Kink Obscurity: A Sexual Politics Beyond Visibility and Comprehension." *Sexualities.* https://doi.org/10.1177/13634607221124401.

Sundén, Jenny. 2023b. "Tracing Sexual Otherness in Sweden: The Opacity of Online Kink." *Lambda Nordica* 28 (1): 76–100.

Sundén, Jenny, and Jelisaveta Blagojevic. 2019. "Dis/Connections: Toward an Ontology of Broken Relationality." *Configurations* 27 (1): 37–57.

Sundén, Jenny, and Malin Sveningsson. 2012. *Gender and Sexuality in Online Game Cultures: Passionate Play.* Routledge.

Sundén, Jenny, Susanna Paasonen, Katrin Tiidenberg, and Maria Vihlman. 2024. "Locating Sex: Regional Geographies of Sexual Social Media." *Gender, Place & Culture* 31 (4): 424–440.

Suominen, Jaakko, Sari Östman, Petri Saarikoski, and Riikka Turtiainen. 2013. *Sosiaalisen Median Lyhyt Historia.* Gaudeamus.

Suzor, Nicolas, Tess Van Geelen, and Sarah Myers West. 2018. "Evaluating the Legitimacy of Platform Governance: A Review of Research and a Shared Research Agenda." *International Communication Gazette* 80 (4): 385–400. https://doi.org/10.1177/174804 8518757142.

Taffel, S. 2019. *Digital Media Ecologies: Entanglements of Content, Code and Hardware.* Bloomsbury.

Taylor, T. L. 2018. *Watch Me Play: Twitch and the Rise of Game Live Streaming.* Princeton University Press.Thor Tureby, Malin. 2019. "Makten över kunskapsproduktionen: Den institutionaliserade etikprövningen och humanistisk och kulturvetenskaplig forskning" [The power over knowledge production: Institutionalized ethics review in the humanities and cultural studies]. *Kulturella perspektiv* 28 (1–2): 17–29.

Tiidenberg, Katrin. 2014. "Bringing Sexy Back: Reclaiming the Body Aesthetic Via Self-Shooting." *Cyberpsychology: Journal of Psychosocial Research on Cyberspace* 8 (1). https://doi.org/10.5817/CP2014-1-3.

Tiidenberg, Katrin. 2016. "Boundaries and Conflict in a NSFW Community on Tumblr: The Meanings and Uses of Selfies." *New Media & Society* 18 (8): 1563–1578.

Tiidenberg, Katrin. 2018. "Ethics in Digital Research." In *The Sage Handbook of Qualitative Data Collection*, edited by Uwe Flick, 466–481. Sage.

Tiidenberg, Katrin. 2019. "Research Ethics, Vulnerability, and Trust on the Internet." In *Second International Handbook of Internet Research*, edited by Jeremy Hunsinger, Lisbeth Klastrup, and Matthew Allen, 1–15. Springer.

Tiidenberg, Katrin. 2021. "Sex, Power and Platform Governance." *Porn Studies* 8 (4): 381–393.

Tiidenberg, Katrin, and Edgar Gómez-Cruz. 2015. "Selfies, Image and the Re-making of the Body." *Body and Society* 21 (5): 77–102.

Tiidenberg, Katrin, and Emily van der Nagel. 2020. *Sex and Social Media*. Emerald Publishing.

Tiidenberg, Katrin, Natalie Ann Hendry, and Crystal Abidin. 2021. *Tumblr*. Polity.

Tiidenberg, Katrin, Susanna Paasonen, Jenny Sundén, and Maria Vihlman. 2023. "Vanilla Normies and Fellow Pervs: Boundary Work on Sexual Platforms." *Sexualities*. https://doi.org/10.1177/13634607231215763.

Tilastokeskus. 2023. "Välituloksia eurooppalaisesta vertailututkimuksesta: Naisiin kohdistuva väkivalta hyvin yleistä Suomessa" [Interim results from a European comparative study: Violence against women is very common in Finland]. June 7. https://stat.fi/uutinen/valituloksia-eurooppalaisesta-vertailututkimuksesta-naisiin -kohdistuva-vakivalta-hyvin-yleista-suomessa.

Timmermans, Elisabeth, Anne-Mette Hermans, and Suzanna J. Opree. 2021. "Gone with the Wind: Exploring Mobile Daters' Ghosting Experiences." *Journal of Social and Personal Relationships* 38 (2): 783–801.

Tracy, Sarah J. 2013. *Qualitative Research Methods: Collecting Evidence, Crafting Analysis, Communicating Impact*. Wiley-Blackwell.

Triggs, Anthony Henry, Kristian Møller, and Christina Neumayer. 2021. "Context Collapse and Anonymity Among Queer Reddit Users." *New Media & Society* 23 (1): 5–21.

Tsing, Anna Lowenhaupt. 2005. *Friction: An Ethnography of Global Connection*. Princeton University Press.

U.S. Congress. *Allow States and Victims to Fight Online Sex Trafficking Act of 2017*. Public Law 115–164. U.S. Statutes at Large 132 (2018): 1253–1261.

Valentine, Gill. 2008. "The Ties That Bind: Towards Geographies of Intimacy." *Geography Compass* 2 (6): 2097–2110.

van der Nagel, Emily. 2017. "From Usernames to Profiles: The Development of Pseudonymity in Internet Communications." *Internet Histories* 1 (4): 312–331.

van der Nagel, Emily. 2020. "Verifying Images: Deepfakes, Control, and Consent." *Porn Studies* 7 (4): 424–429. https://doi.org/10.1080/23268743.2020.1741434.

van der Nagel, Emily, and Jordan Frith. 2015. "Anonymity, Pseudonymity, and the Agency of Online Identity: Examining the Social Practices of r/Gonewild." *First Monday* 20 (3). http://dx.doi.org/10.5210/fm.v20i3.5615.

van Dijck, José. 2013. *The Culture of Connectivity: A Critical History of Social Media*. Oxford University Press.

Vihlman, Maria. 2022. "Läheisyyksiä ja etäisyyksiä nautinnon kansallisgalleriassa: Alaston Suomi tilana ja paikkana" [Proximities and distances in the national gallery of pleasure: Naked Finland as space and place]. *Kulttuurintutkimus* 39 (2): 19–34.

Vihlman, Maria. 2023. "'Mä koen että naisellehan se on taivas:' Alastoman Suomen sukupuolittuneet nautinnot" ["I feel that for a woman, it's heaven": The gendered pleasures of Naked Finland]. *Sukupuolentutkimus-Genusforskning* 36 (2): 19–31.

Wakeford, Nina. 1996. "Sexualized Bodies in Cyberspace." In *Beyond the Book: Theory, Culture, and the Politics of Cyberspace*, edited by Warren Chernaik, Marilyn Deegan, and Andrew Gibson, 93–104. Office for Humanities Communication Publications.

Waling, Andrea, and Tinonee Pym. 2019. "'C'mon, No One Wants a Dick Pic': Exploring the Cultural Framings of the 'Dick Pic' in Contemporary Online Publics." *Journal of Gender Studies* 28 (1): 70–85.

Wang, Shuaishuai. 2020. "Live Streaming, Intimate Situations, and the Circulation of Same-Sex Affect: Monetizing Affective Encounters on Blued." *Sexualities* 23 (5–6): 934–950.

Wang, Yidong. 2021. "The Twink Next Door, Who Also Does Porn: Networked Intimacy in Gay Porn Performers' Self-Presentation on Social Media." *Porn Studies* 8 (2): 224–238.

Warner, Michael. 2000. *The Trouble with Normal: Sex, Politics and the Ethics of Queer Life*. Harvard University Press.

Waskul, Dennis D. 2003. *Self-Games and Body-Play: Personhood in Online Chat and Cybersex*. Peter Lang.

Waskul, Denis D., and Justin A. Martin. 2010. "Now the Orgy Is Over." *Symbolic Interaction* 33 (2): 297–318.

Weeks, Jeffrey. 2017. *Sexuality*. 4th ed. Routledge.

Weiner, Joshua J., and Damon Young. 2011. "Introduction: Queer Bonds." *GLQ: A Journal of Lesbian and Gay Studies* 17 (2–3): 223–241.

Weiss, Margot. 2006. "Mainstreaming Kink: The Politics of BDSM Representation in U.S. Popular Media." *Journal of Homosexuality* 50 (2-3): 103–130.

Weiss, Margot. 2011. *Techniques of Pleasure: BDSM and the Circuits of Sexuality*. Duke University Press.

Wignall, Liam. 2022. *Kinky in the Digital Age: Gay Men's Subcultures and Social Identities*. Oxford University Press.

Wilson, Ara. 2016. "The Infrastructure of Intimacy." *Signs: Journal of Women in Culture and Society* 41 (2): 247–280.

Wolf, Tabea, and Lisa Nusser. 2022. "Maintaining Intimacy During the COVID-19 Pandemic." *Applied Cognitive Psychology* 36 (4): 954–961.

Xiao, Sijia, Danaë Metaxa, Joon Sung Park, Karrie Karahalios, and Niloufar Salehi. 2020. "Random, Messy, Funny, Raw: Finstas as Intimate Reconfigurations of Social Media." In *CHI '20: Proceedings of the 2020 CHI Conference on Human Factors in Computing Systems*, 1–13. https://doi.org/10.1145/3313831.3376424.

Yan, Eric G., and Kerim M. Munir. 2004. "Regulatory and Ethical Principles in Research Involving Children and Individuals with Developmental Disabilities." *Ethics & Behavior* 14 (1): 31–49.

Zappavigna, Michele. 2023. "Digital Intimacy and Ambient Embodied Copresence in YouTube Videos: Construing Visual and Aural Perspective in ASMR Role Play Videos." *Visual Communication* 22 (2): 297–321.

Zattoni, Fabio, Murat Gül, Matteo Soligo, et al. 2021. "The Impact of COVID-19 Pandemic on Pornography Habits: A Global Analysis of Google Trends." *International Journal of Impotence Research* 33 (8): 824–831.

Zelizer, Viviana A. 2019. *The Purchase of Intimacy*. Princeton University Press.

Zolides, Andrew. 2021. "Gender Moderation and Moderating Gender: Sexual Content Policies in Twitch's Community Guidelines." *New Media & Society* 23 (10): 2999–3015. https://doi.org/10.1177/1461444820942483.

Index

Publisher contact:
The MIT Press
Massachusetts Institute of Technology
77 Massachusetts Avenue, Cambridge, MA 02139
mitpress.mit.edu

EU Authorised Representative:
Easy Access System Europe, Mustamäe tee 50,
10621 Tallinn, Estonia
gpsr.requests@easproject.com

Printed by Integrated Books International,
United States of America

GENERATION CHIPS

Computer und Fastfood – was unsere Kinder in die Fettsucht treibt!

Edmund Fröhlich, Susanne Finsterer

KRENN

Inhalt

Vorwort

Dicke Kinder, Jugendliche und Erwachsene gab es schon immer – allerdings selten. Das änderte sich meiner Erinnerung nach mit der „Fresswelle" in den fünfziger Jahren: als Zeichen für Wohlstand galten wohlgenährt bis dick, Zigarre, fettes Auto.

Dass dies keine singuläre Erscheinung gewesen ist, zeigt sich heutzutage in wirtschaftlich ebenfalls aufstrebenden Ländern wie z. B. China. Auch hier präsentiert man seinen Wohlstand dadurch, dass man anders und mehr isst, dicker wird, und sich nicht mehr bewegen „muss", das Fahrrad durch das Auto ersetzen „kann".

Das starke Interesse, das heutzutage die Adipositas und Fettsucht hervorruft, entspringt primär keinen gesundheitlichen Überlegungen. Auslöser ist vielmehr, dass abzusehen ist, dass bzw. ab wann die Folgen der Adipositas nicht mehr zu bezahlen sind. Diese umfassen neben den unmittelbaren gesundheitlichen Schäden auch die Kosten der Frühberentung, das Nichtgewähren von Ausbildungsplätzen etc.

Wir Ärzte haben geglaubt, es genügt, einer Epidemie Herr zu werden, indem man die Erkrankten behandelt oder wenigstens versucht, die Folgekrankheiten aufzuhalten bzw. einen für die Ursache verantwortlichen Erreger dingfest zu machen. Dies entspricht unserer Schulung in der westlichen Medizin.

Es mangelt nicht an Initiativen, die irgendwo angesetzt haben, irgendwie gegen die Fett-Sucht vorzugehen – und auch irgendetwas erreicht haben. Sogar Geld lässt sich damit verdienen.

Das drohende epidemische Ausmaß der Adipositas ist aber nur durch eine gemeinsame gesellschaftliche und damit auch politische Anstrengung zu lösen. Ich wünsche diesem Buch, dass es dazu beiträgt.

Dr. med. Hanspeter Goldschmidt

Vorwort der Autoren

Warum wir ein Buch über fettsüchtige Kinder und Jugendliche, die „Generation Chips" schreiben

Fettsucht ist ein weltweites Problem. In den Industrienationen, aber auch in Schwellenländern gibt es immer mehr sogenannte adipöse Kinder und Jugendliche. Wissenschafter unterschiedlicher Fachrichtungen sprechen von einer Epidemie.

Die Verbreitung der Fettsucht führt zu einer enormen Belastung des Gesundheitsbudgets der betroffenen Länder. Insofern sind wir alle von der Krankheit betroffen. Zudem müssen wir aus sozialer Verantwortung erkennen, dass die erkrankten Kinder und Jugendlichen unter ihren Kilos körperlich und seelisch zusammenbrechen. Die meisten kommen aus sozial schwachen Verhältnissen und erhalten von ihren Eltern keine Unterstützung

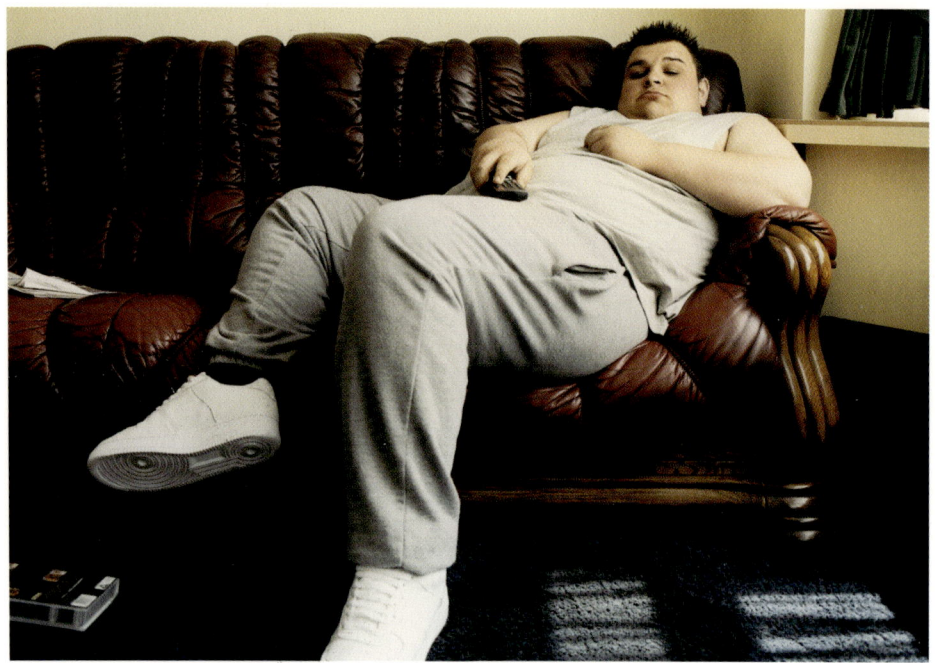

im Kampf gegen den stigmatisierenden körperlichen Zustand. Im Gegenteil: oft sind auch die Eltern fettsüchtig und möchten nicht auch noch mit dem eigenen Problem konfrontiert werden. Da überlässt man die Kids lieber der Spielkonsole oder dem Fernsehprogramm. Die Kinder brauchen unseren Schutz, eine Chance, aus der Krankheit auszubrechen oder sie bei entsprechender Disposition frühzeitig zu bekämpfen.

In einer demokratischen Gesellschaft sollte die Politik dafür sorgen, dass sich alle Kinder positiv entwickeln können. Glücklicherweise ist die Forschung schon sehr weit und hilft, vieles zu verstehen und entsprechend zu reagieren. Kinder- und Jugendärzte, Sportmediziner, Psychologen, Therapeuten in Spezialkliniken und ambulanten Zentren sind gut aufgestellt und möchten lieber prophylaktisch arbeiten, als bedauernswerte Kinder von 150 auf 50 Kilo abzuspecken. Es gibt auch Wachstumsmärkte, die keiner haben möchle.

Was fehlt, ist das Bewusstsein und ein breites Wissen in der Gesellschaft und damit auch in der Politik. Denn ohne die Gesamtverantwortung beginnt die Behandlung erst beim Arzt. Und die Erfahrung zeigt, dass die betroffenen Kinder und Eltern erst in einem fortgeschrittenen und damit teuren Stadium nach Hilfe suchen.

Der Begriff „Generation Chips"

1. KAPITEL

Der Begriff „Generation Chips"

Die **Generation Chips** wird diejenige Generation sein, die kränker sein wird als frühere Generationen und früher sterben wird als ihre Eltern. Wir verwenden den Begriff **Generation Chips** in Anspielung auf die fatale Mischung ungesundes Essen (KartoffelCHIPS) plus Computerspiele (MikroCHIPS). Dabei geht es nicht darum, Kindern beide Genüsse rigoros zu verbieten, sondern einen verantwortlichen Umgang zu lernen. Zu warnen ist aber vor der katastrophalen demografischen Entwicklung, die uns in den nächsten Jahrzehnten angesichts der Anzahl der dicken Kinder, die dann noch dickere Erwachsene werden, bevorsteht.

Gesellschaftspolitisch und zunehmend auch kulturhistorisch werden Generationen über gemeinsame Lebensumstände oder Merkmale definiert (zum Beispiel die Kriegsgeneration, 68er Generation). Begriffe wie Generation Golf oder Generation X sind inzwischen zu viel zitierten Schlagwörtern geworden, die freilich unzulässig verallgemeinern.

Die in den 60er und 70er Jahren Geborenen werden von manchen als Generation X bezeichnet, die sich erstmals ohne Kriegseinwirkung mit weniger ökonomischem Wohlstand begnügen muss als die Elterngenerationen, die aber gleichzeitig für deren ökologische und ökonomische Sünden büßen muss. Etwas später wurde dieselbe Generation in Westdeutschland als Generation Golf charakterisiert, die sich im Vergleich zu ihrer Vorgängergeneration unpolitisch verhält, mode- und markenbewusst ist und materiell weitgehend sorgenfrei sei.

Anfang 2005 war ein Artikel in der „Zeit" mit „Generation Praktikum" überschrieben, als lebensprägendem Trend vieler junger Akademiker, die lediglich ein Praktikum nach dem anderen absolvieren, anstatt eine feste Anstellung zu erhalten.

Die „jüngste" Generation wird gelegentlich als XXL-Generation bezeichnet aufgrund der starken Zunahme übergewichtiger Kinder und Jugendlicher. „XXL" umschreibt dabei jedoch lediglich den äußeren Zustand, in Anlehnung an Kleidungsgrößen. Dagegen bezieht sich der Begriff **Generation Chips** auf die komplexen Ursachen, nämlich mangelnde Bewegung durch zu viel Medienkonsum, einseitige Ernährung sowie die genetisch bedingte Disposition (Software), dass der menschliche Körper Energiereserven speichert für Notzeiten, obwohl in der westlichen Gesellschaft heute überall und ständig Nahrungsmittel zur Verfügung stehen.

Nach Einschätzung der Deutschen Adipositasgesellschaft sollten bereits heute ein Drittel der erwachsenen Bundesbürger aus medizinischen Gründen abnehmen, weil sie deutlich übergewichtig sind. Wie wird sich dieser Anteil erst noch erhöhen, wenn die **Generation Chips**, bei denen bereits grob geschätzt zehn Prozent als adipös gelten, voll im Erwachsenenalter steht? Zurzeit werden schon heute knapp fünf Prozent aller Gesundheitsausgaben laut Deutscher Adipositasgesellschaft für die Behandlung der Adipositas und ihrer Folgen aufgewendet.

Die Betroffenen – es handelt sich um die Altersgruppe der Mitte der 80er Jahre (und später) Geborenen – erkranken früher an den Gelenken (aufgrund der schweren Last), belasten den Kreislauf durch mangelnde Bewegung, haben oft „schon Alterszucker" und leiden unter sozialer Ausgrenzung, die regelmäßig zu den für das Gesundheitssystem sehr kostspieligen psychosomatischen Erkrankungen führen. Zudem haben sie eher Schwierigkeiten beim Lernen und angesichts des unattraktiven Äußeren schlechtere Chancen nicht nur auf dem Arbeitsmarkt.

Wir müssen ein Bewusstsein für diese Kinder und Jugendlichen schaffen, bevor es zu spät ist, denn bereits heute ist jedes fünfte Kind in Deutschland zu dick!

2. KAPITEL

Was ist Fettsucht (Adipositas)?

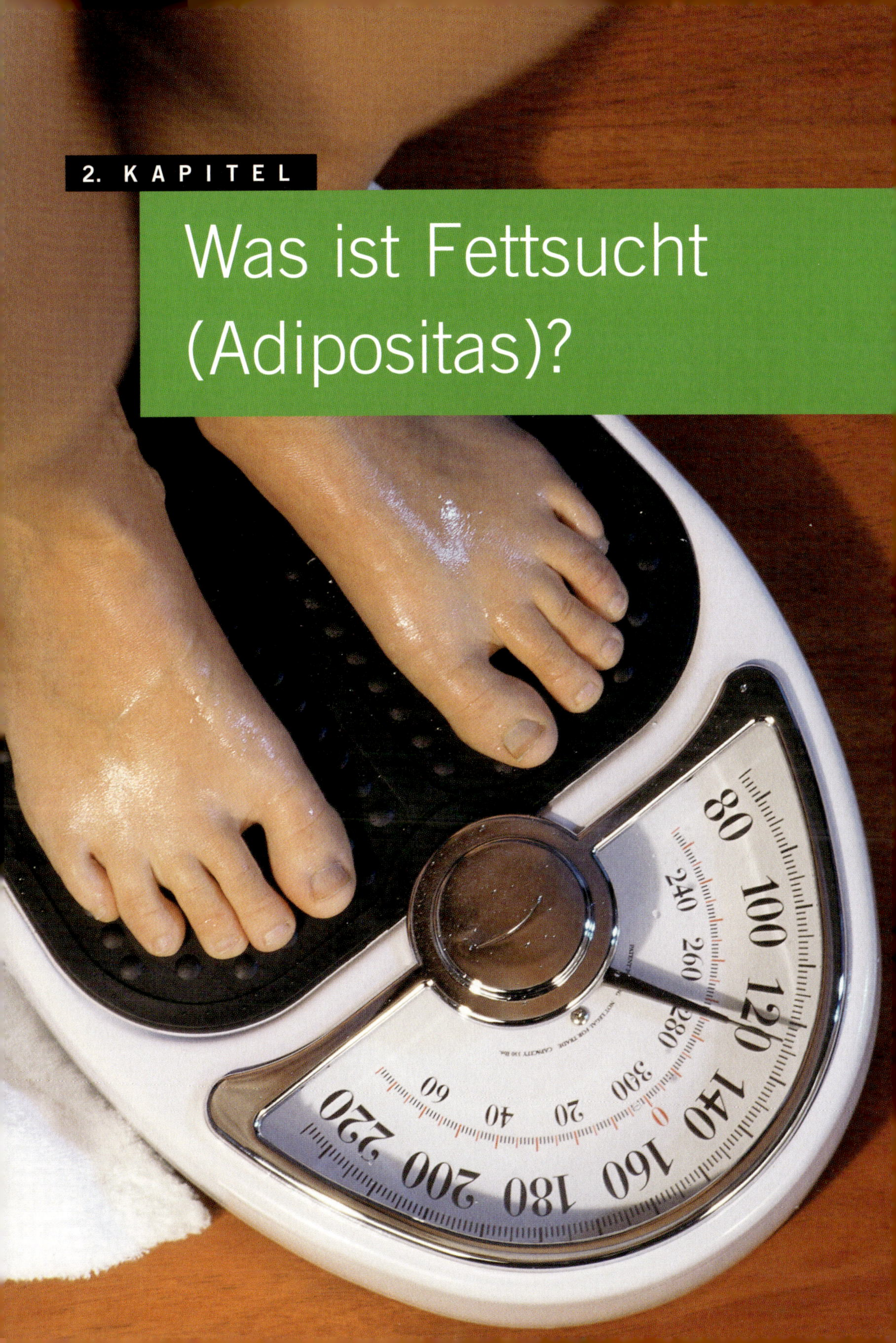

2. KAPITEL

Was ist Fettsucht (Adipositas)?

Fettsucht heißt, dass der Körperfettanteil an der Gesamtkörpermasse pathologisch erhöht ist. Unterschiedliche Ursachen sind es, die zu diesem Krankheitsbild führen. Nur bei ei etwa fünf Prozent der Patienten liegen Stoffwechselerkrankungen vor, Störungen im Hormonhaushalt oder andere körperliche Gegebenheiten, auf die der Lebensstil des Patienten keinen Einfluss hat. Der Körper gibt eine Krankheit vor. Bei etwa 95 Prozent der an Fettsucht erkrankten beruht der erhöhte Fettanteil auf einem falschen Lebensstil – auf einem Leben zwischen Pommes mit Mayo und Computerspielen. Diese Mehrheit der Fettsüchtigen ist unsere Generation Chips.

Kaum eine Krankheit ist so deutlich erkennbar wie Fettsucht. Dennoch müssen Kinder- und Hausärzte klar definieren können, ab welcher

errechneten Größe aus den Faktoren Geschlecht, Alter, Gewicht und Größe die Einstufung „adipös" erfolgt. Der Hintergrund ist von bürokratischer oder – positiver formuliert – organisatorischer Bedeutung, denn mit der Diagnose „Fettsucht" wird eine Reihe von medizinischen Maßnahmen ausgelöst, die von den Krankenkassen und der Rentenversicherung bezahlt werden. Eine Definition der Krankheit erleichtert das Zusammenspiel von Ärzten, Krankenversicherungen, Ernährungsberatern oder Psychologen. Der

Begriff „Fettsucht" stellt keine Stigmatisierung dar, hätte aber sicherlich aufgrund der Grausamkeit der Assoziationen das Potenzial, zum Unwort gewählt zu werden. „Fettsucht" (= Adipositas) beinhaltet zu Recht den Hinweis auf den unbeherrschbaren und vereinnehmenden Faktor der Krankheit, den man von „anderen" Süchten wie Drogensucht, Nikotinsucht, Tablettensucht, Alkoholsucht oder Spielsucht kennt.

Uns erscheint es wichtig, die Fettsucht immer wieder auch als solche beim Namen zu nennen. Eine Beschönigung der Situation durch eine freundliche Wortwahl lenkt ab von der Schwere des Problems und unterstützt ein lethargisches Verhalten aufseiten der Eltern („Nur Babyspeck, wächst sich raus" oder „Das nimmt sie schon wieder ab, wenn sie in die Pubertät kommt und verliebt ist"). Ein dickes fettsüchtiges Kind hat ohne Einwirken eines Haus- oder Kinderarztes eine fast 100%ige Chance, ein fettsüchtiger Erwachsener zu werden. Deswegen: Die Kinder und Jugendlichen sind süchtig. Wir haben es mit einer tief gehenden Sucht zu tun. Wenn ein Kind drogensüchtig ist, raucht, Klebstoffe schnüffelt, gefährdet es seine Gesundheit und seine Lebensperspektive. Wenn es fettsüchtig ist, hat es ein „schweres" Leben und geht einem frühen Tod entgegen.

Der aktuelle Stand der Forschung besagt, dass ein extrem adipöser 20- bis 30-jähriger Mann 13 Jahre seines Lebens an die Krankheit verliert. Frauen im selben Alter blicken beim vergleichbaren Ausmaß der Adipositas auf acht Jahre weniger Lebenserwartung. (Quelle: Österreichischer Adipositasbericht).

Die Weltgesundheitsorganisation hat im Jahr 1997 festgelegt, dass Fettsucht anhand des sogenannten Body-Mass-Index definiert wird:

$$\text{BMI} = \frac{\text{Körpergewicht in kg}}{(\text{Körpergröße in m})^2}$$

Das Normalgewicht liegt laut der Definition der WHO bei Erwachsenen zwischen 18,5 und 24,9 kg/m^2. Von Übergewicht spricht man bei 25,0 bis 29,0 kg/m^2, Fettsucht beginnt bei 30 kg/m^2.

Für Kinder und Jugendliche gelten wegen des Wachstums andere Werte. Die Arbeitsgemeinschaft Adipositas im Kindes- und Jugendalter (AGA) empfiehlt eine Einteilung, die einige deutsche Experten in Gemeinschaftsarbeit erstellt haben. Sie orientieren sich auch am Body-Mass-Index, legen aber für jede Altersstufe einen eigenen Grenzwert fest und unterscheiden auch noch nach Geschlecht. Um die folgende Grafik in einfache Worte zu fassen: Wenn ein zwölfjähriger Junge einen BMI über 22 hat, gehört er zur Gruppe der Übergewichtigen. Hätte er einen BMI von 26 oder mehr, gilt er als adipös, weil er zu den zehn Prozent bzw. drei Prozent Schwerstgewichtigen seiner Altersklasse gehört.

Eine Fettsucht beinhaltet nicht nur, dass das Kind äußerlich entstellt ist. Fettsucht ist viel mehr. Die beiden häufigsten Ursachen für Adipositas – Bewegungsmangel und falsche Ernährung – bewirken in der Regel noch weitere gesundheitliche Beeinträchtigungen und Krankheiten, die zur Einschaltung einer ganzen Reihe von Ärzten führen. Zu den „Risiken und Nebenwirkungen" gehören Bluthochdruck, Herz-Kreislauf-Erkrankungen, Diabetes mellitus, Fettstoffwechselstörungen, chronische Erkrankungen der Verdauungsorgane, Erkrankungen des Bewegungsapparates und Osteoporose.

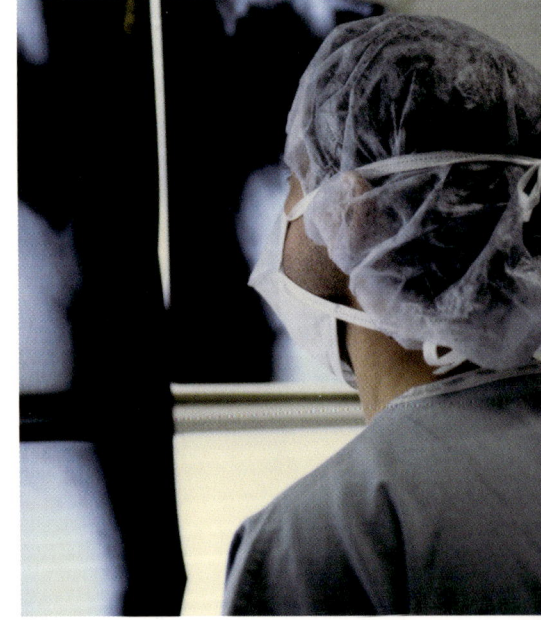

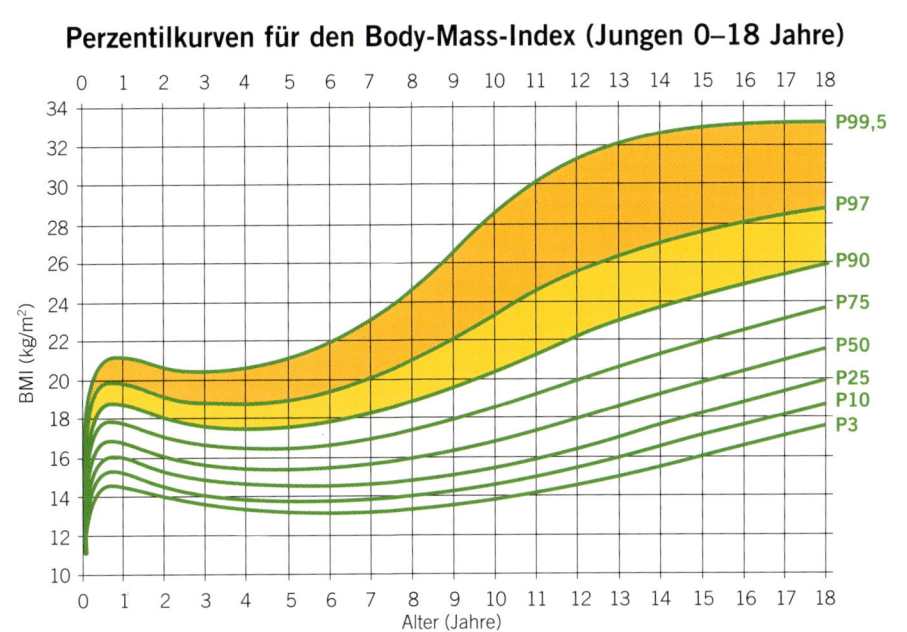

Perzentilkurven für den Body-Mass-Index (Jungen 0–18 Jahre)

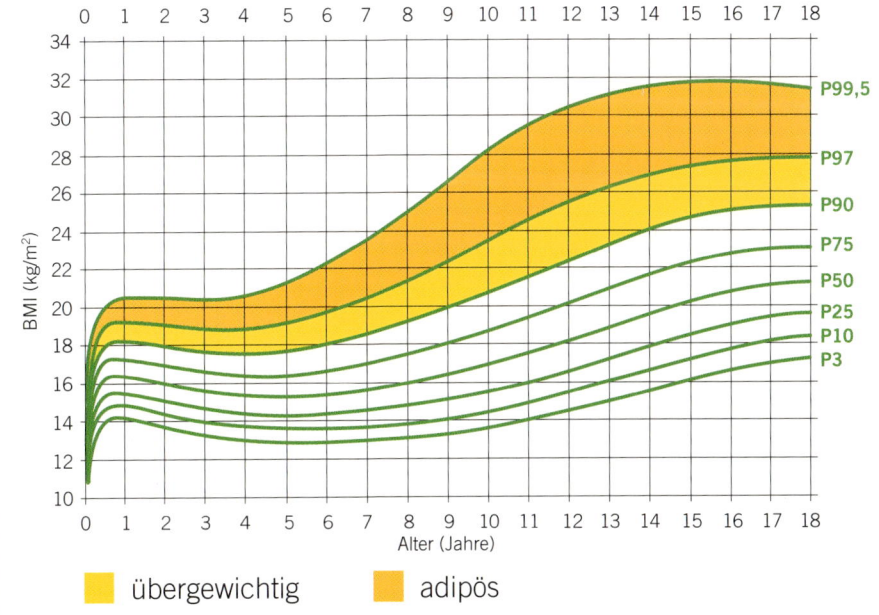

Perzentilkurven für den Body-Mass-Index (Mädchen 0–18 Jahre)

übergewichtig   adipös

(Abb. mit freundlicher Genehmigung von Danone und der AG Adipositas im Kinder- und Jugendalter)

Man kann getrost davon ausgehen, dass ein Kleinkind, das schon als Baby dauernd zuckerhaltige Lebensmittel bekommt, auch Probleme mit den Milchzähnen hat und einer lebenslangen unerwünschten Partnerschaft mit dem Zahnarzt entgegensieht.

Relativ häufig tritt bei starker Adipositas bei dunkelhaarigen Patienten zudem eine grau-braune Verfärbung der Haut mit samtartiger Oberfläche auf. Von diesem Effekt berichtet die Berliner Dermatologin Dr. Brigitte Roesler. Befallen sind meist der Hals- und Nackenbereich sowie Achseln und Leisten.

Viele Begleiterscheinungen sind es, die die Fettsucht mit sich bringt. Ein weites Feld für Kinder- und Hausärzte, die täglich neue Erfahrungen machen können und sich angesichts der Epidemie eigentlich permanent fortbilden müssten. Ein Beispiel: Dr. Hanspeter Goldschmidt, einer der verdientesten Kinderärzte im Bereich der Behandlung von Adipositas, weist außerhalb der üblichen Liste auf ein Risiko hin, das sofort plausibel erscheint und adipöse Mädchen betrifft: „Besonders problematisch ist die Kombination: Adipositas, Nikotinabusus und die Einnahme der Pille. Bei diesen Patientinnen ist das Thromboserisiko sehr stark erhöht." Im Laufe seiner langjährigen Berufserfahrung stellt der Chefarzt der Spessart-Klinik jedoch immer wieder fest, dass seine jungen Patienten vor allem unter dem Spott der Mitschüler leiden und das Unwohlsein im eigenen Körper genauso schwer wiegt wie die auf den Knochen lastenden Pfunde.

Die besondere psychische Belastung ist wissenschaftlich erwiesen. Fettsucht macht unglücklich: Mit zunehmendem BMI nimmt die Lebensqualität ab – so steht es im Österreichischen Adipositasbericht. Adipöse Patienten leiden meist auch unter Depressionen: je größer der Körperumfang, desto umfangreicher die Tristesse.

Weltweite Bedeutung der Fettsucht

3. K A P I T E L

Die weltweite Bedeutung der Fettsucht

Wie entsteht eine Epidemie?

Wenig tröstlich erscheint die Tatsache, dass Fettsucht bei Kindern und Jugendlichen ein internationales Problem darstellt. Experten sprechen von einer epidemischen Ausbreitung – eine Einstufung, die zuletzt im Zusammenhang mit HIV-Infektionen getroffen wurde.

Weltweit sind Schätzungen zufolge eine Milliarde Menschen übergewichtig und etwa 300 Millionen Erdbürger adipös. Die höchsten Prävalenzen weisen Amerika und Europa auf, die niedrigsten Südostasien. In den USA rechnet man mit einem Anteil von 35 Prozent Übergewichtiger in der Gesamtbevölkerung; 31 Prozent sind fettsüchtig. Die niedrigsten Quoten werden in Japan vermutet: 22 Prozent der dort lebenden Menschen sind demnach übergewichtig und nur drei Prozent adipös. (Quelle: Österreichischer Adipositasbericht)

Ein sprunghafter Anstieg ist vor allem in boomenden Städten wie Peking, Shanghai und Hongkong zu verzeichnen. Die Gründe liegen auf der Hand, wenn man die Formel Bewegungsmangel + reichhaltiges Essen = Fettsucht anwendet. Die Veränderung zur mobilen, gut ernährten Gesellschaft erfolgt in den neuen Wirtschaftsmetropolen in wesentlich kürzerer Zeit als in den Zentren der Alten Welt. Die Sozialisation per Computerspiel bei gleichzeitig

veränderter Ernährung bereitet einen fruchtbaren Boden für die Fettsucht. Die Hessische Arbeitsgemeinschaft für Gesundheitserziehung (hage) hat eine Übersicht erstellt, in der sehr lebensnah die Faktoren einer „mangelhaften Ernährung" und „mangelnder Bewegung" dargestellt sind. Einfache Hinweise, die zu Beginn unserer Ausführungen umreißen sollen, warum sich eine Krankheit ohne Bakterien und Viren so schnell verbreiten und eine Wohlstandsgesellschaft gefährlicher als jeder Krankheitserreger sein kann. Man möge in Deutschland nur einmal an die rasante Wandlung vieler Faktoren denken, wie sie in den neuen Bundesländern stattgefunden hat. Innerhalb kurzer Zeit wurde eine ganze Bevölkerung zu Autofahrern und Fastfood-Essern.

Insgesamt geht in den vergangenen zwanzig Jahren der Trend dahin, dass die schweren Kinder eher noch schwerer werden, sich jedoch bei den normalgewichtigen und zarteren Kindern keine Veränderungen feststellen lassen. Das an sich schon schwer zu bekämpfende Problem wird damit auch immer weniger in den Griff zu bekommen sein. Jedes Kilo, das abgenommen werden muss, erfordert ein hohes Maß an individuellem und gesellschaftlichem, finanziellem und therapeutischem Einsatz. Der Sprung von hundert auf sechzig Kilo ist leichter zu vollziehen als der von 140 auf 60. Eine banale, aber wichtige Erkenntnis, die uns im Rahmen politischer Forderungen beziehungsweise der Lösungsmodelle noch beschäftigen wird.

Das sind nur einige der harten Fakten und Hinweise auf die weltweite Bedeutung der Fettsucht. So beschäftigt sich auch die WHO seit über einem Jahrzehnt nicht nur mit Unterernährung, sondern auch mit Übergewicht und Fettsucht. Wie viele Experten haben wohl weltweit schon viel früher auf die anstehende Ausbreitung der Krankheit hingewiesen? Wie viele Anträge sind über Jahre hinweg aus wie vielen Ländern gestellt worden, damit sich ein internationales Gremium des Themas annahm – immer vor dem Hintergrund, dass der Kampf gegen den Hunger in den Entwicklungsländern schon lange – zu Recht – eine starke Lobby gefunden hat und emotional so berührt, dass neben ihm kaum ein weiteres Ernährungsthema Platz zu haben scheint.

Ursachen für Adipositas (Quelle: hage e.V.)

Ernährung:

- *mangelnde Einkaufs- und Ernährungskompetenz*

- *Überangebot von Nahrungs- und Genussmitteln*

- *unverständliche Lebensmittel- kennzeichnung*

- *mangelndes Ernährungswissen*

- *zunehmender Konsum von Fertignahrung*

- *unregelmäßige und ungesunde Essenseinnahme*

- *zunehmender Konsum von Fastfood*

- *zu süße und zu fette Ernährung*

- *fehlendes bzw. ernährungsphysiologisch unausgewogenes Angebot in Kitas, Schulen, Unternehmen u. a. Institutionen*

- *abnehmender Anteil stillender Mütter*

- *hohe psychische Belastungen im Alltag*

Bewegung:

- *Bewegungsinaktivität*

- *fehlende Motivation zur aktiven Bewegung*

- *Zunahme bewegungsarmer Freizeitbeschäftigungen bzw. bewegungseinseitiger Tätigkeiten: Fernsehen, PC, Gameboy*

- *Zunahme der Autonutzung im Arbeitsalltag und in der Freizeit*

- *Abnahme bewegter Lebensräume: Fahrstuhl statt Treppe, Auto statt Fahrrad*

- *fehlende „zeitgemäße" und zielgruppengerechte Bewegungsangebote in Sportvereinen*

4. KAPITEL

Internationale Anerkennung

4. KAPITEL

Internationale Aner-
kennung der Fettsucht
als Krankheit

Das Europaparlament in Brüssel forderte im Januar 2007, Fettleibigkeit als chronische Krankheit anzuerkennen – mit der Konsequenz, deren Behandlung durch die Krankenkassen erstatten zu lassen. Grundlage des Beschlusses war die für die Politiker offenbar erschreckende Erkenntnis, dass jedes vierte Kind in der Staatengemeinschaft zu dick ist. Dass Adipositas keine schicksalhafte Fügung, sondern auch eine hausgemachte Krankheit darstellt, wurde mit begleitenden Vorschlägen gleich mit anerkannt: Softdrinks an Schulen sollten künftig verboten, der kindliche Geschmackssinn durch Kochkurse gefördert, die Kinder in Ernährungskunde geschult und für mehr Bewegung gesorgt werden. Europa hat die Fettsucht als Wohlstandskrankheit anerkannt. (Quelle: Ärzteblatt)

Angesichts der schwierigen finanziellen Situation fast aller Gesundheits- und Sozialsysteme in Europa ist die prinzipielle Frage nach der KRANKHEIT Adipositas von gesundheitspolitischer und volkswirtschaftlicher Bedeutung. Wir werden später noch auf die Tatsache hinweisen, dass die meisten Krankenversicherungen erst dann Maßnahmen bezahlen, wenn das Kind schon massiv übergewichtig ist – ein später Eingriff, der die Behandlung zuerst lange aufschiebt und dann hohe Kosten auslöst.

Die WHO hat die Fettsucht im Jahr 1997 mithilfe des BMI definiert (vgl. Kapitel 2). In Deutschland hat das Bundessozialgericht 2003 die versicherungsrechtliche Pflicht bescheinigt, und im Mai 2006 beschloss der Gemeinsame Bundesausschuss die Integration der Adipositas als chronische Krankheit in Disease-Management-Programme. Der Bundes-ausschuss setzt sich aus Vertretern aller Rentenversicherungsträger, aller Krankenkassen und aller Ärztevereinigungen zusammen. Was dort be-schlossen wird, wirkt für alle Beteiligten verpflichtend. Es werden keine Gesetze wie im Bundestag verabschiedet, aber durch die Zusammen-setzung der so unterschiedlichen Interessengruppen wiegt ein Beschluss schwer, denn es geht immer ums Geld. Die einen wollen so viel wie mög-lich bekommen, die anderen so wenig wie möglich ausgeben. Disease-Management-Programme beinhalten Richtlinien zur Behandlung einer Krankheit, Leitlinien, die die Fachgesellschaften erstellen. Eine klare Orientierung für zum Beispiel den Kinderarzt oder Hausarzt. Was hier steht, wird bezahlt. Insofern ist im Jahr 2006 ein großer Durchbruch bei der Behandlung von Adipositas erfolgt.

Ärzte wissen um solche Richtlinien. Was fehlt, ist die Erkenntnis bei den Betroffenen – bei den Kindern und ihren Eltern. Sie suchen in der Regel erst dann einen Arzt auf, wenn die Kilos schwer auf den Knochen lasten und – ein häufiger Effekt – Schäden und damit Schmerzen in den Knien verursachen. Dann gehen die Leidenden gerne zum Orthopäden, der die Gewichtsabnahme empfiehlt und auch in eine Klinik überweisen kann. Ärztliche Leistung kann aber schon viel früher abgerufen werden – lange vor den körperlichen Schmerzen. Wenn ein Kind oder ein Jugendlicher sein Übergewicht nicht „erträgt", die Seele wegen der Hänseleien in der Schule Schaden genommen hat, ist dies ebenfalls eine Grundlage, auf der der Arzt einen Behandlungsplan erstellen kann. Damit ist der psychische Schmerz dem körperlichen Schmerz gleichgestellt. Die Absonderung vor anderen und die Ablenkung durch Computerspiele, die nicht das Gewicht des Spielers wahrnehmen und bewerten, führt immer weiter in die Isolation und in die Krankheit. Die Anerkennung der Adipositas muss noch mit Leben erfüllt werden, um tatsächlich gesellschaftlich zu wirken. Und: Die Prävention müsste genauso ernsthaft betrieben werden wie die Behandlung (siehe dazu auch Kapitel 14 und 16).

Einige Gesellschaften machen sich hier bereits verdient. Vor allem der Deutschen Adipositas Gesellschaft ist die Aufmerksamkeit für die Adipo-sitas zu verdanken. Die Behandlung im Gemeinsamen Bundesausschuss ist ein junger Erfolg für eine Krankheit mit epidemischer Ausbreitung, die schon früher mehr Beachtung hätte finden können.

Parallel zur Deutschen Adipositas Gesellschaft engagieren sich unter anderem die Deutsche Gesellschaft für Essstörungen (DGESS, gegründet März 2006) und der Bundesfachverband für Essstörungen (BfE) sozusagen auf „einer Ebene darüber" um Interessenvertretung und internationale Vernetzung. In Juni 2006 nahm man an einem Kongress der Internationalen Gesellschaft für Essstörungen teil, der erstmals in seiner Geschichte in Europa stattfand – vorher konferierten die Experten verschiedener Fachrichtungen ausschließlich in Nordamerika. Und: Ähnlich wie bei der Europäischen Ministerkonferenz in Istanbul wurde eine – hier jedoch weltweite (!) – Patientencharta mit dem Titel „Action on Eating Disorders" aufgestellt. Diese enthält unter anderem die folgenden Forderungen:

- **Right to accessible, fully-informed, high quality, fully funded, specialised care** (Das Recht auf eine leicht zugängliche, hochqualifizierte, bezahlte und spezialisierte Behandlung.)

- **Right to respectful, fully-informed, age-appropriate, safe levels of care** (Das Recht auf respektvolle, transparente, altersgemäße und sichere Form der Behandlung.)

Die Forderungen zeigen, dass Essstörungen in der medizinischen Praxis nicht überall mit demselben Respekt begegnet wird wie etwa Beinbrüchen oder Virusgrippen. „Wichtig ist, dass der Arzt den Betroffenen, der Familie oder dem Partner Fragen zur Krankheit und Möglichkeiten der Behandlung erläutert. So erklärt Prof. Dr. Manfred Fichter, Präsident der DGESS die Charta, die eben auch Patienten betrifft, bei denen eine Diskrepanz zwischen der Selbsteinschätzung und der Expertenmeinung gegeben ist. „Es geht um einen wertschätzenden Umgang mit Betroffenen und Angehörigen in der Behandlung."

Fettsucht in Zahlen

5. KAPITEL

Fettsucht in Zahlen

Deutschland, Österreich und die Schweiz

In der Bundesrepublik Deutschland leiden rund sieben Prozent der Kinder und Jugendlichen an Fettsucht; etwa 15 bis 18 Prozent sind übergewichtig – Tendenz steigend. Die Zahlen sind das Ergebnis einer Erhebung aus dem Jahr 2001. Ausgewertet wurden Daten von 128.000 Jugendlichen aus 227 Kinderarztpraxen. Dr. Hanspeter Goldschmidt, Chefarzt der medi-net Spessart-Klinik, kommt am Ende seines Berufslebens auf eine „persönliche", alarmierende Statistik: „Im Vergleich zu vor zehn Jahren haben die Patienten im Durchschnitt heute zehn Kilo mehr Übergewicht." Sein schwerster Patient wog 168 Kilo im Alter von 14 Jahren. Bei der Behandlung nahm er rund 70 Kilo ab.

Schätzungen für Österreich gehen in dieselbe Richtung: Zehn bis 29 Prozent der Jungen sind übergewichtig, fünf bis elf Prozent adipös, bei den Mädchen liegen die Quoten bei sechs bis 42 Prozent Übergewicht und drei bis vier Prozent Fettsucht. Schätzungen zufolge sind in Wien 19,2 Prozent der Kinder zwischen 0,5 und zehn Jahren und 24,9 Prozent der Zehn- bis 17-Jährigen übergewichtig, fünf Prozent der unter Zehnjährigen und 6,1 Prozent der über Zehnjährigen gelten als fettsüchtig. Wie in Deutschland tritt bei Familien mit geringem sozioökonomischem Status Fettsucht häufiger auf.

Für die Schweiz liegen folgende Schätzungen vor: 15 bis 20 Prozent aller Sechs- bis Zwölfjährigen leiden an Übergewicht, acht bis zehn Prozent der Altersgruppe sind adipös. Da es keine staatlichen Erhebungen auf der Basis von Reihenuntersuchungen gibt, macht die einfache Anwendung der Formel „ein Viertel übergewichtig, ein Fünftel fettsüchtig" Sinn.

Als Leser dieses Buches wird Sie diese Zahl vermutlich überraschen, da Sie in Ihrem Umfeld nicht einen derart hohen Anteil an dicken Kindern wahrnehmen. Richtig! Mit dem Lesen dieses Buches zeigen Sie ja auch schon ein gesellschaftliches Interesse und gehören von daher kaum zur sozial schwachen Schicht. Erwiesen ist die Tatsache, dass die fettsüchtigen Kinder in ihrer Mehrheit dieser – gerade für sie – chancenlosen Schicht angehören.

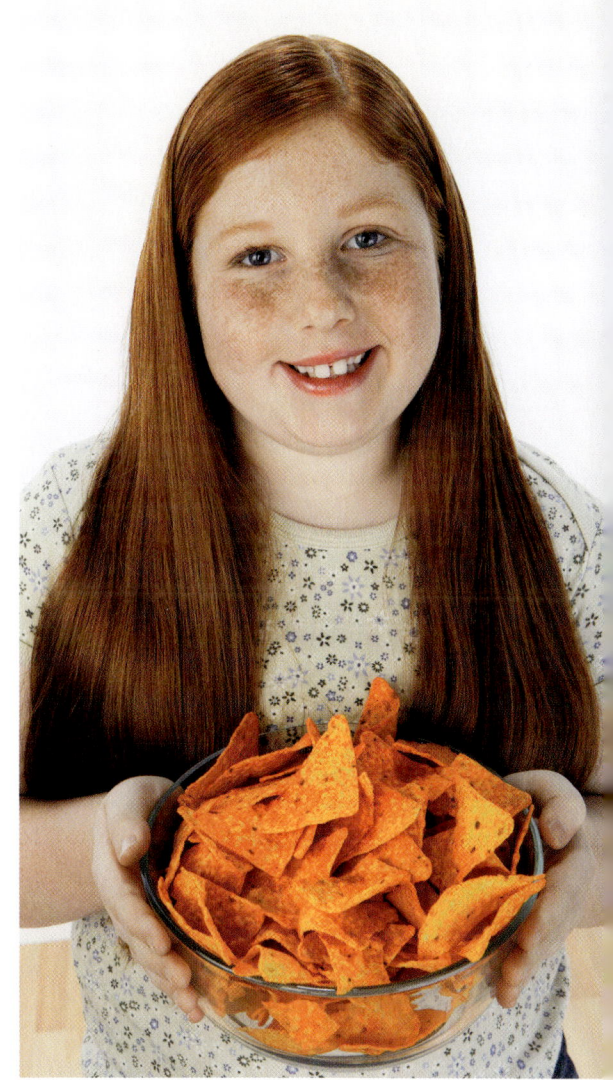

Der Anteil der Jungen überwiegt bei den adipösen Kindern und Jugendlichen; bei den „nur" Übergewichtigen liegen die Mädchen vorne. (Alle Zahlen: Arbeitsgemeinschaft Adipositas). Zudem fällt auf, dass die Krankheit in Deutschland anteilig besonders viele Immigrantenkinder betrifft.

6. KAPITEL

Die Last des Steuerzahlers

6. **K A P I T E L**

Die Last des Steuerzahlers

Gesundheitskosten + Sozialkosten = volkswirtschaftlicher Horror

Gesundheitsbudget

Die Fettsucht (und damit meinen wir die Gesamtbevölkerung) wiegt schwer in den Gesundheitsbudgets der Nationen. Experten gehen davon aus, dass die direkt mit Adipositas assoziierten Gesundheitsausgaben etwa ein bis fünf Prozent des Gesundheitsbudgets ausmachen.

Eine Schätzung besagt, dass in Deutschland im Gesundheitssystem mehr als 70 Milliarden Euro jährlich infolge falscher Ernährung ausgegeben werden müssen – das ist ein Drittel der Gesamtausgaben (Quelle: Bundesministerium für Ernährung, Landwirtschaftsministerium und Verbraucherschutz). Das Bremer Institut für Prävention und Sozialmedizin koordiniert Europas größte Studie zur Adipositas. Der Startschuss fiel am 1. September 2006. Die Ausgangsdaten stellen fest, dass jedes achte Kind in der Bundesrepublik bei der Einschulung Übergewicht aufweist und in der Folge mit Diabetes, Gallensteinen, Nierenschäden, Plattfüßen, einer Fettleber und Gelenkschädigungen leben muss. Die mittelbaren Folgekosten werden dabei auf zwölf Milliarden Euro pro Jahr beziffert.

Zu Österreich liegen uns folgende Zahlen vor: Im Jahr 2004 sollen Übergewicht und Fettsucht zwischen 227,7 und 1.138,5 Millionen Euro verschlungen haben, das entspricht 0,1 bis 0,5 Prozent des Bruttoinlandsprodukts.

Für die konkrete Behandlung der Adipositas werden in der Schweiz nach einer Schätzung zwei bis sieben Prozent der anfallenden Gesundheits-kosten ausgegeben, das sind drei Milliarden Schweizer Franken im Jahr.

Verschiedene Quellen, vage Schätzungen. Was zählt, ist die Erkenntnis, dass es um viel Geld, einen relevanten Anteil der Versichertenbeträge und vor allem um Summen geht, auf die Politiker und Steuer- beziehungsweise Beitragszahler Einfluss nehmen können. Welches Leid ließe sich verhindern, wenn man nur einen winzigen Bruchteil dieser Summe in Vorsorgemaßnah-men investieren würde?

Ausfall am Arbeitsmarkt

Fettsüchtige bekommen kaum Arbeit oder – um es wissenschaftlich auszudrücken: „Adipösen Jugend-lichen ist die Möglichkeit, einen Ausbildungsplatz oder eine Arbeits-stelle zu finden, die ihren Berufs-wünschen entspricht oder zumindest nahe kommt, deutlich erschwert." Zu diesem Ergebnis kommt eine Pilotstudie der medinet Spessart-Klinik (2007).

Die Ursache ist zum einen, dass viele Berufe hohe körperliche und konditionelle Anforderungen stellen, die häufig nicht erfüllt werden kön-nen, und zum anderen, dass die Konkurrenz durch schlanke Be-werber für adipöse Jugendliche oft-mals übermächtig ist. Vorurteile der Arbeitgeber beruhen vor allem in einem vom gängigen Schönheits-ideal stark abweichenden Äußeren, das den Kundenkontakt nicht nur in Dienstleistungsberufen negativ

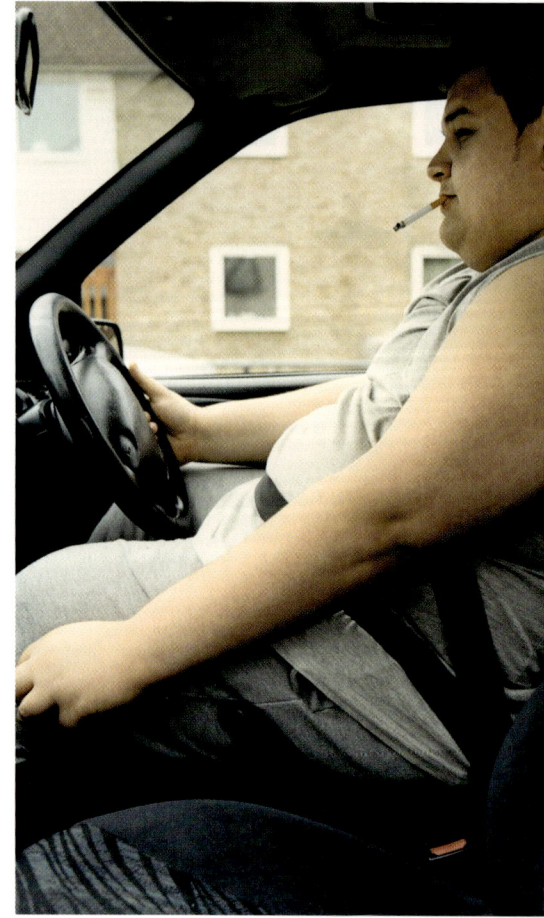

beeinflussen könnte. Empirische Belege dafür gibt es zwar nicht, aber die eigene Lebenserfahrung schließt – da sollte man sich selbst gegenüber ehrlich sein – den Gedanken nicht aus, dass man sich wahrscheinlich auch für einen attraktiveren Bewerber entscheiden würde – in einer Zeit, in der interessante Stellen sowieso schon von sehr vielen Bewerbern nachgefragt werden.

Im Konkreten heißt dies, dass der adipöse Arbeitslose eher in der Fabrik verschwindet und dort sein Selbstbewusstsein wohl auch nicht gefördert wird. Die Krankheit fordert Tribut. Fehlzeiten aufgrund von Diabetes oder zum Beispiel aufgrund der sicheren Gelenkschäden sind die Folge, der Verlust des Arbeitsplatzes nicht weit. Dank Hartz 4 ist man damit angekommen in der Spirale nach unten!

Ergebnis: volkswirtschaftlicher Wahnsinn! Mit dem zynischen Beigeschmack: Fettsüchtige haben eine niedrigere Lebenserwartung als ihre normalgewichtigen Mitmenschen.

Das Ergebnis: die doppelte Last

Erschreckend ist das Zusammentreffen zweier Faktoren: Adipöse Jugendliche bekommen viele Leistungen aus dem Sozialbudget, sind als Einzahler aber zu vernachlässigen. Dies ist nur eine Facette bei der großen volkswirtschaftlichen Betrachtung, denn Gesundheit und Armut korrelieren traditionell auf hohem Niveau. Die Relevanz des Sachverhalts betrifft die fettsüchtigen Kids doppelt. Sie sind an sich schon chronisch krank und gehören mehrheitlich auch noch der sozialen Unterschicht an – heute als „abgehängtes Prekariat" bezeichnet. Der Berliner Public-Health-Forscher Prof. Rolf Rosenbrock stellte bereits im Jahr 2005 als Mitglied des Sachverständigenrats für das Gesundheitswesen in einer Expertise Folgendes fest: „Menschen aus dem untersten Viertel der Gesellschaft, die keine Perspektiven haben und denen es an Bildung, Sozialkontakten und einem ausreichenden Einkommen mangelt, haben ein doppelt so hohes Risiko zu erkranken und sterben im Durchschnitt sieben Jahre früher (Männer zehn, Frauen fünf Jahre) als Menschen aus oberen Gesellschaftsschichten. Zudem manifestieren sich auch chronische Erkrankungen bei diesen Gruppen im Durchschnitt mehrere Jahre früher im Leben." Der mit Armut und Aussichtslosigkeit verbundene Lebensstil führe zu schlechter Ernährung, Bewegungsmangel und Kontaktarmut und damit langfristig zu chronischen Krankheiten und Depression.

Politische Maßnahmen müssen also auch diejenigen erreichen, die sich von der Gesellschaft schon ausgeschlossen fühlen: Adipöse Hauptschulabgänger, denen neben einer besseren Zukunft die Chance projiziert werden muss, den Übergang von der Schule ins ersehnte und (oftmals nicht realisierbare) Wunsch-Berufsleben für die eigene Gesundheit zu nutzen. Die Chance besteht in diesem Lebensabschnitt im Wegfall eines herablassenden, verspottenden Umfelds in der Schule. Eine Befreiung, die die vielleicht letzte Möglichkeit darstellt, die Kids doch noch einmal zu erreichen. In unser aller volkswirtschaftlichen Sinne.

Wie entsteht Fettsucht?

7. KAPITEL

Wie entsteht Fettsucht?

 Falsche Ernährung – die KartoffelCHIPS

Indem man mehr isst, als man verbraucht, und nach heutigem Forschungsstand auch aufgrund einer bestimmten genetischen Disposition. Das klingt so einfach, dass man sich fragt, warum es noch keinen wirklichen Durchbruch in der Behandlung der Krankheit gibt. Zum einen steigt die Anzahl der Betroffenen ständig an – obwohl die heutige Elterngeneration genau um den Zusammenhang von Essen und Gewichtszunahme weiß –, zum anderen erreichen die meisten Patienten trotz vieler Maßnahmen eher eine Linderung als eine Heilung.

Die Ursachen für Fettsucht scheinen demnach tatsächlich sehr komplex zu sein. Vielleicht gibt es ja auch *die eine* Ursache – und alles, was wir jetzt auflisten, sind Minifaktoren in einem Ganzen. Das ungünstige Zusammenspiel basiert nach dem aktuellen Erklärungsmodell auf einem Zusammenhang, den wir alle in der Schule gelernt haben oder lernen: Der Körper benötigt Energie, um sich selbst zu erhalten und um sich zu bewegen. Je mehr er sich bewegt, desto mehr Energie benötigt er. Je weniger er sich bewegt, desto weniger Energie braucht er. Die Energie wird mit Kilokalorien und Kilojoules beziffert – zwei in der Bevölkerung so geläufige Maßeinheiten wie Meter oder Liter.

Wir sind alle aufgewachsen mit Kalorientabellen und Richtwerten für den täglichen Kalorienverbrauch, an denen sich in den letzten Jahrzehnten nichts geändert hat.

Solche Tabellen sind sicherlich hilfreich für eine Einordnung von „zu viel", könnten heute aber um die neuere Erkenntnis ergänzt werden, dass Fett ein wichtiger Maßstab diätischen Denkens ist. Im Durchschnitt gilt: Wer mehr als 60 g Fett am Tag zu sich nimmt, nimmt zu. Wer abnehmen muss, sollte nach heutigem Kenntnisstand nicht mehr als 30 g Fett am Tag zu sich nehmen!*

Es ergibt sich also eine einfache Rechnung, die jedem übergewichtigen Kind nahe legt, ab sofort mit mehr Bewegung viel zu verbrauchen und dabei nach vernünftigen Diätgrundsätzen zu essen. Das schaffen wir dauerhaft kaum als Erwachsene. Die Sehnsucht nach Essen stellt offensichtlich ein übergroßes Verlangen nach etwas dar, dessen Erfüllung eine besondere oder zumindest eine schnelle Befriedigung verschafft – auch jenseits aller Vernunft.

Ein Trieb, der angeboren ist? Dagegen spricht, dass eine entsprechende Erziehung zum Beispiel Heißhunger auf Süßes verhindert (vgl. dazu „Kinder lernen essen", Krenn Verlag) und jeder, der sich ein bisschen mit der menschlichen Seele beschäftigt, weiß, dass Magersucht – als eine andere

Aktivität	kcal pro 10 min
Fernsehen	13
Computerspielen	17
Gehen (langsam, 4 km/h)	31
Laufen (9 km/h)	100
Radfahren (10 km/h)	28
Radfahren (15 km/h)	78
Brustschwimmen (50 m/min)	113
Kraulen (50 m/min)	140
Fußball	93
Tennis oder Badminton	80
Tanzen	70
Tischtennis	53
Eislaufen (12 km/h)	47
Skifahren (Abfahrt)	87
Handball, Basketball, Ringen, Judo oder Trampolin	140
Fechten	100

Quelle: Trainermanual – „Leichter, aktiver, gesünder – interdisziplinäres Konzept für Schulung übergewichtiger oder adipöser Kinder und Jugendlicher", aid

* Die Ernährungsberater der Spessart-Klinik arbeiten fast ausschließlich auf der Grundlage von Fettberechnungen (siehe dazu Serviceteil).

Ausprägung einer Essstörung – häufig auf eine gestörte Eltern-Kind-Beziehung zurückzuführen ist. Die empirischen Werte über die Bulimie oder Anorexie legen nahe, dass seelisches Leid auch eine Fettsucht auslösen oder begünstigen könnte.

Ein Experte, der wegen der Oberflächlichkeit seiner Aussage nicht benannt sein wollte, berichtete aus seinem beruflichen Alltag von dem Eindruck, dass Kinder, die keine elterliche Liebe verspüren, dazu tendieren, zu hungern oder in sich hineinzustopfen. Die Frage, was den

Ausschlag für die jeweilige Richtung geben könnte, beantwortete er folgendermaßen: „Die Intelligenten hungern, die weniger Intelligenten fressen." Harte Worte, die an den Volksmund „Intelligenz säuft, Dummheit frisst" erinnern. Die Erfahrungen aller befragten Experten deuten jedoch tatsächlich darauf hin, dass mit dem Essen versucht wird, ein seelisches Defizit zumindest kurzfristig zu kompensieren.

Ein weiterer Aspekt: Internationale Vergleiche zeigen, dass Fettsucht ein Wohlstandsproblem ist, das uns erst in dem Moment erreicht, in dem wir es mit einem doch eigentlich wunderbaren Überangebot an Lebensmitteln zu tun haben, aus dem man ja auch bewusst auswählen könnte. Entscheidend erscheint hierbei die Frage, warum manche trotz besseren Wissens das Bedürfnis haben, mehr beziehungsweise fetter oder süßer zu essen als andere. An dieser Stelle findet wahrscheinlich die Verknüpfung mit der psychischen und/oder genetisch bedingten Komponente statt (zur genetischen kommen wir noch). Es geht also nicht um Befriedigung von Hunger, sondern um einen sehr ausgeprägten Appetit und ein anders als bei Normalgewichtigen empfundenes Sättigungsgefühl.

Parallel dazu stellen wir unterschiedlich ausgeprägte Verhaltensmuster bezüglich des Bedürfnisses nach Bewegung fest.

Bevor wir im Folgenden konkreter werden, sei vorab zusammenfassend festgestellt:

Grundsätzlich gibt es nach aktuellem Wissensstand tatsächlich eine genetische Komponente, die kein einfaches Vererbungsmuster bedingt, sich aber in Zusammenhang mit Umweltfaktoren einstellt. Das heißt, dass äußere Faktoren (Nahrungsaufnahme/Bewegung) bestimmte Gene „einschalten" oder „ausschalten". Manche nehmen mit Sport sehr schnell ab, manche weniger, manche nehmen in einer Woche All-inclusive-Urlaub mit fünfmal Buffet am Tag mehr zu als andere mit der identen Nahrungsaufnahme. Dies bedeutet nicht, dass das 100-Kilo-Kind, das träge ist und langsam abnimmt, in eine Resignation entlassen werden darf. Im Gegenteil: Das von Natur und Umwelt benachteiligte Kind muss mehr gefördert werden als andere. Es wird sein Leben lang die Schlanken beneiden, die scheinbar alles essen können – und genau auf diese Situation hin muss es gecoacht werden.

Die Welt der Gene ist ungerecht und die Umwelt, in die man hineingeboren wird, auch. Die Shell Jugendstudie 2006 zeigt, wie das gesamte Gesundheitsverhalten nach sozialer Schicht der Jugendlichen variiert. So sind gesundheitsgefährdende Verhaltensweisen wie ungesunde Ernährung (täglicher Konsum von Cola/Limonade: 46 Prozent in der Unterschicht zu zwölf Prozent in der Oberschicht), mangelnde körperliche Bewegung (38 zu 14 Prozent) und regelmäßiges Zigarettenrauchen (37 zu 15 Prozent) unter Jugendlichen aus der Unterschicht weit häufiger verbreitet als in mittleren und oberen Sozialschichten.

Die mutmaßlichen Gründe werden in der Studie wie folgt benannt: „Durch eine Zunahme kultureller und sozialer Spannungsfelder, einer ständig wachsenden Zahl Jugendlicher, die von relativer Armut betroffen sind, und gleichzeitig hohen gesellschaftlichen Erwartungen an Leistung und Qualifikationen wächst der Druck auf Jugendliche. Es ist zu erwarten, dass sich drohende Arbeitslosigkeit, eingeschränkte Bildungschancen und schlechte Wohnverhältnisse weiterhin negativ auf die Gesundheit und das Gesundheitsverhalten Jugendlicher auswirken werden."

⊙ Hunger, Sättigung und Appetit

Weltweit gibt es über zwei Millionen Lebensmittel, Hunderttausende von Mahlzeiten nimmt jeder im Laufe seines Lebens zu sich. Statistiker könnten gigantische Zahlen über die Variationsmöglichkeiten der Nahrungsaufnahme jedes Einzelnen berechnen. Ein weites Feld für universitäre Studien.

Auch die Gefühle „Hunger" und „Sättigung" sind noch nicht hundertprozentig erforscht. Deswegen seien an dieser Stelle aktuelle Erkenntnisse erwähnt, die für den Umgang mit der Krankheit Fettsucht notwendig sind.

Hunger ist ein Urinstinkt und entsteht durch ein Zusammenspiel zwischen dem Hypothalamus (= ein kleiner Bereich im Zwischenhirn) und Leber, Magen und Darm. Die Organe verfügen über eine Art Sensoren, die vor allem Informationen über den Status des Zuckerspiegels weitergeben. Beteiligt sind sowohl beim subjektiven Empfinden von Hunger als auch Sättigung Hormone, sodass es im Rahmen des gesamten, komplexen biochemischen Vorgangs gut vorstellbar ist, dass Medikamente den Kreislauf regulieren oder steuern könnten. Klar ist auch, dass – vereinfacht ausgedrückt – Pillen zum Abnehmen durch Reduktion des Hungeroder Steigerung des Sättigungsgefühls auf einen großen Nachfragermarkt treffen und möglicherweise Fettsüchtigen helfen würden.

Bezüglich unserer Problemstellung „Behandlung von Fettsucht" muss erst einmal festgestellt werden, dass unser Hungerempfinden körperlichen

Prozessen unterliegt, die in der Geschichte der Menschheit lange Zeit vorherrschend waren. Eine andere Entwicklung sei an dieser Stelle vergleichend erwähnt: die abnehmende Beweglichkeit in den letzten Jahrzehnten. Auch unser Hungergefühl ist nach aktuellem Forschungsstand eigentlich nicht zeitgemäß, denn Nahrung gibt es in den westlichen Industrienationen in mehr als ausreichender Form. Die fettsüchtigen Kinder, Jugendlichen und Erwachsenen scheinen also auch an einer Irritation im System der Steuerung von Hunger und Sättigung zu leiden. Möglicherweise verspüren sie keine Sättigung oder erleben ein besonders befriedigtes Gefühl bei Übersättigung.

Ein in der Menschheitsgeschichte eher neues Thema ist der „Appetit", der auf die Befriedigung eines besonderen Geschmacksbedürfnisses ausgerichtet ist. Was einmal als besonders geschmackvoll empfunden wurde, ruft immer wieder das Bedürfnis nach positivem Wiedererleben hervor – auch unabhängig von einem aktuell wahrgenommenen Geruch oder Anblick. Wird versucht, mit einem vergleichsweise gesünderen Lebensmittel darauf zu reagieren, wird die bereits vom Gehirn suggerierte Wunschbefriedigung nicht ausgelöst – eine gefährliche Situation, die schon gesunde Erwachsene jede Disziplin bei der Diät vergessen lässt. Deswegen wird die Befriedigung des individuellen Appetits und das Auslösen des damit verbundenen Glücksgefühls von Ernährungsexperten sehr ernst genommen.

Horst Bauer, Diätassistent in der Spessart-Klinik und renommierter Experte in der Behandlung der Adipositas bei Kindern und Jugendlichen, rührt für seine kleinen Patienten zusätzlich zu einem sehr fettarmen Burger eine Mayonnaise-ähnliche – fettarme – Sauce, die er auch noch ähnlich wie in Burger-Restaurants verpackt. Mit diesem Doppeltrick, begehrte Mahlzeiten so zu verpacken wie das fette Original, erreicht er die höchste Stufe an Bedürfnisbefriedigung bei gleichzeitigem Einhalten der diätischen Grundsätze. Deswegen gibt es bei ihm auch Pizza mit fettarmer Salami für die Kinder, die ein starkes Bedürfnis nach dem Geschmack von pikanter Wurst verspüren. Eine sehr banale, aber im Umgang mit den Betroffenen extrem wertvolle Erkenntnis, denn Fettsucht ist zwar ein gesellschaftliches, aber im Kern individuelles Problem.

Der Appetit auf Süßes ist offensichtlich auch anerzogen. Viele Eltern wissen dies und handeln entsprechend, versuchen also, das Baby oder Kleinkind außerhalb der natürlichen Fruchtsüße nicht noch zusätzlich mit Zucker oder Zuckeraustauschstoffen zu versorgen. Bei Fertigprodukten muss auch aus diesem Grund auf die Altersangabe geachtet werden.

⊙ Getränke

Obstsäfte, Milchmixgetränke, heiße Schokoladen. Gesund im Vergleich zu Cola und zuckerhaltigen Limonaden diverser Geschmacksrichtungen, aber „optimal wäre es natürlich, wenn die Kinder so viel Wasser wie möglich trinken würden – einfaches Mineralwasser", so Ernährungsberater Horst Bauer, der darauf verweist, dass man die Kids auch an den Geschmack des Wassers von klein auf gewöhnen muss.

Studien ergaben, dass Kinder, die häufig Süßgetränke konsumieren, zu einem höheren Körpergewicht neigen. Im Forschungsinstitut für Kinderernährung (FKE) in Dortmund wird daher ausdrücklich vor Cola und Limonade gewarnt. Hauptsächlich sei der hohe Zuckergehalt für die Gewichtszunahme verantwortlich, wobei bei den sogenannten Softdrinks auch noch ein geringeres Sättigungsgefühl hinzukomme. Als gesund gelten Wasser und Früchtetees, weniger empfehlenswert sind Säfte (hoher Kaloriengehalt!). Auf Softdrinks sollten Kinder zwar nicht ganz verzichten, auch das FKE empfiehlt, keine Verbote auszusprechen, um die Genüsse nicht noch reizvoller zu gestalten.

In den USA werden in Grund- und mittleren Schulen künftig ausschließlich ungesüßter Saft, Magermilch und Wasser angeboten. Die Getränkeautomaten werden von den großen Firmen wie Coca Cola, Schweppers PLC und PepsiCo Inc nur noch mit kalorienarmen Getränken bestückt. Das Ergebnis eines Abkommens mit der Industrie, nachdem Studien ergaben, dass Softdrinks zur übermäßigen Kalorienaufnahme der Kinder beitragen und damit die Verbreitung von Übergewicht und Fettsucht begünstigen. Interessanterweise ist die Amerikanische Herzgesellschaft (American Heart Association, AHA) sehr engagiert, wenn es um solche Maßnahmen zur frühen Prophylaxe des Übergewichts geht.

Der Einfluss der MikroCHIPS
Computerspiele und immer noch der Fernseher

Die Kids träumen vom USB-Stick hinter dem Ohr, mit dem sie ihre MP3s direkt in die grauen Zellen laden können, und sie sehen die Welt beim Internetspiel „Second Life" als virtuelle Realität. Sie machen ihr eigenes Fernsehen auf YouTube. Sie bloggen, sie chatten, sie rippen. Neue Welten erschließen sich den Kindern und Jugendlichen. Bunt und spannend und durch die eigene Anonymisierung alles schöner und attraktiver machend – auch die eigene Person. Ideale Fluchtwelten ergänzen das Fernsehen und gestalten den Aufenthalt zuhause oder bei Freunden extrem unterhaltsam. Diese Entwicklung kann man nicht mehr rückgängig machen, und sie wird den Medienkonsum der Kinder eher noch steigern als vermindern.

Computerspiele, die Nutzung des Internets oder Fernsehen – drei völlig unterschiedliche Freizeitbeschäftigungen, die für uns, die wir uns mit Adipositas beschäftigen, jedoch dieselbe Dimension haben: Sie halten die Kinder von Bewegung ab. Vielleicht liegt in der Nutzung von Blogs oder Mails aber auch die Chance, von ärztlicher und therapeutischer Seite mit den Kids direkt zu kommunizieren. In der medinet Spessart-Klinik gibt es erste positive Erfahrungen – dazu später mehr.

Erfahrungswerte gibt es viele, wenn es um Medienkonsum geht. Deutliche Hinweise auf eine umfassende Veränderung der Gesellschaft. Aktuell und aufschlussreich ist eine Studie des Kriminologischen Forschungsinstituts Niedersachen, in der 2005 unter anderem der Zusammenhang zwischen Mediennutzung und schulischer Leistung untersucht wurde. In aufwändigen und fein differenzierten Untersuchungen (u. a. auch aufgeschlüsselt nach Städten und Regionen) wurden 17.000 Neuntklässler und 6000 Viertklässler unter Einbindung ihrer Lehrer befragt. Die Ergebnisse sind deutlich relevant (siehe nächste Seite).

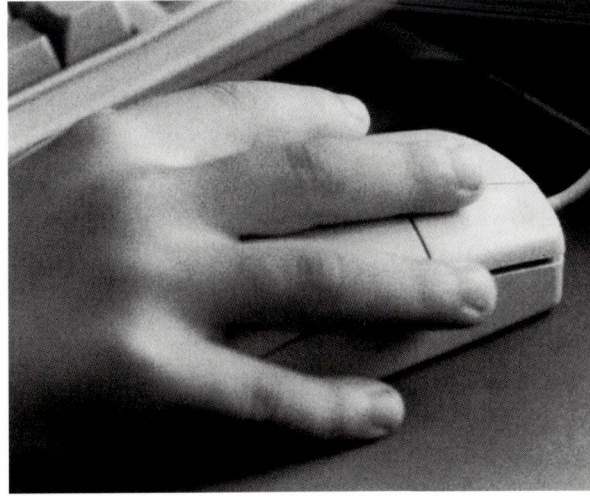

● Seit 1991 gibt es in Deutschland eine stetig anwachsende Leistungsdivergenz zwischen Jungen und Mädchen, die negativ mit der Mediennutzung korreliert. Mehr Mädchen als Jungen legen seitdem ihr Abitur ab. Die Entwicklung deutet sich dabei schon Jahre früher an, wenn zum Ende der vierten Klasse die von den Lehrern ausgesprochenen Schullaufbahnempfehlungen für die Mädchen positiver ausfallen als für die Jungen. Bereits zu diesem Zeitpunkt verfügen 38 Prozent der Jungen über eine eigene Spielkonsole; bei den Mädchen sind es nur 15,6 Prozent.

● Kinder aus Familien mit niedrigem Bildungsniveau sind erheblich stärker mit Bildschirmgeräten ausgestattet als Kinder aus Familien mit höherem Bildungsniveau. Zudem ergibt das niedrige Bildungsniveau zusammen mit einer „sozialen Randlage" eine hohe Wahrscheinlichkeit, dass Kinder schon früh eine eigene Spielkonsole besitzen. Dieses Aufeinandertreffen mehrerer Faktoren führt zu solch alarmierenden Einzelergebnissen wie dem folgenden: Die zehnjährigen Jungen aus Dortmund (aus einem Umfeld mit niedrigerem Bildungsniveau) verbringen pro Jahr mehr Zeit vor dem Fernseher und ihrer Playstation als im Schulunterricht (1430 Stunden zu 1140 Stunden). Türkische 10-jährige Dortmunder Jungen verbringen im Durchschnitt 4,2 Stunden täglich vor der Playstation.

● Die Qualität der mit der Playstation genutzten Spiele korreliert ebenso mit dem Bildungshintergrund. 50 Prozent aller Jungen im Alter von zehn Jahren haben schon Computerspiele genutzt, die von den Obersten Landesjugendbehörden wegen ihres Inhaltes mit brutalen Gewaltszenen erst ab 16 Jahren freigegeben sind. Bei den 14-/15-Jährigen spielen ein Drittel häufig solche Spiele. Bei Letztgenannten fällt zudem auf, dass diejenigen aus Elternhäusern mit geringem Bildungshintergrund besonders viel Zeit mit Fernsehen und Computerspielen verbringen und dann auch noch häufig mit Spielen, die als entwicklungsbeeinträchtigend bewertet werden. Bei einem hohen formalen Bildungshintergrund der Eltern kommen die Kinder auf durchschnittlich 77 Minuten Fernseh- und Computerspielkonsum täglich, bei den Kindern mit einem niedrigen formalen Bildungshintergrund der Eltern sind es im Schnitt 175 Minuten.

Nur einige Zahlen aus einer um-
fangreichen Studie, nach deren Ab-
schluss Prof. Dr. Christian Pfeiffer
von einer „Medienverwahrlosung"
spricht und davon, dass es noch
nicht gelungen ist, den Medienkon-
sum positiv zu kanalisieren. Als
Beispiel für eine glückliche Entwicklung nennt er Neuseeland, wo sich
Lehrer und Schüler auch per Mail
austauschen und der Computer als
hilfreiches, attraktives Tool beim Unterricht genutzt wird.

Dass die totale Mediennutzung eine Erhöhung des Körperfettanteils und
damit Übergewicht bewirkt, ist im Übrigen auch wissenschaftlich anerkannt.
Verschiedene Untersuchungen aus den vergangenen Jahren belegen sowohl
für das Fernsehen als auch für Computerspiele deutliche negative Zusammenhänge (vgl. Marshall, Biddle, Gorely, Cameron und Murdey, 2004).
Forschungen aus dem Bereich der Neurobiologie bestätigen den Verdacht,
dass Bewegung in direktem Zusammenhang mit der Entwicklung der
Intelligenz steht. Der Sport begünstigt dabei die Hirndurchblutung und die
Vernetzung der Hirnzellen untereinander, wobei den frühen Lebensjahren
eine besondere Bedeutung zukommt (Kubesch, 2002).

Um es mit Prof. Berthold Koletzko, Vorsitzender der Stiftung Kindergesundheit, zu sagen: „Es gibt immer mehr Nachweise dafür, dass der Anteil des Fernsehens mit Bewegungsmangel, Übergewicht, Verhaltensauffälligkeiten, Leseschwäche und mit einer insgesamt verzögerten mentalen Entwicklung korreliert."

Fernsehen ist nicht gleich Fernsehen, Internetnutzung nicht gleich Internetnutzung und Computerspiel nicht gleich Computerspiel. Der Familienabend mit Spielfilm nach dem gemeinsamen Nachmittag am Tennis- oder Golfplatz macht Kinder nicht dick. Auch nicht drei Stunden alleiniges Chatten im eigenen Zimmer, nachdem der fast erwachsene Jugendliche den Nachmittag mit Freunden in frischer Luft verbracht hat. Das Zusammenwirken von Alter, Menge und den Umständen „machen es" aus. Und natürlich die Eltern. Da geht es nicht nur um harte mediale Konkurrenz, sondern auch um willkommene Freizeit und Freiheit für Eltern. Wie viele geben hinter vorgehaltener Hand zu, „dass man mal ganz froh ist, das Kind mit dem Fernseher ruhig zu stellen"?

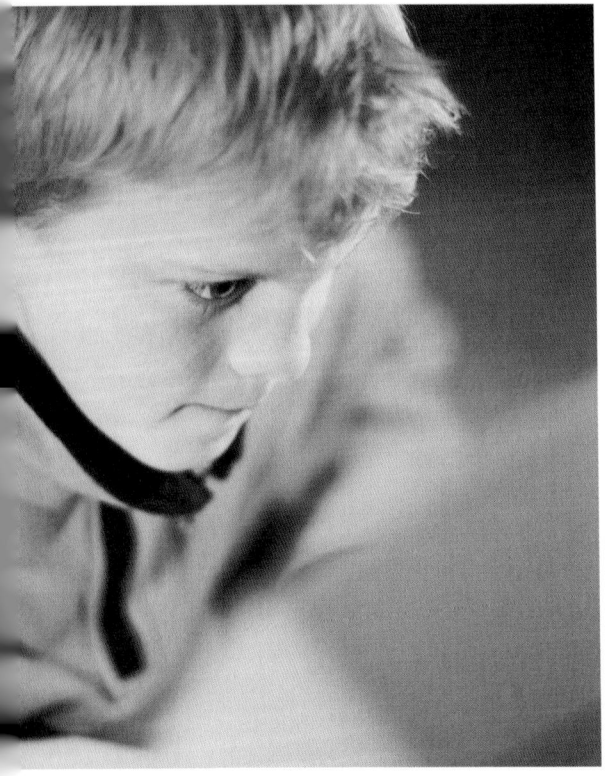

Die Macht von Fernsehen und Computerspielen wird sich nicht eindämmen lassen. Die Deutsche Gesellschaft für Ernährung fokussiert auf einen Medienkonsum, der mit „nebenbei verzehrten Snacks" einhergehe und Werbung im TV beinhalte, die ein „sehr schlechtes Bild der Ernährung" vorführe. Die Vorbildfunktion ist wichtig. Eine Gesellschaft, in der sich in den westlichen Demokratien die meisten ein Leben ohne Handy und Mails nicht mehr vorstellen könnten, in der der „leere Akku" schon innere Unruhe auslöst wie früher die vergessene Uhr, bringt auch Medienkinder hervor – im positiven wie im negativen Sinne. Für die einen hält sie neue kreative Spielfelder vor, für die anderen einen Lebensinhalt, den die Eltern nicht teilen und auch nicht teilen möchten. Ein gefährlicher Rausch, der für viele den Traum einer neuen Freiheit realisiert, Unabhängigkeit von Bürozeiten, schnelle Kommunikation. Für die anderen eine Droge mit der Anmutung von Klebstoffschnüffeln. Eine stupide Ablenkung, ruhig gestellt, die Eltern nicht anstrengend, pflegeleicht. Eine sehr demokratische Angelegenheit. Wir alle bezahlen die Dealer. Manche bezahlen auch noch mit einer hässlichen Krankheit und alle zusammen dann wieder in Form von Krankenkassenbeiträgen.

Wir stehen ohnmächtig vor dem Sog einer Spirale, die manche auch noch bis hin zu Amokläufen und realisierten Gewaltfantasien nach unten zieht. Die Lösung einer Vereinnahmung wird nicht in deren Verdammung oder Verdrängung liegen, die die Medien für Kinder nur noch interessanter gestalten. Im Mittelpunkt einer gesellschaftlichen Lösung müssen attraktive und kostenfreie oder günstige Alternativen stehen, mit denen die Bedürfnisse von Kindern und Eltern befriedigt und mediale Reize ergänzt werden. Lösungen, die ALLE erreichen und nicht wieder nur diejenigen, die schon per Erziehung vielseitig interessiert sind, deren Mediennutzung positiv zu bewerten ist.

Die medinet Spessart-Klinik hat auf ihrer Website ein Forum eingerichtet, in denen sich ehemalige Patienten und interessierte Jugendliche über ihre Erfahrungen austauschen. Der Anstieg der Nutzung ist relevant: Waren es im September 2005 gerade zwölf Einträge, so wurden allein im Januar 2007 schon 448 Beiträge verfasst und das Forum cirka 6000-mal besucht. Derzeit wird ein Programm zur Optimierung der Nachhaltigkeit von Rehabilitation erstellt, das die Kinder da abholen soll, wo sie sich souverän und wohlfühlen: die internetgestützte Kommunikation zur Nachbetreuung – ein kleines Experiment, aber möglicherweise hilfreich in der nachhaltigen Behandlung der adipösen Kinder und Jugendlichen.

Adipositas und Sport

8. KAPITEL

Adipositas
und Sport

Ein echtes Problem-Verhältnis

„Mach doch einfach Sport." Einer der zynischsten Ratschläge, den man dicken Kindern und Jugendlichen geben kann. Sport ist für sie nicht „einfach". Das Fett bremst, erschwert den Einstieg, das Kind weiß um seine unästhetische Unbeweglichkeit – Unsicherheit und körperliche Defizite machen schon Treppensteigen zum Kraftakt. Das Schlimmste: Sport macht keinen Spaß – im Übrigen nicht einmal vielen Normalgewichtigen, die sich allerdings wenigstens noch zu sonntäglichen Wanderungen oder Gartenarbeit motivieren.

Eine Zehnjahresstudie in der Durchschnittsbevölkerung macht indirekt deutlich, wie schwierig es sein muss, fettsüchtige Kids zum Sport zu bewegen, wenn dies nicht einmal im Sinne der Erhaltung der Gesundheit bei mittleren Gewichtsklassen möglich zu sein scheint. 15.200 Menschen wurden von Forschern der Uniklinik Heidelberg beobachtet und dabei wurde festgestellt, dass zwischen 1992 und 2001 die Anzahl derjenigen, die regelmäßig sportlich aktiv sind, anstieg – unter den Frauen stärker als unter den Männern. Der Anteil der Männer, die *nie* Sport machen, stieg dabei ebenfalls auffallend an (von 39 Prozent 1996 auf 45 Prozent 2001). Insgesamt kam die Studie zu dem Ergebnis, dass vor allem junge, ledige, gut ausgebildete Menschen deutscher Nationalität in Deutschland sportlich aktiv sind. Das erstaunt nicht, da in den großen Städten viele Fitnessketten immer mehr Filialen eröffnen, um ein offensichtlich zahlungskräftiges Publikum zu bedienen. Dort sieht man auch Menschen, die einige Kilos abnehmen wollen, aber sicherlich nicht „unsere" adipösen Kinder, denn diese müssten ab dem zweiten Gerät schon wegen Überforderung passen. Die gesellschaftliche Schere geht also auch beim Sport auseinander – nicht überraschend, aber hier kann der Staat eingreifen, denn uns geht es um Kinder und Jugendliche, die immerhin mit dem Schulsport erreicht werden können. Der muss allerdings anders aussehen als bisher.

„Als Letzter gewählt, als Erster ausgeschieden und dann auch noch ausgelacht und verspottet", beschreibt Christian Eilers den harten Alltag der betroffenen Kinder und Jugendlichen im heutigen Schulsport. Der Sportwissenschafter und Therapeut in der Spessart-Klinik berichtet von einem „Teufelskreislauf", bei dem die beschriebenen Erlebnisse „Angst- und Schamgefühle" hervorrufen, die in der Konsequenz dazu führten, dass sportliche Aktivität und körperliche Anstrengung gemieden würden, um eben diesen Situationen aus dem Weg zu gehen. „Der Kreis schließt sich, denn infolge der Inaktivität ist die Energiebilanz positiv, das Leistungsvermögen nimmt weiter ab und das Körpergewicht zu."

Von außen lassen sich die sportlichen Aktivitäten also unterstützen, die Last der langwierigen und mühevollen Behandlung kann dem Kind jedoch niemand abnehmen. Höchstens optimieren. Die Spessart-Klinik verfügt durch glückliche historische Umstände über ein Schwimmbad in halbolympischem Ausmaß – ein Segen für die dort behandelten adipösen Jugendlichen, denn das Wasser nimmt beim Sport zumindest etwas von der körperlichen Last. Doch: würden sich diese Kinder auch zuhause im Badeanzug oder Shorts zeigen wollen? Schwimmunterricht ist schon für viele „normale" Kinder im Rahmen des Schulsports ein Grauen. Die Medien – und sie formen das ästhetische Bewusstsein der Kinder – zeigen auch den Kleinen, was Schönheit ist. Casting-Shows für Kinder machen nur den schönen und selbstbewussten Kids Spaß. Den von den Eltern und gemessen am aktuellen Schönheitsideal von Natur aus Vernachlässigten wird hingegen ein Ideal präsentiert, das nicht zu erreichen ist und zur Frustration führt.

Jede sportliche Therapie ist erst einmal darauf ausgelegt, die kleinen Patienten von extern vorgegebenen Maßstäben zu befreien. „Eine dauerhafte Verhaltensänderung im Sinne einer erhöhten körperlichen Aktivität ist nur dann möglich, wenn das Sichbewegen um seiner selbst willen geschieht, die Kinder das Erlebnis haben: Ich fühle mich gut, wenn ich Sport treibe, lautet der Ansatz von Christian Eilers. Intrinsische Motivation nennt man diesen Ansatz. Eine extrinsische Motivation („Ich muss das machen, weil der Arzt gesagt hat, dass ich abnehmen soll.") führt erfahrungsgemäß nicht zum anhaltenden Erfolg.

Die Sportmedizin verfügt über Testmöglichkeiten, die an die RTL-Erfolgsserie „Dr. House" mit ihrem Feuerwerk an Knowhow und Hightech-Untersuchungen erinnern. Prof. Dr. med. Klaus Jung von der Universität Mainz verweist auf Tests zur Bestimmung der aerob-anaeroben Schwelle, Laktatmessungen, Spirometrie, Lungenfunktionstests, Körperzusammensetzungsanalysen, tragbare metabolische Aktivitäts- und Lebensstilmonitorings und und und. Sensationelle Möglichkeiten zur Auswertung der körperlichen Gegebenheiten. Vorlagen für eine Leistungsoptimierung, die wir aus dem Spitzensport kennen. Computergestützte Möglichkeiten, die – vielleicht ein Glücksfall – die Generation Chips nachhaltig faszinieren und beim Einstieg ins Abspecken motivieren können. Ausgewertete Testreihen mögen vor allem die Jungs durchhalten lassen. Sehr hilfreich! Schöner wäre es, wenn all diese Untersuchungen

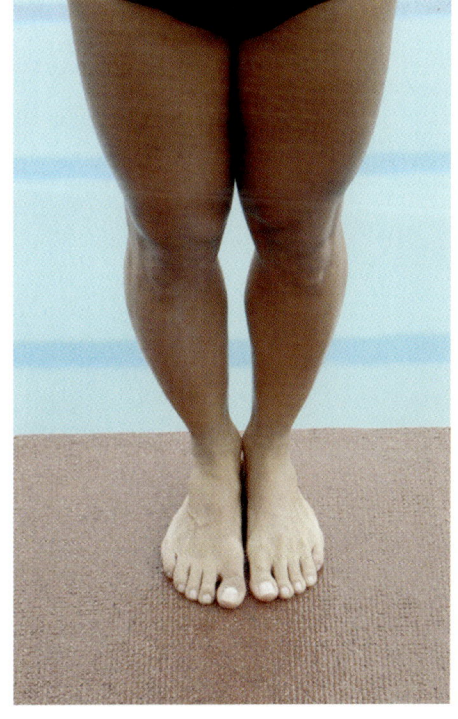

schon bei einem niedrigeren Übergewicht eingesetzt werden könnten. Hohe Ausgaben, aber im Endeffekt wesentlich günstiger als die lebenslange Behandlung nach Erreichen der Adipositas. „Wenn wir die Kinder und Jugendlichen bereits bei einem Übergewicht von maximal zehn Prozent erreichen könnten, wäre mir um die Finanzierung unseres Gesundheitswesens in den nächsten fünfzig Jahren nicht bange", so Prof. Dr. med. Claus Jung.

Die Berliner Sportlehrerin Anja Blaku hat die Trainingsmethode Medical Move („Medical Move – Gesundheitstraining der Zukunft", siehe Inhaltsverzeichnis) erfunden, die durch effektivste Gestaltung der einzelnen Trainingselemente zu einem raschen Fortschritt bei Kondition und Beweglichkeit führt. Die schnelle Befriedigung der Motivation ist wichtig für Menschen, die nicht von sich aus zum Sport drängen, sondern herangeführt werden möchten oder müssen. Das gilt für Junge und Alte nach längerer Krankheit, für Ältere, die ihre Beweglichkeit konsolidieren müssen, und eben auch für Übergewichtige.

Bei fettsüchtigen Kindern und Jugendlichen betont Sportlehrerin Blaku ähnlich wie Christian Eilers noch eine zusätzliche Behandlungsdimension: „Am wichtigsten ist es, dass man den Kindern Vertrauen in sich selbst gibt." Für das Training bedeutet dies, dass die Kids von jedem Leistungsdruck befreit werden müssen. Die Vorgabe, eine Übung in einer bestimmten Anzahl zu wiederholen, sei schon kontraproduktiv, da das Kind sofort ein negatives Erfolgserlebnis verspürt und schneller aufgibt. Anja Blaku empfiehlt für den Einstieg Übungen im Sitzen. Hierbei wird den Kindern ein Teil der körperlichen Last genommen. Ideal sind Bewegungen mit leichten Bällen jeder Größe. Gewichtige Medizinbälle sind ungeeignet, da deren Bewegung viel Kraft

Anja Blaku in ihrem Studio
www.medicalmove.de

erfordert und damit die Atemtechnik der fetten Kinder überfordert. Prinzipiell müsse man bei den kleinen Patienten immer mit einer eingeschränkten Belastungsfähigkeit der Atmung rechnen – ein Fakt, der zum Beispiel auch Übungen im Liegen ausschließt, da in dieser Position Atmen im wahrsten Sinne des Wortes schwerer fällt als im Sitzen.

Alles was dem Körper einen Teil des Gewichts nimmt, ist bei der Konzeption von sportlichen Übungen hilfreich. Alternativ zum Sitzen können Bewegungen einbezogen werden, bei denen der Rücken an eine Wand gelehnt wird. Auch dies führt zu einer realen und gefühlten Erleichterung. Wer an Schwimmen denkt (s. o.), liegt natürlich richtig, denn was sollte den Körper umfangreicher erleichtern als der Auftrieb. Bedenken muss man dabei jedoch, dass auch das Abschwimmen ganzer Bahnen viel „Luft" erfordert und sich die Kinder im Beisein Schlanker schämen. Damit hat sich die Motivation nach der Premiere im Schwimmbad schon wieder erledigt. Sinn macht da schon eher Aquarobic – und bitte unter Ausschluss der Öffentlichkeit.

Insofern fordern auch wir aus Sicht der adipösen Kinder und Jugendlichen ein Umdenken bei der Struktur des Schulsports. Mit Blick auf die adipösen Schüler behaupten wir, dass diesen Kindern geholfen wäre, wenn sie klassenübergreifend extra unterrichtet werden würden. Das macht pro Schule zwei Sportlehrerstunden zusätzlich pro Woche. Die Kosten dafür sind nichts im Vergleich zum volkswirtschaftlichen Aufwand, der durch die unzulängliche Behandlung der kranken Kinder und Jugendlichen entsteht – vom verhinderten persönlichen Leid ganz zu schweigen.

Würden wir uns in einem prosperierenden Land wie Dubai befinden, könnten wir ein visionäres Konzept vorschlagen, bei dem alle fettsüchtigen Kinder einer Stadt – aufgeteilt nach Altersgruppen – Aquarobicstunden in Schwimmbädern verordnet bekommen, die zum Trainingszeitpunkt für andere geschlossen werden. Selbst wenn man „nur" Unterricht anbietet und die fettsüchtigen Kinder dabei unter sich bleiben, wird in Deutschland und Österreich keiner kommen. Warum? Die Kinder müssten für sich alleine lange Wege in Kauf nehmen, um überhaupt erst zum Schwimmbad zu gelangen. Bei allem Bedürfnis, den Kindern zu helfen, darf nie die Tatsache außer Acht gelassen werden, dass wir es in der Regel mit uninteressierten und unmotivierten Eltern zu tun haben, die ihr Kind eher nicht zum Schwimmbad bringen oder begleiten würden. Die vielleicht effektivste aller Möglichkeiten wird es deswegen realistischerweise nur im Rahmen von stationären Heilverfahren geben können, bei denen sich engagierte Therapeuten anstelle der Eltern um die Kleinen kümmern. Die zweiteffektivste sind Schulsport und Adipositaszentren, die wenigstens schon von Eltern adipöser Kinder aufgesucht werden, die das Problem aktiv angehen – weil sie es selbst möchten oder von anderen dazu gezwungen werden.

Eine weitere wunderbare „Trainingsmethode" außerhalb von Aquarobic lässt sich bedauerlicherweise nicht als Ansatz ohne staatliches Umfeld konzipieren – aufgrund der vernachlässigenden Haltung vieler Eltern von adipösen Kindern muss die Möglichkeit, mit sehr feinfühligen Übungen bereits Babys zu lustvollen Bewegungen hinzuführen, in politische Maßnahmen eingebettet werden: Anja Blaku weist auf motivierende Reize durch die Eltern hin, die das Kleinkind dazu bringen, Muskeln aufzubauen. Das kann zum Beispiel eine Rassel sein, die dem Baby nicht direkt in die Hand gedrückt,

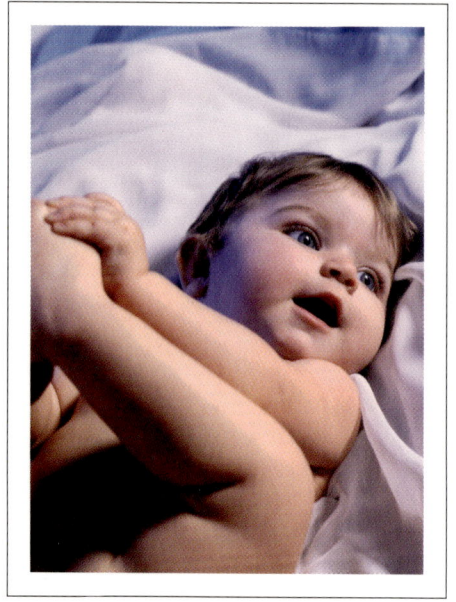

sondern ein kleines Stückchen weiter vor die Finger gehalten wird, damit es sich danach strecken muss. Auch könnte man das Baby beim Aufrichten mit weniger Kraft unterstützen, damit sich der kleine Körper selbst schon so weit einbringen kann, wie es ihm möglich ist. Eine Prophylaxe-Methodik, die nach einer hohen Sensibilität aufseiten der Eltern verlangt und nicht zu erwarten ist, wenn man zu einer Bindung vielleicht gar nicht erst fähig ist und sich für das Kind sowieso nur marginal interessiert. Eine traurige Tatsache, die immer wieder daran erinnert, dass die politische Beschäftigung mit dem Thema im Rahmen staatlicher Möglichkeiten stattfinden muss. Auf verantwortungsvolle Liebe der Eltern kann in Zusammenhang mit adipösen Kindern nicht unreflektiert gebaut werden.

Die sportlichen, gut gebildeten Eltern nehmen das Kind mit zum Tennisplatz und zum Skifahren, die Kinder der sozialen Unterschicht sind längst schon zu übergewichtig, wenn man mit den Nachbarkindern im Hof Fußball spielen könnte.

Wird Fettsucht vererbt?

9. KAPITEL

Wird Fettsucht vererbt?

Ja, zum Teil, wie bereits erwähnt: An dieser Stelle wird nun der genetische Zusammenhang ausgeführt.

Etwa 80 Prozent der übergewichtigen Kinder haben ein übergewichtiges Elternteil, 25 Prozent der übergewichtigen Kinder haben zwei übergewichtige Elternteile (Quelle: Goldschmidt). Das heißt noch nicht, dass Fettsucht vererbt wird, denn die Kinder übernehmen das Ess- und Ernährungsverhalten der Eltern – Fettsucht könnte also anerzogen sein.

Aus der Genforschung weiß man, dass 250 Gene gesteigerte Nahrungsaufnahme, verminderten Energieumsatz und Energiespeicherung verantworten. Ein solch komplexes System legt den Verdacht nahe, dass es schlanke Menschen mit „günstigen" Genen und dicke Menschen mit „ungünstigen" Genen gibt. Nicht umsonst gibt es Models – und dafür verbürgen wir uns aufgrund persönlicher Erfahrung –, die dauerhaft üppig essen ohne zuzunehmen.

Der aktuelle Stand der Forschung besagt, dass die Fähigkeit, das Gewicht regulieren zu können, angeboren ist. Zu diesem Ergebnis kommen wissenschaftliche Studien aus der Familien- und Zwillingsforschung. Festgestellt wurde zum Beispiel, dass adoptierte Kinder im Körpergewicht (in Relation zu Alter und Größe) ihren leiblichen Eltern ähneln, nicht jedoch den Adoptiveltern. Untersuchungen mit eineiigen und zweieiigen Zwillingen, die getrennt beziehungsweise gemeinsam aufgewachsen sind, belegen ebenfalls den Einfluss der genetischen Programme.

Prof. Volker Pudel, Leiter der Ernährungspsychologischen Forschungsstelle in der Klinik für Psychiatrie und Psychotherapie der Universität Göttingen, weist dabei jedoch darauf hin, dass die Vererbung immer nur zum Teil das Körpergewicht beeinflusst. „Zwischen Umwelteinflüssen und Genetik besteht eine Wechselwirkung, das heißt, die genetischen Programme benötigen eine bestimmte Umwelt, um wirken zu können. So war der Genpool in der Nachkriegszeit so wie heute, doch gab es keine Übergewichtigen. Erst die moderne Umwelt, die Bewegung an die Technik delegiert und die Supermärkte überfüllt hat, gibt dem „genialen Fettspeicherprogramm" der Evolution die Chance, permanent Energiereserven für Notzeiten zu speichern, die nicht mehr eintreffen. So gesehen sind die ausbleibenden Notzeiten der eigentliche Grund für die Übergewichtigkeit, die auf Programmen der Evolution beruht, die den Menschen auch unter Zeiten knapper Versorgung das Überleben möglich gemacht hat."

In der Shell Jugendstudie 2006 wurde unter anderem das Freizeitverhalten von Jugendlichen untersucht. Bewiesen wurde dabei eine These, die wahrscheinlich alle, die sich beruflich mit Kindern und Jugendlichen beschäftigen, auch aufstellen würden: WIE DIE ELTERN, SO DIE KINDER!

„Jugendliche aus den oberen Sozialschichten beschäftigen sich in ihrer Freizeit besonders häufig mit Lesen, mit kreativen oder künstlerischen Aktivitäten und pflegen ihre sozialen Kontakte: Wir haben diese Gruppe als „kreative Freizeitelite" bezeichnet. Bei den Jugendlichen aus sozial benachteiligten Familien hingegen hat das Abtauchen in die Gleichaltrigengruppe mit ihrer spezifischen Freizeitkultur eine andere Bedeutung.

Insbesondere männliche Jugendliche aus der Unterschicht bilden die Gruppe der Technikfreaks, die ihre Freizeit vorrangig mit Computerspielen und Fernsehen verbringen. Verbindet sich dies mit einer Abwendung von Schule und Berufsausbildung, liegt ein riskantes Abrücken von gesellschaftlichen Konditionen vor." (Shell Jugendstudie 2006).

Wenn das Verhalten der Eltern das ihrer Kinder vorprägt, heißt das auch, dass die Kinder fettsüchtiger Eltern kaum eine Chance haben, schlanke Erwachsene zu werden. Sie werden mit Genen geboren, die die Fettsucht begünstigen, und auch noch von Eltern ernährt, die wahrscheinlich ihre Fettsucht unbewusst fördern werden.

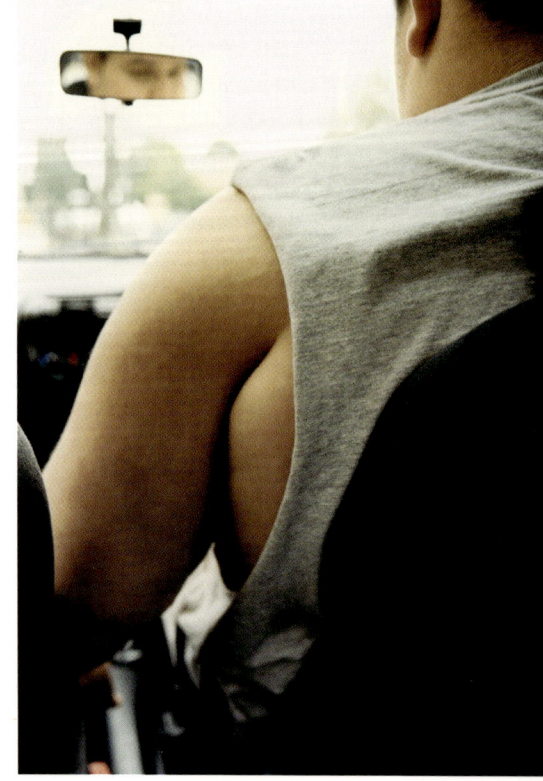

Der gerne gebrauchte Hinweis, dass man sich bei der Verehelichung mit dem geliebten Wunschpartner erst einmal den jeweiligen Körperumfang der künftigen Schwiegereltern zur visionären Projektion in die Zukunft betrachten soll, zeigt, dass intuitiv ein Wissen um das Zusammenspiel von Erbgut und Lebensgestaltung weit verbreitet ist.

Dass fettsüchtige Kinder in der Regel zumindest einen fettsüchtigen Elternteil haben, erklärt auch, warum sie überhaupt erst an Fettsucht erkranken. Eine „gesund" lebende Mutter hat wahrscheinlich das Bedürfnis, ihren Kindern das eigene Bewusstsein für Ernährung und Bewegung zu vermitteln. Auch Eltern mit ästhetischem Anspruch möchten sich wohl kaum mit einem übergewichtigen Kind zeigen. Für übergewichtige Eltern bedeutet das immer dicker werdende Kind aber ein Abbild ihrer selbst.

Dr. Hanspeter Goldschmidt stellt nach 30 Jahren als Chefarzt der Spessart-Klinik fest, dass die Jugendlichen erst dann zur Behandlung kommen, wenn Adipositas „weh tut", wenn die Gelenke aufgrund des Gewichts schmerzen, keine Lehrstelle gefunden wird oder die Demütigungen durch andere Jugendliche unerträgliche Ausmaße annehmen. „Es ist ein erstaunliches Phänomen, dass bei 16-jährigen Jugendlichen 120 kg vorher nicht bemerkt wurden, Striae (Dehnungsstreifen) am ganzen Körper oder extreme Gynäkomastie (Vergrößerung der männlichen Brustdrüse) bei Jungen niemanden veranlassten, etwas dagegen zu unternehmen", so Goldschmidt, der zuallererst die ignoranten Eltern kritisiert.

Sowohl der Stoffwechsel als auch das allgemeine situationsübergreifende Verhalten sind also auch genetisch bedingt. Der aktuelle Stand der Forschung besagt, dass fünfzig bis achtzig Prozent der Varianz des BMI genetisch erklärbar sind. Umweltfaktoren wirken sich nicht bei allen Kindern und Jugendlichen gleich aus – an dieser Stelle denke man wieder an all diejenigen, die offensichtlich ohne Reue genießen können. Gerne spricht man als Laie dann von „guten Verbrennern", weil es offensichtlich in der Allgemeinbevölkerung das Bedürfnis gibt, einem auffallenden Phänomen eine Begründung zuzuordnen.

Die Tatsache, dass fettsüchtige Elternpaare in der Regel fettsüchtige Kinder haben und fettsüchtige Erwachsene oftmals nur fettsüchtige Partner finden, bedeutet, dass sich Adipositas – andere Umweltfaktoren einmal außer Acht lassend – auch wie eine Erbkrankheit ausbreitet. Und: dass mit Fortschritten in der Genforschung möglicherweise auch Methoden gefunden werden, Adipositas zu lindern. Forschung und Pharmaindustrie stoßen hier auf einen weltweiten Markt. Vielleicht eine Hilfe für diejenigen, die an einer besonders negativen genetischen Konstellation leiden. Ganz sicher jedoch keine Hoffnung, die davon abhalten sollte, jetzt alles zu versuchen, die Krankheit bei jedem Einzelnen zu stoppen und die Lawine der Ausbreitung der Erkrankung aufzuhalten.

Die adipösen Kids und ihre Eltern

10. KAPITEL

Die adipösen Kids und ihre Eltern

Noch ein Problem-Verhältnis

Die Therapeuten in der Spessart-Klinik berichten alle von einer auffallenden Anzahl psychisch belasteter Kinder und Jugendlicher unter ihren adipösen Schützlingen. „In vielen Familien scheint durch Berufstätigkeit beider Eltern wenig Zeit für die Familie da zu sein. Oft haben wir auch Kinder, bei denen Scheidung, Trennung, Verlust oder Krankheit eines Elternteils eine große Rolle spielt", sagt Marion Tschirschwitz, die in der Klinik psychosoziale Arbeit leistet und mit den adipösen Kindern und Jugendlichen einige Stunden am Tag in einer familienähnlichen Situation zusammenlebt. Zudem fällt im klinischen Alltag und in der näheren Begegnung mit den

kleinen Patienten auf, dass die Zugehörigkeit zur sozial schwachen Schicht eine relevante Rolle zu spielen scheint.

Eine aktuelle Studie des Robert Koch Instituts belegt die Erfahrungswerte. Es wurde festgestellt, dass Übergewicht und Adipositas häufiger bei Kindern aus sozial benachteiligten Schichten und bei jenen mit Migrations-hintergrund auftritt. Insgesamt ergab die Untersuchung, dass *„bei Jugend-lichen mit Essstörungen der Anteil der Auffälligen mit niedrigem sozioöko-nomischem Status mit 27,6 Prozent fast doppelt so hoch ist wie der in der oberen Sozialschicht (15,5 Prozent)". Bei den als auffällig eingestuften Kindern wurde eine höhere Quote an „psychischen Auffälligkeiten und Depressivitätsneigung" erhoben. Die Betroffenen seien „weniger zufrieden mit ihrem Körperselbstbild, rauchen mehr und berichten häufiger über die Erfahrung sexueller Belästigung". Umfragewerte mit traurigen Er-gebnissen, die zum wiederholten Mal unterstreichen, dass man den Kindern frühzeitig helfen muss, denn auch ein jahrelanges Verbleiben in einer Talsohle psychischer Belastung und Anspannung ist äußerst schwie-rig zu behandeln – unabhängig vom Körpergewicht. Die schrecklich* *aktuellen Nachrichten um Kinder, die von ihren Eltern dem Hungertod überlassen oder zu Tode geschlagen werden, machen auf brutale Weise die Zustände bewusst und mahnen die Pflicht ein, die Lebenszustände der Kleinen zu verändern.*

Eine verletzte oder beschwerte Kinderseele ist nach allem, was man heute vom Seelenleben weiß, empfänglich für Essstörungen. Caroline Raasch spricht von Resignation im Verhältnis zu den Eltern oder einem Elternteil, die mit einer (in der Doppeldeutigkeit gemeinten) Unbeweglichkeit einhergeht. In ihrer homöopathischen Praxis in Berlin erlebt sie übergewichtige Mütter und Kinder und stellt fest, dass die Kids spüren, wenn sie anstelle echter liebevoller Zuwendung Ersatzgaben wie Essen oder eben Computerspiele erhielten. Häufig seien die Mütter emotional nicht in der Lage, dem Kind die für die psychische

Stabilität notwendige Mutterliebe zu geben, was das Bedürfnis auslöse, das Kleine eben anderweitig zu versorgen. „Es hat doch alles, es geht ihm doch gut", lautet dann das Fazit zur Selbstberuhigung.

11. KAPITEL

Die Verantwortung der Eltern

11. KAPITEL

Die Verantwortung der Eltern

WANTED!

Prinzipiell muss man davon ausgehen, dass Eltern heutzutage wissen, welche Ernährung gesund ist und welche ungesund. Im Medienzeitalter wird seit Jahrzehnten überall aufgeklärt – Fernsehformate, die die „breite Masse" ansprechen, beschäftigen sich besonders gerne mit Diäten, denn aufgrund des in sozial schwächeren Schichten weit verbreiteten Übergewichts lassen sich hier besonders gute Quoten erzielen. Der Zuschauer schwelgt in „Das-kann-ich-auch-Träumen", identifiziert sich für die Zeit des Beitrags mit der Hauptperson der Geschichte, die 50 kg abgenommen hat – und stopft sich eine halbe Stunde danach mit fettem Essen zu.

Prof. Dr. Volker Pudel stellt fest, dass sogar der Begriff des Jo-Jo-Effekts, der die schnelle Gewichtszunahme nach der Diät beschreibt, allgemein bekannt ist. Für ihn haben Ernährungsaufklärung und Ernährungsberatung in den vergangenen fünfzig Jahren „ihr Ziel nicht erreicht": „Die Menschen essen nicht anders, aber das, was sie essen, essen sie oft mit schlechtem Gewissen. Die Ernährungsaufklärung hat den Kopf, aber nicht den Bauch erreicht." Dies könnte auch erklären, warum adipöse Eltern im Umgang mit sich selbst und im Umgang mit ihren Kindern nicht konsequent handeln.

Und dabei sollte Eltern doch so viel an ihren adipösen Kindern liegen, dass sie alle Kraft darauf verwenden, sie zu gesundem Essen und Bewegung anzuleiten. (vgl. „Starke Kinder lernen essen", Krenn Verlag) Eine hohe Anforderung, die eigentlich eine 24h-Beobachtung beinhaltet, denn der fette Nussriegel ist schnell gekauft und noch schneller verzehrt. Die Chance liegt in der Früherkennung – in den ersten Jahren, in denen die Handhabe der Eltern am größten ist und der Grundstein für Appetit und Lust auf Bewegung gelegt wird. Hier begünstigen auch noch Wachstumsschübe eine retardierte

Motivation, denn dann geht es „nur" darum, das Gewicht zu halten. Der Ausgleich kommt mit der wachsenden Körpergröße. In dieser Zeit gibt es auch noch regelmäßige Besuche beim Kinderarzt.

Je jünger das Kind ist, umso mehr können die Eltern erfolgreich Verantwortung übernehmen. Die Möglichkeiten, noch weitgehend ungestört von medialen und gesellschaftlichen Einflüssen zu erziehen, ist groß. In den Grundschul- und Jugendjahren prallen die Gesellschaft und das Kind aufeinander. Damit verteilt sich die Verantwortung dann auch auf mehr Schultern. Deswegen möchten wir feststellen, dass den Eltern immer eine Verantwortung zukommt, die sich mit Älterwerden des Kindes jedoch komplex vermischt und schon beginnt, wenn sich das Baby noch im Bauch der Mutter befindet.

Eine verpflichtende Teilnahme an Workshops zur Ernährung für Schwangere sorgt für Aufklärung, zu deren Aufmerksamkeit manche erst angestoßen werden müssen. Müssen ist ein Wort, das wir als Autoren selbst nicht schätzen. Wir ahnen auch die negative Reaktion, denn hier geht es um eine Art Eltern-Führerschein, der mit kontinuierlichen Reihenuntersuchungen abgefragt wird. Aber ganz ehrlich: Alles was bisher geschehen ist, hat die Epidemie nicht im Geringsten aufgehalten. Mit mehr Aufklärung wurden die Gesunden gesünder. Das ist schön – wir als Autoren gehören auch zu dieser privilegierten Gruppe. Wir machen Sport und essen gesund – weil wir auf diese Art von Leben Lust haben. Und wir

beschäftigen uns mit einer Epidemie, die aufgehalten werden MUSS. Wir fordern die konsequente Anwendung von strafrechtlichen Sanktionen, wenn Eltern ihrem Kind ein ungesundes Leben aufbürden.

Nun zur gesellschaftlichen elterlichen Verantwortung. Ohne Ironie möchten wir feststellen, dass die deutsche Gesellschaft sich selbst schon gut organisiert hat. Umso mehr, seit via Internet global Bedürfnisse geäußert werden können und sich unter Millionen von Nutzern leichter Befriedigung oder Hilfe finden lässt als mit der Kleinanzeige in der Heimatzeitung. Portale für Mitfahrgelegenheiten und ebay sind die besten Beispiele.

Auch Eltern kranker oder belasteter Kinder recherchieren über das Leid ihrer Kinder und finden schneller dort Anschluss, wo es traditionell kompetente Hilfe gibt: bei den ebenso betroffenen Eltern, die sich schon in Selbsthilfegruppen zusammengefunden haben. Ein bewährtes System, das wie so oft aus der Bevölkerung entstanden und nicht politisch oktroyiert ist. Vielleicht deswegen auch eine Erfolgsstory. „Nach entsprechenden Studien fühlen sich Eltern am besten in Selbsthilfegruppen aufgehoben", sagt Julia von

Seiche vom Aktionskomitee Kind im Krankenhaus (AKIK e.V.). Aus ihrem Alltag berichtet sie von „Verständnis für Alltagssorgen, praktischen Rat und Hilfe im Umgang mit der Krankheit ihres Kindes" und „Problembewältigung", wenn es etwa um Verhandlungen mit den Kostenträgern geht. Unterstützen könne man diese Eltern vor allem durch Bereitstellung von Räumlichkeiten oder Unterstützung beim Schriftverkehr.

Bei den Eltern von fettsüchtigen Kindern müssten sich Eltern organisieren, die in ihrer Mehrheit über einen Bildungshintergrund verfügen, der nur wenige Erfahrungswerte zum Einstarten einer Initiative liefert. Meist sind die Eltern auch übergewichtig bzw. können sich selbst nicht von der körperlichen Last befreien. Dies kann eine Chance sein, weil man in einer Betroffenengruppe die Probleme der Eltern und Kinder gleichzeitig angehen kann – ein großer Kraftakt, der schon viel soziale und fachliche Kompetenz und auch noch Disziplin erfordert. Aber kann man diese Eltern und Kinder sich selbst überlassen?

Die Verantwortung der Lebensmittelindustrie

12. KAPITEL

Die Verantwortung der Lebensmittel- industrie

Die Lebensmittelindustrie wehrt sich gegen Vorwürfe, die Fettsucht zu schüren. Und sie hat längst den gesunden Markt erkannt. Der Boom der Entwicklung nahezu fettfreier Lebensmittel wird abgelöst vom Bio- boom, von vitalisierenden Lebens- mitteln, von Functional Food, von fruchtigen Desserts ohne zusätzliche Zugabe von Zucker und Farbstoffen. Lifestyle-Lebensmittel, nachgefragt, gekauft und gegessen von gesund- heitsbewussten Kunden, die auch gerne einmal Süßes essen oder Burger im pappigen Brötchen, weil

sie Sünden mit Bewegung und Sport ausgleichen. Nachfrager, deren Lebens- einstellung Gesundheit *und* Genuss ist, die Schokolade mit einem hohen Kakaoanteil essen, seit überall zu lesen ist, dass dies gesund ist.

Presse und Käufer arbeiten hier gut zusammen. Wir möchten an dieser Stelle den Bioboom als Positivbeispiel anführen, der auch den Weg zeigen kann, „vernünftige" Lebensmittel am Markt durchzusetzen. Über viele Jahre hinweg haben unzählige Journalisten in noch mehr TV-Sendungen und Artikeln über lebensunwürdige Massentierhaltung berichtet, über Schadstoffe in Lebensmitteln bzw. Nährstoffgehalte in biologisch angebauten Rohstoffen. Jahrzehnte später verdrängen große Bioketten nun die kleinen Bioläden, die irgendwann unter der Risikobereitschaft von Idealisten der ersten Stunde den Bedarf der nur partiell interessier-

ten Bevölkerung an möglichst unbelasteten Nahrungsmitteln bedienten. Die ersten Biobauern hatten noch den Status von Spinnern, heute sind einige davon mittelständische Unternehmer. Der nächste Schritt werden Bioskandale sein, in denen unsaubere Geschäftsleute geoutet werden, die Lebensmittel als biologisch angebaut verkaufen, die gar nicht „bio" sind (vgl. „Die 50 größten Bio-Lügen", Krenn Verlag). Übrig bleibt dann ein Markt mit echten Aussagen und sicherlich immer noch wenigen schwarzen Schafen – ein Sieg der Vernunft, des Geschmacks und des Glaubens an eine bessere Welt für Mensch und Tier. An die überbordende Biowelle in herkömmlichen Supermärkten haben vor zehn Jahren nur wenige geglaubt.

Zusätzlich zur Presse ist die Sucht der Nahrungsmittelindustrie nach PR eine Chance auf ein breiteres Spektrum an wertvollen Lebensmitteln. In einer Zeit, in der große und kleine PR-Agenturen alles tun, um ihre Kunden bei den Endkunden als Gutmenschen mit einzigartigen Produkten und Dienstleistungen unterzubringen und Auftraggeber auch einen Wert in der Verbreitung entsprechender Nachrichten sehen, lässt sich vorauseilender Gehorsam gut nutzen – eine subtile Einflussnahme durch Presse und Markt. Ein Beispiel, um direkt zu unserem Thema zurückzukehren:

Die Wirtschaftsvereinigung Alkoholfreie Getränke e.V. (wafg) geht Anfang 2007 in die Offensive und bietet von sich aus an, „ihren Beitrag zur Bekämpfung dieses großen gesellschaftlichen Problems [Übergewicht, d. Autoren] zu leisten" (Martin Möller, Präsident der wafg). Beginnend ab dem Frühjahr 2007 werden auf den Etiketten von Erfrischungsgetränken detaillierte Nährstoffangaben – bezogen auf den Tagesbedarf, sogenannte GDAs (Guideline Daily Amount) – ausgewiesen. Neben der Ausweisung der GDAs für Energie (Kilokalorien) auf der Vorderseite der Verpackung werden auf der Rückseite zusätzlich die GDAs für alle Nährstoffe, die in der Diskussion um die öffentliche Gesundheit stehen (Fett, gesättigte Fettsäuren, Zucker, Natrium), ausgewiesen. Darüber hinaus bekennen sich die wafg-Mitgliedsunternehmen, insbesondere die internationalen Markenhersteller, zum Ver-

haltenskodex für Erfrischungsgetränke des europäischen Dachverbandes der Erfrischungsgetränke-Industrie UNESDA. Dieser beinhaltet als wesentliche Bestandteile den verantwortungsvollen Umgang bei Werbemitteilungen gegenüber Kindern, die Werbeaktivitäten an Schulen (inkl. Getränkeautomaten) sowie eine entsprechende Evaluation (Monitoring). Die Vereinigung verdient sich deswegen keinen Heiligenschein, aber Anerkennung für den klugen Schritt zur Selbstverpflichtung und einer sympathischen Eigen-PR, bevor staatliche Auflagen greifen.

Nestlé gibt ein mehrseitiges fundiertes Thesenpapier zur Adipositas heraus, Nahrungsmittelhersteller rekrutieren gesundheitsorientierte Experten der Ernährungswissenschaften für ihre Entwicklungs-, Marketing- und PR-Abteilungen. Die Industrie ist auf einen gesellschaftlichen Wandel vorbereitet. Produziert wird, was nachgefragt wird.

Die Europäische Union plant, ab 2009 deutlichere Kennzeichnungen zu Inhaltsstoffen bei Lebensmitteln einzuführen. Der Unesda, Dachverband der Lebensmittelbranche, setzt dem bereits eine Art Charta entgegen, in der sich die Unterzeichner – ähnlich wie Zeitungen im Pressekodex – selbst gewählten Regeln unterwerfen. Dazu gehört, Getränkeautomaten in Grundschulen gegen markenfreie Geräte auszutauschen, die auch Wasser und Säfte bereithalten. Manche Nahrungsmittelhersteller kooperieren auch mit den Hochschulen, um höherwertige Lebensmittel herzustellen.

Wir verdammen das im Übrigen nicht, denn der Zusammenschluss mit der Wirtschaft bringt den Studenten Marktpraxis und allen gegenseitigen Input. Im Sinne unserer eigenen Forderungen an die Politik stellen wir fest, dass es ein großes funktionierendes Netz an Handelnden in Sachen Herstellung und Vertrieb von gesunden Nahrungsmitteln gibt, das die Basis für die Ein- dämmung der epidemischen Fettsucht sein kann. Die Lebensmittelindustrie reagiert auf den Markt. Wenn flächendeckend alle Familien durch öffentliche Aufklärung und individuelle Unterstützung erkennen, welche Lebensmittel gesund und schmackhaft sind, werden diese bevorzugt gekauft und Unter- nehmen der Lebensmittelbranche ihr Sortiment entsprechend ändern. Gesellschaftlich ist dies erfreulich, denn den gesundheitsbewussten Ver- brauchern wird die Befriedigung ihres eigenen Bedürfnisses erleichtert. Zudem entdecken die Übergewichtigen, die sich bereits mit Ernährung und Nährwerttabellen beschäftigen, durch eine klare Deklarierung immer mehr fett- und/oder zuckerarme Lebensmittel, um die sich ihr Spektrum an mögli- chen Mahlzeiten erweitert. Dies bedeutet mehr Genuss, und das ist ja schon einmal sehr erfreulich! Dass man mit klaren Auflagen an die Lebens- mittelbranche alleine schon das Problem der Zunahme an Adipositasfällen nicht löst, ist klar.

Die Spessart-Klinik hat in einem Pilot- projekt in Kooperation mit dem Berli- ner Bio-Vollkornkonditor Bernd Till- mann nahrhafte und schmackhafte Bio-Muffins auf den Markt gebracht, bei deren Vertrieb Folgendes deutlich wurde: Eltern greifen dann gerne für ihre Kinder zu, wenn sie in direkter Ansprache über die Wertigkeit der In- haltsstoffe informiert werden. Ein Bei- spiel, das den mühsamen Prozess der Aufklärung zeigt. Diesen Erkenntnispro- zess gilt es jedoch zu beschleunigen.

Die Behandlung der Adipositas

13. KAPITEL

Die medizinische und therapeutische Behandlung der Adipositas

Die einfache wie banale Erkenntnis lautet: Ein Kind nimmt nicht über Nacht fünfzig Kilo zu. Irgendwann ist es erst einmal pummelig. Für den Kinderarzt bedeutet dies, dass er die Eltern schon bei den ersten Anzeichen von Übergewicht ansprechen muss. Eine Ernährungsberatung übt er dabei freiwillig aus, denn er kann sie in der Regel nicht bei den Krankenversicherungen abrechnen. Eine Überweisung an eine kommunale Ernährungsberatung oder an einen Verein macht daher Sinn. Die Erfahrung zeigt jedoch, dass die Eltern von Kindern, die früh zu Adipositas neigen, kein offenes Ohr für die Problematik haben (vgl. Interview mit Dr. Wolfram Hartmann, Präsident des Verbandes der Kinder- und Jugendärzte).

Das heißt, dass der Kinderarzt erst mit Unterstützung der Krankenversicherungen eingreift, wenn die Adipositas sozusagen schon ausgebrochen ist – nämlich ab der 97. Perzentile. Hat er den Eindruck, dass das familiäre Umfeld zuhause eine Diät ermöglicht, so führen die Kinder und Jugendlichen Ernährungs- und Bewegungsprotokolle, damit der Kinderarzt die

Schwachstellen erkennt und mit dem kranken Kind die Gegenmaßnahmen erläutert. Ambulant ist es auch noch möglich, bei Bedarf einen Kinderpsychologen einzuschalten, der in Absprache mit dem Arzt arbeitet.

In vielen Städten gibt es bereits ambulante Adipositaszentren, in denen die besorgten Eltern oder Hilfe suchenden Kinder und Jugendlichen schnell kompetente Unterstützung finden. Für die Zukunft ist zu erwarten, dass es immer mehr solcher Zentren geben wird. Kontaktdaten dazu gibt es zum Beispiel bei der Deutschen Adipositas Gesellschaft.

Wenn eine private Diät nicht zum Erfolg führt, wird der Kinderarzt eine stationäre Rehabilitation beantragen, die je nach Schwere des Falls von unterschiedlicher Dauer sein kann: Manchmal werden drei Wochen genehmigt, im Extremfall drei Monate. Kostenträger sind in der Regel die Krankenversicherungen.

In der Rehabilitation befindet sich das Kind in der Obhut von

- Kinderärzten, die sich auch um die assoziierten Krankheiten wie z. B. Diabetes mellitus kümmern
- Ernährungsberatern/Diätassistenten, die mit den Kindern auch Lebensmittel einkaufen und kochen
- Pädagogen, die die Kinder in einer internatsähnlichen Situation betreuen
- Lehrern, die die Kinder während der Kur unterrichten
- Psychologen, die mit den Kindern vor allem familiäre Probleme erörtern
- Sporttherapeuten, die den Kindern Freude an der Bewegung vermitteln und mit ihnen bis zu drei Mal täglich Sport machen, um die Diät zu unterstützen

Eine solche Rehabilitation kostet zwischen 3500 und 4500 Euro. Solche Beträge werden ausgegeben, um noch Schlimmeres zu verhindern. Würde man anstelle derart nachbetreuender Maßnahmen übergewichtige Kinder in Ferienzeiten zu Spezialkliniken schicken oder sie zuhause in Adipositas- bzw. Ernährungsberatungszentren ambulant betreuen, könnte man früher eingreifen, weitaus mehr erreichen, den Kindern Leid ersparen und uns alle vor gigantischen Gesundheitskosten verschonen.

Die Krankenkassen in Deutschland arbeiten längst wirtschaftlich, soweit dies eben möglich ist. Sie sind interessiert an der Entwicklung nachhaltiger Therapieformen, die langfristig Kosten einsparen.

Als zukunftsweisend gelten Netzwerke wie etwa das Adipositasnetzwerk Hessen und sogenannte sequenzielle Rehabilitationsmaßnahmen, bei denen das Behandlungsziel über bis zu mehrere Jahre gestreut wird und ebenso wie in Netzwerken auf eine langhaltige kontinuierliche Betreuung am Wohnort orientiert wird. Sinn macht dies nicht nur bei Adipositas, sondern auch bei anderen chronischen Krankheiten wie etwa bronchiales Asthma oder Haltungsschäden. Die Kinder und Jugendlichen werden im Idealfall mit dem Knowhow einer Spezialklinik therapiert, der Kostenträger spart jedoch die Unterbringung ein und ermöglicht eine Betreuung, die Jahre andauern kann. Damit wäre kein idealisierbarer Zustand erreicht, entstehen dabei doch gigantische Kosten. Aber an der gesellschaftlichen Verpflichtung, Maßnahmen zu ergreifen bzw. zu ermöglichen, führt kein Weg vorbei. Wir zahlen alle die Krankenkassenbeiträge, die solch aufwändige Maßnahmen ermöglichen. Fettsüchtige Kinder aber zahlen den höchsten Preis – es raubt ihnen körperlich und psychisch sprichwörtlich den Atem.

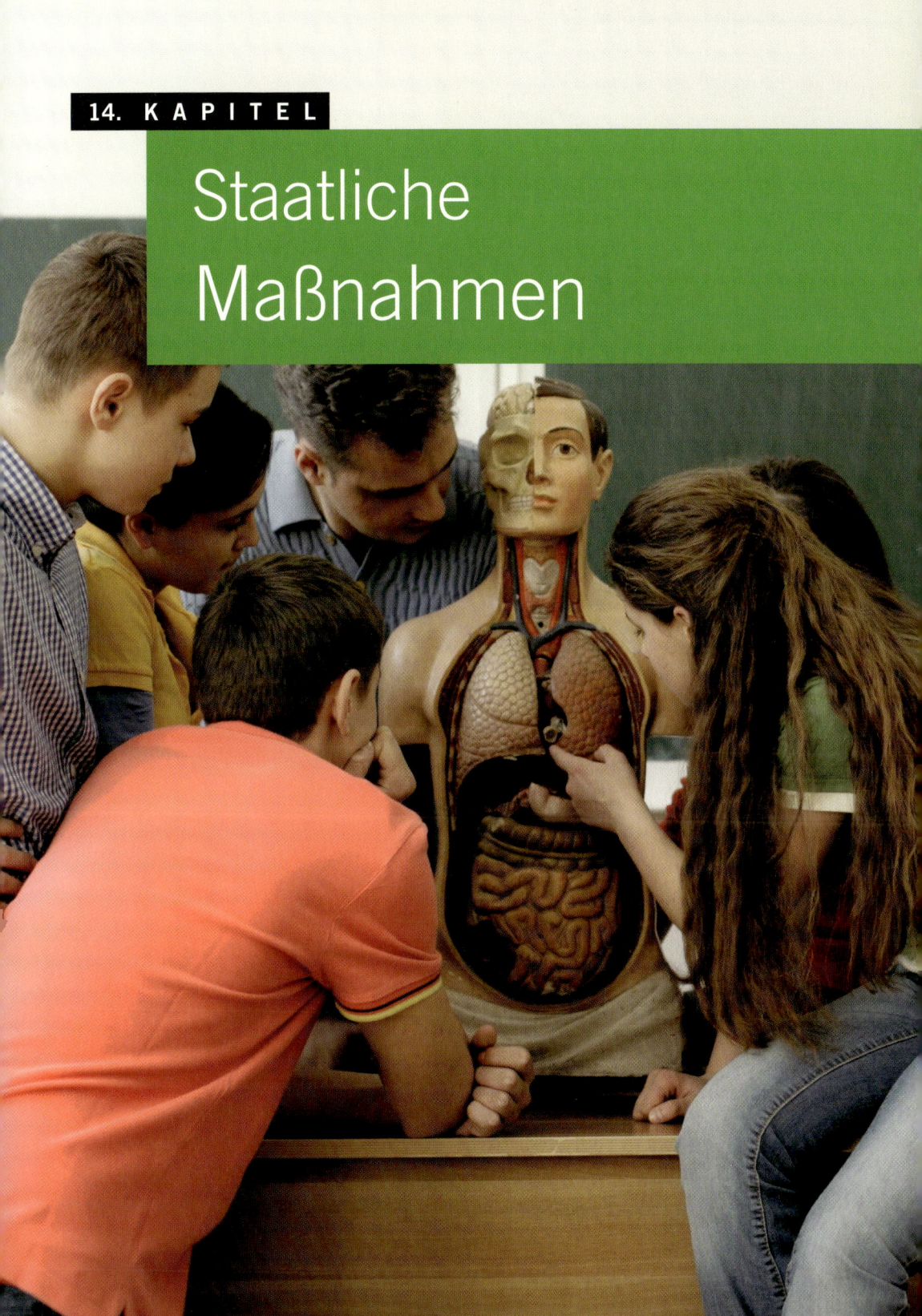

Staatliche Maßnahmen

14. KAPITEL

Staatliche Maßnahmen

Die Politik hat prinzipiell die Bedeutung der Adipositas erkannt. Weltweit, in Europa, in Deutschland und in Österreich. Lösungen oder Maßnahmen zur Eindämmung unterliegen jedoch politischen Vorstellungen, bei denen es im Kern um das Ausmaß des Eingriffs in das Privatleben Betroffener geht. Zudem beschäftigt uns auch die Frage, ob wir uns in Aktionismus erschöpfen oder ob wir wirklich auch diejenigen erreichen, die staatliche Hilfe nötig haben. Um es vorwegzunehmen: Aktionismus gibt es, und sicherlich fließt Geld auch an Stellen, die nicht aus sachlichen Gründen präferiert werden. Aber es gibt auch gute und effiziente Ansätze und Maßnahmen. Wir werden noch darauf zu sprechen kommen, dass diese angesichts der Dimension des Problems nicht ausreichend sind.

Im November 2006 fand in Istanbul die Europäische Ministerkonferenz der WHO zur Bekämpfung der Adipositas statt, als deren Ergebnis eine Europäische Charta zur Bekämpfung der Adipositas verabschiedet wurde. Dabei wurden erschreckende Zahlen veröffentlicht: Jährlich werden allein in Europa eine Million Todesfälle mit der Adipositas assoziiert. Spätestens 2015 soll es keine Zunahme der Fälle, sondern eine Abnahme geben.

Die Europäische Kommission finanziert im Rahmen ihrer Forschungspolitik das Projekt IDEFICS (Identification and prevention of dietary- and lifestyle-induced health effects in children and infants), die bislang größte europaweit durchgeführte Studie zur Erforschung der Ursachen und zur Prophylaxe von Übergewicht bei Kindern. Die Studie fokussiert auf Kinder im Alter von zwei bis zehn Jahren, ist auf eine Dauer von fünf Jahren ausgelegt und vernetzt Wissenschafter verschiedenster Fachrichtungen. Untersucht wird unter anderem die These, dass Geschmackspräferenzen und -empfindungen große Auswirkungen auf die Ausbildung der Krankheit haben. Langfristig sollen unter dem Dach von IDEFICS Präventionsprogramme für Schulen und Kindergärten angebo-

ten werden. In einem Partnerprojekt unter dem Namen HELENA (Healthy lifestyles in Europe by nutrition in adolescents) wird die Fettleibigkeit bei Jugendlichen erforscht. Die Federführung für IDEFICS liegt beim Bremer Institut für Präventionsforschung und Sozialmedizin.

Das in Deutschland für das Thema Adipositas zuständige Bundesministeriums für Ernährung, Landwirtschaft und Verbraucherschutz veröffentlichte eine Presseerklärung mit der mit der WHO-Charta übereinstimmenden Feststellung: „Übergewicht wird zu einer der größten gesundheitspolitischen Herausforderungen der nächsten Jahre werden" heraus. (Dr. Gerd Müller, Parlamentarischer Staatssekretär im Bundesministerium für Landwirtschaft, Ernährung und Verbraucherschutz) Maßnahmen dagegen werden als „Aktionsschwerpunkte" des Ministeriums deklariert – und tatsächlich flossen im Jahr 2006 rund 4,5 Millionen Euro allein in Projekte zur Verbraucheraufklärung im Ernährungsbereich. Darüber hinaus fördert das Bundesernährungsministerium zahlreiche Forschungsvorhaben und finanziert die Deutsche Gesellschaft für Ernährung e.V., den aid-Infodienst sowie den Verbraucherzentrale Bundesverband. Das Ministerium verfolgt dabei einen eher individualistischen Zugang, wenn es darauf hinweist, dass „Verantwortung für Leben und Gesundheit in (der) Verantwortung jedes Einzelnen stehen". (Staatssekretär Müller) Staatliche Maßnahmen wie z. B. Werbeverbote werden ausgeschlossen. Seine Priorität liegt auf der Bewusstseinsschaffung wie etwa beim „Nationalen Aktionsplan Ernährung", der immerhin im Sinne der „Stärkung einer Ernährungsbildung" die Einführung von „Ernährungskunde" und gesonderten Sportkursen an Schulen vorsieht. Dies wäre dann allerdings Ländersache – auch was die Finanzierung betrifft.

Dennoch kann man der Bundesregierung nicht vorwerfen, untätig zu sein. Im Gegenteil. Bereits im Jahr 2003 wurde die Kampagne „Besser essen. Mehr bewegen. Kinderleicht." lanciert. Hier werden im Moment 24 Projekte bezuschusst, die sich in einem nationalen Wettbewerb durchsetzten. In der Regel geht es dabei um kommunale Initiativen, die ihr Budget aus Spenden, kommunalen Zuschüssen und Mitteln aus dem Modellvorhaben zusammenstellen.

Dieses Miteinander aus ehrenamtlichem Einsatz und verschiedenen staatlichen Förderungen entspricht dem allgemeinen Politikverständnis und sei an dieser Stelle auch deutlich positiv hervorgehoben. Im selben Jahr gründete sich die Plattform Ernährung und Bewegung (peb) mit Vertretern aus Politik, Wirtschaft und Verbänden. Neben den üblichen Willensbekundungen geht es dabei auch um handfeste Zuschüsse für Aufklärungsmaßnahmen in Schulen, Kindergärten, Kindertagesstätten und Familien.

So bietet zum Beispiel die Deutsche Gesellschaft für Ernährung ein kostenloses Beratungs- und Informationsservice für Pädagogen an, die dann eben rund um das Thema Ernährung geschult werden, um die Kenntnisse an ihre eigenen Schützlinge weiterzugeben. Auch unter dem Dach FIT KID können sich Vertreter von Schulen im Projekt „Schule + Essen = Note 1" beraten lassen. Hier geht es vor allem darum, Input und Informationen zu erteilen, wenn eine Schule ihr Ernährungsangebot ausweiten oder auf Ganztagsbetrieb umstellen möchte. Daneben gibt es noch „Kinderleicht in Bibliotheken" mit Bücherpaketen für zum Beispiel Schulbibliotheken und viele Einzelaktionen. (siehe Serviceteil)

Was kann man sich unter diesen Projekten konkret vorstellen? Eines der im Rahmen von „Besser essen. Mehr bewegen. Kinderleicht" geförderten Projekte ist „KIKS UP". Hierbei handelt es sich um ein Präventionskonzept, das von engagierten Bürgern und kommunalen Stelleninhabern in Bad Nauheim entwickelt wurde. Im Zentrum steht dabei nicht nur die Prophylaxe von Adipositas, sondern auch jene von Süchten wie Alkohol, Nikotin bzw. Gewalt. Einbezogen sind werdende Eltern, Eltern, Kindertagesstätten, Grundschulen und Sportvereine mit dem Ziel, die Erziehungskompetenz aller zu stärken und sie in der Ausprägung der wichtigen Vorbildrolle zu unterstützen. Es geht um Lebensfreude und Vielfalt der Genüsse – ein insgesamt sehr positiv orientiertes Konzept, das von einem Kardiologen initiiert wurde, der in seinem Beruf mit den Folgen von beispielsweise Bewegungsarmut konfrontiert ist und offensichtlich den gesamtgesellschaftlichen Zusammenhang erkennt. Entscheidend ist, dass es ohne erhobenen Zeigefinger um eine direkte Kommunikation in Workshops und Vorträgen geht und um gemeinsame Veranstaltungen mit Kindern und deren Eltern in Anbindung an Kindergärten, Kindertagesstätten und Grundschulen. Die Teilnahme adipöser Kinder an „KIKS UP"-Camps wird bereits von den ersten Krankenkassen bezuschusst.

Ein Positivbeispiel kommunaler Verantwortung, aus dem heraus es sich die Stadt Bad Nauheim bereits zum Ziel gemacht hat, auch andere Städte für ein ebensolches Projekt zu gewinnen und selbst ein Schulungszentrum für „KIKS UP"-Maßnahmen zu errichten.

Auch bei der Plattform „Ernährung und Bewegung" (peb) geht es um Bündelung verschiedener Kräfte. So kooperiert man je nach Projekt in verschiedene Richtungen – je nach Zielgruppe. Herausgehoben sei ein Vorhaben, das sich noch im Anfangsstadium befindet und sich konkret an sozial Schwache richtet, unter denen auch die meisten

Adipositasfälle zu finden sind. In einer Kooperation aus peb und difu (Deutsches Institut für Urbanistik) werden Übergewichtsprävention und Gesundheitsförderung mit bereits bestehenden Maßnahmen zur Stadtteilentwicklung und Quartiersmanagement verknüpft. Letztere arbeiten seit Jahren an sozialen Brennpunkten, sind also schon da, wo man sich mit neuen Beratungsstellen erst einmal langwierig etablieren müsste. Weil uns dieser Ansatz Hoffnung macht, hier ein Beispiele aus der Praxis: das Kursangebot im Sprengelhaus in Berlin. Angeboten werden „Turnen für Kinder im Kita-Alter", „Offenes Mutter/Vater-Kind-Turnen", „HipHop für Mädchen", „Shiatsu-Atmen, Bewegung, Entspannen", „Fahrrad fahren für Frauen mit Migrationshintergrund", „Gymnastik für türkische Frauen", „Apfel, Möhre und Co. in Kitas – Kochen mit Kindern". Auch denkt man bei peb zeitgemäß: TV-Werbespots wurden entwickelt, in denen es ausschließlich um gesunde Ernährung geht.

Bei aller positiven Erwähnung sei darauf hingewiesen, dass peb auch renommierte Kritiker findet, die sich nicht wohl dabei fühlen, mit Vertretern der Wirtschaft (Nahrungsmittelbranche) über Positionierung von gesundem Essen nachzudenken, während in deren Fabriken die Produktion von süßen und fetten Riegeln auf Hochtouren läuft.

15. KAPITEL

Die Verantwortung der Medien

15. KAPITEL

Die Verantwortung der Medien

Unglaublich, was manche Eltern ihren Kindern antun: Sie treiben sie zur Prostitution, sie lassen sie verhungern, sie schlagen sie. Die Spitze des Eisbergs entnehmen wir der Presse. Als Journalistin stand ich (in diesem Fall eine Ausführung der Autorin) in einer Winternacht bei minus 20 Grad vor einem Haus, in dem der Vater gerade die Mutter getötet hatte und die drei kleinen Kinder bei der Mutter Totenwache

hielten, bis ein weiterer Verwandter die Tat entdeckte und die Polizei informierte. Ich wartete zusammen mit meinem Kamerateam und vielen weiteren Kollegen vor der Tür auf den Bestatter, damit wir Bilder vom Abtransport der Leiche einfangen konnten. Man reicht sich dann gegenseitig Heißgetränke aus Thermoskannen zu und versucht irgendwie, den professionellen Ansatz zu finden und anderes zu verdrängen. Solche Bilder vergisst man selbst sein Leben lang nicht. Zuschauer und Leser sind vergleichsweise nicht ganz so nah dran – aber nahe genug, um immer wieder aufs Neue zu erschrecken über die Alltagskriminalität in den Familien.

Wenn Eltern ihren Kinder fettes Essen verabreichen oder unbeteiligt zuschauen, wie die Kleinen immer fetter werden, steht keine Kamera vor der Tür. Die Misshandlung ist schleichender. Und auch hier schauen alle zu wie die Nachbarn der Familie, in der die Mutter niedergestochen wurde. Mehr Courage wird häufig eingefordert. Immerhin ist man endlich so weit, abgemagerte Models als Gesellschaftsproblem wahrzunehmen, als falsche Ikonen für junge Mädchen, die einem gesundheitsschädigenden Schönheitsideal verfallen.

Auch die dicken Kinder gehen die Medien an – ebenso wie Fleischskandale oder korrupte Manager. Wen das Schicksal der adipösen Kids nicht berührt, der kann vielleicht darüber, dass die Kinder mit ihrer Fresssucht die Krankenkassen und damit letztendlich auch das eigene Budget belasten, einen Zugang finden. Die Raucher sind bereits gerade deswegen kriminalisiert. Kinder sind die Opfer, nicht die Täter. Wer nie Disziplin und das Erkennen der zwei unterschiedlich zu gewichtenden Ansätze von Nahrung als Lebensmittel und – deutlich seltener – als Genussmittel gelernt hat, muss an die Thematik herangeführt werden.

Dicke Kinder wecken keine Emotionen! Das bringt keine Quote, keine Leser, keine Werbekunden. Erst in letzter Zeit, in der langsam das epidemische Ausmaß ersichtlich wird, ändert sich das mediale Interesse. In den Medien dargestellte Dicke sind nicht mehr nur ehemalige Dicke, die ihre Erfolgsstory erzählen – man denke an die US-Schauspielerin Kirsty Alley oder an die ehemalige britische Prinzessin Fergie, die von den Weight Watchers als Werbeikone aufgebaut wurde. Solche Frauen verschaffen sich Respekt und laden zu einer Du-schaffst-es-auch-Identifikation ein. Und sehen zudem auf Bildern auch besser aus als dicke Kinder.

Agenda-Setting in Medien ist eine komplexe Angelegenheit: Die mediale Karriere einer Bemerkung: „Die Beschäftigung mit Mager-Models lenkt von der Thematik der Fettsucht ab" vermag den Zusammenhang beim Thema Adipositas ein wenig zu erhellen. Eine einzige Bemerkung, die eine ganze Reihe von Medienberichten auslöste. Offensichtlich hat dieser von uns geäußerte Neben-Satz ins Schwarze getroffen. Das Thema „Dicke Kinder" ist bekannt, doch das Thema „Dünne Models" ist attraktiver. Dafür gibt es zwei Gründe (siehe Seite 91 und 92).

Das heißt nicht, dass es gar keine mediale Berichterstattung gibt. RTL hat eine ganze Woche lang sehr aufmerksam und fair über einen Jungen und ein Mädchen berichtet, die in der Spessart-Klinik therapiert wurden. Ein an sich hübsches Mädchen und ein selbstbewusster Junge, beide sehr reflektiert und sympathisch – ein medialer Glücks- und Ausnahmefall. Fettsüchtige Kids sind leider auch nicht niedlich. Die Lobby der Tierschützer dürfte größer sein.

1. ÄSTHETIK

Das Model

Ein abgemagertes Model ist immer noch ein Model. Ein Mädchen mit einem schönen Gesicht. Ein Mädchen, das ein Leben führt, das die Leser und Zuschauer nicht kennen und sich zumindest für einige Momente herbeisehnen: die perfekte Frisur, das beste Make-up, der teure Designer, Champagner, schicke Restaurants, seltene Kreditkarten, berühmte Bekannte – ein Traum. Reich und schön!

Die tragische Geschichte beruhigt Zuschauer und Leser: auch das privilegierte Mädchen, das im Gegensatz zu einem selbst mit einem perfekten Gesicht zur Welt gekommen ist, hat Probleme. Der Zuschauer bzw. Leser will nicht nur Traumhochzeiten, er will auch Schicksal – aber bitte schön verpackt. Dieter Bohlen hat eine attraktive neue Freundin. Nett! Dieter Bohlen wird zusammen mit seiner attraktiven neuen Freundin überfallen. Super!

Das fettsüchtige Kind

Ein dickes Kind kann noch so gut fotografiert werden, es bleibt immer hässlich. Ein unattraktiver kleiner Mensch, der ein Leben führt, das die Leser und Zuschauer nicht kennen möchten. Ein Leben, das sie vielleicht ihrem ärgsten Feind wünschen: fettige Haare, schlechte Haut, schlecht sitzende Outfits, schlechte Getränke in nach Fett stinkenden Pommes-Buden – ein Alptraum.

Chancenlos und fett! Die traurige Geschichte will man nicht sehen. „Diese Kinder haben ausschließlich Probleme. Es gibt zu viele fettsüchtige Kinder." Schlecht! „Wir zeigen Ihnen einige in den nächsten fünf Minuten." Noch schlechter!

2. PRAKTISCHE GRÜNDE

Das Model

Stellen Sie sich ein Model auf dem Laufsteg eines bekannten Designers bei der Mailänder Modewoche vor. Dieses Mädchen hat es in seinem Beruf schon einigermaßen weit gebracht: Es präsentiert hochpreisige Outfits in der Öffentlichkeit. Das war ja auch das Lebensziel der kleinen Schönheit: gesehen werden, identifiziert werden mit Reichtum und Unerreichbarem. Jeder Abdruck in einem Hochglanzmagazin ist ein Mehrwert, ein echter Gewinn, denn dann wird das Mädchen nicht nur von den geladenen Gästen der Show gesehen, sondern von hunderttausenden von Lesern.

Medienrechtlich ist das ein geschlossener Kreislauf – die junge Frau unterzeichnet den Projektvertrag und alle Welt darf Bilder von ihr zeigen. Auch mit der Überschrift: „Kein schöner Anblick – Magermodels ..." Das Mädchen hat seine Bildrechte abgetreten. Selbst wenn es keinen Vertrag hätte, tritt es in der Öffentlichkeit auf. In einer Öffentlichkeit, zu der Journalisten und Fotografen eingeladen sind.

Das fettsüchtige Kind

Wenn Journalisten adipöse Kinder in einer Klinik oder bei einer Behandlung beim Hausarzt zeigen, gibt es keine bereits vorhandenen Rechte zur Veröffentlichung. Da müssen Drehgenehmigungen oder Fotorechte eingeholt werden – bei allen Eltern der beteiligten Kinder, die dann zu sehen sein werden. Wenn es auch noch ein längerer Fernsehbericht sein soll, muss das Kind auch etwas „in die Kamera sagen", das heißt, es muss klar verständliche Sätze sprechen können, idealerweise auch noch dialektfrei. Natürlich nimmt man lieber ein sympathisches Kind, damit der Zuschauer überhaupt noch irgendwie bereit ist, hinzuhören.

Unsere politische Agenda

16. KAPITEL

Unsere politische Agenda

Prophylaxe und „Keine Angst vor dem Strafrecht!"

Man muss davon ausgehen, dass jedes vierte Kind übergewichtig bzw. jedes fünfte fettsüchtig ist und nach Schätzungen auch noch jedes fünfte Kind in Deutschland an einer psychischen Störung leidet (hier gibt es sicherlich auch eine Schnittmenge). Angesichts dieses epidemischen Kinderleids erscheint uns die Forderung nach Einsatz des Staates gerechtfertigt. Ansätze gibt es, aber sie sind so zaghaft, dass sie nur wenig bewirken werden. Ärzte und Therapeuten auf der einen und Eltern auf der anderen Seite können viel tun, allerdings immer mit dem Gegenwind der Gesellschaft. Die kleinen Patienten sind stigmatisiert und viele von ihnen erhalten keine elterliche Unterstützung – im Gegenteil, sie werden in der Ausbildung der Krankheit von denselben bewusst oder unbewusst noch gefördert.

Wir stellen fest, dass wir bei der Bekämpfung der Adipositas so früh wie möglich ansetzen müssen, damit die Neigung zur Krankheit bei den Patienten in einem Stadium erkannt wird, in dem noch das Leben mit einem Normalgewicht ermöglicht werden kann. Prophylaxe steht also an erster Stelle, und hier gibt es einiges zu tun, denn wir blicken auf ein großes Vakuum innerhalb der Gesellschaft. Selbstverständlich anerkennen wir Aktionen, die von der Industrie oder Verbänden gesteuert werden und die

Beweglichkeit der Kinder fördern sollen. Das ist erfreulich und unterstützenswert. Nur werden sie die schon übergewichtigen Kinder nicht erreichen, weil sie von solchen Aktionen nichts wissen oder nicht den Mut finden, teilzunehmen. Die adipösen Kids schämen sich ihrer Schwerfälligkeit bei der Bewegung und können mit den anderen Kindern nicht mithalten. Eine doppelte bedauernswerte Frustration.

▶▶▶ Wie kann der Staat Einfluss nehmen?

Prinzipiell durch Maßnahmen, die

▶ die Früherkennung der Krankheit fördern

▶ der Aufklärung, die ein Verständnis beim Umfeld schafft und damit die Stigmatisierung eingrenzt, dienen

▶ die Vernetzung der medizinischen und therapeutischen Versorgung stärken

▶ die Eltern verstärkt in die Sorgfaltspflicht der Erziehung einbinden.

Die am politischen Prozess Beteiligten verfügen über einen reichen Erfahrungsschatz bei der Bekämpfung von Epidemien von Süchten. Der Staat zeigt bereits große Präsenz bei der Eindämmung der Nikotinsucht und kleineren Maßnahmen im Bereich Drogen und Alkohol. Immer geht es dabei auch um den Schutz von Kindern und Jugendlichen.

Bei der Bekämpfung von Adipositas muss dieser Aspekt in den Vordergrund gestellt werden. Die frühe Weichenstellung entscheidet über das spätere Gewicht des Kindes.

▶▶▶   **Deswegen fordern wir:**

▶ Verpflichtende Ernährungsberatung während der Schwangerschaft

▶ Die Einführung des Schulfachs „Gesundheitskunde" in der Grundschule (mit dem Schwerpunkt „Ernährung")

▶ die schulische Erziehung zum Trinken von Wasser. Wasser sollte auch während des Unterrichts getrunken werden

▶ Die Kontrolle von Essen in Kitas und Ganztagsschulen nach gesundheitlichen Mindestanforderungen, die sich z. B. am Fettgehalt orientieren

▶ Die Erweiterung des Schulsports (hier könnte man jeweils zwei Jahrgangsstufen zusammenpacken und verschiedene Sportarten zur Wahl anbieten, damit Übergewichtige nicht stigmatisiert werden und sich zumindest eine Sportart aussuchen können, in der sie sich am ehesten zurechtfinden)

▶ Die Ergänzung des Schulsports um Fördergruppen, die stadtteilbezogen unter kommunaler Verantwortung angeboten werden müssen und von den Kinderärzten verpflichtend vermittelt werden

▶ Die Wiedereinführung schulmedizinischer Untersuchungen im zweijährigen Rhythmus. Übergewichtige Kinder müssen sich von da an quartalsmäßig zusammen mit mindestens einem Elternteil beim Kinderarzt einfinden

▶ Die Aufnahme der Ernährungsberatung durch Kinderärzte bereits bei Feststellung des Übergewichts

▶ Die Sensibilisierung und umfassende Aufklärung der Kinderärzte (z. B. durch verpflichtende Fortbildungen), damit gewährleistet ist, dass die fettsüchtigen Kinder durch den Kinderarzt an das Jugendamt überstellt werden, wenn über einen langen Zeitraum hinweg die Eltern erkennbar die Unterstützung bei der Gewichtsabnahme verwehren

▶ Die Sensibilisierung zur aktiven Einbindung der Straftatbestände „Unterlassene Hilfestellung", „Vernachlässigung" und „Kindesmisshandlung", wenn sich unter Obhut des Jugendamtes die Ernährungssituation in einer betroffenen Familie nicht ändert.

Der letzte Punkt ist am kontroversiellsten. Denn wer wünscht schon eine Einmischung ins Privatleben? Gurtpflicht, Rauchverbote, Geschwindigkeitsbegrenzungen – alles schwer durchsetzbar. Wenn es um das Wohl von Kindern geht, gerät die öffentliche Meinung jedoch in Schieflage. Jugendliche Amokläufer, Eltern, die ihre Kinder an die Heizung binden, schlagen, verhungern lassen, töten oder ermorden. Schnell wird recherchiert, ob das Jugendamt nicht doch schon einen Hinweis von Nachbarn oder der Schule bekommen hat, rasch wünscht man sich den „Eingreifer-Staat". Umso mehr, wenn schon erwogen worden war, das Sorgerecht zu entziehen und das Kind dann doch bei der gewalttätigen Mutter verblieb. Dann

gibt es Fälle, da hätte man das Kind vielleicht doch lieber bei den Eltern belassen sollen. Ein fürchterlich komplexer Bereich mit sehr differenzierten individuellen Problemstellungen. Und dennoch sagen wir:

Wenn Eltern ihr fettsüchtiges Kind trotz kinderärztlicher Hinweise oder Ansprache von Lehrern und Ärzten des schulmedizinischen Dienstes nicht kompetent behandeln lassen, ist dies – je nach Schweregrad und Uneinsichtigkeit – eine Form von „Vernachlässigung" oder „Unterlassener Hilfeleistung" und damit ein Straftatbestand. „Nicht kompetent behandeln

lassen" heißt, dass die Hinzuziehung weiterer Therapeuten abgelehnt oder eine Kur verweigert wird – obwohl der Hausarzt oder Kinderarzt auf die Gefahren von Übergewicht und Fettsucht beim eigenen Kind deutlich hinweist. Das erscheint uns wichtig, damit der Kinderarzt eine Handhabe hat, eine Sanktionsmöglichkeit. Einen Ansatz von Autorität, der weit über die ärztliche Schweigepflicht hinausreicht.

Kindesmisshandlung sehen wir gegeben, wenn die Eltern mehr tun, als untätig zuzuschauen. Wenn zuhause bewusst fett gekocht wird, weil man sich „von einem Arzt keine Vorschriften machen lassen will", „weil man besser weiß, was gut für das Kind ist". Die Verletzungen sind nicht durch Blutergüsse ersichtlich, auch nicht durch gebrochene Knochen. Aber die Schädigung der Gesundheit kann so nachhaltig sein, dass sie zu einem früheren Tod führt und auf jeden Fall zu einer Reihe von assoziierten Krankheiten. *Eine besonders perfide Art der Misshandlung.*

Ältere Kinder und Jugendliche können Ernährungsprotokolle führen und im Gespräch mit Vertretern von Jugendämtern Auskunft über das vorgegebene Essverhalten geben. Eine mögliche Sorge aufgrund einer Nichtüberprüfbarkeit haben wir nicht.

Jahrzehntelange Aufklärung über die Notwendigkeit einer gesunden Lebensführung ging an den betroffenen Familien scheinbar spurlos vorüber. Wir freuen uns über staatliche Maßnahmen zur Förderung von Bewegung und hochwertigem Essen, möchten aber das Bewusstsein dort schärfen, wo der Brennpunkt liegt: bei Menschen, die sich nicht mit den schicken Ball spielenden Familien auf ermunternden Werbeplakaten identifizierten.

INTERVIEWS

Interviews mit Ernährungsexperten

Während der Erstellung dieses Buches haben wir festgestellt, dass wir manchen Experten gerne mehr Raum geben möchten, uns ihr Fachwissen und ihre Erfahrungen mitzuteilen. Im Folgenden lesen Sie nun von persönlichen Eindrücken und von Wissenswertem, das den ersten Teil ergänzen soll.

Dr. med. Gerd Claußnitzer

Kinder- und Jugendarzt in der medinet Spessart-Klinik

● *Dr. Claußnitzer, wie muss man sich die Aufnahme der Kinder und Jugendlichen in der Klinik vorstellen?*

▶ Zum Erstgespräch kommen die Kinder und Jugendlichen mit ihren Eltern oder einem Elternteil. In dem Arztgespräch geht es darum, den psychosozialen Hintergrund kennenzulernen. Wo gibt es soziale Konflikte, gibt es Probleme zwischen den Eltern und den Kindern oder frustrale Erlebnisse, was ist die Motivation, eine Kur zu machen, und welche Krankengeschichte liegt zugrunde? Wenn die psychosozialen Probleme überwiegen, findet noch ein gemeinsames Gespräch mit dem Psychologen und dem Pädagogen statt. Nach dem Zusammentragen aller Informationen und der Aufnahmeuntersuchung werden ein Therapieplan erstellt und Regeln vereinbart, in denen es zum Beispiel um das Anrufen der Eltern geht.

● *In welchem Zustand kommen die Kinder und Jugendlichen zu Ihnen?*

▶ In der Regel kommen sie hoch motiviert. Für viele sind wir so etwas wie die letzte Hoffnung, nachdem schon einige Diäten gescheitert sind. Manchmal gibt es auch überzogene Vorstellungen, Ideen von einem schnellen Erfolg. Da müssen wir aufklären über die Langzeitrelevanz einer Verhaltensänderung.

● *Wie oft sehen Sie als Arzt die Kinder?*

▶ Der Therapieplan beinhaltet eine Untersuchung in der Woche, wobei es noch zweimal täglich die Möglichkeit gibt, uns als Ärzte zu konsultieren. Die regelmäßigen Untersuchungen sind wichtig, um Ergebnisse zu besprechen, um notwendige Änderungen des Therapieplans vorzunehmen und die Ziele eventuell zu modifizieren.

● *Haben Sie schon am Anfang der Kur eine Ahnung davon, wie sich der Patient entwickeln wird – eine Art intuitiver Prognose?*

▶ Ja. Die familiäre Situation weist auf die Ressourcen hin, über die der Patient verfügt. Wir haben ein Schema für Prognosen erstellt, das sich immer wieder bewahrheitet. Darin geht es um die Dimensionen Motivation, Selbsteinschätzung, psychosoziale Familiensituation und realistische Zielplanung.

● *Hatten Sie auch schon Patienten, die Sie gerade aufgrund einer bestimmten Prognose gerne länger in der Klinik behalten hätten?*

▶ Ja, aber das kann man dann auch beim Kostenträger durchsetzen. Eine beantragte Verlängerung wird selten abgesagt. Meistens werden drei bis vier Wochen Klinikaufenthalt bewilligt, häufig auch sechs Wochen. Bei schweren Fällen können es acht bis zehn Wochen sein; die Höchstdauer in unserer Klinik liegt bei zwölf Wochen.

● *Hatten Sie auch schon Fälle, die Ihnen nahe gingen?*

▶ **Ich erinnere mich an einen Jungen, dessen Mutter direkt nach der Geburt starb. Der Vater war drogenabhängig, die Großeltern überfordert, und der Bub kam ins Heim. Wenn man mit solch einer Lebensgeschichte befasst ist, berührt einen das schon. Dann gibt es aber auch sehr positives Feedback, wenn etwa ehemalige Patienten anrufen oder schreiben und über ihren weiteren Erfolg berichten.**

● *Wie sehr beschäftigen Sie sich mit der Nachhaltigkeit, also mit dem Leben nach dem stationären Aufenthalt, wenn weiter abgenommen werden oder das Gewicht gehalten werden muss?*

▶ Diese Zeit ist sehr wichtig. Wir haben als Modellprojekt eine ambulante Nachsorge in der Klinik über drei Jahre hinweg in vierwöchigen Abständen angeboten, zu denen ungefähr ein Drittel der ehemaligen

Patienten mit Wohnsitz in Hessen mit ihren Familien gekommen sind, um gemeinsam zu kochen oder familientherapeutische Angebote zu nutzen. Gewünscht hätten wir uns eine höhere Zahl, die allerdings nicht zu erreichen ist, wenn man Patienten aus dem gesamten Bundesgebiet hat, für die die Anreise einfach zu aufwändig ist. Nun haben wir das Adipositasnetzwerk Hessen gegründet, um näher an den Patienten zu sein. Ziel ist es, flächendeckend interdisziplinäre Therapiezentren vorzuhalten, die auch Ernährungsberatung und familientherapeutische Maßnahmen vermitteln oder anbieten. In Hessen haben wir bereits sechzig Mitglieder.

● *Sie sind selbst Vorsitzender des Netzwerks, warum liegt Ihnen die Behandlung der Adipositas so sehr am Herzen?*

▶ Es reizt mich, dass ich als Arzt bei der Behandlung der Adipositas von Kindern und Jugendlichen noch so viel erreichen kann. Kinder und Jugendliche verfügen über Verhaltensgewohnheiten, die noch nicht zu sehr eingeschliffen sind. Sie lassen sich gut zu körperlicher Aktivität motivieren und können einiges durch ihr Wachstum noch ausgleichen. Da lässt sich das Ruder noch einmal herumreißen.

● *Sie sind Vater eines kleinen Sohnes. Denken Sie, dass Sie Ihr Kind mehr als andere zu Bewegung und gesundem Essen motivieren?*

▶ Im Kindergarten bin ich der einzige Vater, der seinen Sohn nicht mit dem Auto bringt. Ganz sicher strahlt mein Beruf auch auf meine Familie ab. Ich achtete von Anfang an auf Bewegung und gesundes Essen. Die Großmutter ist immer ganz überrascht, dass der Junge keinen Appetit auf Schokolade hat.

● *Was wäre Ihre politische Forderung zur breiten Bekämpfung der Adipositas?*

▶ Ich denke an keine Einzelforderung, sondern an ein notwendiges Umdenken in der Gesellschaft. Unser ganzer Alltag ist auf Unbeweglichkeit ausgerichtet, dies muss sich komplett ins Gegenteil verkehren. Zusätzlich noch ein stärkeres Bewusstsein für gesünderes Essen – dann haben wir schon viel erreicht.

● *Dr. Claußnitzer, herzlichen Dank für das Gespräch!*

Thomas Kukula

ist Pädagogischer Leiter in der medinet Spessart-Klinik und arbeitet dort seit 22 Jahren mit adipösen Jugendlichen

● *Herr Kukula, in welchem emotionalen Zustand kommen die Jugendlichen zu Ihnen?*

▶ Unsere jugendlichen Patienten stehen in den ersten Tagen in der Regel unter starkem Druck und Stress, die aus mannigfachen Gründen resultieren. Da gibt es Mitschüler, die die adipösen Kinder zuhause wegen ihrer Figur verspotteten, Konfektionsgrößen, die zu klein geworden sind, und ein Spiegelbild, das man selbst nicht mehr mag. Dies löst einen derart großen Leidensdruck aus, dass die Jugendlichen zu 85 Prozent aus einer Eigenmotivation heraus kommen. Sie haben aus der Presse oder durch Bekannte von der Spessart-Klinik gehört und erwarten Hilfe und Unterstützung.

● *Kommen die Jugendlichen in Begleitung ihrer Eltern oder zumindest eines Elternteils?*

▶ Die meisten werden gebracht, allerdings auch häufig im Sinne von abgegeben. Ich habe tatsächlich einmal einen Vater erlebt, der uns seine Tochter mit den Worten: „Ich hole sie dann runderneuert wieder ab" anvertraute.

● *Damit bestätigen Sie die These, dass eine gestörte Eltern-Kind-Beziehung einer der Auslöser für Fettsucht ist.*

▶ **Ganz bestimmt. Viele Eltern nehmen für sich auch nicht wahr, dass sie ihr Kind isolieren. Sie verwechseln die Versorgung mit einem eigenen Fernseher oder Autofahrten zu einer Party mit einer echten Zuneigung zur Tochter oder zum Sohn. Häufig wissen sie nicht, was ihr Kind beschäftigt. Sich auch nur 20 Minuten Zeit zu nehmen hat eine andere Qualität als eine unreflektierte Dienstleistung – im Übrigen ein Problem, das sich durch alle Schichten zieht. Die Kinder sehen zwar, was ihre Eltern für sie leisten, empfinden aber keine emotionale Bindung. Dies gilt auch für Familien, die für sich große Aufgeschlossenheit und Modernität beanspruchen. „Wir sind doch ganz locker", sagen Eltern dann, wenn sie ihre 14-jährige Tochter zur Diskothek bringen, sie aber**

nicht wirklich in ihrer Entwicklung wahrnehmen. Häufig erleben wir, dass die Jugendlichen sehr davon berührt sind, dass ihnen in der Klinik zum ersten Mal jemand lange zuhört.

● *Wie entsteht dann die konkrete Fettsucht?*

▶ Die Kinder und Jugendlichen haben kein Gegenüber, kein Regulat, das sie zu mehr Bewegung und gesundem Essen anregt. Sie fahren mit der U-Bahn zur Schule, treffen sich am Nachmittag mit Freunden, mit denen sie nur zusammensitzen, und verbringen den Abend mit zwei Tüten Kartoffelchips vor dem eigenen Fernseher. Es fehlt das Modell, die Eltern, die selbst Sport machen oder sich bewegen. Stellen Sie sich am besten einen Vater vor, der sein Kind mit den Worten „Sei nicht so laut!" anschreit. Das ist kein Modell und auch kein Leitbild. Aus dieser unkontrollierten und nicht positiv beeinflussten Bequemlichkeit heraus entsteht die Fettsucht, und sie entsteht eben sehr schnell, wenn man über einen gewissen Zeitraum hinweg mehr konsumiert, als man verbraucht.

● *Die Kinder erleben also in einer Reha erstmals den Idealzustand?*

▶ Ja und nein, denn auch die Klinik ist eine Scheinwelt. Deswegen ist es so wichtig, dass wir als Therapeuten authentisch sind. Wir werden ja auch dafür bezahlt, dass wir den Jugendlichen zuhören und sie wahrnehmen, aber wir dürfen zum Beispiel nicht besonders cool sein, um bei den Patienten besser anzukommen. Auch in der Scheinwelt muss es einen echten Zustand geben. Wir sind oft die Ersten, die die Jugendlichen so wahrnehmen, wie sie sind. Ich kenne Eltern, die können zwei Stunden lang über ihr Kind reden, ohne es zu kennen. Problematisch wird es, wenn die Jugendlichen in einer Reha selbstbewusster werden, dann aber zuhause auf einen unveränderten Zustand treffen.

● *Kann man hier nicht gegensteuern?*

▶ Und ob, und das ist uns auch ganz wichtig. In jeder Reha findet ein Elternseminar statt, das dann auch sehr gut angenommen wird, wenn die Eltern sich erst ein paar Stunden in der Klinik aufhalten und sich oft zum ersten Mal intensiv mit der Krankheit der Kinder befassen. Entscheidend ist es, den Eltern nicht mit erhobenem Zeigefinger zu begegnen. Inhaltlich arbeiten wir familientherapeutisch, zeigen aber auch, wie wir mit den Kindern kochen. Zusätzlich telefonieren wir regelmäßig mit den Eltern – und natürlich vor allem dann, wenn etwas Besonderes vorgefallen ist.

● *Was können Sie den Eltern noch auf den Weg mitgeben? Echte Zuneigung kann doch auch durch einen Rehatag oder Familientherapie nicht entstehen?*

▶ Unser Vorbild ist es, konsequent zu sein. Regeln zu vereinbaren – zum Beispiel zum Rauchen – und die Einhaltung auch zu kontrollieren und entsprechend zu behandeln. Die Konsequenz zeigt den Jugendlichen, dass es uns ernst ist, wir sie aber auch ernstnehmen. Diese Verhalten bekommen wir genauso zurück. Wahrnehmen und ernstnehmen – das ist im Umgang miteinander entscheidend. Auch kleine Vorfälle wichtig nehmen, um dem Gegenüber die Ernsthaftigkeit der Wahrnehmung zu spiegeln.

● *Gibt es einen Unterschied in der Therapie von Jungen und Mädchen?*

▶ Im Prinzip nicht, wobei bei Mädchen hinsichtlich Konfektionsgrößen der Leidensdruck schneller beginnt. Das Grundmuster ist immer: Ich muss den anderen wahrnehmen.

● *Wenn Sie politisch etwas zur Bekämpfung der Fettsucht bewegen könnten: Welche Maßnahme würden Sie ergreifen?*

▶ Schnellere Präventionsmaßnahmen, die Familienunterstützung vorantreiben, mehrere kostenlose Elternseminare. Elternarbeit sollte auch innerhalb der Kinderreha bezahlt werden.

● *Herr Kukula, danke für das Gespräch!*

Dr. med. Wolfram Hartmann

Präsident des Verbands der Kinder- und Jugendärzte und seit 28 Jahren praktizierender Kinderarzt

● *Dr. Hartmann, man mag die Zahlen über die Verbreitung der Adipositas kaum glauben. Stellen Sie in Ihrer ärztlichen Praxis tatsächlich eine Zunahme der fettsüchtigen und übergewichtigen Kinder fest?*

▶ Dr. med. Wolfram Hartmann: Ja, dieses Phänomen nimmt seit etwa zehn Jahren auffallend zu. Die Eltern sprechen das Übergewicht in der Regel nicht an, sondern kommen wegen anderer Krankheiten mit dem Kind in die Praxis. Bei nur etwa einem Prozent der betroffenen Kinder ergreifen Mutter oder Vater die Initiative, den Arzt auf die Problematik anzusprechen.

● *Das heißt, dass der Arzt von sich aus auf die Eltern zugeht?*

▶ Ja, und in dem Moment, in dem er die Eltern auch noch über gesunde Ernährung und Bewegung berät, tut er dies ohne Bezahlung. Nur in seltenen Ausnahmefällen (Sonderverträge) gehören solche Beratungsgespräche zum Leistungskatalog der Krankenversicherungen. **Ein Arzt, der von sich aus den Befund objektiviert, indem er ein sogenanntes Somatogramm zur Feststellung des BMI aufstellt und zusammen mit den Eltern das Ergebnis erörtert, tut dies freiwillig und unentgeltlich. Wir als Kinder- und Jugendärzte machen mehr, als wir tun müssten.** Die Krankenversicherung ist erst ab der 97. Perzentile zuständig. Da ist das Kind schon so massiv übergewichtig, dass man eigentlich nur noch auf Beibehaltung des Gewichts und nicht mehr an Abnehmen denken kann.

● *Wie reagieren die Eltern denn, wenn man sie auf die Notwendigkeit zu mehr Bewegung und gesünderem Essen anspricht?*

▶ **Bewegung und gesundes Kochen machen Arbeit – das möchten die meisten nicht übernehmen. Viele nehmen sich auch einfach nicht die Zeit, sich mit der Problematik zu beschäftigen, und scheuen die Kämpfe mit ihrem Kind.** Häufig versuchen die Eltern, das Problem nur beim Kind zu sehen, und wollen im Alltag der Familien und bei sich selbst nichts verändern; Erfolg wird es aber nur geben, wenn auch die Eltern sich entsprechend verhalten. Wir plädieren für Modelle der positiven Verstärkung. Krankenversicherungen könnten Bonusprogramme für Familien anbieten, in denen etwa Jahresgebühren für den Sportverein oder die Kosten für einen Fahrradhelm erstattet werden, wenn die Kinder regelmäßig an den gesetzlichen Früherkennungsuntersuchungen und den öffentlich empfohlenen Impfungen teilgenommen haben.

● *Das heißt, dass Sie schwerpunktmäßig nicht auf eine freiwillige positive Einflussnahme der Eltern setzen?*

▶ Nein, vielmehr muss überall dort angesetzt werden, wo der Staat über seine Einrichtungen selbst in der Pflicht ist. In den Kindergärten, in Kindertagesstätten und in Schulen. Da gibt es Ganztags-Kindergärten, in denen ungesundes Essen vorgehalten wird, weil man nur auf den Preis des Caterers schaut. Sinn würde es machen, wenn im Kindergarten zusammen mit den Kindern gesundes Essen gekocht wird, um Ihnen auch gleich das richtige Wissen zu vermitteln. Oder denken Sie an Kioske in Schulen. Hier ist das Ernährungsangebot in der Regel katastrophal. Verkauft wird vor allem das, was Übergewicht begünstigt. Dann fehlen oft auch die Bewegungsräume in den Kindergärten – sowohl in den Häusern als auch im Freien. Ein nächster Punkt sind Schuluntersuchungen. In Bayern und Baden-Württemberg wurden die Schuleingangsuntersuchungen abgeschafft. Kinder im Alter zwischen sechs und zehn Jahren werden bundesweit – von wenigen Ausnahmen abgesehen – überhaupt nicht mehr vom jugendmedizinischen Dienst der Gesundheitsämter untersucht. **Hier hat es in den letzten Jahren massive Sparmaßnahmen zulasten der Kinder und Jugendlichen gegeben, gegen die wir uns wehren. Die Politik hat hier eine sehr große Verantwortung, die sie unbedingt nutzen muss.**

● *Dr. Hartmann, haben Sie herzlichen Dank für das Gespräch!*

Georg Ehrmann

Rechtsanwalt und Geschäftsführender Vorsitzender der Deutschen Kinderhilfe Direkt e.V.

● *Herr Ehrmann, könnte man die Straftatbestände „Vernachlässigung", „Unterlassene Hilfeleistung" und „Kindesmisshandlung" bei Eltern adipöser Kinder anwenden, die in einer Trotzreaktion gegenüber Kinderärzten und Lehrern ihre Kinder weiterhin ungesund versorgen und nicht zu Bewegung anleiten?*

▶ In letzter Konsequenz kann man dies aus heutiger Sicht schon tun. Prinzipiell befürworte ich auch Sanktionsmöglichkeiten gegen Eltern, wenn es um das Wohl des Kindes geht. Ich rate jedoch Kinderärzten und Erzieherinnen, den Weg zum Jugendamt einzuschlagen, denn dort verfügt man über einen umfangreichen Maßnahmenkatalog in Anwendung des Kinder- und Jugendhilfegesetzes und könnte, wenn keine Maßnahmen greifen, immer noch ein Strafverfahren in Gang setzen. Es muss doch in erster Hinsicht um Hilfe für das Kind und die Familie gehen. Das heißt, dass die Jugendämter mit den Familien einen nachhaltigen Hilfeplan aufstellen und ihr gesamtes Netzwerk wie etwa Selbsthilfegruppen, Vereine oder Ernährungsberatungsstellen einbringen. Dies kann dann durch Auflagen und Hausbesuche auch kontrolliert werden. **Die Jugendämter sind sehr erfahren im Umgang mit schwierigen familiären Situationen, allerdings sicherlich noch nicht im Umgang mit Adipositas. Hier liegt auch das eigentliche Problem. Die bestehende Rechtslage ist eindeutig, in den von Ihnen geschilderten Fällen stellt das unkooperative Verhalten eindeutig eine Kindesmisshandlung und damit eine Beeinträchtigung des Kindeswohls dar – da haben die Jugendämter eine Eingriffspflicht.** Unser Ziel muss es sein, dass diese Erkenntnis in den Köpfen der Beteiligten ankommt. Das war auch so bei der Kindesmisshandlung, lange wurden eindeutige Zeichen wie verdächtige Brandnarben bei Kindern ignoriert. Heute sind Ärzte und Jugendämter sensibilisiert und sehen deutlich, welche Verletzungen von Bügeleisen oder Zigaretten kommen und offensichtlich auf eine Kindesmisshandlung hinweisen. Da steht der Arzt unter Meldepflicht – die dann auch über der Schweigepflicht steht: Er muss den Fall beim Jugendamt anzeigen.

● *Herr Ehrmann, wenn es dieses Netz schon gibt, müsste man wohl „nur" noch für Aufklärung und Öffentlichkeit sorgen?*

▶ Ja, und da gibt es zahlreiche Beispiele, bei denen im Sinne des Kinderschutzes über Jahre hinweg aufgeklärt wurde, um dann auch Maßnahmen und eingespielte Verfahren zu erwirken. Wir müssen aber auch die bestehenden Hilfsangebote ausbauen und auch die Jugendämter mit dem Wissen und auch den Mitteln ausstatten, dass sie diesen Familien helfen können. Weitere Kürzungen im Bereich der Kinder- und Jugendhilfe darf es da nicht geben.

● *Herr Ehrmann, haben Sie herzlichen Dank für das Gespräch!*

Prof. Dr. Volker Pudel

Leiter der Ernährungspsychologischen Forschungsstelle in der Klinik für Psychiatrie und Psychotherapie der Universität Göttingen

● *Prof. Dr. Pudel, welche Bedeutung hat die Verbreitung der Adipositas für die Volkswirtschaft?*

▶ Die WHO bewertet die Adipositas weltweit (!) als eines der größten Gesundheitsprobleme. Damit sind erhebliche Auswirkungen (Kosten) auf die Gesundheitssysteme zu erwarten. Bereits heute werden die Kosten auf ca. fünf bis sechs Prozent der Gesamtausgaben im Gesundheitssystem geschätzt. Experten der International Obesity Task Force prognostizieren, dass sich die Prävalenz der Adipositas weltweit in den nächsten 30 Jahren verdoppeln wird.

● *Sie weisen immer wieder darauf hin, dass die Behandlung von Adipositas nicht zureichend abgerechnet werden kann. Wie sind hier die Zusammenhänge?*

▶ Das Problem ist – vor allem in Deutschland –, dass Adipositas „versicherungstechnisch" nicht als Krankheit definiert ist. Damit sind die Behandlungskosten nicht erstattungsfähig, und die Statistiken der Gesundheitssurveys – was Adipositas angeht – unvollständig, ebenso wie die Berechnung der volkswirtschaftlichen Kosten, die durch Adipositas verursacht werden (auch indirekte Kosten wie Arbeitsausfall etc.). Übergewicht (BMI zwischen 25 und 30), insbesondere aber Adipositas (BMI > 30) gelten unbestritten als Risikofaktor für Diabetes, Herz-Kreislauf-Erkrankungen, Schlafapnoe, Gelenkbeschwerden, psychischen Leidensdruck etc. Daher ist es auch volkswirtschaftlich nicht weise, die Ursache dieser Erkrankungen nicht als erstattungsfähige Krankheitsbehandlung zu betrachten. Adipöse müssen erst „richtig krank werden", damit sie behandelt werden können. Besonders deutlich stellt sich diese paradoxe Auffassung dar, wenn Kinder und Jugendliche nicht behandelt werden, bei denen dann lebenslang die Kosten für chronische Krankheiten übernommen werden müssen, die durch Adipositas ausgelöst werden.

● *In welchen Bereichen könnte man heute schon auf der Basis der aktuellen versicherungstechnischen Grundlage die Behandlung verbessern?*

▶ Es stellt sich ernsthaft die Frage, ob eine Intensivierung der Therapie der Adipositas sinnvoll und überhaupt möglich ist. Um 16 Millionen Menschen in Deutschland effektiv zu therapieren, sind die therapeutischen Potenziale nicht einmal verfügbar. Ganz abgesehen davon, dass Adipositastherapie – auch wenn sie optimiert durchgeführt werden kann – lange keine zufriedenstellenden langfristigen Resultate zeigt. Als Anforderung an eine optimierte Adipositastherapie gilt heute: (1) Multimodales Therapieprogramm mit (2) interdisziplinärem Team aus Arzt, Psychologe, Ernährungs- und Bewegungsfachkraft über (3) mindestens zwölf Monate mit (4) nachfolgendem Anschlussprogramm über möglichst lange Zeit. Diese Kriterien werden aber bei weitem nicht von allen angebotenen Programmen erfüllt. Alle Kurzzeitinterventionen (so z. B. mit Diäten) sind nutzlos, oft sogar kontraproduktiv. **Die optimale Behandlung der Adipositas besteht darin, sie nicht entstehen zu lassen. Doch breit angelegte, wirksame Präventionsprogramme stehen nicht zur Verfügung bzw. werden nicht realisiert.** Gerade für Kinder und Jugendliche wäre es von elementarer Wichtigkeit, durch Prävention die Gewichtszunahme zu verhindern.

● *Sie möchten aufgrund der erschreckenden Verbreitung der Adipositas den Staat mehr in die Pflicht nehmen. Wie lauten Ihre konkreten Vorstellungen?*

▶ „Ernährung" ist in Deutschland ein unreglementierter Bereich. Daher arbeitet die Prävention mit Hinweisen auf das Verhalten, könnte aber zusätzlich auch Verhältnisse ändern, um dem Individuum zu helfen, die Empfehlungen der Verhaltensprävention auch zu realisieren. Doch dazu müsste der Ernährungsbereich in gewisser Weise auch reglementiert werden – z. B. durch gesetzliche Rahmenrichtlinien, die vorgeben, welche Speisen in der Gemeinschaftsverpflegung angeboten werden. Die Empfehlungen zur Nährstoffzufuhr der Deutschen Gesellschaft für Ernährung könnten die Grundlage bilden, die im Verlauf einer Woche von der Gemeinschaftsverpflegung erfüllt werden muss. Wer die Hygiene in Kindergärten reglementiert und überwacht, kann auch das Speisenangebot regulieren. Ähnliche Vorgaben könnten sich auf Snacks beziehen, die in den letzten Jahren in immer größeren Verpackungseinheiten angeboten wurden. Es stimmt nachdenklich, dass in jedem Kindergarten, falls eine Zugangsstufe abbricht, sofort ein gelb-schwarzer Warnstreifen aufgeklebt wird, um Haftpflichtansprüche abzuweisen, aber keine Vorgabe existiert, um zu vermeiden, dass die den Kindern angebotenen Speisen den Tatbestand der Körperverletzung erfüllen. Gleiches gilt für die gesamte Gemeinschaftsverpflegung.

● *Als Ernährungswissenschafter fokussieren Sie auf gesunde Ernährung. Welchen Stellenwert hat für Sie die Bewegung?*

▶ In die Verhältnisprävention muss natürlich das Bewegungsverhalten ebenfalls einbezogen werden. Die Immobilität, ausgelöst durch TV und PC im Kinderzimmer, stellt in den letzten Jahren einen entscheidenden Faktor für die kindliche und jugendliche Adipositasentwicklung dar. Hier könnten Moden entwickelt werden, um aktive Bewegung im Alltag „in" zu gestalten, ihr Prestigewert zu verleihen. Auch hier sind gesellschaftliche Konsensbildungen nötig, die veranlassen, dass Bewegungsräume (auch Radwege) geschaffen werden.

● *Sind Ihre Forderungen realistisch oder doch eher eine schöne Vision?*

▶ **Ein gutes Beispiel liefert der deutsche Straßenverkehr, der Anfang der 60er Jahre jährlich über 24.000 Verkehrstote forderte. Hier wurde so gut wie keine Verhaltensprävention (Gespräch mit dem Autofahrer) vorgenommen, sondern intensiv auf Verhältnisprävention gesetzt. Im letzten Jahr sanken die Verkehrstoten auf unter 5.000 Opfer, obschon seither viel mehr und viel schnellere Autos in Deutschland fahren. Durch Beplankungen der Autobahnen, Geschwindigkeitsbeschränkungen, Techniken wie ABS oder ESP, intelligente Leitsysteme, Rückhaltesysteme etc. wurden die Verhältnisse günstig geändert, um auf das Verhalten durch die Bedingungen einzuwirken.**

● *Prof. Dr. Pudel, wir danken Ihnen für das Gespräch.*

Diana, 19 Jahre

Ehemalige Patientin der Spessart-Klinik

● *Diana, wie kam es, dass du so zugenommen hast?*

▶ Ich habe in einem Jahr fünfzehn bis zwanzig Kilo zugenommen, das ging „einfach so". Bis zum Alter von zwölf konnte ich alles essen, was ich wollte, und dann wog ich plötzlich immer mehr. Ich habe gar nichts Besonderes gegessen, nur eher aus Langeweile. Dann bin ich eben zum

Kühlschrank gegangen. Manchmal auch aus Kummer. Zu wenig Bewegung hatte ich nie, ich habe immer Sport gemacht. Im Nachhinein denke ich, dass ich wegen der Snacks zwischendurch zugenommen habe.

● *Warst du nicht eitel? Hast du nicht versucht, schon die ersten fünf Kilo wieder abzunehmen?*

▶ Na ja, ich war bei allem nie hässlich. Manche sagten auch, dass mir meine Rundungen ganz gut stehen. Und als ich bewusst abnehmen wollte, hat sich auf der Waage überhaupt nichts bewegt. Im Gegenteil: Ich hatte den Eindruck, dass ich da dann auch noch einmal zugenommen habe. Ich konnte das alles gar nicht verstehen. Ich habe doch auch immer Sport gemacht.

● *Wie bist du auf die Idee gekommen, eine Kur zu beantragen?*

▶ An eine Kur dachte ich gar nicht. Ich habe meinem Hausarzt mein Leid geklagt. Ich war immer verzweifelter, konnte gar nicht mehr in den Spiegel schauen. Psychisch war ich total am Ende. Ich fand das alles so ungerecht. Ich hatte doch nicht einmal Schokolade gegessen – nie. Mein Hausarzt war dann sehr engagiert und hat irgendwann die Kur für mich beantragt. Der erste Antrag wurde abgelehnt. Dann haben wir Widerspruch eingelegt, und schließlich hat es geklappt.

● *In der Kur in der Spessart-Klinik hast du in vier Wochen zehn Kilo abgenommen. Was war da anders als zuhause?*

▶ Zuerst einmal habe ich mein Trinkverhalten komplett umgestellt. Es gab nur Wasser und Tee. Wasser tranken wir auch vor dem Essen. Immer zwei Gläser, das gab schon einmal ein Gefühl der Sättigung. Dann habe ich viel weniger Fleisch und Kartoffeln gegessen. Verzichten musste ich nie – das hält man auf Dauer auch nicht durch –, aber satt wurde ich von der Gemüsebeilage. Das Fleisch war dann für den Genuss. Und natürlich gab es zwischendurch nichts zu essen. Ich glaube, es hat auch geholfen, dass wir alle miteinander bewusst gegessen haben.

● *Zuhause hast du dann wieder fünf Kilo zugenommen. Was ist da falschgelaufen?*

▶ Das überlege ich mir immer wieder. Mir kommt es so vor, als würde ich schon vom Hinschauen zunehmen. Ich koche jetzt zusammen mit meiner Mutter so, wie ich es in der Klinik gelernt habe, und mache auch noch fast jeden Tag Sport. Was anders ist als in der Klinik, ist, dass ich zuhause nicht schwimmen gehen kann. Das heißt, ich könnte natürlich schon, aber dann würde ich mich schämen. In der Klinik war es super, weil da hatten wir alle keine perfekte Figur. Ich glaube, das Schwimmen hat's total gebracht.

● *Ist dein Alltag zuhause so schwierig?*

▶ Ja, ich wurde und werde viel gehänselt, wobei ich es wahrscheinlich von allen, die ich in der Kur getroffen habe, am leichtesten habe. Weil ich eigentlich ganz gut aussehe und mit 1,73 auch groß bin.

Aber mir tut es jedes Mal weh, wenn ich zusammen mit meinem Freund ein schlankes Mädchen sehe. Er sagt zwar nichts, aber ich spüre doch, dass er kuckt. Ich bin völlig am Ende. Ich möchte so gerne noch einmal abnehmen, und es gelingt mir einfach nicht.

● *Diana, wir danken dir für das Gespräch.*

Muhammed, 18 Jahre

Ehemaliger Patient der Spessart-Klinik

Muhammed war vier Monate Patient in der Spessart-Klinik und hat in dieser Zeit 40 Kilo abgenommen. Sein Ausgangsgewicht waren 150 Kilo – heute, knapp ein Jahr nach Therapieende hat er wieder fünf Kilo zugenommen.

● *Muhammed, warum wurden Sie so stark übergewichtig?*

▶ Ich war schon als Kind sehr krank und habe nach einigen Jahren endlich mit der richtigen Therapie schmerzfrei leben können. Die Therapie beinhaltete jedoch eine lange Einnahme von Cortison, und dabei nahm ich zu. Ich gewöhnte mich damit schon als Kind an meine zu vielen Kilos. Man könnte fast sagen, dass ich mich mit ihnen anfreundete.

● *Das heißt, dass Sie gar nicht unter Ihrem Gewicht litten?*

▶ Nein, ich war immer zufrieden mit mir selbst. Viele andere, die ich bei der Kur kennenlernte, litten tatsächlich.

● *Warum kamen Sie dann auf die Idee, im Rahmen einer Kur abzunehmen?*

▶ Das war eine Entscheidung, die die Familie getroffen hat. Es lag ja auf der Hand, dass das starke Übergewicht nicht gesund ist, und man muss ja auch an die Zukunft denken. Ich werde irgendwann eine Familie gründen und möchte gesund sein. Meine Eltern haben Druck gemacht, und wir haben dann mit dem Hausarzt gesprochen.

● *Und dieser hat direkt der Versicherungsantrag gestellt?*

▶ Ja, aber die Versicherung hat ihn zweimal abgewiesen. Ich bin dann zu einem Professor ins Krankenhaus gegangen, der sich sehr gut mit Magenverkleinerungen auskennt. Fragen Sie mich nicht, wie er es gemacht hat, aber durch ihn kam ich in die Spessart-Klinik. Und da möchte ich gerne auch noch ein zweites Mal hin.

● *Schaffst du es zuhause nicht, weiter abzunehmen oder zumindest dein Gewicht zu halten? Du könntest doch Sport machen und für dich kochen?*

▶ Nein, zuhause ist es anders. Ich bin jetzt berufstätig. In der Klinik habe ich fünf Stunden Sport am Tag gemacht. Das bemerkte ich gar nicht. Wenn ich jetzt fünf Stunden Sport am Tag machen würde, dürfte ich nur noch drei Stunden schlafen. Ich schaffe es auch nicht, konsequent für mich zu kochen. In der Klinik konzentriert man sich aufs Abnehmen. Deswegen klappt es auch so gut.

● *Muhammed, wir danken Ihnen für das Gespräch.*

Dr. med. Susanne Wiesner

Clinical Research Center Franz Volhard der
Universitätsmedizin Berlin Charité Campus Buch

● *Frau Dr. Wiesner, welche Therapie/welcher Therapiemix ist aus Ihrer Sicht am wirkungsvollsten bei der Behandlung adipöser Kinder und Jugendlicher?*

▶ Aus meiner Erfahrung und auch aus aktuellen Studien ist der Therapieeinstieg mittels Bewegungstherapie am sinnvollsten. Hier konnte gezeigt werden, dass problematische Aspekte im Verlauf der Gewichtsreduktion, wie zum Beispiel der Reduktion des Grundumsatzes, reduziert werden können und die Aufrechterhaltung der Gewichtsreduktion besser funktioniert.

Die Therapie muss dann zu einem bestimmten Zeitpunkt immer durch ernährungsmedizinische Maßnahmen ergänzt werden. Aus wissenschaftlichen Untersuchungen ist anzumerken, dass zur Gewichtszunahme gerade bei Kindern der übermäßigen Fettzufuhr eine bedeutende Rolle zukommt. Häufig ist es aber so, dass zur effektiven Gewichtsreduktion die alleinige Reduktion der Fettmenge nicht ausreicht. Insbesondere gibt es immer mehr Jugendliche, die infolge eines chronischen Bewegungsmangels eine verminderte Stoffwechselfunktion ihrer Muskeln aufweisen, wodurch es dringend erforderlich ist, zunächst die Qualität der Kohlenhydrate, aber auch den Zeitpunkt des Verzehrs und die Menge der Kohlenhydrate zu bedenken.

Gerade bei Kindern spielt das soziale Umfeld eine besonders große Rolle. Kinder aus sozial schwachen Familien und auch Immigrantenkinder sind besonders von Adipositas betroffen. Leider sind die verfügbaren Studien zur Verhaltensprävention, sprich: verhaltenspsychologische Unterstützung nicht sehr Erfolg versprechend verlaufen. Hier muss prinzipiell über Verhältnisprävention, also Verbesserung des sozialen Umfeldes diskutiert werden. Trotzdem ist wichtig, die Kinder verhaltenspsychologisch zu stärken. Es sollte zumindest zeitweise eine derartige Therapiekomponente vorhanden sein.

Zusammenfassend möchte ich sagen, dass mit einer Bewegungstherapie gestartet und dann die Umstellung der Ernährung (erst Reduktion der Fette, dann Optimierung der Kohlenhydrate) erfolgen sollte – dies in der Gesamtheit bei kontinuierlicher verhaltenspsychologischer Unterstützung.

● *Frau Dr. Wiesner, gibt es im Speziellen auch Medikamente, die unterstützen?*

▶ Anzumerken ist hier, dass alle Medikamente zur Adipositastherapie erst ab dem 18. Lebensjahr zugelassen sind. Es liegen aber durchaus Studien, sowohl mit Sibutramin als auch mit Orlistat, bei jugendlichen Patienten ab dem zwölften Lebensjahr vor. Nach meiner Erfahrung – ich verordne im Einverständnis der Eltern nach Unterschrift „aut idem" ab dem 16. Lebensjahr, gibt es besonders gefährdete Patienten, die bereits eine Störung der Glukosetoleranz oder sogar einen Diabetes mellitus Typ 2 bzw. weitere Erkrankungen des Stoffwechsels (Fettstoffwechsel) und Herz-Kreislauf-Systems aufweisen. Hier sollte sehr rasch eine medikamentöse Begleittherapie der Adipositas initialisiert werden, da hier immer mit schweren Folgeerkrankungen wie Nierenschwäche (Dialysenotwendigkeit), Herzschwäche zu rechnen ist, die dann in einem noch sehr jungen Alter (< 40. LJ) auftreten. Sind diese Erkrankungen einmal vorhanden, können Basismaßnahmen zur Gewichtsreduktion, wie z. B. eine effektive

Bewegungstherapie bei bereits eingetretener Herzschwäche oder Durchblutungsstörungen in den Beinen bzw. bei schwer einstellbarer Zuckerkrankheit mit Insulinpflicht, nur noch bedingt durchgeführt werden. Auch sind hier ernährungsmedizinische Interventionen nicht mehr unendlich ausdehnbar. Die Reduktion der Energiezufuhr stellt nur eine Seite der Medaille dar, da sie später oft ausgeschöpft ist! Die Steigerung des Energieverbrauches ist die andere Seite – und sie ist dann nicht mehr möglich.

Adipositas ist durch eine Interaktion von Genen und Umwelt bedingt, wie die meisten anderen Erkrankungen auch, die einer medikamentösen Therapie bedürfen. Vergleichen Sie hierzu durchaus auch aus ethischen Abwägungen einmal das Colon-Karzinom mit Adipositas. Auch hier sind fettreiche bzw. ballaststoffarme Ernährung, Bewegungsmangel und familiäre Disposition für das Auftreten der Erkrankung verantwortlich, nach Hereditätsstudien mit ähnlicher Gewichtung wie bei Adipositas – fünfzig Prozent Genetik; fünfzig Prozent Umwelt. Selbstverständlich soll der Betroffene seinen Lebensstil ändern – das allein würde aber den Krebs wohl kaum heilen bzw. eine Lebensverlängerung/Verbesserung der Lebensqualität bewirken. Dem Adipösen verwehrt man aber eine Therapie, da dieser „selbst schuld" ist. Hier wird nach Auffassung vieler Adipositasforscher mit zweierlei Maßstab gemessen. Auch aus meiner Sicht ist es vernünftiger, die Adipositas zu behandeln, auch medikamentös, da hier genügend wissenschaftliche und molekularbiologische Daten vorliegen – und nicht die Folgen der Adipositas mit zehn weiteren Medikamenten. Auch aus wirtschaftlichen Gründen ist dies nicht effizient.

Andere Krankenkassensysteme, wie z. B. in Schweden und auch in England, die durchaus nicht finanziell besser dastehen als das deutsche Gesundheitssystem, finanzieren eine solche Therapie (bei Erwachsenen). Hier haben gesundheitsökonomische Evaluationen einen Nutzen der medikamentösen Adipositastherapie nachgewiesen.

● *Was sind die Ursachen für Adipositas?*

▶ Die Ursachen der Adipositas sind, wie bereits genannt und wie bei vielen anderen Erkrankungen auch, ein gewisser Anteil genetische Disposition und Umwelteinflüsse. Unsere Gene haben sich in den letzten 50 Jahren nicht geändert, aber unsere Umwelt hat sich bedeutend geändert, sodass es hier zum Einschalten von ganz bestimmten Genen gekommen ist, die dann zu dieser exponentiellen Zunahme der Adipositas geführt haben.

Bei Kindern muss insbesondere erwähnt werden, dass das Zusammen-treffen von sehr energiedichter Nahrung als auch von deutlichem Be-wegungsmangel, und in den letzten Jahren besonders die Zunahme des Bewegungsmangels durch Fernsehen und Computer, als auslösende Faktoren zu bewerten sind. Wie bereits erwähnt, gibt es Unterschiede zwi-schen den einzelnen sozialen Gruppen. Es gibt Studien, die die Adipo-sitashäufigkeit von Kindern und Jugendlichen in sozial schwächer gestell-ten Familien nachweisen, zumindest für die westliche Hemisphäre.

Der Verquickung von Umwelt und genetischen Aspekten kommt man immer mehr auf die Spur. Dies ermöglicht neue Therapiekonzepte. Aus philosophischen Gesichtspunkten muss man sich aber auch damit aus-einandersetzen, dass es schwerlich möglich sein wird, unsere Umwelt wieder so zu verändern, dass wir uns zu dem Bewegungsumfang hin ent-wickeln, den wir vor 20.000 Jahren hatten. Denn die Weiterentwicklung der Technik und insbesondere von Information- und Datenverarbeitung ist ein Teil der menschlichen Evolution und so logisch wie die Evolution selbst, sodass ich hier durchaus kühn behaupten möchte, dass wir uns selbst technisch so verändern müssen, damit wir durch diese neue Umwelt nicht mehr erkranken. Doch bis es so weit ist, gilt es, die Erkenntnisse zu nutzen und Therapiekonzepte anzubieten, gerade auch für Kinder und Jugendliche. Adipositas hat gerade für Kinder deutliche psychosoziale gesundheitliche Konsequenzen, von den gesellschaftlichen gesundheitsökonomischen Problemen ganz zu schweigen.

- *Sehr geehrte Frau Dr. Wiesner, wir danken Ihnen für das Gespräch.*

SERVICETEIL

Rezepte & Hinweise für betroffene Familien

⊙ ESSEN IN DER FAMILIE

Die Eltern sind das Vorbild der Kinder. Sportliche, sich gesund ernährende Eltern haben in der Regel keine adipösen Kinder. Familientherapeutische Maßnahmen beziehen den Doppeleffekt mit ein, bei dem Eltern die Chance nutzen, gemeinsam mit dem Kind abzuspecken. Sinn macht es, Regeln für die ganze Familie aufzustellen:

▶▶▶ Täglich werden nur fünf Mahlzeiten – davon zwei Zwischenmahlzeiten – eingenommen. Verboten sind Snacks und Naschereien zwischendurch.

▶▶▶ Einmal am Tag gibt es eine warme Familienmahlzeit, bei der Essen als Genuss bewusst zelebriert wird. Der psychologische Nebeneffekt: Wenigstens in dieser Zeit findet ein intensiveres Gespräch innerhalb der Familie statt.

▶▶▶ Ein Tag am Wochenende wird gemeinsam aktiv genutzt – für Wanderungen, Schlittschuhlaufen etc.

▶▶▶ Fahrdienste werden bewusst öfter durch Fahrten mit dem Rad oder Zu-Fuß-Gehen ersetzt.

In Bad Orb haben die Gesundheits-Pädagogin Birgit Schäfer-Labude und die Ernährungs-Therapeutin Ingrid Ström die „Kochlöffelbande" gegründet, die Kindern den Genuss am Essen vermittelt. Gekocht wird zusammen mit den Kindern und immer mit frischen Zutaten, die die Kleinen auch riechen sollen. Essen wird als positives Erlebnis zelebriert, im Laufe dessen die Kinder einen Sinnesparcours durchlaufen:

SINNESPARCOURS

Sehen – Mit den Augen essen

Riechen – Immer der Nase nach

Schmecken – Mit Zunge & Gaumen

Tasten – Wie fühlt es sich an

Hören – Das Ohr isst mit

Wichtig ist es, die Bedeutung des Essens derart sinnlich zu vermitteln. Eine positive Herangehensweise, bei der die Kinder verstehen können, dass speisen viel mehr ist als snacken während des Spielens am Computer. Den Kleinen wird eine höherwertige Einstellung zum Essen vermittelt – ein positives Vorbild, das als Anregung für die vielen Kindergärten und Kitas dienen könnte. Es werden bereits Weiterbildungen für Lehrer im Auftrag vom Schulamt angeboten.

Nun vom positiven zum negativen Ansatz:

Für die Versorgung während der Baby- und Kleinkindjahre sind Eltern schon gut damit beraten, wenn sie beim Kauf von Fertigprodukten auf die Aufschrift „Für Kinder bis drei Jahre" achten. Dieser Hinweis ist keine werbliche Aussage, sondern eine Deklaration im Rahmen der Deutschen Diätverordnung. Diese regelt unter anderem die Zusammensetzung (Nährstoffe), die Verwendung von Zusatzstoffen oder Grenzen von Belastung durch Keime oder Pestizide für diätetische Lebensmittel – und verbietet den Zusatz von chemischen Konservierungsstoffen, künstlichen Farb- und Aroma- sowie Süßstoffen und Zuckeraustauschstoffen. Wichtig ist die erwähnte Aufschrift, denn angeboten und entsprechend beworben werden auch Lebensmittel ohne diesen Zusatz. Die Arbeiterkammer hat bei vielen dieser angeblich auf Kinder zugeschnittenen Produkte eine übertriebene Süße und/oder einen zu hohen Fettgehalt festgestellt. Achten Sie in der Werbung auf die gesunden Zwischenmahlzeiten und lesen Sie die Inhaltsstoffe!

Wenn die selbst zubereitete Nahrung frei von Zucker, Süß- und Zuckeraustauschstoffen ist, haben Eltern in prägenden Jahren schon viel dafür getan, dass das Kind erst gar keinen Appetit auf Süßes entwickelt. Bei der Anregung zur Prophylaxe mag der zusätzliche Hinweis auf die Gefahr der Karies von der Notwendigkeit der sorgsamen Auswahl der Nahrung überzeugen.

⊙ ABNEHMEN DURCH FETTKONTROLLE

Das Hauptaugenmerk beim Abspecken der adipösen Kids ist auf die Zufuhr von Fetten und Kohlehydraten auszurichten – prinzipiell keine überraschende Erkenntnis, da viele bekannte Diäten für Erwachsene auch auf dem Wissen über die beiden Parameter aufgebaut sind.

Horst Bauer, Diätassistent und renommierter Experte in der Adipositas-Therapie, wendet als Grundlage die Formel: „Nicht mehr als 30 g Fett täglich" an. Mit „seinen" Kindern in der Spessart-Klinik spricht er über Fettpunkte, wobei 1 g Fett = 1 Fettpunkt gilt – eine für die Kids freundlichere Sprachregelung. Und es ist ihm wichtig, dass die Kinder auch ihren Appetit befriedigen können. Wer eine fettarme Pizza mit fettarmer Salami isst, wird eine Diät eher durchhalten, als den eigentlichen Wunsch-Belag durch Gemüse zu ersetzen.

Die folgenden Rezepte sind dem Kochbuch der Spessart-Klinik entnommen. Ein Buch, das ohne eine entsprechende Erwartungshaltung ein Bestseller wurde, weil die ehemaligen Patienten der Klinik aus derselben nach der Entlassung kochen und sich so eine Mund-zu-Mund-Propaganda ergab, die auch für die Erfinder der Rezepte eine schöne Bestätigung darstellt.

⊙ REZEPTE

Tortellinigratin mit Goldbarsch (Rezept für 4 Personen)

Zutaten: 1 TL Öl, 1 Zwiebel, 2 Knoblauchzehen, 1 große Dose gestückelte Tomaten, 300 g Goldbarsch, 500 g Tortellini, 6 Scheiben Käse (20 %), 1 Zucchini, Salz, Pfeffer, Kräuter, Zitronensaft

Zubereitung: Den Fisch waschen, in etwa 1 cm dicke Scheiben schneiden, mit Zitronensaft beträufeln, salzen und pfeffern. Zucchini putzen, waschen und klein schneiden. Das Öl erhitzen, die Zucchini andünsten, die Tomaten und den gepressten Knoblauch zugeben, ca. 5 min schmoren lassen. Mit Salz und Pfeffer würzen. Die Tortellini garen. Den Fisch zum Gemüse geben, etwa 5 min garen und danach in eine Auflaufform füllen. Die Tortellini abgießen, gleichmäßig auf der Gemüse-Fisch-Mischung verteilen und die Käsescheiben darüberlegen. Das Gratin ca. 15 min bei 225° C überbacken.

PRO PORTION: 11 FETTPUNKTE

Apfel-Zimt-Muffins (Rezept für 12 Stück)

Zutaten: 1 Ei, 150 g Zucker, 1 Pk. Vanillezucker, 300 g Buttermilch, 275 g Mehl, 2 TL Backpulver, 1½ TL Zimt, 2 Äpfel (250 g)

Zubereitung: Das Ei, das Salz und den Vanillezucker in eine Schüssel geben, cremig rühren und die Buttermilch dazugeben. Mehl und Backpulver mischen und vorsichtig unterheben. Die Äpfel reiben, mit dem Zimt vermischen und unter den Teig ziehen. Den Teig gleichmäßig auf die Muffinsförmchen verteilen und auf mittlerer Schiene ca. 25 min bei 180° C backen.

PRO STÜCK: 1 FETTPUNKT

Bunter Fischtopf (Rezept für 4 Personen)

Zutaten: 300 g Lauch, 2 rote Paprikaschoten, 2 Kartoffeln, 2 Knoblauchzehen, 2 Dosen Mais (Abtropfgewicht pro Dose ca. 140 g), 2 EL Öl, 2 EL Tomatenmark, 2 EL Gemüsebrühe, 1,5 l Wasser, 200 g Erbsen, 2 TL Stärke, 200 g Seelachsfilet, 2 EL Zitronensaft, Salz, Pfeffer, 4 Brötchen

Zubereitung: Den Lauch putzen, waschen und in Ringe schneiden. Die Paprikaschoten halbieren, entkernen, waschen und würfeln. Kartoffeln schälen, waschen und ebenfalls würfeln, den Mais auf einem Sieb abtropfen lassen und den Knoblauch schälen. Lauch in heißem Öl anschwitzen. Tomatenmark und den gepressten Knoblauch dazugeben und kurz andünsten. Mit 1,5 l Wasser aufgießen, aufkochen lassen und die Gemüsebrühe einrühren. Paprika, Kartoffeln, Mais und Erbsen in die Suppe geben und ca. 15 min kochen lassen. Stärke in etwas Wasser anrühren, unter Rühren zur Suppe geben und 1 min kochen lassen. Seelachs waschen, trockentupfen, in Würfel schneiden, mit Zitronensaft beträufeln, zur Suppe geben und ca. 10 min gar ziehen lassen. Nach Belieben mit Salz und Pfeffer abschmecken. Mit Brötchen servieren.

PRO PORTION: 8 FETTPUNKTE

Chicken-Burger (Rezept für 4 Personen)

Zutaten: 4 Hähnchenbrustfilets, Salz, Pfeffer, Kräuter (z. B. Oregano, Thymian), 1 Fladenbrot. Für die Soße: 1 kleine Flasche Ketchup, 1 TL Curry, 1 kleine Zwiebel, 1 Gewürzgurke

Zubereitung: Das Fleisch in dünne Streifen schneiden und portionsweise in einer beschichteten Pfanne ohne Öl kräftig anbraten. Mit den Gewürzen und Kräutern abschmecken. Das Fleisch herausnehmen, in eine Schüssel geben und im Backofen bei 70 °C warm halten. Das Fladenbrot vierteln, eine Tasche hineinschneiden und im Backofen erwärmen. Für die Soße die Zwiebel und die Gewürzgurke fein würfeln. Das Ketchup in eine Schüssel geben, Curry, die Zwiebel und die Gewürzgurke unterrühren. Die Tasche des Fladenbrots mit dem Fleisch und der Soße füllen.

PRO BURGER: 2 FETTPUNKTE

Erdbeereis (Rezept für 4 Personen)

Zutaten: 400 g Erdbeeren (tief gefroren), 160 ml fettarme Milch (1,5 %), Zitronensaft, Zucker, Süßstoff

Zubereitung: Die tief gefrorenen Erdbeeren in 2 cm große Stücke schneiden und in die Milch geben. Mit Zitronensaft (ca. 1 TL), Zucker und Süßstoff nach Belieben abschmecken. Alles zusammen mit dem Mixer zu einem cremigen Eis pürieren. Bis zum Verzehr in die Tiefkühltruhe stellen.

PRO PORTION: 1 FETTPUNKT

Feine Kartoffelsuppe mit Lachs (Rezept für 4 Personen)

Zutaten: 700 g Kartoffeln, 80 g Sellerieknolle, 2 mittelgroße Zwiebeln, 300 g Möhren, 200 g Lauch, 2 TL Keimöl, 250 ml fettarme Milch (1,5 %), 2 EL gehackte Petersilie, 2 Würfel Gartenkräuterlinge, Pfeffer, Jodsalz, Zitronensaft, 160 g Räucherlachs, fein gehackter Dill, 1 Baguette

Zubereitung: Kartoffeln und Sellerie schälen, waschen und in Stücke schneiden. Die Möhren und den Lauch putzen, waschen und in Scheiben schneiden. Die Zwiebeln schälen, würfeln und in heißem Keimöl andünsten. Kartoffeln und Gemüse dazugeben, 600 ml Wasser zugießen und aufkochen lassen. Die Suppe ca. 20 min bei schwacher Hitze garen. Milch dazugießen und aufkochen lassen. Petersilie und Kräuterlinge Gartenkräuter zur Suppe geben und fein pürieren. Mit Pfeffer, Salz und Zitronensaft abschmecken. Den Lachs in feine Streifen schneiden. Die Suppe mit Lachs und Dill garniert servieren. Dazu das Baguette reichen.

PRO PORTION: 9 FETTPUNKTE

Geflügelfilet an Blattspinat (Rezept für 4 Personen)

Zutaten: 4 kleine Hähnchenbrustfilets, 1 TL Öl, 2 Zwiebeln, 200 ml Wasser und 1 gehäufter TL gekörnte Gemüsebrühe, 200 ml fettarme Milch (1,5 %), 4 TL Stärke, 4 EL saure Sahne (10 %), 450 g Spinat (TK), Salz, Pfeffer, Muskat, 100 g Schmelzkäse (20 % F.i.T.)

Zubereitung: Hähnchenbrustfilet in Öl anbraten, würzen und durchgaren lassen. Das Fleisch herausnehmen und die gewürfelten Zwiebel in der Pfanne anbraten. Gemüsebrühe und Milch dazugeben und mit der Stärke andicken. Die saure Sahne einrühren, das Filet hineinlegen und warm halten. Den Spinat erwärmen, würzen und den Schmelzkäse unterrühren.

PRO PORTION: 7 FETTPUNKTE

Gnocchi in Thunfischsoße (Rezept für 4 Personen)

Zutaten: 1 EL Olivenöl, 1 Zwiebel, 2 Knoblauchzehen, 750 g frische Gnocchi aus dem Kühl-regal, 1 Dose Tomaten (850 g), 2 Dosen Thunfisch in Wasser, Salz, Pfeffer, Basilikum, Oregano oder andere Kräuter

Zubereitung: Die Zwiebel und den Knoblauch schälen, in kleine Würfel schneiden und zu-sammen mit den Gnocchi in Olivenöl in einer beschichteten Pfanne bei großer Hitze ca. 5 min anbraten. Die Tomaten und den Thunfisch hinzufügen und mit den Gewürzen abschmecken.

PRO PORTION: 5 FETTPUNKTE

Hawaiibaguette (Rezept für 4 Personen)

Zutaten: 4 Baguettebrötchen zum Aufbacken, 8 EL Tomato al Gusto, 4 Scheiben fettarmen Käse (30 % F.i.T.), 4 Scheiben gekochter Schinken, 4 Scheiben Ananas

Zubereitung: Baguettebrötchen aufschneiden und mit Tomato al Gusto bestreichen. Zuerst den gekochten Schinken, dann die Ananas und zum Schluss den Käse auf das Baguette legen und im Backofen bei 180° C ca. 15 min überbacken.

PRO BAGUETTE: 5 FETTPUNKTE

Pasta-Salat „Alla Caprese" (Rezept für 4 Personen)

Zutaten: 150 g Nudeln (z. B. Farfalle), 400 g Tomaten, 125 g Mozzarella (45 % Fett), 1 EL Par-mesan, 1 kleine Zwiebel, Basilikumblätter, 1 TL Olivenöl, 2 EL Balsamico-Essig, Salz, Pfeffer

Zubereitung: Die Pasta in kochendem Salzwasser nach Packungsanweisung garen. Die Tomaten vierteln, entkernen und längs in Spalten schneiden. Den Mozzarella grob würfeln und die Zwiebeln in Scheiben schneiden. Die Pasta mit Tomaten, Mozzarella, Zwiebelringen, Parmesan (gehobelt) und den Basilikumblättern mischen. Für die Vinaigrette Öl und Balsamico-Essig verrühren, mit Salz und Pfeffer würzen und über den Salat geben.

PRO PORTION: 8 FETTPUNKTE

Schinken-Käse-Soße (Rezept für 6 Personen)

Zutaten: 1 l fettarme Milch (1,5 %), 40 g Stärke, 100 g Schmelzkäse (20 % Fett), 200 g ge-kochter Schinken, 1 TL Gemüsebrühe, Salz, Pfeffer, Muskat

Zubereitung: Einen Teil der Milch (ca. 300 ml) mit der Stärke anrühren und die restliche Milch zum Kochen bringen. Die angerührte Milch zugeben und einmal aufkochen lassen. An-schließend den Schmelzkäse in die Soße geben und so lange rühren, bis er geschmolzen ist. Den in Streifen geschnittenen Schinken in die Soße geben, mit den Gewürzen und der Gemüsebrühe abschmecken.

PRO PORTION: 5 FETTPUNKTE

▶ **Küchenmaße – Wiegen ohne Waage**

Wenn es schnell gehen soll, kann man auch ohne zeitaufwändiges Messen und Wiegen mit der Küchenwaage die benötigten Zutaten in der richtigen Menge abmessen. Kleine Mengen kann man genauso gut mit Löffeln und Tassen abmessen. Gebräuchliche Maße – Löffelweise abgewogen:

1 TL = 5 ml	1 TL ger. Käse = 3 g	1 EL Öl = 10 g
1 TL Butter = 4 g	1 EL Sahne = 15 g	1 Suppenteller = 250 ml
1 TL Zucker = 5 g	1 EL ger. Käse = 6 g	1 TL ger. Nüsse = 3 g
1 EL Butter = 10 g	1 Kaffeetasse = 125 ml	1 EL ger. Nüsse = 6 g
1 EL Zucker = 15 g	1 TL Crème frâiche = 5 g	
1 EL = 10 ml	1 TL Senf = 4 g	
1 TL Milch = 5 g	1 EL Crème frâiche = 15 g	
1 TL Mehl = 3 g	1 EL Senf = 12 g	
1 EL Milch = 15 g	1 Wasserglas = 200 ml	
1 EL Mehl = 8 g	1 TL Salz = 5 g	
1 Schnapsglas = 20 ml	1 TL Öl = 4 g	
1 TL Sahne = 5 g	1 EL Salz = 15 g	

◉ SERVICE

Als Quelle diente uns unter anderem eine sehr gut gemachte „Ernährungsmedizinische Information" mit dem Titel „NutriFacts" von Nestlé:
www.nestle.ch

Die Kochlöffelbande:
www.kochloeffelbande.de
Birgit Schäfer: bschaefer06@aol.com

Medical Move: Die Trainings- und Fitnessmethode der Berlinerin Anja Blaku löst schon innerhalb von zehn Wochen mit nur einem Trainingstermin pro Woche erstaunliche Verbesserungen im Bereich Beweglichkeit, Körperwahrnehmung, alltagsnotwendige Kraft und grundlegende Belastungsfähigkeit aus.

Da dieses Gesundheitsportkonzept fünf Intensitätsstufen umfasst, kann jeder je nach seinem aktuellen Stand optimal trainieren, ohne über- oder auch unterfordert zu werden. Letzteres stellt einen besonders wichtigen Aspekt heraus, der bei Gesundheitssport meist gar keine Berücksichtigung erfährt und logischerweise dann auch keine nennenswerten Effekte bei den Teilnehmern auslöst.
www.medicalmove.de

„Medical Move" von Anja Blaku, erschienen im Hubert Krenn Verlag

Fakten zur Adipositas in Österreich und Hinweise zur Gesundheitsförderung findet man unter www.alternmitzukunft.at und www.fgoe.org

Quellen zum Kapitel 7:

Kubesch, S. (2002). Sportunterricht: Training für Körper und Geist. Nervenheilkunde, 21, 487-490.

Marshall, S. J., Biddle, S. J. H., Gorely, T., Cameron, N. & Murdey, I. (2004). Relationships between media use, body fatness and physical activity in children and youth: a meta-analysis. International Journal of Obesity, 28, 1238-1246.

DER WEG ZUR REHA

Wenn Sie als Eltern für Ihr Kind oder als Jugendlicher zur Rehabilitation in eine Klinik möchten, sprechen Sie zunächst mit Ihrem Hausarzt oder Kinderarzt. Dieser stellt einen medizinisch begründeten Antrag (E65–E68 „Adipositas" nach dem ICD 10) für ein stationäres Kinderheilverfahren mit Diagnose und Rehabilitationsziel. Dann füllen Sie und Ihr behandelnder Arzt diesen Antrag aus und benennen eine Rehabilitationsklinik als Wunscheinrichtung.

Eine stationäre Rehabilitation bei krankhaftem Übergewicht wird in der Regel dann bewilligt, wenn bereits Folgeerkrankungen des Übergewichtes (wie zum Beispiel orthopädische Erkrankungen, Bluthochdruck, Stoffwechselerkrankungen oder psychische Probleme bzw. Störungen) auftreten, auch wenn Grunderkrankungen festzustellen sind, die das Übergewicht erst ausgelöst haben, wie Bewegungseinschränkungen nach Operationen, angeborene oder erworbene Stoffwechselstörungen (Diabetes mellitus).

Während bei Erwachsenen ein BMI über 30 als Adipositas definiert ist, werden bei Kindern und Jugendlichen die so genannten Perzentilkurven ergänzend herangezogen. Nach der Berechnung des BMI wird das Ergebnis in Abhängigkeit von Alter und Geschlecht in ein Diagramm nach Kromeyer-Hausschild et al (2001) übertragen. Liegt der Wert über der 90. Perzentile, spricht man von Übergewicht, liegt der Wert über der 97. Perzentile, spricht man von Adipositas. Wichtig ist, dass der Arzt den Antrag fachlich begründet.

Der Antrag wird dann bei Ihrer Krankenkasse eingereicht. Der Antrag wird von dem Kostenträger – das kann die Krankenversicherung oder die Deutsche Rentenversicherung (ehemals BfA oder LVA) oder die Beihilfe sein – geprüft. Wenn der Antrag abgelehnt wird, haben Sie die Möglichkeit, Widerspruch einzulegen. Eventuell ist ein Gutachten des medizinischen Dienstes notwendig. In der Regel zahlt die Sozialversicherung den Klinikaufenthalt für Kinder und Jugendliche ohne Selbstbeteiligung.

Wenn Sie von dem Kranken- oder Rentenversicherungsträger die Zustimmung erhalten, dass das stationäre Heilverfahren genehmigt wird, erhalten Sie von der Klinik eine Terminbestätigung und die Aufnahmeunterlagen. Es ist nicht auszuschließen, dass Kostenträger eine andere als die von Ihnen gewünschte Einrichtung bewilligen. Dann haben Sie die Möglichkeit, Widerspruch einzulegen, indem Sie auf § 9 SGB IX hinweisen, welcher Ihnen als Versicherten ein Wunsch- und Wahlrecht zubilligt. Darin wird geregelt, dass berechtigten Wünschen der Leistungsberechtigten entsprochen wird, u. a. unter Berücksichtigung der persönlichen Lebenssituation, des Alters, des Geschlechts oder der Familie. Ein solches Widerspruchsverfahren dauert in der Regel vier bis fünf Wochen, also meist nicht länger als der Zeitraum zwischen Bewilligung und Vorschlag für eine Aufnahme. Dies klingt komplizierter, als es in Wirklichkeit ist. Sollten Sie Unterstützung oder Rat brauchen, sind Ihnen die Kliniken gerne auch behilflich.

Folgende Kinderrehabilitationskliniken haben sich auf Adipositas spezialisiert
(die Liste erhebt keinen Anspruch auf Vollständigkeit):

Fachklinik Hochried
82418 Murnau
www.klinikhochried.de

Fachklinik Sylt für Kinder und Jugendliche
Steinmannstraße 52-54
25980 Westerland/Sylt
www.fachklinik-sylt.de

Kinderrehaklinik „Am Nikolausholz"
Elly-Kutscher-Straße 16 · 06628 Bad Kösen
www.rehaklinik.de

Klinik Schönsicht Berchtesgaden
Oberkälberstein 1-13
83471 Berchtesgaden
www.klinikschoensicht.de

medinet Spessart-Klinik Bad Orb
Würzburger Straße 7-11
63619 Bad Orb
www.spessartklinik.de

Viktoriastift
Cecilienhöhe 3
55543 Bad Kreuznach
www.viktoriastift.de

Fachkliniken Wangen
Kinderklinik
Am Vogelherd 14
88239 Wangen/Allgäu
www.fachkliniken-wangen.de

Fachklinik Gaißach
Dorf 1
83674 Gaißach/bei Bad Tölz
www.fachklinik-gaissach.de

Edelstein Klinik
Lindenstraße 46-48
55758 Bruchweiler
www.edelstein-klinik.de

Folgende Institutionen können Ihnen ebenfalls weiterhelfen:

Adipositasnetzwerk Hessen e.V. – Vorstand
Würzburger Straße 7-11 · 63619 Bad Orb
www.adipositas-hessen.de

Arbeitsgemeinschaft Adipositas im Kindes- und Jugendalter
c/o Vestische Kinder- und Jugendklinik
Uni Witten-Herdecke
Dr.-F.-Steiner Straße 5 · 45711 Datteln
www.a-g-a.de

Arbeitsgemeinschaft Kinderrehabilitation BRD – Geschäftsstelle
Cecilienhöhe 3 · 55543 Bad Kreuznach
www.arbeitsgemeinschaft-kinderrehabilitation.de

Deutsche Adipositasgesellschaft e. V.
Lohbrügger Kirchstraße 65
21033 Hamburg
www.adipositas-gesellschaft.de

Plattform Ernährung und Bewegung e.V.
Wallstraße 65 · 10179 Berlin
www.ernaehrung-und-bewegung.de

Deutsche Adipositashilfe e.V.
Am Hellberg 29 · 32760 Detmold
Adipositas-hilfe@t-online.de

Deutsche Kinderhilfe Direkt e.V.
Wilmersdorfer Straße 94 · 10629 Berlin
www.dkhd.de

aid infodienst Verbraucherschutz-Ernährung
Friedrich-Ebert-Straße 3 · 35117 Bonn
www.aid.de

KgAS – Konsensusgruppe Adipositasschulung
www.adipositasschulung.de

Kinderleicht
Besser essen – mehr bewegen
Kampagne des Bundesministeriums für Ernährung, Landwirtschaft und Verbraucherschutz
Wilhelmstraße 54 · 10117 Berlin
www.kinder-leicht.net

Aus unserem Programm

Hanni Rützler
Kinder lernen essen
Strategien gegen das Zuviel
240 Seiten, gebunden
Format: 16,5x23 cm
Preis: € 24,90 (A)/SFR 42,70
ISBN: 978-3-902351-94-4

Kinder lernen essen

260.000 Artikel im Supermarkt – das Leben im Schlaraffenland ist für viele Esser zur größten Herausforderung geworden. Die renommierte Ernährungswissenschafterin Hanni Rützler beschäftigt sich mit aktuellen Ernährungsproblemen und entwickelt eine Strategie gegen das Zuviel, in der Freude am Essen und Trinken im Mittelpunkt steht.

Starke Kinder lernen essen

Wer glaubt, dass starke Kinder zu viel essen, wird mit Karin Lobners Buch seine Überraschungen erleben. Und auch mit der scheinbar ewigen Regel: „Morgens wie ein Kaiser ..." wird den Jüngsten keine (allgemein) gültige Anleitung auf den Essensweg mitgegeben. Wie's richtig geht, wird anhand zahlreicher Beispiele, Arbeitsblätter und erprobter Schritt-für-Schritt-Programme praxisnahe und spielerisch vermittelt.

Karin Lobner
Starke Kinder lernen essen
128 Seiten, broschiert
Format: 16,5x23 cm
Preis: € 16,95 (A)/SFR 31,60
ISBN: 978-3-902532-31-2

Markus Groll, Gernot Loitzl
Die 50 größten Bio-Lügen
Die gängigsten Irrtümer rund um glückliche Kühe & gesunde Geschäfte
144 Seiten, broschiert
durchgehend farbig bebildert
Preis: € 16,90 (A)/SFR 31,60
ISBN: 978-3-902532-29-9

Alles Bio, oder was?

Längst sind die Zeiten vorbei, als Biokost nur in kleinen Bioläden zu haben war. Inzwischen sind die Discounter in das Geschäft mit biologisch erzeugten Lebensmitteln eingestiegen. Kein Wunder: „Bio" klingt nach mehr – mehr Gesundheit, mehr Geschmack, mehr Natur. Was ist faul an „Bio"? Mit „Bio" lässt sich sehr gut Geld verdienen. Das verleitet zu unseriösen Geschäftspraktiken. Dr. Markus Groll, Autor und Redakteur des österreichischen Wirtschaftsmagazins „trend", und Gernot Loitzl, Ernährungswissenschafter und Ex-Prüfer bei Österreichs führender Bio-Kontrollstelle, analysieren den aktuellen Ernährungstrend und decken dabei die 50 größten Bio-Lügen auf.

KRENN ⚙
Hubert Krenn Verlag

Hubert Krenn Verlag
Gußhausstraße 18 · A-1040 Wien
Tel.: +43-(0)1-585 34 72 · Fax: +43-(0)1-585 04 83 · E-Mail: hwk@buchagentur.at
Auslieferungen: Österreich: Hain · Deutschland: Herold
www.hubertkrenn.at